EDUCATIONAL
—THEORY—

EDUCATIONAL
—THEORY—

PHILOSOPHICAL AND POLITICAL PERSPECTIVES

Edited by
Edmund Wall

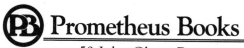 Prometheus Books
59 John Glenn Drive
Amherst, New York 14228-2197

KH

Published 2001 by Prometheus Books

Educational Theory. Copyright © 2001 by Edmund Wall. All rights reserved. No part of this publication may be reproduced, stored in a retrieval system, or transmitted in any form or by any means, digital, electronic, mechanical, photocopying, recording, or otherwise, or conveyed via the Internet or a Web site without prior written permission of the publisher, except in the case of brief quotations embodied in critical articles and reviews.

Inquiries should be addressed to
Prometheus Books
59 John Glenn Drive
Amherst, New York 14228–2197
VOICE: 716–691–0133, ext. 207
FAX: 716–564–2711
WWW.PROMETHEUSBOOKS.COM

04 03 02 01 00   5 4 3 2 1

Library of Congress Cataloging-in-Publication Data

Educational theory: philosophical and political perspectives / edited by
Edmund Wall.
    p. cm.
Includes bibliographical references.
ISBN 1–57392–838–0 (pbk. : alk. paper)
1. Education–Philosophy. 2. Education and state. I. Wall, Edmund.

LB14.7 .E397 2000
370'.1–dc21
                          00–046448

Printed in the United States of America on acid-free paper

12/21/04

*Dedicated to my children, Ryan and Alicia,
and to my wife, Robin*

CONTENTS

PART II: POLITICS AND EDUCATION

PART III: FREE SPEECH ON CAMPUS

ACKNOWLEDGMENTS

I could never offer adequate thanks to my mentor, Burleigh T. Wilkins. His constant encouragement on this project has meant much to me. My association with him throughout the years not only has contributed considerably to my work, but has enriched my life in many other ways as well.

The patience and helpful advice of Keith M. Ashfield and his assistant, Cindy Kaufman-Nixon, have been greatly appreciated. I would also like to thank the anonymous reader for Humanities Press for insightful comments on the introductions.

At some point into this project, Prometheus Books picked up the publication of this book from Humanities Press, which, for financial reasons, had to close its doors. However, Paul Kurtz, Steven L. Mitchell, Christine Kramer, Meghann French, and others at Prometheus Books were very helpful in facilitating that transition.

I am also very grateful to the College of Arts and Sciences at East Carolina University for giving me the opportunity to serve on its "Great Books" Executive Committee. My association with that committee has deepened my own understanding of the "Great Books" approach to education.

I would like to acknowledge all of the individuals and organizations who granted permission to reprint the following materials contained in this volume:

Selections from Karl Marx and Friedrich Engels, *The German Ideology: Part One.* Copyright © 1947 by International Publishers Co., Inc. By permission of International Publishers, Co. Inc.

PREFACE

This anthology combines classic and contemporary approaches to educational theory. One would think that such a project would have been undertaken many times. This is not the case. Despite the obvious importance of scholars defining their educational mission and thoughtfully expressing their educational objectives, we find few attempts to combine original classic sources with contemporary offerings. If there are basic questions in, say, political theory or in ethical theory, scholars generally insist on a grounding in the classics as well as a careful scrutiny of contemporary work. It is important to consider why this is not the case in the philosophy of education.

There have been bitter ideological contests between traditionalists and reconstructionists who seek extensive alterations in our educational system. These feuds can, perhaps, be traced back to the 1960s, when student protests against the "establishment," with all the narrowness and intolerance it represented, became commonplace. The animosity has not abated, as later generations have taken up the struggle for what they take to be creative freedom and social equality. The disagreements may no longer be accompanied by threats of violence, as they often were during the '60s and '70s, but, for many, the outcome of the disagreements is every bit as important.

Unlike other work offered today in the philosophy of

education, this anthology takes a first step toward integrating the major contributions found in both traditional and nontraditional scholarship. The selections not only provide an introduction to some of the major trends of thought in contemporary educational theory, but also suggest provisional solutions to some of the problems that have fueled the quarrel between the two camps. These solutions depend both on historical texts and on a broad range of contemporary contributions.

The zealous struggles between traditionalists and nontraditionalists have, to some extent, contributed to the deterioration of our educational system. Not only are many of our young (and older) students ill-equipped and unmotivated, but all too many of our advanced students are unfamiliar with the general purposes of their education and their role within the educational system. This should not surprise us, as a significant number of their instructors are less than committed to a genuine search for the objectives and principles of education. We owe our youth more than that. We can begin to remedy the inadequacies of our educational system only if we are willing to consider a variety of possible objectives and methods in educational theory. If such a commitment has no other effect, it will at least encourage reasoned debate. This will provide a preferable alternative to the current gridlock.

The words of Walter Kaufmann are especially appropriate here, even though they are found in his philosophy of religion anthology:

> If a demon came to me and offered me, without exacting any price, that all of mankind might accept *my* faith, my views, my standards, I should not even be tempted. Demon, I might say, I have no wish for mankind to conform to any single faith or set of views or standards: but if you are intent on granting me such a great favor, make men's disagreements more responsible and more humane.[1]

We know that many nontraditional scholars have recklessly ignored the historical lineage of contemporary perspectives on education. But even though some scholars have neglected the theoretical roots of education, the brilliant insights of a Plato or a Dewey cannot be considered obsolete. The classics continue to delineate many of the basic challenges and parameters of educational theory.

Many traditionalists exhibit a recklessness of their own by completely dismissing reconstructionism and other nontraditional approaches to education. This rejection opens onto an intellectual abyss that divides classic scholarship from contemporary thought. These traditionalists are left with an educational theory that lacks the relevance and sophistication indicative of a more open-minded inquiry. Consider, for example, the attention now given the view that cultural and personal experiences shape the content of social theories. If cultural and other environmental factors are said to determine theoretical content, then that claim requires serious attention. Among other things, such a position raises questions about the very possibility of objectivity in the formation of social theories.

Questions about objectivity and social relevance are not the private domain of nontraditionalists, however. Classic approaches such as those of John Dewey or Karl Marx or even Plato provide helpful suggestions on these matters. For example, as selection 5 indicates, Dewey's educational theory *specifically* addresses educational problems associated with cultural diversity. By steering a middle course between traditional and nontraditional approaches, his theory offers enlightening advice on issues prominent in nontraditional analyses. The fact is that both classic and contemporary sources provide valuable insights into the aims, methods, and principles of education. Perhaps the reluctance to integrate traditional and nontraditional scholarship is not so much the result of insurmountable theoretical or cultural differences as it is a stubborn refusal to consider alternative approaches.

Educators who defend a "Great Books" curriculum with Western classics at its core tend to overlook the contribution of reconstructionists who plan to alter our educational system in order to facilitate constructive improvements in society. Reconstructionists view schools and curricula as instruments of dominant classes, but believe that the educational system can be changed so that it is more equitable.

In one selection, Mortimer Adler defends the "Great Books" approach for students K–12. He contends that the curriculum for these grades should revolve around the Western classics and that traditional principles of good citizenship should be drilled into our children. The reconstructionists whose work is presented here strongly disagree with approaches such as Adler's, which they feel are out of touch with social reality. Nobuo Shimahara, Paulo Freire, and Michael Apple all oppose the continuation of a traditional education. Under the influence of Marx and Dewey, their reconstructionist writings maintain that as new needs and interests arise in society, corresponding changes ought to be made in the educational system.

Consider, again, the disagreement between reconstructionists and traditionalists on the possibility of objectivity in education. The objectivity/relativity debate was at the forefront of Marx and Dewey's thought. If truth is relative to environmental and social factors, as they believed, then there can be no perennial texts and lessons. Curricula and educational principles are to be adjusted to meet the needs of society. Education thus becomes a useful tool for solving current social problems. The selections here offer some of the major arguments in the objectivity debate. Adler and Allan Bloom presuppose objective truths and values while the reconstructionists, following the lead of Marx and Dewey, view truth and value as relative to an ever-changing social environment. Bloom is critical of the latter's open-ended approach. Against Bloom's criticisms, however, Sidney Hook argues that adherence to relativism need not translate into subjectivism or into an "anything goes" approach.

One of the questions suggested by the objectivity/relativity debate is whether any knowledge is intrinsically worthwhile. "Great Books" proponents would answer affirmatively, despite the influence of Dewey's instrumentalism and the reconstructionist writings. The latter believe that unless there is some useful purpose to be served by seeking the "knowledge" in question, such a quest is pointless. Bloom and Adler, on the other hand, hark back to the ancient Greek classics of Plato and Aristotle which set out to identify eternal objective truths and values. Plato, the most influential metaphysical idealist, found objective truth in the immutable and invisible "forms" of another world, whereas Aristotle, an early realist, found objective truth in this world through reflection and sense knowledge. Both philosophers, however, held that objective moral, social, and political values could be discovered by rational attention to the workings of human nature. This is one of the ancient themes inherited by Bloom.

Henry Aiken's paper addresses another interesting question in education: Can and should a university education be politically neutral? Adler and Bloom openly acknowledge their acceptance of classic democratic values, which they wish to see inculcated in our youth. The reconstructionists, on the other hand, push for new values and lessons to accommodate an ever-changing society. Aiken argues that a university education cannot be politically neutral. In this, he agrees with the reconstructionists. He also shares their belief that university policies ought to reflect certain political values. Like them, he views the practice of student rallies and political protests as a significant part of the university experience. But unlike the reconstructionists, his position is consciously shaped by adherence to some central Aristotelian assumptions. Aiken and Hook's essays suggest that the debate between reconstructionists and classical scholars may not be as irreconcilable as many of them believe.

In contrast to Aiken's analysis (and to the reconstructionists), Robert Simon's paper offers a definition of neutrality that he believes can legitimately be expected in universities. He argues that, except in urgent situations, the university is a place for impartial reflection and not political protests. Of course, there is considerable disagreement concerning if and when campus demonstrations would be justified and what form the demonstrations should take. It would seem that academic freedom is paramount in a democratic society. Yet, as events of the '60s and '70s suggest, some demonstrations appear to "cross the line" and ought to be prohibited. The selections by Amy Gutmann, Thomas Grey, Alan Keyes, Charles

Lawrence III, and Nadine Strossen address the issue of freedom of speech on campus. Even though these selections are contemporary, the problem of freedom versus security dates back to the ancient world. As Gutmann's paper indicates, the discussion of freedom and security has been made much richer by the works of Plato as well as Mill.

Not all of the troublesome questions revolve around a university education, however. The discussions by Plato, Aristotle, Locke, Dewey, Freire, and Adler address the education of very young students as well as the very advanced ones. These thinkers find themselves grappling with the problem of whether to grant children the freedom to help determine their educational tasks and inquiries or to insist on a formal structure designed to lead them to important truths. All of these thinkers, except Dewey and Freire, endorse the latter approach. They assume that there is an objective body of knowledge, rich in wisdom and insight, that ought to be instilled in our youth. Freire and Dewey, however, want to suggest a problems approach to education, one which centers on a child's interaction with his environment. According to Freire and Dewey, with some assistance, a child is more than capable of determining relevant questions and issues.

Like Dewey's approach to education, the approach currently found in Montessori schools has been shaped by realist influences (of which Aristotle and Locke are early representatives). Montessori schools operate on the assumptions, shared by Dewey, that children are naturally curious and, with limited guidance, can engage in fruitful explorations of their physical and social environments. According to the Montessori approach, formal instruction tends to stifle a child's creativity and desire to learn.

NOTE

1. Walter Kaufmann, ed., *Religion from Tolstoy to Camus* (New Brunswick, N.J.: Transaction Publishers, 1994), p. 42.

Part I

CLASSICS

Introduction

Plato's thought still has considerable influence on educational theory. In addition to contemporary Platonists such as Allan Bloom (see selection 6) and those critics who openly acknowledge their debt to Plato, some of the philosophical struggles of Plato and his contemporaries greatly resemble our own.

Plato and his contemporaries struggled with attempts to reconcile *phusis* and *nomos*. The latter referred to the customs, practices, and positive laws of a society; the former, to the unchanging natural order of the world. The sophists, immortalized in Plato's dialogues, maintained that morality and law are both exclusively the product of human creation (i.e., of *nomos*). At the other extreme, of course, was Plato's position that defended a world of unchangeable and invisible forms that were said to provide the exclusive foundation for morality and legal systems. Among other things, the two positions clashed on the capability of human beings to obtain certain and absolute knowledge. The sophists vehemently denied such knowledge, whereas Plato maintained that if philosophers cleared away nagging misconceptions about the world, such knowledge could be obtained.

The sophists were itinerant teachers who offered practical tutorials in rhetoric, law and politics–provided the prospective student could afford it, that is. The students were primarily wealthy aristocrats in a society of very modest means. So while this confrontation between *nomos* and *phusis* was taking place, most of Athens was busy eking out an existence. Nevertheless, discussions about law, politics, and society still held considerably more interest for ancient Athenians than they do now for those in our society.

There were no "lawyers" as such in those days. Plaintiffs and defendants presented their own cases in front of a large group of judges who themselves were fellow citizens. These judges were chosen by lot. In fact, most executive officers also were chosen by lot. These facts help us to understand why subjects such as rhetoric and politics were important to many of these citizens. They realized that they would be called on to participate in their political system and that, some day, they might have to plead their own legal case in front of peers.

Athens was, for a while, a participatory democracy. This was made possible by the fact that its population and territorial dimensions were relatively small. The number of active participants in this city-state was even smaller than one might think. Approximately half of the population were slaves, and women, along with slaves, were excluded from political affairs.

Plato was, therefore, challenging the status quo when he maintains in book 5 of his *Republic* that the guardians of his state are to include both women and men (see selection 1). They are to undergo physical training together so that they will be able to protect the state from invasion. But even though women participate as citizens in Plato's state, the state is hardly democratic. Plato subjects all citizens, women and men alike, to a rigorous education that includes extensive censorship of literature, music, plays, and so on (books 2 and 3) as well as a program of human breeding which requires leaders to control their citizens' marriages (book 5) and to tell "useful" lies to them (book 2). Along with poetry and music, Plato even wants to regulate the amount of humor in his city-state (book 3). State intervention reaches its zenith when Plato compares the "training" of the citizens to the training of dogs and recommends the execution of citizens who are found to have unhealthy bodies or souls (book 3).

This censorship and social control is designed by Plato to help lead his state to justice. But Plato's notion of justice is anything but commonplace. According to him, the world of *nomos* or convention has an ephemeral ontological status. In fact, all of the objects of sense experience are said to comprise a shadow world that derives its existence from the realm of immutable forms. It is in the unchanging natural order (i.e., *phusis*) that Plato finds the blueprint for human happiness. Intimate knowledge of the true form of justice entails a harmonious soul, and happiness is defined as the harmony of the soul (book 4). Plato does not, however, limit his investigation to justice in the individual. Plato views the entire state as a kind of organism whose happiness depends on its harmonious organization. Philosophers who have knowledge of true justice are to lead a state in which each citizen performs his or her own task. Such a state, in Plato's view, is just and happy.

The reader will notice that Plato's investigation of the definition of justice is more or less a search for "the good" of the soul and of the state. He did not employ "justice" in the narrower sense in which it is used today. Note also that the typical Greek in Plato's time would not have accepted his account of a soul. The soul was not thought to be the seat of the moral and intellectual faculties, but, rather, a breath or vapor that somehow animates the body and which exits the body upon death. But, as we said earlier, Plato was not content with the flux and changes of the world of *nomos* and therefore sought refuge in a realm of unchanging reality. He thought that the education of the soul in this world would prepare it for eternal bliss.

Plato's stance on *nomos* left an enormous impression on Aristotle, who refused to surrender *nomos* to *phusis*. Aristotle based the education of citizens on the lessons of concrete human experience, not on an unchanging, supersensible reality. His political and educational proposals are therefore more flexible than those of Plato. However, Aristotle does admit *phusis* through the back door. His position is that morality is guided by inner principles of human nature such as reason. These principles are said to provide guidance and continuity to human development, even if nature or reality is itself subject to change.

Aristotle grounds his ethical theory on a single highest good (i.e., happiness), but this ultimate end of human action is not fixed in some other realm. It constitutes the all-inclusive final end or purpose of human actions. In other words, it is rooted solely in what takes place in this life (or at least primarily in what takes place in this life; see book 10 of the *Nicomachean Ethics* in which Aristotle defines human happiness as "theoretical contemplation" and relates this to the activity of the gods).

In book 1 of his *Nicomachean Ethics,* Aristotle defines happiness as an activity of soul expressing complete virtue. Obviously, not just anybody can attain this. Aristotle offers extensive prerequisites for prospective students of ethics. We are told that students must not be too young (or at least not immature); must not have had a bad upbringing; must not be poor, very ill, or repulsive in physical appearance; and must have friends. (Aristotle is not exactly clear whether these restrictions are meant to be necessary conditions for being morally educable or are offered as considerations that must be weighed before people can plausibly embark on a moral education.)

Aristotle offers a more detailed statement of his educational theory in the *Politics.* He meant for his *Nicomachean Ethics* and *Politics* to be read together, as he never drew a sharp distinction between the two areas. In the *Ethics*, Aristotle defines politics as the master science of the practical good. In book 7 of the *Politics*, he tells us that the happiness of the individual is the same as that of the city-state, and equates the virtue of citizens and rulers with that of the "good man."

In books 7 and 8 of the *Politics*, Aristotle maintains that the purpose of the state is to educate citizens to become virtuous. He defines education as the formation of good habits and good character through the use of reason. He believes that a good and effective program of education by the state will lead to its happiness. On these general points, Aristotle and Plato would agree. However, Aristotle also maintains that the legislator "makes" the citizens good by constructing laws that prompt them to form good habits of conduct. At first glance, we might be tempted to view this as a mere extension of Plato's *Republic*. However, in truth, the *Republic* opposes a system of extensive laws in the state and, instead, turns to training, censorship, and social breeding for the practical means to the state's happiness. Aristotle therefore places much greater importance than Plato on the role of the law in education. Indeed, Aristotle seems to suggest that the state can legislate morality.

Aristotle's approach to education also includes state censorship, albeit to a lesser degree than that of Plato. But we should acknowledge that the call for censorship in the *Republic* and the *Politics* would not have struck the same ominous tone in ancient Greece that it does for us today. Our own society includes many conflicting (sub)cultures, and we sharply distinguish mere social censure and voluntary procedures from the bureaucratic machinery of government. The social burdens and benefits of a given culture in our society do not, as a general rule, reflect those of our government. In ancient Athens, however, the social practices of citizens were not sharply distinguished from legal and political matters. Given the city-state's emphasis on direct participation in political affairs, the moral consciousness of the citizens was bound up with the state's legal and political system.

Yet, like his contemporaries, Aristotle defends both participatory government and slavery. We are told that some people are natural slaves whose task it is to provide citizens with sufficient leisure to further the moral life of the state. Moreover, Aristotle was less impressed than Plato with the issue of equality for women. In the *Politics*, he opposes the emancipation of women because he believes they are needed in individual households to help their families run smoothly.

The selections from John Locke fit our expectations of a social theory much more readily than does the work of Plato and Aristotle. Locke acknowledges natural and contractual rights and presents them from a natural-law perspective. Moreover, despite the legal, political, and cultural differences between seventeenth-century English society and our own, the resemblance between the two societies is undeniable. Unlike ancient Athenian culture, Locke's society distinguished between social practice and the workings of legal and political institutions. For Locke, legal and political affairs are carried on by professional politicians who are confronted by the need to reconcile effective governing with individual liberty.

The attempt at such a reconciliation by Locke's contemporaries was not always a smooth one. Locke himself lived through a civil war and a revolution. The main struggle revolved around the Crown and Parliament. The supporters of the Crown's extensive authority included the Protestant Church of England and Tories such as the country gentry (i.e., a distinguished class of not-so-wealthy landowners). The Whigs, on the other hand, were Protestant dissenters who opposed the kingship of the Catholic James II, and who wished to see a less dictatorial person assume the throne. Locke's personal contacts were with these dissidents.

The Glorious Revolution of 1688, a swift and bloodless Whig rebellion, marked the end of James II's reign and the rise of the more liberal William of Orange to the throne. Among other changes, the Crown's policies would now depend upon a majority vote in Parliament and a "Declaration of Right" would help secure the constitutional liberties of the people. From these changes, we can see that the Locke who would come to have enormous influence on the formation of our government was himself in the midst of events which were not dissimilar from what our Founding Fathers would encounter.

Locke opens his *Second Treatise* with the assumption that people are free from each other and equal to each other. This freedom, however, is not genuine unless it is used to further the "law of nature" or reason. According to Locke, individuals are free to preserve their lives and health, and to protect their estates and belongings. Individuals have a natural right to execute the law of nature and to punish offenders. But because individuals in a state of nature tend to execute the law of nature arbitrarily and unfairly, they agree to establish a government to perform these tasks.

Locke insists that citizens do not renounce their natural rights to life and property when they agree to establish a governing authority. Government always acts "in trust" for the governed. Similarly, parents are to act in trust for their children when they educate them. The law of nature makes it a parent's duty to educate his children until they become rational adults. Parents never have arbitrary authority over their children.

Given Locke's view that parents have a duty to educate their children, it should come as no surprise that Locke recommends private home schooling in *Some Thoughts Concerning Education*. Locke confesses that such an approach may lead to a child's ignorance about wordly affairs, but it also paves the way for the cultivation of virtue in children.

Among the virtues that Locke includes here are good manners, independence, generosity, sobriety, and industry. These virtues are to be nur-
tured through a tutorial method of teaching which is tailored to the abilities
and interests of the pupil in question. This is important. We will see in section 2 that many contemporary theorists emphasize the role of group identity or culture in the educational process. Locke, on the other hand, makes
the individual the central concern. Education is a personal matter between
tutor and pupil. Through private instruction and by setting a good example
the tutor can guide a pupil to virtue.

Not surprisingly, in section 217 of *Some Thoughts Concerning Education*,
Locke says that a pupil is like "white Paper or Wax, to be moulded and fashioned as one pleases." However, this only purports to tell us that the virtues
can be taught. The question remains: Should the cultivation of virtue be the
main concern of education? Locke assigns the virtues a central role in education because, as he sees it, success in both practical and academic pursuits
requires an ability to control one's desires and avoid distractions. If, as the
Second Treatise says, a citizen's duty is to protect human life, property, and
freedom, *Some Thoughts Concerning Education* is designed to tell us how to prepare a young person for such a duty.

Locke's general position on the cultivation of virtue and the role of
reason in controlling desire coincides with what Plato and Aristotle said
about education. Indeed, Locke's natural-law theory can be seen as a reformulation of the *phusis* theme. According to Locke, morality and the aims of
education are grounded in an unchanging natural order. Specific rules and
applications may change, but the fundamental laws of nature are permanent
fixtures of the universe.

Karl Marx specifically rejects the idea that there are permanent,
unchanging moral laws. As the selection from *The German Ideology* indicates,
Marx maintains that morality, law, politics, and other social institutions
depend on material forces of production. He argues that social institutions,
ideology, and culture constitute a superstructure that is built upon a given
mode of production (i.e., the forces and relations of production which may
include agriculture, handicrafts, industry, and so on). The superstructure of
a society owes both its existence and its form to the mode of production
within which it operates. However, according to Marx, there is also movement in the other direction. Although social institutions depend on productive modes, social institutions regulate and condition productive modes so
that there is a dynamic interplay between the productive life of human
beings and the configuration of their social institutions.

Modes of production differ between societies, and they change within
societies. So, given that all social institutions, including morality, depend on
modes of production, Marx concludes that there are no permanent and uni-

versal moral laws. The values and norms that are necessary for a particular society to function at a particular time may not be required of a different society. Since Marx also believes that concerted social action can effect alterations in social institutions, it appears that *nomos* reasserts itself through Marx's writing. However, the ancient sophist was likely to say that morality is merely a matter of convention, whereas Marx would not attempt to account for morality so simplistically. He would say that the dialectic between social structures and productive modes accounts for the formation of moral values, with social structures and productive modes themselves being very complex systems of human activity.

As we will see in section 2, contemporary educational theorists such as Paulo Freire and Michael Apple owe much to Marx. Not only does Marx say that a capitalist system alienates people from the raw materials, tools, and products of their labor, but he emphasizes that a capitalist system alienates people from all of their basic activities. According to Marx, people are creative and productive beings. The capitalist system exploits a laborer's creative activities and treats the laborer as if he or she were a mere commodity. With today's emphasis on the social inequities between groups, the malleability of social values, and the recognition of social and economic influences on these values, it is not difficult to recognize Marx's handwriting on contemporary literature.

Marx envisions a future in which the worldwide division between the owners of the means of production (i.e., bourgeoisie) and the class of laborers (i.e., the proletariat) will be replaced by one cooperative society where a creative being is free from price tags and meddling power structures. How does Marx specifically advise us to prepare younger generations to reach this goal? Here it should be said that Marx does not so much offer a theory of education as he does a general explanation of and prescription for reshaping society. Nevertheless, the selection here does reveal that Marx was a strong advocate of technological training. He wanted the proletariat to receive such training so that they could understand the means of production and thereby expedite the overthrow of the bourgeoisie. Marx thought that the proletariat's control of the means of production was a crucial step toward social liberation.[1]

John Dewey shared Marx's distrust of idealism and, like Marx, sought to ground social thought on concrete human experience rather than on a permanent, unchanging reality. According to both philosophers, human beings naturally seek to express their creative intelligence and ought to be offered the social environment for doing so. Neither of these thinkers thought that this would be a simple task. Both of them based their accounts of social life on dynamic processes. Marx, of course, saw a dialectic between the material forces of production and social institutions. He believed that social institutions expire, flourish, and undergo other changes, depending on the outcome of this dialectic. Dewey, likewise, believed that social life should be thought of as dynamic. He pictured a world in which people constantly are interacting with the physical and social environments.

According to Dewey, pragmatism is not a system of principles and values. He maintains that no set of rules and explanations could possibly do justice to the ever-changing experiences of human beings. Pragmatism is instead a method. It is an approach to a constant barrage of human problems which run the gamut from heating a house to establishing peace between nations. Dewey's pragmatism purports to offer an intelligent way for humans to adjust to their physical and social environments. This adjustment is to take place through an experimental method that tests and retests various possible solutions to obstacles, inconsistencies, and unexplained occurrences in human experience. The experimental method requires that various types of behavior be considered as possible solutions to such problems. The types of behavior that are most likely to have the best consequences with regard to the problems in question are then to be accepted as tentative solutions.

Dewey maintains that growth and progress are the central aims of education. In fact, for Dewey, growth is the main characteristic of human life. He defines it as the enlargement of our capacity to learn and to benefit from our experiences. Thus, like Marx, Dewey wants educational institutions to keep pace with technological and scientific advances. He is confident that most problems can be surmounted if people select the appropriate methods and instruments for each problem.

Although Dewey stresses the need for practical solutions to new problems, it would be a mistake to say that he is opposed to tradition and to the lessons of history. Old values and solutions are to be retained, provided that they help solve problems in contemporary society. Indeed, Dewey insists that society would collapse in the absence of some intellectual continuity between generations. This brings us to what was said in the preface about Dewey's contribution to multiculturalism in education.

As chapters 2 and 7 of *Democracy and Education* suggest, Dewey opposes the complete cultural assimilation of Americans. Not only does he believe that each and every social group has something positive to offer education, but he also wants individuals to cultivate what is unique to their culture and unique to them as individuals. What is it, then, that holds society together? We are told that differing cultures are united by shared common goals which include intellectual development and adjustment to the physical and social environments.

This is important. On the one hand, Dewey's approach acknowledges the significance of what we now call cultural diversity. But, on the other hand, cultural diversity is not to be emphasized at the expense of individuality or social progress. Dewey calls for an intelligent estimation of those features of one's personal background that will promote desirable solutions to current problems. This appears to offer a fertile middle ground between today's traditional and nontraditional approaches to education. Unlike traditionalists, Dewey acknowledges the significance of change and personal background. Unlike nontraditionalists, he stresses individualism and social cohesion. Against both, he warns that the useful lessons from any and all sources need to be integrated into a whole so that the grand purpose of education comes into focus: the promotion of the moral and intellectual growth of society.

Social continuity both within subcultures and within the larger society is made possible by communication. Communication is, for Dewey, the lifeblood of education. It is, in his view, a process of sharing experiences until they become a common possession. It is true that genuine communication is not possible without some common ground, but when people discuss issues and problems with each other, they traverse new ground and often grow together in their beliefs, inclinations, goals, and methods.

Dewey insists that educational theory is part of an ongoing process of social adjustment. He held that experience determines the content of theoretical principles. Dewey's lesson here is that theories may have to be adjusted to fit the facts. This dynamic aspect of pragmatism makes it difficult to apply "Dewey's theory" to today's educational problems. Each new problem situation is unique and may require theoretical reappraisal. Still, we can identify Dewey's influence on today's educational theory.

Consider the selection in part 2 by Paulo Freire. Freire's educational theory centers on individuals looking at their own specific problems within a social context and then offering their creative responses to those problems. Indeed, this "problems approach" to education is Deweyan. The purpose of education is not to impart abstract ideas to passive minds. A genuine quest for knowledge begins with a specific concrete problem that requires attention. The wisdom of old and new sources can then be creatively applied to the particular problem. Notice that this Deweyan approach to education centers on people as unique individuals with personal histories. The curriculum is built around their unique problems, but then includes any useful solutions that may be forthcoming.

NOTE

1. In "Marxism and Schooling: The Limits of Radical Discourse," *Educational Theory* 34, no. 2 (1984): 113–35, Henry A. Giroux rejects Marxism as a basis for

social theory. Giroux maintains that Marx's method of critical theory should be retained, but he argues that Marx's focus on economic interests and class structures is much too narrow to do justice to the cultural mores, practices, and personal histories that also shape social institutions and educational practices.

1

FROM *THE REPUBLIC*

Plato

[Socrates, recounting his dialogue with Glaucon and Adeimantus, says]

Then he who is to be a really good and noble guardian of the state will require to unite in himself philosophy and spirit and swiftness and strength?

Undoubtedly.

Then we have found the desired natures; and now that have found them, how are they to be reared and educated? Is not this an inquiry which is our final end—How do justice and injustice grow up in States? for we do not want either to omit what is to the point or to draw out the argument to an inconvenient length.

Adeimantus thought that the inquiry would be of great service to us.

Then, I said, my dear friend, the task must not be given up, even if somewhat long.

Certainly not.

Come then, and let us pass a leisure hour in story-telling, and our story shall be the education of our heroes.

By all means.

And what shall be their education? Can we find a better than the traditional sort?—and this has two divisions, gymnastics for the body, and music for the soul.

True.

Shall we begin education with music, and go on to gymnastics afterward?

By all means.

And when you speak of music, do you include literature or not?

I do.

And literature may be either true or false?

Yes.

And the young should be trained in both kinds, and we begin with the false?

I do not understand your meaning, he said.

You know, I said, that we begin by telling children stories which, though not wholly destitute of truth, are in the main fictitious; and these stories are told them when they are not of an age to learn gymnastics.

Very true.

That was my meaning when I said that we must teach music before gymnastics.

Quite right, he said.

You know also that the beginning is the most important part of any work, especially in the case of a young and tender thing; for that is the time at which the character is being formed and the desired impression is more readily taken.

Quite true.

And shall we just carelessly allow children to hear any casual tales which may be devised by casual persons, and to receive into their minds ideas for the most part the very opposite of those which we should wish them to have when they are grown up?

We cannot.

Then the first thing will be to establish a censorship of the writers of fiction, and let the censors receive any tale of fiction which is good, and reject the bad; and we will desire mothers and nurses to tell their children the authorized ones only. Let them fashion the mind with such tales, even more fondly than they mould the body with their hands; but most of those which are now in use must be discarded.

Of what tales are you speaking? he said.

You may find a model of the lesser in the greater, I said; for they are necessarily of the same. type, and there is the same spirit in both of them.

Very likely, he replied; but I do not as yet know what you would term the greater.

Those, I said, which are narrated by Homer and Hesiod, and the rest of the poets, who have ever been the great storytellers of mankind.

But which stories do you mean, he said; and what fault do you find with them?

A fault which is most serious, I said; the fault of telling a lie, and, what is more, a bad lie.

But when is this fault committed?

Whenever an erroneous representation is made of the nature of gods and heroes—as when a painter paints a portrait not having the shadow of a likeness to the original.

Yes, he said, that sort of thing is certainly very blamable; but what are the stories which you mean?

First of all, I said, there was that greatest of all lies in high plates, which the poet told about Uranus, and which was a bad lie too—I mean what Hesiod says that Uranus did, and how Cronus retaliated on him. The doings of Cronus, and the sufferings which in turn his son inflicted upon him, even if they were true, ought certainly not to be lightly told to young and thoughtless persons; if possible, they had better be buried in silence. But if there is an absolute necessity for their mention, a chosen few might hear them in a mystery, and they should sacrifice not a common [Eleusinian] pig, but some huge and unprocurable victim; and then the number of the hearers will be very few indeed.

Why, yes, said he, those stories are extremely objectionable.

Yes, Adeimantus, they are stories not to be repeated in our State; the young man should not be told that in committing the worst of crimes he is far from doing anything outrageous; and that even if he chastises his father when he does wrong, in whatever manner, he will only be following the example of the first and greatest among the gods.

I entirely agree with you, he said; in my opinion those stories are quite unfit to be repeated.

Neither, if we mean our future guardians to regard the habit of quarrelling among themselves as of all things the basest, should any word be said to them of the wars in heaven, and of the plots and fightings of the gods against one another, for they are not true. No, we shall never mention the battles of the giants, or let them be embroidered on garments; and we shall be silent about the innumerable other quarrels of gods and heroes with their friends and relatives. If they would only believe us we would tell them that quarrelling is unholy, and that never up to this time has there been any quarrel between citizens; this is what old men and old women should begin by telling children; and when they grow up, the poets also should be told to compose them in a similar spirit. But the narrative of Hephaestus binding Here his mother, or how on another occasion Zeus sent him flying for taking her part when she was being beaten, and all the battles of the gods in Homer—these tales must not be admitted into our State, whether they are supposed to have an allegorical meaning or not. For a young person cannot judge what is allegorical and what is literal; anything that he receives into his mind at that age is likely to become indelible and unalterable; and therefore it is most important that the tales which the young first hear should be models of virtuous thoughts.

There you are right, he replied; but if anyone asks where are such models to be found and of what tales are you speaking–how shall we answer him?

I said to him, You and I, Adeimantus, at this moment are not poets, but founders of a State: now the founders of a State ought to know the general forms in which poets should cast their tales, and the limits which must be observed by them, but to make the tales is not their business.

Very true, he said; but what are these forms of theology which you mean?

Something of this kind, I replied: God is always to be represented as he truly is, whatever be the sort of poetry, epic, lyric, or tragic, in which the representation is given.

Right.

And is he not truly good? and must he not be represented as such?

Certainly.

And no good thing is hurtful?

No, indeed.

And that which is not hurtful hurts not?

Certainly not.

And that which hurts not does no evil?

No.

And can that which does no evil be a cause of evil?

Impossible.

And the good is advantageous?

Yes.

And therefore the cause of well-being?

Yes.

It follows, therefore, that the good is not the cause of all things, but of the good only?

Assuredly.

Then God, if he be good, is not the author of all things, as the many assert, but he is the cause of a few things only, and not of most things that occur to men. For few are the goods of human life, and many are the evils, and the good is to be attributed to God alone; of the evils the causes are to be sought elsewhere, and not in him.

That appears to me to be most true, he said.

Then we must not listen to Homer or to any other poet who is guilty of the folly of saying that two casks

"Lie at the threshold of Zeus, fall of lots, one of good. the other of evil lots,"

and that he to whom Zeus gives a mixture of the two

"Sometimes meets ts with evil fortune, at other times with good;"

but that he to whom is given the cup of unmingled ill,

"Him wild hunger drives o'er the beauteous earth."

And again

"Zeus, who is the dispenser of good and evil to us."

And if anyone asserts that the violation of oaths and treaties, which was really the work of Pandarus, was brought about by Athene and Zeus, or that the strife and contention of the gods were instigated by Themis and Zeus, he shall not have our approval; neither will we allow our young men to hear the words of Aeschylus, that

"God plants guilt among men when he desires utterly to destroy a house."

And if a poet writes of the sufferings of Niobe—the subject of the tragedy in which these iambic verses occur—or of the house of Pelops, or of the Trojan War or on any similar theme, either we must not permit him to say that these are the works of God, or if they are of God, he must devise some explanation of them such as we are seeking: he must say that God did what was just and right, and they were the better for being punished; but that those who are punished are miserable, and that God is the author of their misery—the poet is not to be permitted to say; though he may say that the wicked are miserable because they require to be punished, and are benefited by receiving punishment from God; but that God being good is the author of evil to anyone is to be strenuously denied, and not to be said or sung or heard in verse or prose by anyone whether old or young in any well-ordered commonwealth. Such a fiction is suicidal, ruinous, impious.

I agree with you, he replied, and am ready to give my assent to the law.

Let this then be one of our rules and principles concerning the gods, to which our poets and reciters will be expected to conform—that God is not the author of all things, but of good only.

That will do, he said.

And what do you think of a second principle? Shall I ask you whether God is a magician, and of a nature to appear insidiously now in one shape, and now in another—sometimes himself changing and passing into many forms, sometimes deceiving us with the semblance of such transformations; or is he one and the same immutably fixed in his own proper image?

I cannot answer you, he said, without more thought.

Well, I said; but if we suppose a change in anything, that change must be effected either by the thing itself or by some other thing?

Most certainly.

And things which are at their best are also least liable to be altered or discomposed; for example, when healthiest and strongest, the human frame is least liable to be affected by meats and drinks, and the plant which is in the fullest vigor also suffers least from winds or the heat of the sun or any similar causes.

Of course.

And will not the bravest and wisest soul be least confused or deranged by any external influence?

True.

And the same principle, as I should suppose, applies to all composite things—furniture, houses, garments: when good and well made, they are least altered by time and circumstances.

Very true.

Then everything which is good, whether made by art or nature, or both, is least liable to suffer change from without?

True.

But surely God and the things of God are in every way perfect ?

Of course they are.

Then he can hardly be compelled by external influence to take many shapes?

He cannot.

But may he not change and transform himself?

Clearly, he said, that must be the case if he is changed at all.

And will he then change himself for the better and fairer, or for the worse and more unsightly?

If he change at all he can only change for the worse, for we cannot suppose him to be deficient either in virtue or beauty.

Very true, Adeimantus; but then, would anyone, whether God or man, desire to make himself worse?

Impossible.

Then it is impossible that God should ever be willing to change; being, as is supposed, the fairest and best that is conceivable, every God remains absolutely and forever in his own form.

That necessarily follows, he said, in my judgment.

Then, I said, my dear friend, let none of the poets tell us that

"The gods, taking the disguise of strangers from other lands, walk up and down cities in all sorts of forms;"

and let no one slander Proteus and Thetis, neither let anyone, either in tragedy or in any other kind of poetry, introduce Here disguised in the likeness of a priestess asking an alms

"For the life-giving daughters of Inachus the river of Argos;"

—let us have no more lies of that sort. Neither must we have mothers under the influence of the poets scaring their children with a bad version of these myths—telling how certain gods, as they say, "Go about by night in the likeness of so many strangers and in divers forms"; but let them take heed lest they make cowards of their children, and at the same time speak blasphemy against the gods.

Heaven forbid, he said.

But although the gods are themselves unchangeable, still by witchcraft and deception they may make us think that they appear in various forms?

Perhaps, he replied.

Well, but can you imagine that God will be willing to lie, whether in word or deed, or to put forth a phantom of himself?

I cannot say, he replied.

Do you not know, I said, that the true lie, if such an expression may be allowed, is hated of gods and men?

What do you mean? he said.

I mean that no one is willingly deceived in that which is the truest and highest part of himself, or about the truest and highest matters; there, above all, he is most afraid of a lie having possession of him.

Still, he said, I do not comprehend you.

The reason is, I replied, that you attribute some profound meaning to my words; but I am only saying that deception, or being deceived or uninformed about the highest realities in the highest part of themselves, which is the soul, and in that part of them to have and to hold the lie, is what mankind least like;—that, I say, is what they utterly detest.

There is nothing more hateful to them.

And, as I was just now remarking, this ignorance in the soul of him who is deceived may be called the true lie; for the lie in words is only a kind of imitation and shadowy image of a previous affection of the soul, not pure unadulterated falsehood. Am I not right?

Perfectly right.

The true lie is hated not only by the gods, but also by men?

Yes.

Whereas the lie in words is in certain cases useful and not hateful; in dealing with enemies—that would be an instance; or again, when those whom we call our friends in a fit of madness or illusion are going to do some harm, then it is useful and is a sort of medicine or preventive; also in the tales of mythology, of which we were just now speaking—because we do not know the truth about ancient times, we make falsehood as much like truth as we can, and so turn it to account.

Very true, he said.

But can any of these reasons apply to God? Can we suppose that he is ignorant of antiquity, and therefore has recourse to invention?

That would be ridiculous, he said.

Then the lying poet has no place in our idea of God?

I should say not.

Or perhaps he may tell a lie because he is afraid of enemies?

That is inconceivable.

But he may have friends who are senseless or mad?

But no mad or senseless person can be a friend of God.

Then no motive can be imagined why God should lie?

None whatever.

Then the superhuman, and divine, is absolutely incapable of falsehood?

Yes.

Then is God perfectly simple and true both in word and deed; he changes not; he deceives not, either by sign or word, by dream or waking vision.

Your thoughts, he said, are the reflection of my own.

You agree with me then, I said, that this is the second type or form in which we should write and speak about divine things. The gods are not magicians who transform themselves, neither do they deceive mankind in any way.

I grant that.

. . . justice will be admitted to be the having and doing what is a man's own, and belongs to him?

Very true.

Think, now, and say whether you agree with me or not. Suppose a carpenter to be doing the business of a cobbler, or a cobbler of a carpenter; and suppose them to exchange their implements or their duties, or the same person to be doing the work of both, or whatever be the change; do you think that any great harm would result to the State?

Not much.

But when the cobbler or any other man whom nature designed to be a trader, having his heart lifted up by wealth or strength or the number of his followers, or any like advantage, attempts to force his way into the class of warriors, or a warrior into that of legislators and guardians, for which he is unfitted, and either to take the implements or the duties of the other; or when one man is trader, legislator, and warrior all in one, then I think you will agree with me in saying that this interchange and this meddling of one with another is the ruin of the State.

Most true.

Seeing, then, I said, that there are three distinct classes, any meddling of one with another, or the change of one into another, is the greatest harm to the State, and may be most justly termed evildoing?

Precisely.

And the greatest degree of evildoing to one's own city would be termed by you injustice?

Certainly.

This, then, is injustice; and on the other hand when the trader, the auxiliary, and the guardian each do their own business, that is justice, and will make the city just.

I agree with you.

We will not, I said, be over-positive as yet; but if, on trial, this conception of justice be verified in the individual as well as in the State, there will be no longer any room for doubt; if it be not verified, we must have a fresh inquiry. First let us complete the old investigation, which we began, as you remember, under the impression that, if we could previously examine justice on the larger scale, there would be less difficulty in discerning her in the individual. That larger example appeared to be the State, and accordingly we constructed as good a one as we could, knowing well that in the good State justice would be found. Let the discovery which we made be now applied to the individual—if they agree, we shall be satisfied; or, if there be a difference in the individual, we will come back to the State and have another trial of the theory. The friction of the two when rubbed together may possibly strike a light in which justice will shine forth, and the vision which is then revealed we will fix in our souls.

That will be in regular course; let us do as you say.

I proceeded to ask: When two things, a greater and less, are called by the same name, are they like or unlike in so far as they are called the same?

Like, he replied.

The just man then, if we regard the idea of justice only, will be like the just State?

He will.

And a State was thought by us to be just when the three classes in the State severally did their own business; and also thought to be temperate and valiant and wise by reason of certain other affections and qualities of these same classes?

True, he said.

And so of the individual; we may assume that he has the same three principles in his own soul which are found in the State; and he may be rightly described in the same terms, because he is affected in the same manner?

Certainly, he said.

Once more, then, O my friend, we have alighted upon an easy question—whether the soul has these three principles or not?

An easy question! Nay, rather, Socrates, the proverb holds that hard is the good.

Very true, I said; and I do not think that the method which we are employing is at all adequate to the accurate solution of this question; the true method is another and a longer one. Still we may arrive at a solution not below the level of the previous inquiry.

May we not be satisfied with that? he said: under the circumstances, I am quite content.

I, too, I replied, shall be extremely well satisfied.

Then faint not in pursuing the speculation, he said.

Must we not acknowledge, I said, that in each of us there are the same principles and habits which there are in the State; and that from the individual they pass into the State?—how else can they come there? Take the quality of passion or spirit; it would be ridiculous to imagine that this quality, when found in States, is not derived from the individuals who are supposed to possess it, e.g., the Thracians, Scythians, and in general the Northern nations; and the same may be said of the love of knowledge, which is the special characteristic of our part of the world, or of the love of money, which may, with equal truth, be attributed to the Phoenicians and Egyptians.

Exactly so, he said.

There is no difficulty in understanding this.

None whatever.

But the question is not quite so easy when we proceed to ask whether these principles are three or one; whether, that is to say, we learn with one part of our nature, are angry with another, and with a third part desire the satisfaction of our natural appetites; or whether the whole soul comes into play in each sort of action—to determine that is the difficulty.

Yes, he said; there lies the difficulty.

Then let us now try and determine whether they are the same or different.

How can we? he asked.

I replied as follows: The same thing clearly cannot act or be acted upon in the same part or in relation to the same thing at the same time, in contrary ways; and therefore whenever this contradiction occurs in things apparently the same, we know that they are really not the same, but different.

Good.

For example, I said, can the same thing be at rest and in motion at the same time in the same part?

Impossible.

Still, I said, let us have a more precise statement of terms, lest we should hereafter fall out by the way. Imagine the case of a man who is standing and also moving his hands and his head, and suppose a person to say that one and the same person is in motion and at rest at the same moment—to such a mode of speech we should object, and should rather say that one part of him is in motion while another is at rest.

Very true.

And suppose the objector to refine still further, and to draw the nice distinction that not only parts of tops, but whole tops, when they spin round with their pegs fixed on the spot, are at rest and in motion at the same time (and he may say the same of anything which revolves in the same spot), his objection would not be admitted by us, because in such cases things are not at rest and in motion in the same parts of themselves; we should rather say that they have both an axis and a circumference; and that the axis stands still, for there is no deviation from the perpendicular; and that the circumference goes round. But if, while revolving, the axis inclines either to the right or left, forward or backward, then in no point of view can they be at rest.

That is the correct mode of describing them, he replied.

Then none of these objections will confuse us, or incline us to believe that the same thing at the same time, in the same part or in relation to the same thing, can act or be acted upon in contrary ways.

Certainly not, according to my way of thinking.

Yet, I said, that we may not be compelled to examine all such objections, and prove at length that they are untrue, let us assume their absurdity, and go forward on the understanding that hereafter, if this assumption turn out to be untrue, all the consequences which follow shall be withdrawn.

Yes, he said, that will be the best way.

Well, I said, would you not allow that assent and dissent, desire and aversion, attraction and repulsion, are all of them opposites, whether they are regarded as active or passive (for that makes no difference in the fact of their opposition)?

Yes, he said, they are opposites.

Well, I said, and hunger and thirst, and the desires in general, and again willing and wishing—all these you would refer to the classes already mentioned. You would say—would you not?—that the soul of him who desires is seeking after the object of his desire; or that he is drawing to himself the thing which he wishes to possess: or again, when a person wants anything to be given him, his mind, longing for the realization of his desire, intimates his wish to have it by a nod of assent, as if he had been asked a question?

Very true.

And what would you say of unwillingness and dislike and the absence of desire; should not these be referred to the opposite class of repulsion and rejection?

Certainly.

Admitting this to be true of desire generally, let us suppose a particular class of desires, and out of these we will select hunger and thirst, as they are termed, which are the most obvious of them?

Let us take that class, he said.

The object of one is food, and of the other drink?

Yes.

And here comes the point: is not thirst the desire which the soul has of drink, and of drink only; not of drink qualified by anything else; for example, warm or cold, or much or little, or, in a word, drink of any particular sort: but if the thirst be accompanied by heat, then the desire is of cold drink; or, if accompanied by cold, then of warm drink; or, if the thirst be excessive, then the drink which is desired will be excessive; or, if not great, the quantity of drink will also be small: but thirst pure and simple will desire drink pure and simple, which is the natural satisfaction of thirst, as food is of hunger?

Yes, he said; the simple desire is, as you say, in every case of the simple object, and the qualified desire of the qualified object.

But here a confusion may arise; and I should wish to guard against an opponent starting up and saying that no man desires drink only, but good drink, or food only, but good food; for good is the universal object of desire, and thirst being a desire, will necessarily be thirst after good drink; and the same is true of every other desire.

Yes, he replied, the opponent might have something to say.

Nevertheless I should still maintain, that of relatives some have a quality attached to either term of the relation; others are simple and have their correlatives simple.

I do not know what you mean.

Well, you know of course that the greater is relative to the less?

Certainly.

And the much greater to the much less?

Yes.

And the sometime greater to the sometime less, and the greater that is to be to the less that is to be?

Certainly, he said.

And so of more or less, and of other correlative terms, such as the double and the half, or, again, the heavier and the lighter, the swifter and the slower; and of hot and cold, and of any other relatives; is not this true of all of them?

Yes.

And does not the same principle hold in the sciences? The object of science is knowledge (assuming that to be the true definition), but the object of a particular science is a particular kind of knowledge; I mean, for example, that the science of house building is a kind of knowledge which is defined and distinguished from other kinds and is therefore termed architecture.

Certainly.

Because it has a particular quality which no other has?

Yes.

And it has this particular quality because it has an object of a particular kind; and this is true of the other arts and sciences?

Yes.

Now, then, if I have made myself clear, you will understand my original meaning in what I said about relatives. My meaning was, that if one term of a relation is taken alone, the other is taken alone; if one term is qualified, the other is also qualified. I do not mean to say that relatives may not be disparate, or that the science of health is healthy, or of disease necessarily diseased, or that the sciences of good and evil are therefore good and evil; but only that, when the term "science" is no longer used absolutely, but has a qualified object which in this case is the nature of health and disease, it becomes defined, and is hence called not merely science, but the science of medicine.

I quite understand, and, I think, as you do.

Would you not say that thirst is one of these essentially relative terms, having clearly a relation—

Yes, thirst is relative to drink.

And a certain kind of thirst is relative to a certain kind of drink; but thirst taken alone is neither of much nor little, nor of good nor bad, nor of any particular kind of drink, but of drink only?

Certainly.

Then the soul of the thirsty one, insofar as he is thirsty, desires only drink; for this he yearns and tries to obtain it?

That is plain.

And if you suppose something which pulls a thirsty soul away from drink, that must be different from the thirsty principle which draws him like a beast to drink; for, as we were saying, the same thing cannot at the same time with the same part of itself act in contrary ways about the same.

Impossible.

No more than you can say that the hands of the archer push and pull the bow at the same time, but what you say is that one hand pushes and the other pulls.

Exactly so, he replied.

And might a man be thirsty, and yet unwilling to drink?

Yes, he said, it constantly happens.

And in such a case what is one to say? Would you not say that there was something in the soul bidding a man to drink, and something else forbidding him, which is other and stronger than the principle which bids him?

I should say so.

And the forbidding principle is derived from reason, and that which bids and attracts proceeds from passion and disease?

Clearly.

Then we may fairly assume that they are two, and that they differ from one another; the one with which a man reasons, we may call the rational principle of the soul; the other, with which he loves, and hungers, and thirsts, and feels the flutterings of any other desire, may be termed the irrational or appetitive, the ally of sundry pleasures and satisfactions?

Yes, he said, we may fairly assume them to be different.

Then let us finally determine that there are two principles existing in the soul. And what of passion, or spirit? Is it a third, or akin to one of the preceding?

I should be inclined to say—akin to desire.

Well, I said, there is a story which I remember to have heard, and in which I put faith. The story is, that Leontius, the son of Aglaion, coming up one day from the Piraeus, under the north wall on the outside, observed some dead bodies lying on the ground at the place of execution. He felt a desire to see them, and also a dread and abhorrence of them; for a time he struggled and covered his eyes, but at length the desire got the better of him; and forcing them open, he ran up to the dead bodies, saying, Look, ye wretches, take your fill of the fair sight.

I have heard the story myself, he said.

The moral of the tale is, that anger at times goes to war with desire, as though they were two distinct things.

Yes; that is the meaning, he said.

And are there not many other cases in which we observe that when a man's desires violently prevail over his reason, he reviles himself, and is angry at the violence within him, and that in this struggle, which is like the struggle of factions in a State, his spirit is on the side of his reason; but for the passionate or spirited element to take part with the desires when reason decides that she should not be opposed, is a sort of thing which I believe that you never observed occurring in yourself, nor, as I should imagine, in anyone else?

Certainly not.

Suppose that a man thinks he has done a wrong to another, the nobler he is, the less able is he to feel indignant at any suffering, such as hunger, or cold, or any other pain which the injured person may inflict upon him—these he deems to be just, and, as I say, his anger refuses to be excited by them.

True, he said.

But when he thinks that he is the sufferer of the wrong, then he boils and chafes, and is on the side of what he believes to be justice; and because he suffers hunger or cold or other pain he is only the more determined to persevere and conquer. His noble spirit will not be quelled until he either slays or is slain; or until he hears the voice of the shepherd, that is, reason, bidding his dog bark no more.

The illustration is perfect, he replied; and in our State, as we were saying, the auxiliaries were to be dogs, and to hear the voice of the rulers, who are their shepherds.

I perceive, I said, that you quite understand me; there is, however, a further point which I wish you to consider.

What point?

You remember that passion or spirit appeared at first sight to be a kind of desire, but now we should say quite the contrary; for in the conflict of the soul spirit is arrayed on the side of the rational principle.

Most assuredly.

But a further question arises: Is passion different from reason also, or only a kind of reason; in which latter case, instead of three principles in the soul, there will only be two, the rational and the concupiscent; or rather, as the State was composed of three classes, traders, auxiliaries, counsellors, so may there not be in the individual soul a third element which is passion or spirit when not corrupted by bad education in the natural auxiliary of reason?

Yes, he said, there must be a third.

Yes, I replied, if passion, which has already been shown to be different from desire, turn out also to be different from reason.

But that is easily proved: We may observe even in young children that they are full of spirit almost as soon as they are born, whereas some of them never seem to attain to the use of reason, and most of them late enough.

Excellent, I said, and you may see passion equally in brute animals, which is a further proof of the truth of what you are saying. And we may once more appeal to the words of Homer, which have been already quoted by us,

"He smote his breast, and thus rebuked his soul;"

for in this verse Homer has clearly supposed the power which reasons about the better and worse to be different from the unreasoning anger which is rebuked by it.

Very true, he said.

And so, after much tossing, we have reached land, and are fairly agreed that the same principles which exist in the State exist also in the individual, and that they are three in number.

Exactly.

Must we not then infer that the individual is wise in the same way, and in virtue of the same quality which makes the State wise?

Certainly.

Also that the same quality which constitutes courage in the State constitutes courage in the individual, and that both the State and the individual bear the same relation to all the other virtues?

Assuredly.

And the individual will be acknowledged by us to be just in the same way in which the State is just?

That follows of course.

We cannot but remember that the justice of the State consisted in each of the three classes doing the work of its own class?

We are not very likely to have forgotten, he said.

We must recollect that the individual in whom the several qualities of his nature do their own work will be just, and will do his own work?

Yes, he said, we must remember that too.

And ought not the rational principle, which is wise, and has the care of the whole soul, to rule, and the passionate or spirited principle to be the subject and ally?

Certainly.

Men and women alike possess the qualities which make a guardian; they differ only in their comparative strength or weakness.

Obviously.

And those women who have such qualities are to be selected as the companions and colleagues of men who have similar qualities and whom they resemble in capacity and in character?

Very true.

And ought not the same natures to have the same pursuits?

They ought.

Then, as we were saying before, there is nothing unnatural in assigning music and gymnastics to the wives of the guardians–to that point we come round again.

Certainly not.

The law which we then enacted was agreeable to nature, and therefore not an impossibility or mere aspiration; and the contrary practice, which prevails at present, is in reality a violation of nature.

That appears to be true.

We had to consider, first, whether our proposals were possible, and secondly whether they were the most beneficial?

Yes.

And the possibility has been acknowledged?

Yes.

The very great benefit has next to be established?

Quite so.

You will admit that the same education which makes a man a good guardian will make a woman a good guardian; for their original nature is the same?

Yes.

I should like to ask you a question.

What is it?

Would you say that all men are equal in excellence, or is one man better than another?

The latter.

And in the commonwealth which we were founding do you conceive the guardians who have been brought up on our model system to be more perfect men, or the cobblers whose education has been cobbling?

What a ridiculous question!

You have answered me, I replied: Well, and may we not further say that our guardians are the best of our citizens?

By far the best.

And will not their wives be the best women?

Yes, by far the best.

And can there be anything better for the interests of the State than that the men and women of a State should be as good as possible?

There can be nothing better.

And this is what the arts of music and gymnastics, when present in such a manner as we have described, will accomplish?

Certainly.

Then we have made an enactment not only possible but in the highest degree beneficial to the State?

True.

Then let the wives of our guardians strip, for their virtue will be their robe, and let them share in the toils of war and the defence of their country; only in the distribution of labors the lighter are to be assigned to the women, who are the weaker natures, but in other respects their duties are to be the same. And as for the man who laughs at naked women exercising their bodies from the best of motives, in his laughter he is plucking

"A fruit of unripe wisdom,"

and he himself is ignorant of what he is laughing at, or what he is about; for that is, and ever will be, the best of sayings, "that the useful is the noble, and the hurtful is the base."

Very true.

Here, then, is one difficulty in our law about women, which we may say that we have now escaped; the wave has not swallowed us up alive for enacting that the guardians of either sex should have all their pursuits in common; to the utility and also to the possibility of this arrangement the consistency of the argument with itself bears witness.

Yes, that was a mighty wave which you have escaped.

Yes, I said, but a greater is coming; you will not think much of this when you see the next.

Go on; let me see.

The law, I said, which is the sequel of this and of all that has preceded, is to the following effect, "that the wives of our guardians are to be common, and their children are to be common, and no parent is to know his own child, nor any child his parent."

Yes, he said, that is a much greater wave than the other; and the possibility as well as the utility of such a law are far more questionable.

I do not think, I said, that there can be any dispute about the very great utility of having wives and children in common; the possibility is quite another matter, and will be very much disputed.

I think that a good many doubts may be raised about both.

You imply that the two questions must be combined, I replied. Now I meant that you should admit the utility; and in this way, as I thought, I should escape from one of them, and then there would remain only the possibility.

But that little attempt is detected, and therefore you will please to give a defence of both.

Well, I said, I submit to my fate. Yet grant me a little favor: let me feast my mind with the dream as daydreamers are in the habit of feasting themselves when they are walking alone; for before they have discovered any means of effecting their wishes—that is a matter which never troubles them—they would rather not tire themselves by thinking about possibilities; but assuming that what they desire is already granted to them, they proceed with their plan, and delight in detailing what they mean to do when their wish has come true—that is a way which they have of not doing much good to a capacity which was never good for much. Now I myself am beginning to lose heart, and I should like, with your permission, to pass over the question of possibility at present. Assuming therefore the possibility of the proposal, I shall now proceed to inquire how the rulers will carry out these arrangements, and I shall demonstrate that our plan, if executed, will be of the greatest benefit to the State and to the guardians. First of all, then, if you have no objection, I will endeavor with your help to consider the advantages of the measure; and hereafter the question of possibility.

I have no objection; proceed.

First, I think that if our rulers and their auxiliaries are to be worthy of the name which they bear, there must be willingness to obey in the one and the power of command in the other; the guardians themselves must obey the laws, and they must also imitate the spirit of them in any details which are intrusted to their care.

That is right, he said.

You, I said, who are their legislator, having selected the men, will now select the women and give them to them; they must be as far as possible of like natures with them; and they must live in common houses and meet at common meals. None of them will have anything specially his or her own; they will be together, and will be brought up together, and will associate at gymnastic exercises. And so they will be drawn by a necessity of their natures to have intercourse with each other—necessity is not too strong a word, I think?

Yes, he said; necessity, not geometrical, but another sort of necessity which lovers know, and which is far more convincing and constraining to the mass of mankind.

True, I said; and this, Glaucon, like all the rest, must proceed after an orderly fashion; in a city of the blessed, licentiousness is an unholy thing which the rulers will forbid.

Yes, he said, and it ought not to be permitted.

Then clearly the next thing will be to make matrimony sacred in the highest degree, and what is most beneficial will be deemed sacred?

Exactly.

And how can marriages be made most beneficial? that is a question which I put to you, because I see in your house dogs for hunting, and of the nobler sort of birds not a few. Now, I beseech you, do tell me, have you ever attended to their pairing and breeding?

In what particulars?

Why, in the first place, although they are all of a good sort, are not some better than others?

True.

And do you breed from them all indifferently, or do you take care to breed from the best only?

From the best.

And do you take the oldest or the youngest, or only those of ripe age?

I choose only those of ripe age.

And if care was not taken in the breeding, your dogs and birds would greatly deteriorate?

Certainly.

And the same of horses and of animals in general?

Undoubtedly.

Good heavens! my dear friend, I said, what consummate skill will our rulers need if the same principle holds of the human species!

Certainly, the same principle holds; but why does this involve any particular skill?

Because, I said, our rulers will often have to practise upon the body corporate with medicines. Now you know that when patients do not require medicines, but have only to be put under a regimen, the inferior sort of practitioner is deemed to be good enough; but when medicine has to be given, then the doctor should be more of a man.

That is quite true, he said; but to what are you alluding?

I mean, I replied, that our rulers will find a considerable dose of falsehood and deceit necessary for the good of their subjects: we were saying that the use of all these things regarded as medicines might be of advantage.

And we were very right.

And this lawful use of them seeing likely to be often needed in the regulations of marriages and births.

How so?

Why, I said, the principle has been already laid down that the best of either sex should be united with the best as often, and the inferior with the inferior as seldom, as possible; and that they should rear the offspring of the one sort of union, but not of the other, if the flock is to be maintained in first-rate condition. Now these goings-on must be a secret which the rulers only know, or there will be a further danger of our herd, as the guardians may be termed, breaking out into rebellion.

Very true.

Had we better not appoint certain festivals at which we will bring together the brides and bridegrooms, and sacrifices will be offered and suitable hymeneal gongs composed by our poets: the number of weddings is a matter which must be left to the discretion of the rulers, whose aim will be to preserve the average of population? There are many other things which they will have to consider, such as the effects of wars and diseases and any similar agencies, in order as far as this is possible to prevent the State from becoming either too large or too small.

Certainly, he replied.

We shall have to invent some ingenious kind of lots which the less worthy may draw on each occasion of our bringing them together, and then they will accuse their own ill-luck and not the rulers.

To be sure, he said.

And I think that our braver and better youth, besides their other honors and rewards, might have greater facilities of intercourse with women given them; their bravery will be a reason, and such fathers ought to have as many sons as possible.

True.

And the proper officers, whether male or female or both, for offices are to be held by women as well as by men—

Yes—

The proper officers will take the offspring of the good parents to the pen or fold, and there they will deposit them with certain nurses who dwell in a separate quarter; but the offspring of the inferior, or of the better when they chance to be deformed, will be put away in some mysterious, unknown place, as they should be.

Yes, he said, that must be done if the breed of the guardians is to be kept pure.

They will provide for their nurture, and will bring the mothers to the fold when they are full of milk, taking the greatest possible care that no mother recognizes her own child; and other wet nurses may be engaged if more are required. Care will also be taken that the process of suckling shall not be protracted too long; and the mothers will have no getting up at night or other trouble, but will hand over all this sort of thing to the nurses and attendants.

You suppose the wives of our guardians to have a fine easy time of it when they are having children.

Why, said I, and so they ought. Let us, however, proceed with our scheme. We were saying that the parents should be in the prime of life?

Very true.

And what is the prime of life? May it not be defined as a period of about twenty years in a woman's life, and thirty years in a man's?

Which years do you mean to include?

A woman, I said, at twenty years of age may begin to bear children to the State, and continue to bear them until forty; a man may begin at five-and-twenty, when he has passed the point at which the pulse of life beats quickest, and continue to beget children until he be fifty-five.

Certainly, he said, both in men and women those years are the prime of physical as well as of intellectual vigor.

Anyone above or below the prescribed ages who takes part in the public hymeneals shall be said to have done an unholy and unrighteous thing; the child of which he is the father, if it steals into life, will have been conceived under auspices very unlike the sacrifices and prayers, which at each hymeneal priestesses and priests and the whole city will offer, that the new generation may be better and more useful than their good and useful parents, whereas his child will be I the offspring of darkness and strange lust.

Very true, he replied.

And the same law will apply to any one of those within the prescribed age who forms a connection with any woman in the prime of life without the sanction of the rulers; for we shall say that he is raising up a bastard to the State, uncertified and unconsecrated.

Very true, he replied.

This applies, however, only to those who are within the specified age:

after that we will allow them to range at will, except that a man may not marry his daughter or his daughter's daughter, or his mother or his mother's mother; and women, on the other hand, are prohibited from marrying their sons or fathers, or son's son or father's father, and so on in either direction. and we grant all this, accompanying the permission with strict orders to prvent any embryo which may come into being from seeing the light; and if any force a way to the birth, the parents must understand that the off-spring of such a union cannot be maintained, and arrange accordingly.

They will never know. The way will be this, dating from the day of the hymeneal, the bridegroom who was then married will call all the male chil-dren who are born in the seventh and the tenth month afterward his sons, and the female children his daughters, and they will call him father, and he will call their children his grandchildren, and they will call the elder gener-ation grandfathers and grandmothers. All who were begotten at the time when their fathers and mothers came together will be called their brothers and sisters, and these, as I was saying, will be forbidden to intermarry. This, however, is not to be understood as an absolute prohibition of the marriage of brothers and sisters; if the lot favors them, and they receive the sanction of the Pythian oracle, the law will allow them.

Quite right, he replied.

Such is the scheme, Glaucon, according to which the guardians of our State are to have their wives and families in common.

2

●

FROM *NICOMACHEAN ETHICS* AND *POLITICS*

Aristotle

ARISTOTLE'S *ETHICS*

And now let us revert to the Good of which we are in search: what can it be? for manifestly it is different in different actions and arts: for it is different in the healing art and in the art military, and similarly in the rest. What then is the Chief Good in each? Is it not "that for the sake of which the other things are done?" and this in the healing art is health, and in the art military victory, and in that of house building a house, and in any other thing something else; in short, in every action and moral choice the End, because in all cases men do everything else with a view to this. So that if there is some one End of all things which are and may be done, this must be the Good proposed by doing, or if more than one, then these.

Thus our discussion after some traversing about has come to the same point which we reached before. And this we must try yet more to clear up.

Now since the ends are plainly many, and of these we choose some with a view to others (wealth, for instance, musical instruments, and, in general, all instruments), it is clear that all are not final: but the Chief Good is manifestly something final; and so, if there is some one only which is final, this must be the object of our search: but if several, then the most final of them will be it.

Now that which is an object of pursuit in itself we call more final than that which is so with a view to something else; that again which is never an object of choice with a view to something else than those which are so both in themselves and with a view to this ulterior object: and so by the term "absolutely final," we denote that which is an object of choice always in itself, and never with a view to any other.

And of this nature Happiness is mostly thought to be, for this we choose always for its own sake, and never with a view to anything further: whereas honour, pleasure, intellect, in fact every excellence we choose for their own sakes, it is true (because we would choose each of these even if no result were to follow), but we choose them also with a view to happiness, conceiving that through their instrumentality we shall be happy: but no man chooses happiness with a view to them, nor in fact with a view to any other thing whatsoever.

The same result is seen to follow also from the notion of self-sufficiency, a quality thought to belong to the final good. Now by sufficient for Self, we mean not for a single individual living a solitary life, but for his parents also and children and wife, and, in general, friends and countrymen; for man is by nature adapted to a social existence. But of these, of course, some limit must be fixed: for if one extends it to parents and descendants and friends' friends, there is no end to it. This point, however, must be left for future investigation: for the present we define that to be self-sufficient "which taken alone makes life choiceworthy, and to be in want of nothing"; now of such kind we think Happiness to be: and further, to be most choiceworthy of all things; not being reckoned with any other thing, for if it were so reckoned, it is plain we must then allow it, with the addition of ever so small a good, to be more choiceworthy than it was before: because what is put to it becomes an addition of so much more good, and of goods the greater is ever the more choice-worthy.

So then Happiness is manifestly something final and self-sufficient, being the end of all things which are and may be done.

But, it may be, to call Happiness the Chief Good is a mere truism, and what is wanted is some clearer account of its real nature. Now this object may be easily attained, when we have discovered what is the work of man; for as in the case of flute player, statuary, or artisan of any kind, or, more generally, all who have any work or course of action, their Chief Good and Excellence is thought to reside in their work, so it would seem to be with man, if there is any work belonging to him.

Are we then to suppose, that while carpenter and cobbler have certain works and courses of action, Man as Man has none, but is left by Nature without a work? or would not one rather hold, that as eye, hand, and foot, and generally each of his members, has manifestly some special work; so too the whole Man, as distinct from all these, has some work of his own?

What then can this be? not mere life, because that plainly is shared with him even by vegetables, and we want what is peculiar to him. We must separate off then the life of mere nourishment and growth, and next will come the life of sensation: but this again manifestly is common to horses, oxen, and every animal. There remains then a kind of life of the Rational Nature apt to act: and of this Nature there are two parts denominated Rational, the one as being obedient to Reason, the other as having and exerting it. Again, as this life is also spoken of in two ways, we must take that which is in the way of actual working, because this is thought to be most properly entitled to the name. If then the work of Man is a working of the soul in accordance with reason, or at least not independently of reason, and we say that the work of any given subject, and of that subject good of its kind, are the same in kind (as, for instance, of a harp player and a good harp player, and so on in every case, adding to the work eminence in the way of excellence; I mean, the work of a harp player is to play the harp, and of a good harp player to play it well); if, I say, this is so, and we assume the work of Man to be life of a certain kind, that is to say a working of the soul, and actions with reason, and of a good man to do these things well and nobly, and in fact everything is finished off well in the way of the excellence which peculiarly belongs to it: if all this is so, then the Good of Man comes to be "a working of the Soul in the way of Excellence," or, if Excellence admits of degrees, in the way of the best and most perfect Excellence.

And we must add, in a complete life; for as it is not one swallow or one fine day that makes a spring, so it is not one day or a short time that makes a man blessed and happy.

Let this then be taken for a rough sketch of the Chief Good: since it is probably the right way to give first the outline, and fill it in afterwards. And it would seem that any man may improve and connect what is good in the sketch, and that time is a good discoverer and cooperator in such matters: it is thus in fact that all improvements in the various arts have been brought about, for any man may fill up a deficiency.

You must remember also what has been already stated, and not seek for exactness in all matters alike, but in each according to the subject matter, and so far as properly belongs to the system. The carpenter and geometrician, for instance, inquire into the right line in different fashion: the former so far as he wants it for his work, the latter inquires into its nature and properties, because he is concerned with the truth.

So then should one do in other matters, that the incidental matters may not exceed the direct ones.

And again, you must not demand the reason either in all things alike, because in some it is sufficient that the fact has been well demonstrated, which is the case with first principles; and the fact is the first step, i.e., starting point or principle.

And of these first principles some are obtained by induction, some by perception, some by a course of habituation, others in other different ways. And we must try to trace up each in their own nature, and take pains to secure their being well defined, because they have great influence on what follows: it is thought, I mean, that the starting point or principle is more than half the whole matter, and that many of the points of inquiry come simultaneously into view thereby.

We must now inquire concerning Happiness, not only from our conclusion and the data on which our reasoning proceeds, but likewise from what is commonly said about it: because with what is true all things which really are are in harmony, but with that which is false the true very soon jars.

Now there is a common division of goods into three classes; one being called external, the other two those of the soul and body respectively, and those belonging to the soul we call most properly and specially good. Well, in our definition we assume that the actions and workings of the soul constitute Happiness, and these of course belong to the soul. And so our account is a good one, at least according to this opinion which is of ancient date, and accepted by those who profess philosophy. Rightly, too, are certain actions and workings said to be the end, for thus it is brought into the number of the goods of the soul instead of the external. Agreeing also with our definition is the common notion, that the happy man lives well and does well, for it has been stated by us to be pretty much a kind of living well and doing well.

But further, the points required in Happiness are found in combination in our account of it.

For some think it is virtue, others practical wisdom, others a kind of scientific philosophy; others that it is these, or else some one of them, in combination with pleasure, or at least not independently of it; while others again take in external prosperity.

Of these opinions, some rest on the authority of numbers or antiquity, others on that of few, and those men of note: and it is not likely that either of these classes should be wrong in all points, but be right at least in some one, or even in most.

Now with those who assert it to be Virtue (Excellence), or some kind of Virtue, our account agrees: for working in the way of Excellence surely belongs to Excellence.

And there is perhaps no unimportant difference between conceiving of the Chief Good as in possession or as in use, in other words, as a mere state or as a working. For the state or habit may possibly exist in a subject without effecting any good, as, for instance, in him who is asleep, or in any other way inactive; but the working cannot so, for it will of necessity act, and act well. And as at the Olympic games it is not the finest and strongest men who are crowned, but they who enter the lists, for out of these the prizemen are selected; so too in life, of the honourable and the good, it is they who act who rightly win the prizes.

Their life too is in itself pleasant: for the feeling of pleasure is a mental sensation, and that is to each pleasant of which he is said to be fond: a horse, for instance, to him who is fond of horses, and a sight to him who is fond of sights: and so in like manner just acts to him who is fond of justice, and more generally the things in accordance with virtue to him who is fond of virtue. Now in the case of the multitude of men the things which they individually esteem pleasant clash, because they are not such by nature, whereas to the lovers of nobleness those things are pleasant which are such by nature: but the actions in accordance with virtue are of this kind, so that they are pleasant both to the individuals and also in themselves.

So then their life has no need of pleasure as a kind of additional appendage, but involves pleasure in itself. For, besides what I have just mentioned, a man is not a good man at all who feels no pleasure in noble actions, just as no one would call that man just who does not feel pleasure in acting justly, or liberal who does not in liberal actions, and similarly in the case of the other virtues which might be enumerated: and if this be so, then the actions in accordance with virtue must be in themselves pleasurable. Then again they are certainly good and noble, and each of these in the highest degree; if we are to take as right the judgment of the good man, for he judges as we have said.

Thus then Happiness is most excellent, most noble, and most pleasant, and these attributes are not separated as in the well-known Delian inscription

"Most noble is that which is most just, but best is health;
And naturally most pleasant is the obtaining one's desires."

For all these coexist in the best acts of working: and we say that Happiness is these, or one, that is, the best of them.

Still it is quite plain that it does require the addition of external goods, as we have said: because without appliances it is impossible, or at all events not easy, to do noble actions: for friends, money, and political influence are in a manner instruments whereby many things are done: some things there are again a deficiency in which mars blessedness; good birth, for instance, or fine offspring, or even personal beauty: for he is not at all capable of Happiness who is very ugly, or is ill-born, or solitary and childless; and still less perhaps supposing him to have very bad children or friends, or to have lost good ones by death. As we have said already, the addition of prosperity of this kind does seem necessary to complete the idea of Happiness; hence some rank good fortune, and others virtue, with Happiness.

And hence, too, a question is raised, whether it is a thing that can be learned, or acquired by habituation or discipline of some other kind, or whether it comes in the way of divine dispensation, or even in the way of chance.

Now to be sure, if anything else is a gift of the Gods to men, it is probable that Happiness is a gift of theirs, too, and specially because of all human goods it is the highest. But this, it may be, is a question belonging more properly to an investigation different from ours: and it is quite clear, that on the supposition of its not being sent from the Gods direct, but coming to us by reason of virtue and learning of a certain kind, or discipline, it is yet one of the most Godlike things; because the prize and End of virtue is manifestly somewhat most excellent, nay divine and blessed.

It will also on this supposition be widely participated, for it may through learning and diligence of a certain kind exist in all who have not been maimed for virtue.

And if it is better we should be happy thus than as a result of chance, this is in itself an argument that the case is so; because those things which are in the way of nature, and in like manner of art, and of every cause, and specially the best cause, are by nature in the best way possible: to leave them to chance what is greatest and most noble would be very much out of harmony with all these facts.

The question may be determined also by a reference to our definition of Happiness, that it is a working of the soul in the way of excellence or virtue of a certain kind: and of the other goods, some we must have to begin with, and those which are cooperative and useful are given by nature as instruments.

These considerations will harmonise also with what we said at the commencement: for we assumed the End of πολιτική to be most excellent: now this bestows most care on making the members of the community of a certain character; good that is and apt to do what is honourable.

With good reason then neither ox nor horse nor any other brute animal do we call happy, for none of them can partake in such working: and for this same reason a child is not happy either, because by reason of his tender age he cannot yet perform such actions: if the term is applied, it is by way of anticipation.

For to constitute Happiness, there must be, as we have said, complete virtue and a complete life: for many changes and chances of all kinds arise during a life, and he who is most prosperous may become involved in great misfortunes in his old age, as in the heroic poems the tale is told of Priam: but the man who has experienced such fortune and died in wretchedness, no man calls happy.

Now that we have spoken about the Excellences of both kinds, and Friendship in its varieties, and Pleasures, it remains to sketch out Happiness, since we assume that to be the one End of all human things: and we shall save time and trouble by recapitulating what was stated before.

Well then, we said that it is not a State merely; because, if it were, it might belong to one who slept all his life through and merely vegetated, or to one who fell into very great calamities: and so, if these possibilities displease us and we would rather put it into the rank of some kind of Working (as was also said before), and Workings are of different kinds (some being necessary and choiceworthy with a view to other things, while others are so in themselves), it is plain we must rank Happiness among those choiceworthy for their own sakes and not among those which are so with a view to something further: because Happiness has no lack of anything but is self-sufficient.

By choiceworthy in themselves are meant those from which nothing is sought beyond the act of Working: and of this kind are thought to be the actions according to Virtue, because doing what is noble and excellent is one of those things which are choiceworthy for their own sake alone.

And again, such amusements as are pleasant; because people do not choose them with any further purpose: in fact they receive more harm than profit from them, neglecting their persons and their property. Still the common run of those who are judged happy take refuge in such pastimes, which is the reason why they who have varied talent in such are highly esteemed among despots; because they make themselves pleasant in those things which these aim at, and these accordingly want such men.

Now these things are thought to be appurtenances of Happiness because men in power spend their leisure herein: yet, it may be, we cannot argue from the example of such men: because there is neither Virtue nor Intellect necessarily involved in having power, and yet these are the only sources of good Workings: nor does it follow that because these men, never having tasted pure and generous Pleasure, take refuge in bodily ones, we are therefore to believe them to be more choiceworthy: for children too believe that those things are most excellent which are precious in their eyes.

We may well believe that as children and men have different ideas as to what is precious so too have the bad and the good: therefore, as we have many times said, those things are really precious and pleasant which seem so to the good man: and as to each individual that Working is most choiceworthy which is in accordance with his own state to the good man that is so which is in accordance with Virtue.

Happiness then stands not in amusement; in fact the very notion is absurd of the End being amusement, and of one's toiling and enduring hardness all one's life long with a view to amusement: for everything in the world, so to speak, we choose with some further End in view, except Happiness, for that is the End comprehending all others. Now to take pains and to labour with a view to amusement is plainly foolish and very childish: but to amuse one's self with a view to steady employment afterwards, as Anacharsis says, is thought to be right: for amusement is like rest, and men want rest because unable to labour continuously.

Rest, therefore, is not an End, because it is adopted with a view to Working afterwards.

Again, it is held that the Happy Life must be one in the way of Excellence, and this is accompanied by earnestness and stands not in amusement. Moreover those things which are done in earnest, we say, are better than things merely ludicrous and joined with amusement: and we say that the Working of the better part, or the better man, is more earnest; and the Working of the better is at once better and more capable of Happiness.

Then, again, as for bodily Pleasures, any ordinary person, or even a slave, might enjoy them, just as well as the best man living: but Happiness no one supposes a slave to share except so far as it is implied in life: because Happiness stands not in such pastimes but in the Workings in the way of Excellence, as has also been stated before.

Now if Happiness is a Working in the way of Excellence of course that Excellence must be the highest, that is to say, the Excellence of the best Principle. Whether then this best Principle is Intellect or some other which is thought naturally to rule and to lead and to conceive of noble and divine things, whether being in its own nature divine or the most divine of all our internal Principles, the Working of this in accordance with its own proper Excellence must be the perfect Happiness.

That it is Contemplative has been already stated: and this would seem to be consistent with what we said before and with truth: for, in the first place, this Working is of the highest kind, since the Intellect is the highest of our internal Principles and the subjects with which it is conversant the highest of all which fall within the range of out knowledge.

Next, it is also most Continuous: for we are better able to contemplate than to do anything else whatever, continuously.

Again, we think Pleasure must be in some way an ingredient in Happiness, and of all Workings in accordance with Excellence that in the way of Science is confessedly most pleasant: at least the pursuit of Science is thought to contain Pleasures admirable for purity and permanence; and it is reasonable to suppose that the employment is more pleasant to those who have mastered, than to those who are yet seeking for, it.

And the Self-Sufficiency which people speak of will attach chiefly to the Contemplative Working: of course the actual necessaries of life are needed alike by the man of science, and the just man, and all the other characters; but, supposing all sufficiently supplied with these, the just man needs people towards whom, and in concert with whom, to practise his justice; and in like manner the man of perfected self-mastery, and the brave man, and so on of the rest; whereas the man of science can contemplate and speculate even when quite alone, and the more entirely he deserves the appellation the more able is he to do so: it may be he can do better for having fellow-workers but still he is certainly most Self-Sufficient.

Again, this alone would seem to be rested in for its own sake, since nothing results from it beyond the fact of having contemplated; whereas from all things which are objects of moral action we do mean to get something beside the doing them, be the same more or less.

Also, Happiness is thought to stand in perfect rest; for we toil that we may rest, and war that we may be at peace. Now all the Practical Virtues require either society or war for their Working, and the actions regarding these are thought to exclude rest; those of war entirely, because no one chooses war, nor prepares for war, for war's sake: he would indeed be thought a bloodthirsty villain who should make enemies of his friends to secure the existence of fighting and bloodshed. The Working also of the statesman excludes the idea of rest, and, beside the actual work of government, seeks for power and dignities or at least Happiness for the man himself and his fellow-citizens: a Happiness distinct from the national Happiness which we evidently seek as being different and distinct.

If then of all the actions in accordance with the various virtues those of policy and war are preeminent in honour and greatness, and these are restless, and aim at some further End, and are not choiceworthy for their own sakes, but the Working of the Intellect, being apt for contemplation, is thought to excel in earnestness, and to aim at no End beyond itself, and to have Pleasure of its own which helps to increase the Working; and if the attributes of Self-Sufficiency, and capacity of rest, and unweariedness (as far as is compatible with the infirmity of human nature), and all other attributes of the highest Happiness, plainly belong to this Working, this must be perfect Happiness, if attaining a complete duration of life; which condition is added because none of the points of Happiness is incomplete.

But such a life will be higher than mere human nature, because a man will live thus, not insofar as he is man but insofar as there is in him a divine Principle: and in proportion as this Principle excels his composite nature so far does the Working thereof excel that in accordance with any other kind of Excellence: and therefore, if pure Intellect, as compared with human nature, is divine, so too will the life in accordance with it be divine compared with man's ordinary life.

Yet must we not give ear to those who bid one as man to mind only man's affairs, or as mortal only mortal things; but, so far as we can, make ourselves like immortals and do all with a view to living in accordance with the highest Principle in us; for small as it may be in bulk yet in power and preciousness it far more excels all the others [than they it in bulk].

In fact this Principle would seem to constitute each man's "Self," since it is supreme and above all others in goodness: it would be absurd then for a man not to choose his own life but that of some other.

And here will apply an observation made before, that whatever is proper to each is naturally best and pleasantest to him: such then is to Man the life in accordance with pure Intellect (since this Principle is most truly Man), and if so, then it is also the happiest.

And second in degree of Happiness will be that Life which is in accordance with the other kind of Excellence, for the Workings in accordance with this are proper to Man: I mean, we do actions of justice, courage, and the other virtues, towards one another, in contracts, services of different kinds, and in all kinds of actions and feelings too, by observing what is befitting for each: and all these plainly are proper to man. Further, the Excellence of the Moral character is thought to result in some points from physical circumstances, and to be, in many, very closely connected with the passions.

Again, Practical Wisdom and Excellence of the Moral character are very closely united; since the Principles of Practical Wisdom are in accordance with the Moral Virtues and these are right when they accord with Practical Wisdom.

These moreover, as bound up with the passions, must belong to the composite nature, and the Excellences or Virtues of the composite nature are proper to man: therefore so too will be the life and Happiness which is in accordance with them. But that of the Pure Intellect is separate and distinct: and let this suffice upon the subject, since great exactness is beyond our purpose.

It would seem, moreover, to require supply of external goods to a small degree, or certainly less than the Moral Happiness: for, as far as necessaries of life are concerned, we will suppose both characters to need them equally (though, in point of fact, the man who lives in society does take more pains about his person and all that kind of thing; there will really be some little difference), but when we come to consider their Workings there will be found a great difference.

I mean, the liberal man must have money to do his liberal actions with, and the just man to meet his engagements (for mere intentions are uncertain, and even those who are unjust make a pretence of wishing to do justly), and the brave man must have power, if he is to perform any of the actions which appertain to his particular Virtue, and the man of perfected self-mastery must have opportunity of temptation, else how shall he or any of the others display his real character?

(By the way, a question is sometimes raised, whether the moral choice or the actions have most to do with Virtue, since it consists in both: it is plain that the perfection of virtuous action requires both: but for the actions many things are required, and the greater and more numerous they are the more.) But as for the man engaged in Contemplative Speculation, not only are such things unnecessary for his Working, but, so to speak, they are even hindrances: as regards the Contemplation at least; because of course insofar as he is Man and lives in society he chooses to do what Virtue requires, and so he will need such things for maintaining his character as Man though not as a speculative philosopher.

And that the perfect Happiness must be a kind of Contemplative Working may appear also from the following consideration: our conception of the gods is that they are above all blessed and happy: now what kind of Moral actions are we to attribute to them? those of justice? nay, will they not be set in a ridiculous light if represented as forming contracts, and restoring deposits, and so on? well then, shall we picture them performing brave actions, withstanding objects of fear and meeting dangers, because it is noble to do so? or liberal ones? but to whom shall they be giving? and further, it is absurd to think they have money or anything of the kind. And as for actions of perfected self-mastery, what can theirs be? would it not be a degrading praise that they have no bad desires? In short, if one followed the subject into all details all the circumstances connected with Moral actions would appear trivial and unworthy of gods.

Still, every one believes that they live, and therefore that they Work because it is not supposed that they sleep their time away like Endymion: now if from a living being you take away Action, still more if Creation, what remains but Contemplation? So then the Working of the Gods, eminent in blessedness, will be one apt for Contemplative Speculation: and of all human Workings that will have the greatest capacity for Happiness which is nearest akin to this.

A corroboration of which position is the fact that the other animals do not partake of Happiness, being completely shut out from any such Working.

To the gods then all their life is blessed; and to men insofar as there is in it some copy of such Working, but of the other animals none is happy because it in no way shares in Contemplative Speculation.

Happiness then is coextensive with this Contemplative Speculation, and in proportion as people have the act of Contemplation so far have they also the being happy, not incidentally, but in the way of Contemplative Speculation because it is in itself precious.

So Happiness must be a kind of Contemplative Speculation; but since it is Man we are speaking of he will need likewise External Prosperity, because his Nature is not by itself sufficient for Speculation, but there must be health of body, and nourishment, and tendance of all kinds.

However, it must not be thought, because without external goods a man cannot enjoy high Happiness, that therefore he will require many and great goods in order to be happy: for neither Self-sufficiency, nor Action, stand in Excess, and it is quite possible to act nobly without being ruler of sea and land, since even with moderate means a man may act accordance with Virtue.

And this may be clearly seen in that men in private stations are thought to act justly, not merely no less than men in power but even more: it will be quite enough that just so much should belong to a man as is necessary, for his life will be happy who works in accordance with Virtue.

Solon perhaps drew a fair picture of the Happy, when he said that they are men moderately supplied with external goods, and who have achieved the most noble deeds, as be thought, and who have lived with perfect self-mastery: for it is quite possible for men of moderate means to act as they ought.

Anaxagoras also seems to have conceived of the Happy man not as either rich or powerful, saying that lie should not wonder if he were accounted a strange man in the judgment of the multitude: for they judge by outward circumstances of which alone they have any perception.

And thus the opinions of the Wise seem to be accordant with our account of the matter: of course such things carry some weight, but truth, in matters of moral action, is judged from facts and from actual life, for herein rests the decision. So what we should do is to examine the preceding statements by referring them to facts and to actual life, and when they harmonise with facts we may accept them, when they are at variance with them conceive of them as mere theories.

Now he that works in accordance with, and pays observance to, Pure Intellect, and tends this, seems likely to be both in the best frame of mind and dearest to the Gods: because if, as is thought, any care is bestowed on human things by the Gods then it must be reasonable to think that they take pleasure in what is best and most akin to themselves (and this must be the Pure Intellect); and that they requite with kindness those who love and honour this most, as paying observance to what is dear to them, and as acting rightly and nobly. And it is quite obvious that the man of Science chiefly combines all these: he is therefore dearest to the Gods, and it is probable that he is at the same time most Happy.

Thus then on this view also the man of Science will be most Happy.

POLITICA

Book 1

He who thus considers things in their first growth and origin, whether a state or anything else, will obtain the clearest view of them. In the first place there must be a union of those who cannot exist without each other; namely, of male and female, that the race may continue (and this is a union which is formed, not of deliberate purpose, but because, in common with other animals and with plants, mankind have a natural desire to leave behind them an image of themselves), and of natural ruler and subject, that both may be preserved. For that which can foresee by the exercise of mind is by nature intended to be lord and master, and that which can with its body give effect to such foresight is a subject, and by nature a slave; hence master and slave have the same interest. Now nature has distinguished between the female and the slave. For she is not niggardly, like the smith who fashions the Delphian knife for many uses; she makes each thing for a single use, and every instrument is best made when intended for one and not for many uses. But among barbarians no distinction is made between women and slaves, because there is no natural ruler among them: they are a community of slaves, male and female. Wherefore the poets say

"It is meet that Hellenes should rule over barbarians";

as if they thought that the barbarian and the slave were by nature one.

Out of these two relationships between man and woman, master and slave, the first thing to arise is the family, and Hesiod is right when be says

"First house and wife and an ox for the plough,"

for the ox is the poor man's slave. The family is the association established by nature for the supply of men's everyday wants, and the members of it are called by Charondas "companions of the cupboard," and by Epimenides the Cretan, "companions of the manger." But when several families are united, and the association aims at something more than the supply of daily needs, the first society to be formed is the village. And the most natural form of the village appears to be that of a colony from the family, composed of the children and grandchildren, who are said to be "suckled with the same milk." And this is the reason why Hellenic states were originally governed by kings; because the Hellenes were under royal rule before they came together, as the barbarians still are. Every family is ruled by the eldest, and therefore in the colonies of the family the kingly form of government prevailed because they were of the same blood. As Homer says:

"Each one gives law to his children and to his wives."

For they lived dispersedly, as was the manner in ancient times. Wherefore men say that the Gods have a king, because they themselves either are or were in ancient times under the rule of a king. For they imagine, not only the forms of the Gods, but their ways of life to be like their own.

When several villages are united in a single complete community, large enough to be nearly or quite self-sufficing, the state comes into existence, originating in the bare needs of life, and continuing in existence for the sake of a good life. And therefore, if the earlier forms of society are natural, so is the state, for it is the end of them, and the nature of a thing is its end. For what each thing is when fully developed, we call its nature, whether we are speaking of a man, a horse, or a family. Besides, the final cause and end of a thing is the best, and to be self-sufficing is the end and the best.

Hence it is evident that the state is a creation of nature, and that man is by nature a political animal. And he who by nature and not by mere accident is without a state, is either a bad man or above humanity; he is like the

"Tribeless, lawless, hearthless one,"

whom Homer denounces—the natural outcast is forthwith a lover of war; he may be compared to an isolated piece at draughts.

Now, that man is more of a political animal than bees or any other gregarious animals is evident. Nature, as we often say, makes nothing in vain, and man is the only animal whom she has endowed with the gift of speech. And whereas mere voice is but an indication of pleasure or pain, and is therefore found in other animals (for their nature attains to the perception of pleasure and pain and the intimation of them to one another, and no further), the power of speech is intended to set forth the expedient and inexpedient, and therefore likewise the just and the unjust. And it is a characteristic of man that he alone has any sense of good and evil, of just and unjust, and the like, and the association of living beings who have this sense makes a family and a state.

Further, the state is by nature clearly prior to the family and to the individual, since the whole is of necessity prior to the part; for example, if the whole body be destroyed, there will be no foot or hand, except in an equivocal sense, as we might speak of a stone hand; for when destroyed the hand will be no better than that. But things are defined by their working and power; and we ought not to say that they are the same when they no longer have their proper quality, but only that they have the same name. The proof that the state is a creation of nature and prior to the individual is that the individual, when isolated, is not self-sufficing; and therefore he is like a part in relation to the whole. But he who is unable to live in society, or who has no need because he is sufficient for himself, must be either a beast or a god: he is no part of a state. A social instinct is implanted in all men by nature, and yet he who first founded the state was the greatest of benefactors. For man, when perfected, is the best of animals, but, when separated from law and justice, he is the worst of all; since armed injustice is the more dangerous, and he is equipped at birth with arms, meant to be used by intelligence and virtue, which he may use for the worst ends. Wherefore, if he have not virtue, he is the most unholy and the most savage of animals, and the most full of lust and gluttony.

A question may indeed be raised, whether there is any excellence at all in a slave beyond and higher than merely instrumental and ministerial qualities—whether he can have the virtues of temperance, courage, justice, and the like; or whether slaves possess only bodily and ministerial qualities. And, whichever way we answer the question, a difficulty arises; for, if they have virtue, in what will they differ from freemen? On the other hand, since they are men and share in rational principle, it seems absurd to say that they have no virtue. A similar question may be raised about women and children, whether they too have virtues: ought a woman to be temperate and brave and just, and is a child to be called temperate, and intemperate, or not? So in general we may ask about the natural ruler, and the natural subject, whether they have the same or different virtues. For if a noble nature is equally required in both, why should one of them always rule, and the other always be ruled? Nor can we say that this is a question of degree, for the difference between ruler and subject is a difference of kind, which the difference of more and less never is. Yet how strange is the supposition that the one ought, and that the other ought not, to have virtue! For if the ruler is intemperate and unjust, how can he rule well? if the subject, how can he obey well? If he be licentious and cowardly, he will certainly not do his duty. It is evident, therefore, that both of them must have a share of virtue, but varying as natural subjects also vary among themselves. Here the very constitution of the soul has shown us the way; in it one part naturally rules, and the other is subject, and the virtue of the ruler we maintain to be different from that of the subject;—the one being the virtue of the rational, and the other of the irrational part. Now, it is obvious that the same principle applies generally, and therefore almost all things rule and are ruled according to nature. But the kind of rule differs;—the free man rules over the slave after another manner from that in which the male rules over the female, or the man over the child; although the parts of the soul are present in all of them, they are present in different degrees. For the slave has no deliberative faculty at all; the woman has, but it is without authority, and the child has, but it is immature. So it must necessarily be supposed to be with the moral virtues also; all should partake of them, but only in such manner and degree as is required by each for the fulfilment of his duty. Hence the ruler ought to have moral virtue in perfection, for his function, taken absolutely, demands a master artificer, and rational principle is such an artificer; the subjects, on the other hand, require only that measure of virtue which is proper to each of them. Clearly, then, moral virtue belongs to all of them; but the temperance of a man and of a woman, or the courage and justice of a man and of a woman, are not, as Socrates maintained, the same; the courage of a man is shown in commanding, of a woman in obeying. And this holds of all other virtues, as will be more clearly seen if we look at them in detail, for those who say generally that virtue consists in a good disposition of the soul, or in doing rightly, or the like, only deceive themselves. Far better than such definitions is their mode of speaking, who, like Gorgias, enumerate the virtues. All classes must be deemed to have their special attributes; as the poet says of women,

"Silence is a woman's glory,"

but this is not equally the glory of man. The child is imperfect, and therefore obviously his virtue is not relative to himself alone, but to the perfect man and to his teacher, and in like manner the virtue of the slave is relative to a master. Now we determined that a slave is useful for the wants of life, and therefore he will obviously require only so much virtue as will prevent him from failing in his duty through cowardice or lack of self-control. Some one will ask whether, if what we are saying is true, virtue will not be required also in the artisans, for they often fail in their work through the lack of self-control? But is there not a great difference in the two cases? For the slave shares in his master's life; the artisan is less closely connected with him, and only attains excellence in proportion as he becomes a slave. The meaner sort of mechanic has a special and separate slavery; and whereas the slave exists by nature, not so the shoemaker or other artisan. It is manifest, then, that the master ought to be the source of such excellence in the slave, and not a mere possessor of the art of mastership which trains the slave in his duties. Wherefore they are mistaken who forbid us to converse with slaves and say that we should employ command only, for slaves stand even more in need of admonition than children.

Book 7

Since the end of individuals and of states is the same, the end of the best man and of the best constitution must also be the same; it is therefore evident that there ought to exist in both of them the virtues of leisure; for peace, as has been often repeated, is the end of war, and leisure of toil. But leisure and cultivation may be promoted, not only by those virtues which are practised in leisure, but also by some of those which are useful to business. For many necessaries of life have to be supplied before we can have leisure. Therefore a city must be temperate and brave, and able to endure: for truly, as the proverb says, "There is no leisure for slaves," and those who cannot face danger like men are the slaves of any invader. Courage and endurance are required for business and philosophy for leisure, temperance and justice for both, and more especially in times of peace and leisure, for war compels men to be just and temperate, whereas the enjoyment of good fortune and the leisure which comes with peace tend to make them insolent. Those then who seem to be the best-off and to be in the possession of every good, have special need of justice and temperance—for example, those (if such there be, as the poets say) who dwell in the Islands of the Blest; they above all will need philosophy and temperance and justice, and all the more the more leisure they have, living in the midst of abundance. There is no difficulty in seeing why the state that would be happy and good ought to have these virtues. If it be disgraceful in men not to be able to use the goods of life, it is peculiarly disgraceful not to be able to use them in time of leisure—to show excellent qualities in action and war, and when they have peace and leisure to be no better than slaves. Wherefore we should not practise virtue after the manner of the Lacedaemonians. For they, while agreeing with other men in their conception of the highest goods, differ from the rest of mankind in thinking that they are to be obtained by the practice of a single virtue. And since [they think] these goods and the enjoyment of them greater than the enjoyment derived from the virtues . . . and that [it should be practised] for its own sake, is evident from what has been said; we must now consider how and by what means it is to be attained.

We have already determined that nature and habit and rational principle are required, and, of these, the proper *nature* of the citizens has also been defined by us. But we have still to consider whether the training of early life is to be that of rational principle or habit, for these two must accord, and when in accord they will then form the best of harmonies. The rational principle may be mistaken and fail in attaining the highest ideal of life, and there may be a like evil influence of habit. Thus much is clear in the first place, that, as in all other things, birth implies an antecedent beginning, and that there are beginnings whose end is relative to a further end. Now, in men rational principle and mind are the end towards which nature strives, so that the birth and moral discipline of the citizens ought to be ordered with a view to them. In the second place, as the soul and body are two, we see also that there are two parts of the soul, the rational and the irrational, and two corresponding states—reason and appetite. And as the body is prior in order of generation to the soul, so the irrational is prior to the rational. The proof is that anger and wishing and desire are implanted in children from their very birth, but reason and understanding are developed as they grow older. Wherefore, the care of the body ought to precede that of the soul, and the training of the appetitive part should follow: nonetheless our care of it must be for the sake of the reason, and our care of the body for the sake of the soul.

Since the legislator should begin by considering how the frames of the children whom he is rearing may be as good as possible, his first care will be about marriage—at what age should his citizens marry, and who are fit to marry? In legislating on this subject he ought to consider the persons and the length of their life, that their procreative life may terminate at the same period, and that they may not differ in their bodily powers, as will be the case if the man is still able to beget children while the woman is unable to bear them, or the woman able to bear while the man is unable to beget, for from these causes arise quarrels and differences between married persons. Secondly, he must consider the time at which the children will succeed to their parents; there ought not to be too great an interval of age, for then the parents will be too old to derive any pleasure from their affection, or to be of any use to them. Nor ought they to be too nearly of an age; to youthful marriages there are many objections—the children will be wanting in respect to the parents, who will seem to be their contemporaries, and disputes will arise in the management of the household. Thirdly, and this is the point from which we digressed, the legislator must mould to his will the frames of newly born children. Almost all these objects may be secured by attention to one point. Since the time of generation is commonly limited within the age of seventy years in the case of a man, and of fifty in the case of a woman, the commencement of the union should conform to these periods. The union of male and female when too young is bad for the procreation of children; in all other animals the offspring of the young are small and ill-developed, and with a tendency to produce female children, and therefore also in man, as is proved by the fact that in those cities in which men and women are accustomed to marry young, the people are small and weak; in childbirth also younger women suffer more, and more of them die; some persons say that this was the meaning of the response once given to the Troezenians—the oracle really meant that many died because they married too young; it had nothing to do with the ingathering of the harvest. It also conduces to temperance not to marry too soon; for women who marry early are apt to he wanton; and in men too the bodily frame is stunted if they marry while the seed is growing (for there is a time when the growth of the seed, also, ceases, or continues to but a slight extent). Women should marry when they are about eighteen years of age, and men at seven and thirty; then they are in the prime of life, and the decline in the powers of both will coincide. Further, the children, if their birth takes place soon, as may reasonably be expected, will succeed in the beginning of their prime, when the fathers are already in the decline of life, and have nearly reached their term of threescore years and ten.

Thus much of the age proper for marriage: the season of the year should also be considered; according to our present custom, people generally limit marriage to the season of winter, and they are right. The precepts of physicians and natural philosophers about generation should also be studied by the parents themselves; the physicians give good advice about the favourable conditions of the body, and the natural philosophers about the winds; of which they prefer the north to the south.

What constitution in the parent is most advantageous to the offspring is a subject which we will consider more carefully, when we speak of the education of children, and we will only make a few general remarks at present. The constitution of an athlete is not suited to the life of a citizen, or to health, or to the procreation of children, any more than the valetudinarian or exhausted constitution, but one which is in a mean between them. A man's constitution should be inured to labour, but not to labour which is excessive or of one sort only, such as is practised by athletes; he should be capable of all the actions of a freeman. These remarks apply equally to both parents.

Women who are with child should be careful of themselves; they should take exercise and have a nourishing diet. The first of these prescriptions the legislator will easily carry into effect by requiring that they shall take a walk daily to some temple, where they can worship the gods who preside over birth. Their minds, however, unlike their bodies, they ought to keep quiet, for the offspring derive their natures from their mothers as plants do from the earth.

As to the exposure and rearing of children, let there be a law that no *deformed* child shall live, but that on the ground of an *excess* in the number of children, if the established customs of the state forbid this (for in our state population has a limit), no child is to be exposed but when couples have children in excess, let abortion be procured before sense and life have begun; what may or may not be lawfully done in these cases depends on the question of life and sensation.

And now, having determined at what ages men and women are to begin their union, let us also determine how long they shall continue to beget and bear offspring for the state; men who are too old, like men who are too young, produce children who are defective in body and mind; the children of very old men are weakly. The limit, then, should be the age which is the prime of their intelligence, and this in most persons, according to the notion of some poets who measure life by periods of seven years, is about fifty; at four or five years later, they should cease from having families; and from that time forward only cohabit with one another for the sake of health; or for some similar reason.

As to adultery, let it be held disgraceful, in general, for any man or woman to be found in any way unfaithful when they are married, and called husband and wife. If during the time of bearing children anything of the sort occur, let the guilty person be punished with a loss of privileges in proportion to the offence.

After the children have been born, the manner of rearing them may be supposed to have a great effect on their bodily strength. It would appear from the example of animals, and of those nations who desire to create the military habit, that the food which has most milk in it is best suited to human beings; but the less wine the better, if they would escape diseases. Also all the motions to which children can be subjected at their early age are very useful. But in order to preserve their tender limbs from distortion, some nations have had recourse to mechanical appliances which straighten their bodies. To accustom children to the cold from their earliest years is also an excellent practice, which greatly conduces to health, and hardens them for military service. Hence many barbarians have a custom of plunging their children at birth into a cold stream; others, like the Celts, clothe them in a light wrapper only. For human nature should be early habituated to endure all which by habit it can be made to endure; but the process must be gradual. And children, from their natural warmth, may be easily trained to bear cold. Such care should attend them in the first stage of life.

The next period lasts to the age of five; during this no demand should be made upon the child for study or labour, lest its growth be impeded; and there should be sufficient motion to prevent the limbs from being inactive. This can be secured, among other ways, by amusement, but the amusement should not be vulgar or tiring or effeminate. The Directors of Education, as they are termed, should be careful what tales or stories the children hear, for all such things are designed to prepare the way for the business of later life, and should be for the most part imitations of the occupations which they will hereafter pursue in earnest. Those are wrong who in their laws attempt to check the loud crying and screaming of children, for these contribute towards their growth, and, in a manner, exercise their bodies. Straining the voice has a strengthening effect similar to that produced by the retention of the breath in violent exertions. The Directors of Education should have an eye to their bringing up, and in particular should take care that they are left as little as possible with slaves. For until they are seven years old they must live at home; and therefore, even at this early age, it is to be expected that they should acquire a taint of meanness from what they hear and see. Indeed, there is nothing which the legislator should be more careful to drive away than indecency of speech; for the light utterance of shameful words leads soon to shameful actions. The young especially should never be allowed to repeat or hear anything of the sort. A freeman who is found saying or doing what is forbidden, if he be too young as yet to have the privilege of reclining at the public tables, should be disgraced and beaten, and an elder person degraded as his slavish conduct deserves. And since we do not allow improper language, clearly we should also banish pictures or speeches from the stage which are indecent. Let the rulers take care that there be no image or picture representing unseemly actions, except in the temples of those

Gods at whose festivals the law permits even ribaldry, and whom the law also permits to be worshipped by persons of mature age on behalf of themselves, their children, and their wives. But the legislator should not allow youth to be spectators of iambi or of comedy until they are of an age to sit at the public tables and to drink strong wine; by that time education will have armed them against the evil influences of such representations.

Book 8

No one will doubt that the legislator should direct his attention above all to the education of youth; for the neglect of education does harm to the constitution. The citizen should be moulded to suit the form of government under which be lives. For each government has a peculiar character which originally formed and which continues to preserve it. The character of democracy creates democracy, and the character of oligarchy creates oligarchy; and always the better the character, the better the government.

Again, for the exercise of any faculty or art a previous training and habituation are required; clearly therefore for the practice of virtue. And since the whole city has one end, it is manifest that education should be one and the same for all, and that it should be public, and not private—not as at present, when every one looks after his own children separately, and gives them separate instruction of the sort which he thinks best; the training in things which are of common interest should be the same for all. Neither must we suppose that anyone of the citizens belongs to himself, for they all belong to the state, and are each of them a part of the state, and the care of each part is inseparable from the care of the whole. In this particular as in some others the Lacedaemonians are to be praised, for they take the greatest pains about their children, and make education the business of the state.

That education should be regulated by law and should be an affair of state is not to be denied, but what should be the character of this public education, and how young persons should be educated, are questions which remain to be considered. As things are, there is disagreement about the subjects. For mankind are by no means agreed about the things to be taught, whether we look to virtue or the best life. Neither is it clear whether education is more concerned with intellectual or with moral virtue. The existing practice is perplexing; no one knows on what principle we should proceed—should the useful in life, or should virtue, or should the higher knowledge, be the aim of our training; all three opinions have been entertained. Again, about the means there is no agreement; for different persons, starting with different ideas about the nature of virtue, naturally disagree about the practice of it. There can be no doubt that children should be taught those useful things which are really necessary, but not all useful things; for occupations are divided into liberal and illiberal; and to young children should be imparted only such kinds of knowledge as will be useful to them without vulgarizing them. And any occupation, art, or science, which makes the body or soul or mind of the freeman less fit for the practice or exercise of virtue, is vulgar; wherefore we call those arts vulgar which tend to deform the body, and likewise all paid employments, for they absorb and degrade the mind. There are also some liberal arts quite proper for a freeman to acquire, but only in a certain degree, and if he attend to them too closely, in order to attain perfection in them, the same evil effects will follow. The object also which a man sets before him makes a great difference; if he does or learns anything for his own sake or for the sake of his friends, or with a view to excellence, the action will not appear illiberal; but if done for the sake of others, the very same action will be thought menial and servile. The received subjects of instruction, as I have already remarked, are partly of a liberal and partly of an illiberal character.

The customary branches of education are in number four; they are—(1) reading and writing, (2) gymnastic exercises, (3) music, to which is some-times added (4) drawing. Of these, reading and writing and drawing are regarded as useful for the purposes of life in a variety of ways, and gym-nastic exercises are thought to infuse courage. Concerning music a doubt may be raised—in our own day most men cultivate it for the sake of pleasure, but originally it was included in education, because nature herself, as has been often said, requires that we should be able, not only to work well, but to use leisure well; for, as I must repeat once again, the first principle of all action is leisure. Both are required, but leisure is better than occupation and is its end; and therefore the question must be asked, what ought we to do when at leisure? Clearly we ought not to be amusing ourselves, for then amusement would be the end of life. But if this is inconceivable, and amuse-ment is needed more amid serious occupations than at other times (for he who is hard at work has need of relaxation, and amusement gives relax-ation, whereas occupation is always accompanied with exertion and effort, we should introduce amusements only at suitable times, and they should be our medicines, for the emotion which they create in the soul is a relaxation, and from the pleasure we obtain rest. But leisure of itself gives pleasure and happiness and enjoyment of life, which are experienced, not by the busy man, but by those who have leisure. For he who is occupied has in view some end which he has not attained; but happiness is an end, since all men deem it to be accompanied with pleasure and not with pain. This pleasure, however, is regarded differently by different persons, and varies according to the habit of individuals; the pleasure of the best man is the best, and springs from the noblest sources. It is clear then that there are branches of learning and education which we must study merely with a view to leisure spent in intellectual activity, and these are to be valued for their own sake; whereas those kinds of knowledge which are useful in business are to be deemed necessary, and exist for the sake of other things. And therefore our fathers admitted music into education, not on the ground either of its necessity or utility, for it is not necessary, nor indeed useful in the same manner as reading and writing, which are useful in money making, in the management of a household, in the acquisition of knowledge and in political life, nor like drawing, useful for a more correct judgement of the works of artists, nor again like gymnastic, which gives health and strength; for neither of these is to be gained from music. There remains, then, the use of music for intellectual enjoyment in leisure; which is in fact evidently the reason of its introduction, this being one of the ways in which it is thought that a freeman should pass his leisure; as Homer says—

"But he who alone should be called to the pleasant feast,"

and afterwards he speaks of others whom he describes as inviting

"The bard who would delight them all."

And in another place Odysseus says there is no better way of passing life than when men's hearts are merry and

"The banqueters in the hall, sitting in order, hear the voice of the minstrel."

It is evident, then, that there is a sort of education in which parents should train their sons, not as being useful or necessary, but because it is liberal or noble. Whether this is of one kind only, or of more than one, and if so what they are, and how they are to be imparted, must hereafter be determined. Thus much we are now in a position to say, that the ancients witness to us; for their opinion may be gathered from the fact that music is one of the received and traditional branches of education. Further, it is clear that children should be instructed in some useful things—for example, in reading and writing—not only for their usefulness, but also because many other sorts of knowledge are acquired through them. With a like view they may be taught drawing, not to prevent their making mistakes in their own purchases, or in order that they may not be imposed upon in the buying or selling of articles, but perhaps rather because it makes them judges of the beauty of the human form. To be always seeking after the useful does not become free and exalted souls. Now it is clear that in education practice must be used before theory, and the body be trained before the mind; and therefore boys should be handed over to the trainer, who creates in them the proper habit of body, and to the wrestling master, who teaches them their exercises.

3

FROM *SECOND TREATISE OF GOVERNMENT* AND *SOME THOUGHTS CONCERNING EDUCATION*

John Locke

SECOND TREATISE OF GOVERNMENT

Of Paternal Power

It may perhaps be censured as an impertinent criticism, in a discourse of this nature, to find fault with words and names, that have obtained in the world: and yet possibly it may not be amiss to offer new ones, when the old are apt to lead men into mistakes, as this of paternal power probably has done, which seems so to place the power of parents over their children wholly in the *father*, as if the *mother* had no share in it; whereas, if we consult reason or revelation, we shall find, she hath an equal title. This may give one reason to ask, whether this might not be more properly called *parental power*? For whatever obligation nature and the right of generation lays on children, it must certainly bind them equal to both the concurrent causes of it. And accordingly we see the positive law of God every where joins them together, without distinction, when it commands the obedience of children, *Honour thy father and thy mother*, Exod. xx. 12. *Whosoever curseth his father or his mother*, Lev. xx. 9. *Ye shall fear every man his mother and his father*, Lev. xix. 3. *Children, obey your parents*, &c. Eph. vi. 1. is the stile of the Old and New Testament.

Had but this one thing been well considered, without looking any deeper into the matter, it might perhaps have kept men from running into those gross mistakes, they have made, about this power of parents; which, however it might, without any great power of parents; name of absolute dominion, and regal authority, when under the title of *paternal power* it seemed appropriated to the father, would yet have founded but oddly, and in the very name shewn the absurdity, if this supposed absolute power over children had been called *parental*; and thereby have discovered, that it belonged to the *mother* too: for it will but very ill serve the turn of those men, who contend so much for the absolute power and authority of the *fatherhood*, as they call it, that the mother should have any share in it; and it would have but ill supported the *monarchy* they contend for, when by the very name it appeared, that that fundamental authority, from whence they would derive their government of a single person only, was not placed in one, but two persons jointly. But to let this of names pass.

Though I have said above, *Chap. II. That all men by nature are equal*, I cannot be supposed to understand all sorts of *equality*: *age* or *virtue* may give men a just precedency: *excellency of parts* and *merit* may place others above the common level: *birth* may subject some, and *alliance* or *benefits* others, to pay an observance to those to whom nature, gratitude, or other respects, may have made it due: and yet all this consists with the *equality*, which all men are in, in respect of jurisdiction or dominion one over another; which was the *equality* I there spoke of, as proper to the business in hand, being that *equal right*, that every man hath, *to his natural freedom*, without being subjected to the will or authority of any other man.

Children, I confess, are not born in this full state of *equality*, though they are born to it. Their parents have a sort of rule and jurisdiction over them, when they come into the world, and for some time after; but it is but a temporary one. The bonds of this subjection are like the swaddling clothes they art wrapt up in, and supported by, in the weakness of their infancy: age and reason as they grow up, loosen them, till at length they drop quite off, and leave a man at his own free disposal.

Adam was created a perfect man, his body and mind in full possession of their strength and reason, and so was capable, from the first instant of his being to provide for his own support and preservation, and govern his actions according to the dictates of the law of reason which God had implanted in him. From him the world is peopled with his descendants, who are all born infants, weak and helpless, without knowledge or understanding: but to supply the defects of this imperfect state, till the improvement of growth and age hath removed them, *Adam* and *Eve*, and after them all parents were, by the law of nature, *under an obligation to preserve, nourish, and educate the children* they had begotten; not as their own workmanship, but the workmanship of their own maker, the Almighty, to whom they were to be accountable for them.

    The law, that was to govern *Adam*, was the same that was to govern all his posterity, the *law of reason*. But his offspring having another way of entrance into the world, different from him, by a natural birth, that produced them ignorant and without the use of *reason*, they were not presently *under that law*; for no body can be under a law, which is not promulgated to him; and this law being promulgated or made known by *reason* only, he that is not come to the use of his *reason*, cannot be said to be *under this law*; and *Adam's* children, being not presently as soon as born *under this law of reason*, were not presently *free*: for *law*, in its true notion, *is* not so much the limitation as *the direction of a free and intelligent agent* to his proper interest, and prescribes no farther than is for the general good of those under that law: could they be happier without it, the *law*, as an useless thing, would of itself vanish; and that ill deserves the name of confinement which hedges us in only from bogs and precipices. So that, however it may be mistaken, the *end of law* is not to abolish or restrain, but *to preserve and enlarge freedom*: for in all the states of created beings capable of laws, *where there is no law, there is no freedom*: for *liberty* is, to be free from restraint and violence from others; which cannot be, where there is no law: but freedom is not, as we are told, *a liberty for every man to do what he lists*: (for who could be free, when every other man's humour might domineer over him?) but a *liberty* to dispose, and order as he lists, his person, actions, possessions, and his whole property, within the allowance of those laws under which he is, and therein not to be subject to the arbitrary will of another, but freely follow his own.

    The *power*, then, *that parents have* over their children, arises from that duty which is incumbent on them, to take care of their off-spring, during the imperfect state of childhood. To inform the mind, and govern the actions of their yet ignorant nonage, till reason shall take its place, and ease them of that trouble, is what the children want, and the parents are bound to: for God having given man an understanding to direct his actions, has allowed him a freedom of will, and liberty of acting, as properly belonging thereunto, within the bounds of that law he is under. But whilst he is in an estate, wherein he has not *understanding* of his own to direct his *will*, he is not to have any *will* of his own to follow: he that *understands* for him, must *will* for him too; he must prescribe to his will, and regulate his actions; but when he comes to the estate that made his *father a freeman*, the *son is a freeman* too.

    This holds in all the laws a man is under, whether natural or civil. Is a man under the law of nature? *What made him free* of that law? what gave him a free disposing of his property, according to his own will, within the compass of that law? I answer, a state of maturity wherein he might be supposed capable to know that law, that so he might keep his actions within the bounds of it. When he has acquired that state, he is presumed to know how far that law is to be his guide, and how far he may make use of his *freedom*, and so comes to have it; till then, some body else must guide him, who is presumed to know how far the law allows a liberty. If such a state of reason, such an age of discretion *made him free*, the same shall make his son free too. Is a man under the law of *England? What made him free* of that law? that is, to have the liberty to dispose of his actions and possessions according to his own will, within the permission of that law? A capacity of knowing that law; which is supposed by that law, at the age of one and twenty years, and in some cases sooner. If this *made* the father *free*, it shall *make* the son *free* too. Till then we see the law allows the son to have no will, but he is to be guided by the will of his father or guardian, who is to understand for him. And if the father die, and fail to substitute a deputy in his trust; if he hath not provided a tutor, to govern his son, during his minority, during his want of understanding, the law takes care to do it; some other must govern him, and be a will to him, till he hath *attained to a state of freedom*, and his understanding be fit to take the government of his will. But after that, the father and son are equally *free* as much as tutor and pupil after nonage; equally subjects of the same law together, without any dominion left in the father over the life, liberty, or estate of his son, whether they be only in the state and under the law of nature, or under the positive laws of an established government.

But if, through defects that may happen out of the ordinary course of nature, any one comes not to such a degree of reason, wherein he might be supposed capable of knowing the law, and so living within the rules of it, he is *never capable of being a free man*, he is never let loose to the disposure of his own will (because he knows no bounds to it, has not understanding, its proper guide) but is continued under the tuition and government of others, all the time his own understanding is uncapable of that charge. And so *lunatics* and *ideots* are never set free from the government of their parents; *children, who are not as yet come unto those years whereat they may have, and innocents which are excluded by a natural defect from ever having,* thirdly, *madmen, which for the present cannot possibly have the use of right reason to guide themselves, have for their guide, the reason that guideth other men which are tutors over them, to seek and procure their good for them,* says Hooker, Eccl. Pol. *lib.* i. *sect.* 7. All which seems no more than that duty, which God and nature has laid on man, as well as other creatures, to preserve their offspring, till they can be able to shift for themselves, and will scarce amount to an instance or proof of *parents* regal authority.

Thus we are *born free*, as we are born rational; not that we have actually the exercise of either: age, that brings one, brings with it the other too. And thus we see how *natural freedom and subjection to parents* may consist together, and are both founded on the same principle. A *child* is *free* by his father's title, by his father's understanding, which is to govern him till he hath it of his own. The *freedom of a man at years of discretion,* and the *subjection* of a child *to his parents,* whilst yet short of that age, are so consistent, and so distinguishable, that the most blinded contenders for monarchy, *by right of fatherhood,* cannot miss this *difference;* the most obstinate cannot but allow their consistency: for were their doctrine all true, were the right heir of *Adam* now known, and by that title settled a monarch in his throne, invested with all the absolute unlimited power Sir *Robert Filmer* talks of; if he should die as soon as his heir were born, must not the *child,* notwithstanding he were never so free, never so much sovereign, be in subjection to his mother and nurse, to tutors and governors, till age and education brought him reason and ability to govern himself and others? The necessities of his life, the health of his body, and the information of his mind, would require him to be directed by the will of others, and not his own; and yet will any one think, that this restraint and subjection were inconsistent with, or spoiled him of that liberty or sovereignty he had a right to, or gave away his empire to those who had the government of his nonage? This government over him only prepared him the better and sooner for it. If any body should ask me, when my son is *of age to be free?* I shall answer, just when his monarch is of age to govern. *But at what time,* says the judicious *Hooker,* Eccl. Pol. 1. i. sect. 6. *a man may be said to have attained so far forth the use of reason, as sufficeth to make him capable of those laws whereby he is then bound to guide his actions: this is a great deal more easy for sense to discern, than for any one by skill and learning to determine.*

SOME THOUGHTS CONCERNING EDUCATION

A sound mind in a sound body, is a short but full description of a happy state in this world: he that has these two, has little more to wish for; and he that wants either of them, will be but little the better for any thing else. Men's happiness or misery is most part of their own making. He whose mind directs not wisely, will never take the right way; and he whose body is crazy and feeble, will never be able to advance in it. I confess, there are some men's constitutions of body and mind so vigorous, and well framed by nature, that they need not much assistance from others; but, by the strength of their natural genius, they are, from their cradles, carried towards what is excellent; and, by the privilege of their happy constitutions, are able to do wonders. But examples of this kind are but few; and I think I may say, that, of all the men we meet with, nine parts of ten are what they are, good or evil, useful or not, by their education. It is that which makes the great difference in mankind. The little, or almost insensible, impressions on our tender infancies, have very important and lasting consequences: and there it is, as in the fountains of some rivers, where a gentle application of the hand turns the flexible waters into channels, that make them take quite contrary courses; and by this little direction, given them at first, in the source, they receive different tendencies, and arrive at last at very remote and distant places.

Due care being had to keep the body in strength and vigour, so that it may be able to obey and execute the orders of the mind; the next and principal business is, to set the mind right, that on occasions it may be disposed to consent to nothing but what may be suitable to the dignity and excellency of a rational creature.

If what I have said in the beginning of this discourse be true, as I do not doubt but it is, viz. that the difference to be found in the manners and abilities of men is owing more to their education than to any thing else; we have reason to conclude, that great care is to be had of the forming children's minds, and giving them that seasoning early, which shall influence their lives always after. For when they do well or ill, the praise or blame will be laid there: and when any thing is done awkwardly, the common saying will pass upon them, that it is suitable to their breeding.

As the strength of the body lies chiefly in being able to endure hardships, so also does that of the mind. And the great principle and foundation of all virtue and worth is placed in this, that a man is able to deny himself his own desires, cross his own inclinations, and purely follow what reason directs as best, though the appetite lean the other way.

Manners, as they call it, about which children are so often perplexed and have so many goodly exhortations made them, by their wise maids and governesses, I think, are rather to be learned by example than rules; and then children, if kept out of ill company, will take a pride to behave themselves prettily, after the fashion of others, perceiving themselves esteemed and commended for it. But if, by a little negligence in this part, the boy should not put off his hat, nor make legs very gracefully, a dancing-master will cure that defect, and wipe off all that plainness of nature, which the à-la-mode people call clownishness. And since nothing appears to me to give children so much becoming confidence and behaviour, and so to raise them to the conversation of those above their age, as dancing; I think they should be taught to dance, as soon as they are capable of learning it. For, though this consist only in outward gracefulness of motion, yet, I know not how, it gives children manly thoughts and carriage, more than anything. But otherwise I would not have little children much tormented about punctilios, or niceties of breeding.

Never trouble yourself about those faults in them which you know age will cure. And therefore want of well-fashioned civility in the carriage, whilst civility is not wanting in the mind, (for there you must take care to plant it early) should he the parents' least care, whilst they are young. If his tender mind he filled with a veneration for his parents and teachers, which consists in love and esteem, and a fear to offend them; and with respect and good-will to all people; that respect will of itself teach those ways of expressing it which he observes most acceptable. Be sure to keep up in him the principles of good-nature and kindness; make them as habitual as you can, by credit and commendation, and the good things accompanying that state: and when they have taken root in his mind, and are settled there by a continued practice, fear not; the ornaments of conversation, and the outside of fashionable manners, will come in their due time, if, when they are removed out of their maid's care, they are put into the hands of a well-bred man to be their governor.

Whilst they are very young, any carelessness is to be borne with in children, that carries not with it the marks of pride or ill-nature; but those, whenever they appear in any action, are to be corrected immediately, by the ways above-mentioned. What I have said concerning manners, I would not have so understood, as if I meant that those, who have the judgment to do it, should not gently fashion the motions and carriage of children, when they are very young. It would be of great advantage, if they had people about them, from their being first able to go, that had the skill, and would take the right way to do it. That which I complain of is the wrong course that is usually taken in this matter. Children who were never taught any such thing as behaviour, are often (especially when strangers are present) chid for having some way or other failed in good manners, and have thereupon reproofs and precepts heaped upon them, concerning putting off their hats, or making of legs, &c. Though in this those concerned pretend to correct the child, yet, in truth, for the most part, it is but to cover their own shame: and they lay the blame on the poor little ones, sometimes passionately enough, to divert it from themselves, for fear the by-standers should impute to their want of care and skill the child's ill behaviour.

For, as for the children themselves, they are never one jot bettered by such occasional lectures: they at other times should be shown what to do, and by reiterate actions be fashioned beforehand into the practice of what is fit and becoming; and not told, and talked to do upon the spot, what they have never been accustomed to, nor know how to do as they should: to hare and rate them thus at every turn, is not to teach them, but to vex and torment them to no purpose. They should be let alone, rather than chid for a fault, which is none of theirs, nor is in their power to mend for speaking to. And it were much better their natural, childish negligence, or plainness, should be left to the care of riper years, than that they should frequently have rebukes misplaced upon on them, which neither do nor can give them graceful motions. If their minds are well disposed, and principled with inward civility, a great part of the roughness, which sticks to the outside for want of better teaching, time and observation will rub off, as they grow up, if they are bred in good company; but if in ill, all the rules in the world, all the correction imaginable, will not be able to polish them. For you must take this for a certain truth, that let them have what instructions you will, and ever so learned lectures of breeding daily inculcated into them, that which will most influence their carriage will be the company they converse with, and the fashion of those about them. Children (nay, and men too) do most by example. We are all a sort of chameleons, that still take a tincture from things near us: nor is it to be wondered at in children, who better understand what they see than what they hear.

Having named company, I am almost ready to throw away my pen, and trouble you no farther on this subject. For since that does more than all precepts, rules, and instructions, methinks it is almost wholly in vain to make a long discourse of other things, and to talk of that almost to no purpose. For you will be ready to say, "What shall I do with my son? If I keep him always at home, he will be in danger to be my young master; and if I send him abroad, how is it possible to keep him from the contagion of rudeness and vice, which is every where so in fashion? In my house he will perhaps be more innocent, but more ignorant too of the world: wanting there change of company, and being used constantly to the same faces, he will, when he comes abroad, be a sheepish or conceited creature."

I confess, both sides have their inconveniencies. Being abroad, it is true, will make him bolder, and better able to bustle and shift amongst boys of his own age; and the emulation of schoolfellows often puts life and industry into young lads. But till you can find a school, wherein it is possible for the master to look after the manners of his scholars, and can show as great effects of his care of forming their minds to virtue, and their carriage to good breeding, as of forming their tongues to the learned languages; you must confess, that you have a strange value for words, when, preferring the languages of the ancient Greeks and Romans to that which made them such brave men, you think it worth while to hazard your son's innocence and virtue for a little Greek and Latin. For, as for that boldness and spirit which lads get amongst their playfellows at school, it has ordinarily such a mixture of rudeness and an ill-turned confidence, that those misbecoming and disingenuous ways of shifting in the world must be unlearned, and all the tincture washed out again, to make way for better principles, and such manners as make a truly worthy man. He that considers how diametrically opposite the skill of living well, and managing, as a man should do, his affairs in the world, is to that malapertness, tricking, or violence, learnt among school-boys, will think the faults of a privater education infinitely to be preferred to such improvements; and will take care to preserve his child's innocence and modesty at home, as being nearer of kin, and more in the way of those qualities, which make an useful and able man. Nor does any one find, or so much as suspect, that that retirement and bashfulness, which their daughters are brought up in, makes them less knowing or less able women. Conversation, when they come into the world, soon gives them a becoming assurance; and whatsoever, beyond that, there is of rough and boisterous, may in men be very well spared too: for courage and steadiness, as I take it, lie not in roughness and ill breeding.

Virture is harder to be got than a knowledge of the world; and, if lost in a young man, is seldom recoverd. Sheepishness and ignorance of the world, the faults imputed to a private education, are neither the necessary consequences of being bred at home; nor, if they were, are they incurable evils. Vice is the more stubborn, as well as the more dangerous evil of the two; and therefore, in the first place, to be fenced against. If that sheepish softness, which often energetic those who are bred like fondlings at home, be carefully to be avoided, it is principally so for virtue's sake; for fear lest such a yielding temper should be too susceptible of vicious impressions, and expose the novice too easily to be corrupted. A young man, before he leaves the shelter of his father's house, and the guard of a tutor, should be fortified with resolution, and made acquainted with men, to secure his virtue; lest he should be led into some ruinous course, or fatal precipice, before he is sufficiently acquainted with the dangers of conversation, and bits steadiness enough not to yield to every temptation. Were it not for this, a young man's bashfulness and ignorance of the world would not so much need all early care. Conversation would cure it in a great measure; or, if that will not do it early enough, it is only a stronger reason for a good tutor at home. For, if pains be to be taken to give him a manly air and assurance betimes, it is chiefly as a fence to his virtue, when he goes into the world, under his own conduct.

It is preposterous, therefore, to sacrifice his innocency to the attaining of confidence, and some little skill of bustling for himself among others, by his conversation with ill-bred and vicious boys; when the chief use of that sturdiness, and standing upon his own leg, is only for the preservation of his virtue. For if confidence or cunning come once to mix with vice, and support his miscarriages, he is only the surer lost; and you must undo again, and strip him of that he has got from his companions, or give him up to ruin. Boys will unavoidably be taught assurance by conversation with men, when they are brought into it; and that is time enough. Modesty and submission, till then, better fits them for instruction: and therefore there needs not any great care to stock them with confidence beforehand. That which requires most time, pains, and assiduity, is to work into them the principles and practice of virtue and good breeding. This is the seasoning they should be prepared with, so as not easily to be got out again: this they had need to be well provided with. For conversation, when they come into the world, will add to their knowledge and assurance, but be too apt to take from their virtue; which therefore they ought to be plentifully stored with, and have that tincture sunk deep into them.

How they should be fitted for conversation, and entered into the world, when they are ripe for it, we shall consider in another place. But how any one's being put into a mixed herd of unruly boys, and there learning to wrangle at trap, or rook at span-farthing, fits him for civil conversation or business, I do not see. And what qualities are ordinarily to be got from such a troop of playfellows as schools usually assemble together, from parents of all kinds, that a father should so much covet it, is hard to divine. I am sure, he who is able to be at the charge of a tutor at home, may there give his son a more genteel carriage, more manly thoughts, and a sense of what is worthy and becoming, with a greater proficiency in learning into the bargain, and ripen him up sooner into a man, than any at school can do. Not that I blame the schoolmaster in this, or think it to be laid to his charge. The difference is great between two or three pupils in the same house, and three or fourscore boys lodged up and down. For, let the master's industry and skill be ever so great, it is impossible he should have 50 or 100 scholars under his eye any longer than they are in the school together: nor can it be expected, that he should instruct them successfully in any thing but their books; the forming of their minds and manners requiring a constant attention and particular application to every single boy; which is impossible in a numerous flock, and would he wholly in vain, (could he have time to study and correct every one's particular defects and wrong inclinations) when the lad was to be left to himself, or the prevailing infection of his fellows, the greatest part of the four-and-twenty hours.

But fathers, observing that fortune is often most successfully courted by bold and bustling men, are glad to see their sons pert and forward betimes; take it for a happy omen that they will be thriving men, and look on the tricks they play their schoolfellows, or learn from them, as a proficiency in the art of living, and making their way through the world. But I must take the liberty to say, that he that lays the foundation of his son's fortune in virtue and good breeding, takes the only sure and warrantable way. And it is not the waggeries or cheats practised among schoolboys, it is not their roughness one to another, nor the well-laid plots of robbing an orchard together, that makes an able man; but the principles of justice, generosity, and sobriety, joined with observation and industry, qualities which I judge schoolboys do not learn much of one another. And if a young gentleman, bred at home, be not taught more of them than he could learn at school, his father has made a very ill choice of a tutor. Take a boy from the top of a grammar-school, and one of the same age, bred as he should be in his father's family, and bring them into good company together; and then see which of the two will have the more manly carriage, and address himself with the more becoming assurance to strangers. Here I imagine the schoolboy's confidence will either fail or discredit him; and if it be such as fits him only for the conversation of boys, he had better be without it.

Vice, if we may believe the general complaint, ripens so fast now-a-days, and runs up to seed so early in young people, that it is impossible to keep a lad from the spreading contagion, if you will venture him abroad in the herd, and trust to chance, or his own inclination, for the choice of his company at school. By what fate vice has so thriven amongst us these few years past, and by what hands it has been nursed up into so uncontrolled a dominion, I shall leave to others to inquire. I wish that those who complain of the great decay of Christian piety and virtue every where, and of learning and acquired improvements in the gentry of this generation, would consider how to retrieve them in the next. This I am sure, that, if the foundation of it be not laid in the education and principling of the youth, all other endeavours will be in vain. And if the innocence, sobriety, and industry of those who are coming up be not taken care of and preserved, it will be ridiculous to expect, that those who are to succeed next on the stage should abound in that virtue, ability, and learning, which has hitherto made England considerable in the world. I was going to add courage too, though it has been looked on as the natural inheritance of Englishmen. What has been talked of some late actions at sea, of a kind unknown to our ancestors, gives me occasion to say, that debauchery sinks the courage of men; and when dissoluteness has eaten out the sense of true honour, bravery seldom stays long after it. And I think it impossible to find an instance of any nation, however renowned for their valour, who ever kept their credit in arms, or made themselves redoubtable amongst their neighbours, after corruption had once broke through, and dissolved the restraint of discipline; and vice was grown to such a head, that it durst show itself barefaced, without being out of countenance.

It is virtue then, direct virtue, which is the hard and valuable part to be aimed at in education; and not a forward pertness, or any little arts of shifting. All other considerations and accomplishments should give way, and be postponed, to this. This is the solid and substantial good, which tutors should not only read lectures, and talk of; but the labour and art of education should furnish the mind with, and fasten there, and never cease till the young man had a true relish of it, and placed his strength, his glory, and his pleasure in it.

The more this advances, the easier way will be made for other accomplishments in their turns. For he that is brought to submit to virtue, will not be refractory, or resty, in any thing that becomes him. And therefore I cannot but prefer breeding of a young gentleman at home in his father's sight, under a good governor, as much the best and safest way to this great and main end of education; when it can be had, and is ordered as it should be. Gentlemen's houses are seldom without variety of company: they should use their sons to all the strange faces that come there, and engage them in conversation with men of parts and breeding, as soon as they are capable of it. And why those, who live in the country, should not take them with them, when they make visits of civility to their neighbours, I know not: this I am sure, a father that breeds his son at home, has the opportunity to have him more in his own company, and there give him what encouragement he thinks fit; and can keep him better from the taint of servants, and the meaner sort of people, than is possible to be done abroad. But what shall be resolved in the case, must in great measure be left to the parents, to be determined by their circumstances and conveniencies. Only I think it the worst sort of good husbandry for a father not to strain himself a little for his son's breeding; which, let his condition be what it will, is the best portion he can leave him. But if, after all, it shall be thought by some that the breeding at home has too little company, and that at ordinary schools not such as it should be for a young gentleman, I think there might be ways found out to avoid the inconveniencies on the one side and the other.

Besides being well-bred, the tutor should know the world well; the ways, the humours, the follies, the cheats, the faults of the age he is fallen into, and particularly of the country he lives in. These he should be able to show to his pupil, as he finds him capable; teach him skill in men, and their manners; pull off the mask which their several callings and pretences cover them with; and make his pupil discern what lies at the bottom, under such appearances; that he may not, as unexperienced young men are apt to do, if they are unwarned, take one thing for another, judge by the outside, and give himself up to show, and the insinuation of a fair carriage or all obliging application. A governor should teach his scholar to guess at, and beware of, the designs of men he hath to do with, neither with too much suspicion, nor too much confidence; but, as the young man is by nature most inclined to either side, rectify him, and bend him the other way. He should accustom him to make, as much as is possible, a true judgment of men by those marks which serve best to show what they are, and give a prospect into their inside; which often shows itself in little things, especially when they are not in parade, and upon their guard. He should acquaint him with the true state of the world, and dispose him to think no man better or worse, wiser or foolisher, than he really is. Thus, by safe and insensible degrees, he will pass from a boy to a man; which is the most hazardous step in all the whole course of life. This therefore should be carefully watched and a young man with great diligence handed over it; and not, as now usually is done, be taken from a governor's conduct, and all at once thrown into the world under his own, not without manifest danger of immediate spoiling; there being nothing more frequent, than instances of the great looseness, extravagancy, and debauchery, which young men have run into, as soon as they have been let loose from a severe and strict education: which, I think, may be chiefly imputed to their wrong way of breeding, especially in this part; for having been bred up in a great ignorance of what the world truly is, and finding it quite another thing, when they come into it, than what they were taught it should be, and so imagined it was; are easily persuaded, by other kind of tutors, which they are sure to meet with, that the discipline they were kept under, and the lectures that were read to them, were but the formalities of education, and the restraints of childhood; that the freedom belonging to men, is to take their swing in a full enjoyinent of what was before forbidden them. They show the young novice the world, full of fashionable and glittering examples of this every where, and he is presently dazzled with them. My young master, failing not to be willing to show himself a man, as much as any of the sparks of his years, lets himself loose to all the irregularities he finds in the most debauched; and thus courts credit and manliness, in the casting off the modesty and sobriety he has till then been kept in; and thinks it brave, at his first setting out, to signalize himself in running counter to all the rules of virtue which have been preached to him by his tutor.

The showing him the world as really it is, before he comes wholly into it, is one of the best means, I think, to prevent this mischief. He should, by degrees, be informed of the vices in fashion, and warned of the applications and designs of those who will make it their business to corrupt him. He should be told the arts they use, and the trains they lay; and now and then have set before him the tragical or ridiculous examples of those who are ruining, or ruined, this way. The age is not like to want instances of this kind, which should be made landmarks to him; that by the disgraces, diseases, beggary, and shame of hopeful young men, thus brought to ruin, he may be precautioned, and be made see, how those join in the contempt and neglect of them that are undone, who, by pretences of friendship and respect, led them into it, and helped to prey upon them whilst they were undoing that he may see, before he buys it by a too dear experience, that those who persuade him not to follow the sober advices be has received from his governors, and the counsel of his own reason, which they call being governed by others, do it only, that they may have the government of him themselves; and make him believe he goes like a man of himself, by his own conduct, and for his own pleasure, when, in truth, he is wholly as a child, led by them into those vices, which best serve their purposes. This is a knowledge, which, upon all occasions, a tutor should endeavour to instil, and by all methods try to make him comprehend and thoroughly relish.

I know it is often said, that to discover to a young man the vices of the age is to teach them him. That, I confess, is a good deal so, according as it is done; and therefore requires a discreet man of parts, who know the world, and can judge of the temper, inclination, and weak side of his pupil. This farther is to be remembered, that it is not possible now (as perhaps formerly it was) to keep a young gentleman from vice, by a total ignorance of it; unless you will all his life mew him up in a closet, and never let him go into company. The longer he is kept thus hoodwinked, the less he will see, when he comes abroad into open daylight, and be the more exposed to be a prey to himself and others. And an old boy, at his first appearance with all the gravity of his ivy-bush about him, is sure to draw on him the eyes and chirping of the whole town volery; amongst which there will not be wanting some birds of prey, that will presently be on the wing for him.

The only fence against the world, is a thorough knowledge of it: into which a young gentleman should be entered by degrees, as he can bear it; and the earlier the better, so he be in safe and skilful hands to guide him. The scene should be gently opened, and his entrance made step by step, and the dangers pointed out that attend him, from the several degrees, tempers, designs, and clubs of men. He should be prepared to be shocked by some, and caressed by others; warned who are like to oppose, who to mislead, who to undermine him, and who to serve him. He should be instructed how to know and distinguish men; where he should let them see, and when dissemble the knowledge of them and their aims and workings. And if he be too forward to venture upon his own strength and skill, the perplexity and trouble of a misadventure now and then, that reaches not his innocence, his health, or reputation, may not be an ill way to teach him more caution.

When by these gentle ways he begins to be able to read, some easy pleasant book, suited to his capacity, should be put into his hands, wherein the entertainment that he finds, might draw him on, and reward his pains in reading; and yet not such as should fill his head with perfectly useless trumpery, or lay the principles of vice and folly. To this purpose I think Aesop's Fables the best, which being stories apt to delight and entertain a child, may yet afford useful reflections to a grown man; and if his memory retain them all his life after, he will not repent to find them there, amongst his manly thoughts, and serious business. If his Aesop has pictures in it, it will entertain him much the better, and encourage him to read, when it carries the increase of knowledge with it: for such visible objects children hear talked of in vain, and without any satisfaction, whilst they have no ideas of them; those ideas being not to be had from sounds, but from the things themselves, or their pictures. And therefore, I think, as soon as he begins to spell, as many pictures of animals should be got him as can be found, with the printed names to them, which at the same time will invite him to read, and afford him matter of inquiry and knowledge. Reynard the Fox is another book, I think, may be made use of to the same purpose. And if those about him will talk to him often about the stories he has read, and hear him tell them, it will, besides other advantages, add encouragement and delight to his reading, when he finds there is some use and pleasure in it. These baits seem wholly neglected in the ordinary method; and it is usually long before learners find any use or pleasure in reading, which may tempt them to it, and so take books only for fashionable amusements, or impertinent troubles, good for nothing.

The Lord's prayer, the creed, and ten commandments, it is necessary he should learn perfectly by heart; but, I think, not by reading them himself in his primer, but by somebody's repeating them to him, even before he can read. But learning by heart, and learning to read, should not, I think, be mixed, and so one made to clog the other. But his learning to read should be made as little trouble or business to him as might be.

What other books there are in English of the kind of those abovementioned, fit to engage the liking of children, and tempt them to read, I do not know; but am apt to think, that children, being delivered over to the method of schools, where the fear of the rod is to inforce, and not any pleasure of the employment to invite, them to learn; this sort of useful books, amongst the number of silly ones that are of all sorts, have yet had the fate to be neglected; and nothing that I know has been considered of this kind out of the ordinary road of the horn-book, primer, psalter, Testament, and Bible.

These are my present thoughts concerning learning and accomplishments. The great business of all is virtue and wisdom.

"Nullum numen abest, si sit prudentia."

Teach him to get a mastery over his inclinations, and submit his appetite to reason. This being obtained and by a constant practice settled into habit, the hardest part of the task is over. To bring a young man to this, I know nothing which so much contributes, as the love of praise and commendation, which should therefore be instilled into him by all arts imaginable. Make his mind as sensible of credit and shame as may be: and when you have done that, you have put a principle into him, which will influence his actions, when you are not by; to which the fear of a little smart of a rod is not comparable; and which will be the proper stock whereon afterwards to graft the true principles of morality and religion.

I have one thing more to add, which as soon as I mention, I shall run the danger of being suspected to have forgot what I am about, and what I have above written concerning education, all tending towards a gentleman's calling, with which a trade seems wholly to be inconsistent. And yet, I cannot forbear to say, I would have him learn a trade, a manual trade; nay, two or three, but one more particularly.

The busy inclination of children being always to be directed to something that may be useful to them, the advantages proposed from what they are set about may be considered of two kinds; 1. Where the skill itself, that is got by exercise, is worth the having. Thus skill not only in languages, and learned sciences, but in painting, turning, gardening, tempering and working in iron, and all other useful arts, is worth the having. 2. Where the exercise itself, without any consideration, is necessary or useful for health. Knowledge in some things is so necessary to be got by children, whilst they are young, that some part of their time is to be allotted to their improvement in them, though those employments contribute nothing at all to their health: such are reading, and writing, and all other sedentary studies, for the cultivating of the mind, which unavoidably take up a great part of gentlemen's time, quite from their cradles. Other manual arts, which are both got and exercised by labour, do many of them, by that exercise, not only increase our dexterity and skill, but contribute to our health too; especially such as employ us in the open air. In these, then, health and improvement may be joined together; and of these should some fit ones be chosen, to be made the recreations of one, whose chief business is with books and study. In this choice, the age and inclination of the person is to be considered, and constraint always to be avoided in bringing him to it. For command and force may often create, but can never cure an aversion; and whatever any one is brought to by compulsion, he will leave as soon as he can, and be little profited and less recreated by, whilst he is at it.

4

FROM *THE GERMAN IDEOLOGY*

Karl Marx

The first premise of all human history is, of course, the existence of living human individuals. Thus the first fact to be established is the physical organization of these individuals and their consequent relation to the rest of nature. Of course, we cannot here go either into the actual physical nature of man, or into the natural conditions in which man finds himself–geological, orohydrographical, climatic and so on. The writing of history must always set out from these natural bases and their modification in the course of history through the action of man.

Men can be distinguished from animals by consciousness, by religion or anything else you like. They themselves begin to distinguish themselves from animals as soon as they begin to *produce* their means of subsistence, a step which is conditioned by their physical organization. By producing their means of subsistence men are indirectly producing their actual material life.

The way in which men produce their means of subsistence depends first of all on the nature of the actual means they find in existence and have to reproduce. This mode of production must not be considered simply as being the reproduction of the physical existence of the individuals. Rather it is a definite form of activity of these individuals, a definite form of expressing their life, a definite *mode of life* on their part. As individuals express their life, so they are. What they are, therefore, coincides with their production, both with *what* they produce and with *how* they produce. The nature of individuals thus depends on the material conditions determining their production.

This production only makes its appearance with the increase of population. In its turn this presupposes the intercourse of individuals with one another. The form of this intercourse is again determined by production.

The relations of different nations among themselves depend upon the extent to which each has developed its productive forces, the division of labour and internal intercourse.[1] This statement is generally recognized. But not only the relation of one nation to others, but also the whole internal structure of the nation itself depends on the stage of development reached by its production and its internal and external intercourse. How far the productive forces of a nation are developed is shown most manifestly by the degree to which the division of labour has been carried. Each new productive force, in so far as it is not merely a quantitative extension of productive forces already known, (for instance the bringing into cultivation of fresh land), brings about a further development of the division of labour.

The division of labour inside a nation leads at first to the separation of industrial and commercial from agricultural labour, and hence to the separation of town and country and a clash of interests between them. Its further development leads to the separation of commercial from industrial labour. At the same time through the division of labour there develop further, inside these various branches, various divisions among the individuals cooperating in definite kinds of labour. The relative position of these individual groups is determined by the methods employed in agriculture, industry and commerce (patriarchalism, slavery, estates, classes). These same conditions are to be seen (given a more developed intercourse) in the relations of different nations to one another.

The various stages of development in the division of labour are just so many different forms of ownership; i.e., the existing stage in the division of labour determines also the relations of individuals to one another with reference to the material, instrument, and product of labour.

The first form of ownership is tribal ownership. It corresponds to the undeveloped stage of production, at which a people lives by hunting and fishing, by the rearing of beasts or, in the highest stage, agriculture. In the latter case it presupposes a great mass of uncultivated stretches of land. The division of labour is at this stage still very elementary and is confined to a further extension of the natural division of labour imposed by the family. The social structure is therefore limited to an extension of the family; patriarchal family chieftains; below them the members of the tribe; finally slaves.

The slavery latent in the family only develops gradually with the increase of population, the growth of wants, and with the extension of external relations, of war or of trade.

The second form is the ancient communal and State ownership which proceeds especially from the union of several tribes into a city by agreement or by conquest, and which is still accompanied by slavery. Beside communal ownership we already find movable, and later also immovable, private property developing,[2] but as an abnormal form subordinate to communal ownership. It is only as a community that the citizens hold power over their labouring slaves, and on this account alone, therefore, they are bound to the form of communal ownership. It is the communal private property which compels the active citizens to remain in this natural[3] form of association over against their slaves. For this reason the whole structure of society based on this communal ownership, and with it the power of the people, decays in the same measure as immovable private property evolves. The division of labour is already more developed. We already find the antagonism of town and country; later the antagonism between those states which represent town interests and those which represent country, and inside the towns themselves the antagonism between industry and maritime commerce. The class relation between citizens and slaves is now completely developed.

This whole interpretation of history appears to be contradicted by the fact of conquest. Up till now violence, war, pillage, rape and slaughter, etc. have been accepted as the driving force of history. Here we must limit ourselves to the chief points and take therefore only a striking example—the destruction of an old civilization by a barbarous people and the resulting formation of an entirely new organization of society. (Rome and the barbarians; Feudalism and Gaul; the Byzantine Empire and the Turks). With the conquering barbarian people war itself is still, as hinted above, a regular form of intercourse, which is the more eagerly exploited as the population increases, involving the necessity of new means of production to supersede the traditional and, for it, the only possible, crude mode of production. In Italy it was, however, otherwise. The concentration of landed property (caused not only by buying-up and indebtedness but also by inheritance, since loose living being rife and marriage rare, the old families died out and their possessions fell into the hands of a few) and its conversion into grazing-land (caused not only by economic forces still operative today but by the importation of plundered and tribute-corn and the resultant lack of demand for Italian corn) brought about the almost total disappearance of the free population. The very slaves died out again and again, and had constantly to be replaced by new ones. Slavery remained the basis of the whole productive system. The plebeians, midway between freemen and slaves, never succeeded in becoming more than a proletarian rabble. Rome indeed never became more than a city; its connection with the provinces was almost exclusively political and could therefore easily be broken again by political events.

With the development of private property, we find here for the first time the same conditions which we shall find again, only on a more extensive scale, with modern private property. On the one hand the concentration of private property, which began very early in Rome, (as the Licinian agrarian law proves[4]), and proceeded very rapidly from the time of the civil wars and especially under the Emperors; on the other hand, coupled with this, the transformation of the plebeian small peasantry into a proletariat, which, however, owing to its intermediate position between propertied citizens and slaves, never achieved an independent development.

The third form of ownership is feudal or estate-property.[5] If antiquity started out from the town and its little territory, the Middle Ages started out from the country. This different starting-point was determined by the sparseness of the population at that time, which was scattered over a large area and which received no large increase from the conquerors. In contrast to Greece and Rome, feudal development therefore extends over a much wider field, prepared by the Roman conquests and the spread of agriculture at first associated with it. The last centuries of the declining Roman Empire and its conquest by the barbarians destroyed a number of productive forces; agriculture had declined, industry had decayed for want of a market, trade had died out or been violently suspended, the rural and urban population had decreased. From these conditions and the mode of organization of the conquest determined by them, feudal property developed under the influence of the Germanic military constitution. Like tribal and communal ownership, it is based again on a community; but the directly producing class standing over against it is not, as in the case of the ancient community, the slaves, but the enserfed small peasantry. As soon as feudalism is fully developed, there also arises antagonism to the towns. The hierarchical system of land ownership, and the armed bodies of retainers associated with it, gave the nobility power over the serfs. This feudal organization was, just as much as the ancient communal ownership, an association against a subjected producing class; but the form of association and the relation to the direct producers were different because of the different conditions of production.

This feudal organization of land-ownership had its counterpart in the towns in the shape of corporative property, the feudal organization of trades. Here property consisted chiefly in the labour of each individual person. The necessity for association against the organized robber-nobility, the need for communal covered markets in an age when the industrialist was at the same time a merchant, the growing competition of the escaped serfs swarming into the rising towns, the feudal structure of the whole country: these combined to bring about the guilds. Further, the gradually accumulated capital of individual craftsmen and their stable numbers, as against the growing population, evolved the relation of journeyman and apprentice, which brough into being in the towns a hierarchy similar to that in the country.

Thus the chief form of property during the feudal epoch consisted on the one hand of landed property with serf-labour chained to it, and on the other of individual labour with small capital commanding the labour of journeymen. The organization of both was determined by the restricted conditions of production–the small-scale and primitive cultivation of the land, and the craft type of industry. There was little division of labour in the heyday of feudalism. Each land bore in itself the conflict of town and country and the division into estates was certainly strongly marked; but apart from the differentiation of princes, nobility, clergy and peasants in the country, and masters, journeymen, apprentices and soon also the rabble of casual labourers in the towns, no division of importance took place. In agriculture it was rendered difficult by the strip-system, beside which the cottage industry of the peasants themselves emerged as another factor. In industry there was no division of labour at all in the individual trades themselves, and very little between them. The separation of industry and commerce was found already in existence in older towns; in the newer it only developed later, when the towns entered into mutual relations.

The grouping of larger territories into feudal kingdoms was a necessity for the landed nobility as for the towns. The organization of the ruling class, the nobility, had, therefore, everywhere a monarch at its head.

The fact is, therefore, that definite individuals who are productively active in a definite way enter into these definite social and political relations. Empirical observation must in each separate instance bring out empirically, and without any mystification and speculation, the connection of the social and political structure with production. The social structure and the State are continually evolving out of the life-process of definite individuals, but of individuals, not as they may appear in their own or other people's imagination, but as they really are; i.e., as they are effective, produce materially, and are active under definite material limits, presuppositions and conditions independent of their will.

The production of ideas, of conceptions, of consciousness, is at first directly interwoven with the material activity and the material intercourse of men, the language of real life. Conceiving, thinking, the mental intercourse of men, appear at this stage as the direct efflux of their material behaviour. The same applies to mental production as expressed in the language of the politics, laws, morality, religion, metaphysics of a people. Men are the producers of their conceptions, ideas, etc.–real, active men, as they are conditioned by a definite development of their productive forces and of the intercourse corresponding to these, up to its furthest forms. Consciousness can never be anything else than conscious existence, and the existence of men is their actual life-process. If in all ideology men and their circumstances appear upside down as in a *camera obscura*,[6] this phenomenon arises just as much from their historical life-process as the inversion of objects on the retina does from their physical life-process.

In direct contrast to German philosophy which descends from heaven to earth, here we ascend from earth to heaven. That is to say, we do not set out from what men say, imagine conceive, nor from men as narrated, thought of, imagined, conceived, in order to arrive at men in the flesh. We set out from real, active men, and on the basis of their real life-process we demonstrate the development of the ideological reflexes and echoes of this life-process. The phantoms formed in the human brain are also, necessarily, sublimates of their material life-process, which is empirically verifiable and bound to material premises. Morality, religion, metaphysics, all the rest of ideology and their corresponding forms of consciousness, thus no longer retain the semblance of independence. They have no history, no development; but men, developing their material production and their material intercourse, alter, along with this their real existence, their thinking and the products of their thinking. Life is not determined by consciousness, but consciousness by life. In the first method of approach the starting-point is consciousness taken as the living individual; in the second it is the real living individuals themselves, as they are in actual life, and consciousness is considered solely as *their* consciousness.

This method of approach is not devoid of premises. It starts out from the real premises and does not abandon them for a moment. Its premises are men, not in any fantastic isolation or abstract definition, but in their actual, empirically perceptible process of development under definite conditions. As soon as this active lifeprocess is described, history ceases to be a collection of dead facts as it is with the empiricists (themselves still abstract), or an imagined activity of imagined subjects, as with the idealists.

Where speculation ends—in real life—there real, positive science begins: the representation of the practical activity, of the practical process of development of men. Empty talk about consciousness ceases, and real knowledge has to take its place. When reality is depicted, philosophy as an independent branch of activity loses its medium of existence. At the best its place can only be taken by a summing-up of the most general results, abstractions which arise from the observation of the historical development of men. Viewed apart from real history, these abstractions have in themselves no value whatsoever. They can only serve to facilitate the arrangement of historical material, to indicate the sequence of its separate strata. But they by no means afford a recipe or schema, as does philosophy, for neatly trimming the epochs of history. On the contrary, our difficulties begin only when we set about the observation and the arrangement—the real depiction—of our historical material, whether of a past epoch or of the present. The removal of these difficulties is governed by premises which it is quite impossible to state here, but which only the study of the actual life-process and the activity of the individuals of each epoch will make evident. We shall select here some of these abstractions, which we use to refute the ideologists, and shall illustrate them by historical examples.

(a) History

Since we are dealing with the Germans, who do not postulate anything, we must begin by stating the first premise of all human existence, and therefore of all history, the premise namely that men must be in a position to live in order to be able to "make history." But life involves before everything else eating and drinking, a habitation, clothing and many other things. The first historical act is thus the production of the means to satisfy these needs, the production of material life itself. And indeed this is an historical act, a fundamental condition of all history, which today, as thousands of years ago, must daily and hourly be fulfilled merely in order to sustain human life. Even when the sensuous world is reduced to a minimum, to a stick as with Saint Bruno,[7] it presupposes the action of producing the stick. The first necessity therefore in any theory of history is to observe this fundamental fact in all its significance and all its implications and to accord it its due importance. This, as is notorious, the Germans have never done, and they have never therefore had an earthly basis for history and consequently never a historian. The French and the English, even if they have conceived the relation of this fact with so-called history only in an extremely one-sided fashion, particularly as long as they remained in the toils of political ideology, have nevertheless made the first attempts to give the writing of history a materialistic basis by being the first to write histories of civil society, of commerce and industry.

The second fundamental point is that as soon as a need is satisfied, (which implies the action of satisfying, and the acquisition of an instrument), new needs are made; and this production of new needs is the first historical act. Here we recognize immediately the spiritual ancestry of the great historical wisdom of the Germans who, when they run out of positive material and when they can serve up neither theological nor political nor literary rubbish, do not write history at all, but invent the "prehistoric era." They do not, however, enlighten us as to how we proceed from this nonsensical "prehistory" to history proper; although, on the other hand, in their historical speculation they seize upon this "prehistory" with especial eagerness because they imagine themselves safe there from interference on the part of "crude facts," and, at the same time, because there they can give full rein to their speculative impulse and set up and knock down hypotheses by the thousand.

The third circumstance which, from the very first, enters into historical development, is that men, who daily remake their own life, begin to make other men, to propagate their kind: the relation between man and wife, parents and children, the FAMILY. The family which to begin with is the only social relationship, becomes later, when in creased needs create new social relations and the increased population new needs, a subordinate one (except in Germany), and must then be treated and analysed according to the existing empirical data,* not according to "the concept of the family," as is the custom in Germany. These three aspects of social activity are not of course to be taken as three different stages, but just, as I have said, as three aspects or, to I make it clear to the Germans, three "moments,"[8] which have existed simultaneously since the dawn of history and the first men, and still assert themselves in history today.

The production of life, both of one's own in labour and of fresh life in procreation, now appears as a double relationship: on the one hand as a natural, on the other as a social relationship. By social we understand the cooperation of several individuals, no matter under what conditions, in what manner and to what end. It follows from this that a certain mode of production, or industrial stage, is always combined with a certain mode of cooperation, or social stage, and this mode of cooperation is itself a "productive force." Further, that the multitude of productive forces accessible to men determines the nature of society, hence that the "history of humanity" must always be studied and treated in relation to the history of industry and exchange. But it is also clear how in Germany it is impossible to write this sort of history, because the Germans lack not only the necessary power of comprehension and the material but also the "evidence of their senses," for

---

*The building of houses. With savages each family has of course its own cave or hut like the separate family tent of the nomads. This separate domestic economy is made only the more necessary by the further development of private property. With the agricultural peoples a communal domestic economy is just as impossible as a communal cultivation of the soil. A great advance was the building of towns. In all previous periods, however, the abolition of private property, was impossible for the simple reason that the material conditions governing it were not present. The setting up of a communal domestic economy presupposes the development of machinery, of the use of natural forces and of many other productive forces—e.g., of water-supplies, of gaslighting, steam-heating, etc., the removal of the antagonism of town and country. Without these conditions a communal economy would not in itself form a new productive force; lacking any material basis and resting on a purely theoretical foundation, it would be a more freak and would end in nothing more than a monastic economy. What was possible can be seen in the formation of towns and the erection of communal building a for various definite purposes (prisons, barracks, etc.). That the abolition of individual economy is inseparable from the abolition of the family is self-evident.

across the Rhine you cannot have any experience of these things since history has stopped happening. Thus it is quite obvious from the start that there exists a materialistic connection of men with one another, which is determined by their needs and their mode of production, and which is as old as men themselves. This connection is ever taking on new forms, and thus presents a "history" independently of the existence of any political or religious nonsense which would hold men together on its own.

Only now, after having considered four moments, four aspects of the fundamental historical relationships, do we find that man also possesses "consciousness"; but, even so, not inherent, not "pure" consciousness. From the start the "spirit" is afflicted with the curse of being "burdened" with matter, which here makes its appearance in the form of agitated layers of air, sounds, in short of language. Language is as old as consciousness, language is practical consciousness, as it exists for other men, and for that reason is really beginning to exist for me personally as well; for language, like consciousness, only arises from the need, the necessity, of intercourse with other men. Where there exists a relationship, it exists for me: the animal has no "relations" with anything, cannot have any. For the animal, its relation to others does not exist as a relation. Consciousness is therefore from the very beginning a social product, and remains so as long as men exist at all. Consciousness is at first, of course, merely consciousness concerning the immediate sensuous environment and consciousness of the limited connection with other persons and things outside the individual who is growing self-conscious. At the same time it is consciousness of nature, which first appears to men as a completely alien, all-powerful and unassailable force, with which men's relations are purely animal and by which they are overawed like beasts; it is thus a purely animal consciousness of nature (natural religion).

We see here immediately: this natural religion or animal behaviour towards nature is determined by the form of society and *vice versa*. Here, as everywhere, the identity of nature and man appears in such a way that the restricted relation of men to nature determines their restricted relation to one another, and their restricted relation to one another determines men's restricted relation to nature, just because nature is as yet hardly modified historically; and, on the other hand, man's consciousness of the necessity of associating with the individuals around him is the beginning of the consciousness that he is living in society at all. This beginning is as animal as social life itself at this stage. It is mere herd-consciousness, and at this point man is only distinguished from sheep by the fact that with him consciousness takes the place of instinct or that his instinct is a conscious one.

This sheep-like or tribal consciousness receives its further development and extension through increased productivity, the increase of needs, and, what is fundamental to both of these, the increase of population. With these there develops the division of labour, which was originally nothing but the division of labour in the sexual act, then that division of labour which develops spontaneously or "naturally"[9] by virtue of natural predisposition (e.g. physical strength), needs, accidents, etc., etc. Division of labour only becomes truly such from the moment when a division of material and mental labour appears. From this moment onwards consciousness can really flatter itself that it is something other than consciousness of existing practice, that it is really conceiving something without conceiving something real; from now on consciousness is in a position to emancipate itself from the world and to proceed to the formation of "pure" theory, theology, philosophy, ethics, etc. But even if this theory, theology, philosophy, ethics, etc. comes into contradiction with the existing relations, this can only occur as a result of the fact that existing social relations have come into contradiction with existing forces of production; this, moreover, can also occur in a particular national sphere of relations through the appearance of the contradiction, not within the national orbit, but between this national consciousness and the practice of other nations, i.e., between the national and the general consciousness of a nation.

Moreover, it is quite immaterial what consciousness starts to do on its own: out of all such muck we get only the one inference that these three moments, the forces of production, the state of society, and consciousness, can and must come into contradiction with one another, because the division of labour implies the possibility, nay the fact that intellectual and material activity—enjoyment and labour, production and consumption—devolve on different individuals, and that the only possibility of their not coming into contradiction lies in the negation in its turn of the division of labour. It is self-evident, moreover, that "spectres," "bonds," "the higher being," "concept," "scruple," are merely the idealistic, spiritual expression, the conception apparently of the isolated individual, the image of very empirical fetters and limitations, within which the mode of production of life, and the form of intercourse coupled with it, move.

With the division of labour, in which all these contradictions are implicit, and which in its turn is based on the natural division of labour in the family and the separation of society into individual families opposed to one another, is given simultaneously the distribution, and indeed the unequal distribution, (both quantitative and qualitative), of labour and its products, hence property: the nucleus, the first form, of which lies in the family, where wife and children are the slaves of the husband. This latent slavery in the family, though still very crude, is the first property, but even at this early stage it corresponds perfectly to the definition of modern economists who call it the power of disposing of the labour-power of others. Division of labour and private property are, moreover, identical expressions: in the one the same thing is affirmed with reference to activity as is affirmed in the other with reference to the product of the activity.

Further, the division of labour implies the contradiction between the interest of the separate individual or the individual family and the communal interest of all individuals who have intercourse with one another. And indeed, this communal interest does not exist merely in the imagination, as "the general good," but first of all in reality, as the mutual interdependence of the individuals among whom the labour is divided. And finally, the division of labour offers us the first example of how, as long as man remains in natural society,[10] that is as long as a cleavage exists between the particular and the common interest, as long therefore as activity is not voluntarily, but naturally, divided, man's own deed becomes an alien power opposed to him, which enslaves him instead of being controlled by him. For as soon as labour is distributed, each man has a particular, exclusive sphere of activity, which is forced upon him and from which he cannot escape. He is a hunter, a fisherman, a shepherd, or a critical critic, and must remain so if he does not want to lose his means of livelihood; while in communist society, where nobody has one exclusive sphere of activity but each can become accomplished in any branch he wishes, society regulates the general production and thus makes it possible for me to do one thing today and another tomorrow, to hunt in the morning, fish in the afternoon, rear cattle in the evening, criticize after dinner, just as I have a mind, without ever becoming hunter, fisherman, shepherd or critic.

This crystallization of social activity, this consolidation of what we ourselves produce into an objective power above us, growing out of our control, thwarting our expectations, bringing to naught our calculations, is one of the chief factors in historical development up till now. And out of this very contradiction between the interest of the individual and that of the community the latter takes an independent form as the STATE, divorced from the real interests of individual and community, and at the same time as an illusory communal life, always based, however, on the real ties existing in every family and tribal conglomeration (such as flesh and blood, language, division of labour on a larger scale, and other interests) and especially, as we shall enlarge upon later, on the classes, already determined by the division of labour, which in every such mass of men separate out, and of which one dominates all the others. It follows from this that all struggles within the State, the struggle between democracy, aristocracy and monarchy, the struggle for the franchise, etc., etc., are merely the illusory forms in which the real struggles of the different classes are fought out among one another. (Of this the German theoreticians have not the faintest inkling, although they have received a sufficient introduction to the subject in *The German-French Annals*[11] and *The Holy Family*.[12])

Further, it follows that every class which is struggling for mastery, even when its domination, as is the case with the proletariat, postulates the abolition of the old form of society in its entirety and of mastery itself, must first conquer for itself political power in order to represent its interest in turn as the general interest, a step to which in the first moment it is forced. Just because individuals seek only their particular interest, i.e. that not coinciding with their communal interest (for the "general good" is the illusory form of communal life), the latter will be imposed on them as an interest "alien" to them, and "independent" of them, as in its turn a particular, peculiar "general interest"; or they must meet face to face in this antagonism, as in democracy.[13] On the other hand too, the *practical* struggle of these particular interests, which constantly *really* run counter to the communal and illusory communal interests, make *practical* intervention and control necessary through the illusory "general-interest" in the form of the State. The social power, i.e., the multiplied productive force, which arises through the cooperation of different individuals as it is determined within the division of labour, appears to these individuals, since their cooperation is not voluntary but natural, not as their own united power but as an alien force existing outside them, of the origin and end of which they are ignorant, which they thus cannot control, which on the contrary passes through a peculiar series of phases and stages independent of the will and the action of man, nay even being the prime governor of these.

This "estrangement"[14] (to use a term which will be comprehensible to the philosophers) can, of course, only be abolished given two *practical* premises. For it to become an "intolerable" power, i.e., a power against which men make a revolution, it must necessarily have rendered the great mass of humanity "propertyless," and produced, at the same time, the contradiction of an existing world of wealth and culture, both of which conditions presuppose a great increase in productive power, a high degree of its development. And, on the other hand, this development of productive forces (which itself implies the actual empirical existence of men in their *world-historical,* instead of local, being) is absolutely necessary as a practical premise: firstly, for the reason that without it only *want* is made general, and with want the struggle for necessities and all the old filthy business would necessarily be reproduced; and secondly, because only with this universal development of productive forces is a *universal* intercourse between men established, which produces in all nations simultaneously the phenomenon of the "propertyless" mass (universal competition), makes each nation dependent on the revolutions of the others, and finally has put *world-historical,* empirically universal individuals in place of local ones. Without this, (1) Communism could only exist as a local event; (2) The forces of intercourse themselves could not have developed as universal, hence intolerable powers: they would nave remained homebred superstitious conditions; and (3) Each extension of intercourse would abolish local communism. Empirically, communism is only possible as the act of the dominant peoples "all at once" or simultaneously, which presupposes the universal development of productive forces and the world-intercourse bound up with them. How otherwise could property have had a history at all, have taken on different forms, and landed property, for instance, according to the different premises given, have proceeded in France from parcellation to centralization in the hands of a few, in England from centralization in the hands of a few to parcellation, as is actually the case today?[15] Or how does it happen that trade, which after all is nothing more than the exchange of products of various individuals and countries, rules the whole world through the relation of supply and demand—a relation which, as an English economist says, hovers over the earth like the Fate of the Ancients, and with invisible hand allots fortune and misfortune to men, sets up empires and overthrows empires, causes nations to rise and to disappear—while with the abolition of the basis of private property, with the communistic regulation of production (and, implicit in this, the destruction of the alien relation between men and what they themselves produce), the power of the relation of supply and demand is dissolved into nothing, and men get exchange, production, the mode of their mutual relation, under their own control again?

Communism is for us not a stable state which is to be established, an *ideal* to which reality will have to adjust itself. We call communism the *real* movement which abolishes the present state of things. The conditions of this movement result from the premises now in existence. Besides, the world-market is presupposed by the mass of propertyless workers—labour-power cut off as a mass from capital or from even a limited satisfaction—and therefore no longer by the mere precariousness of labour, which, not giving an assured livelihood, is often lost through competition. The proletariat can thus only exist *world-historically*, just as communism, its movement, can only have a "world-historical" existence. World-historical existence of individuals, i.e., existence of individuals which is directly linked up with world history.

The form of intercourse determined by the existing productive forces at all previous historical stages, and in its turn determining these, is *civil society*.[16] This, as is clear from what we have said above, has as its premises and basis the simple family and the multiple, the so-called tribe, the more precise determinants of which are enumerated in our remarks above. Already here we see how this civil society is the true source and theatre of all history, and how nonsensical is the conception of history held hitherto, which neglects the real relationships and confines itself to high-sounding dramas of princes and states. Civil society embraces the whole material intercourse of individuals within a definite stage of the development of productive forces. It embraces the whole commercial and industrial life of this stage and, insofar, transcends the State and the nation, though, on the other hand again, it must assert itself towards foreign peoples as nationality, and inwardly must organize itself as State. The word "civil society" emerged in the eighteenth century, when property relationships had already extricated themselves from the ancient and medieval communal society. Civil society as such only develops with the bourgeoisie; the social organization evolving directly out of production and commerce, which in all ages forms the basis of the State and of the rest of the idealistic superstructure, has, however, always been designated by the same name.

(b) Concerning the Production of Consciousness

In history up to the present it is certainly an empirical fact that separate individuals have, with the broadening of their activity into world-historical activity, become more and more enslaved under a power alien to them (a pressure which they have conceived of as a dirty trick on the part of the so-called universal spirit), a power which has become more and more enormous and, in the last instance, turns out to be the *world-market.* But it is just as empirically established that, by the overthrow of the existing state of society by the communist revolution (of which more below) and the abolition of private property which is identical with it, this power, which so baffles the German theoreticians, will be dissolved; and that then the liberation of each single individual will be accomplished in the measure in which history becomes transformed into world-history. From the above it is clear that the real intellectual wealth of the individual depends entirely on the wealth of his real connections. Only then will the separate individuals be liberated from the various national and local barriers, be brought into practical connection with the material and intellectual production of the whole world and be put in a position to acquire the capacity to enjoy this all-sided production of the whole earth (the creations of man). Universal dependence, this natural form of the world-historical cooperation of individuals, will be transformed by this.

NOTES

1. *Verkehr.* The word, as used by Marx, means "intercourse," with a slight flavour of "commercial" intercourse. I have usually used the word intercourse, but it must be remembered that the word means intercourse based on economic needs; in one or two places the word "commerce" seemed more correct (cf. the earlier use of "commerce" which originally meant social intercourse in general, and only later meant commercial intercourse).

2. *Mobiles* and *immobiles Privateigentum.* The technical translation is "personal

property" and "real property" (or "personality" and "realty"). In a nontechnical work, however, these terms are confusing, and I have preferred "movable" and "immovable" (for which there is good authority). For Marx in this work "movable property" is that which can be estimated in terms of money and turned into money; "immovable" cannot be so transformed.

3. *Naturwuchsig* ("growing naturally"). Marx's use of this term seems not quite consistent. He uses it to distinguish the economic development of precapitalistic times, where the division of labour is determined by "natural predispositions," e.g. physical strength, needs, accidents, etc. Where "natural" capital is attached to the labour and inherited environment of a guildsman, as opposed to the capital of the modern capitalist, which is movable and can be assessed in terms of money. But elsewhere "natural" society is one in which there is a cleavage between the particular and the common interest, hence where men have no control over themselves or society. To this "natural" society he opposes communist society with its planning.

4. The Licinian agrarian law, passed 367 B.C.E. limited the amount of common land which a single Roman citizen could hold, and is a sign of the growth of private ownership in Rome.

5. *Ständisches Eigentum*, property inseparable from the *Stand*, the social estate to which the owner belonged.

6. An instrument perfected in the late Middle Ages, to throw, by means of mirrors, an image of a scene on a plane surface. It was widely used by artists to establish the correct proportions of a natural object or scene. The image appeared on the paper inverted; though the later use of a lens corrected this.

7. Bruno Bauer.

8. *Moment.* A philosophic term which means "a determining active factor."

9. *Naturwuchsig*–see note 3 above.

10. See note 3 above.

11. *Die Deutsch-Französischen Jahrbucher*, Paris 1844, edited jointly by Marx and Ruge. The reference is particularly to Marx's articles *On the Jewish Question* and *A Contribution to the Critique of the Hegelian Philosophy of Law.*

12. *Die Heilige Familie* . . . by Marx and Engels. Frankfurt, 1845.

13. The sentence is imperfect in the original.

14. *Entfremdung.* In the *German Ideology* Marx makes his final reckoning with this concept of "self-estrangement."

For Hegel, the development of society, which is the mode of self-development of the Absolute Idea, occurs through the projection of mind into matter, the self-estrangement of mind in a material form alien to its true nature. Through the struggle between mind and its estranged form higher forms are produced. The process of self-estrangement is the very form of existence of mind, leading to the final stage of absolute knowledge. This concept, which bears the essence of Hegel's idealism and dialectics, is transformed by the Young-Hegelians into the idea of the loss of man, in modern society, of the "essence" of man, his deprivation of a full life, of true justice, freedom, etc. In the works of 1844 Marx wrestles with this concept, and charges it with a new content. The "self-estrangement" of Absolute Mind, or of human essence, comes to be for him an idealistic and perverted expression for the real cleavage of society into classes, for the exploitation of the workers by the owners of property. He makes the conclusion, that to abolish "self-estrangement" one must abolish private property.

The following passages illustrate Marx's use of the concept:

> The possessing class and the class of the proletariat represent the same human self-estrangement. But the former is comfortable in this self-estrangement and finds therein its own confirmation, knows that this self-estrangement is its own power, and possesses in it the semblance of a human existence. The latter feels itself annihilated in this selfestrangement, sees in it its impotence and the reality of an inhuman existence (*Holy Family*, Chap. 4).

> How does it come about that personal interests continually grow, despite the persons, into class-interests, into common interests which win an independent existence over against the individual persons, in this independence take on the shape of general interests, enter as such into opposition with the real individuals, and in this opposition, according to which they are defined as general interests, can be conceived by the consciousness as ideal, even as religious, sacred interests? How does it come about that, within this process of the self-assertion of personal interests as class-interests, the personal behaviour of the individual must become hard and remote, estranged from itself, and at the same time exists apart from him as an independent power produced by intercourse, transforms itself into social relations, into a series of powers which determine and subordinate him and hence, seem conceptually to be "sacred" powers? (*Ideology*–"Saint Max," *Gesamtausgabe*, I, 5, p. 226).

15. Should "England" be put for "France" and "France" for "England"? Marx gives a masterly account of the historical process by which landed property in England went out of the hands of the many into those of the few in *Capital*, vol. 11, chaps. 27–29.

16. *Burgerliche Gesellschaft*. This term is often wrongly translated as "bourgeois society." On the one hand it has the meaning of "civilized society," i.e., society with government, laws, etc., as opposed to "natural" or primitive society; and also serves to denote the personal and economic relations of men as opposed to political relations and forms. In particular it arose and was used in the seventeenth and eighteenth centuries amongst bourgeois theoreticians as a theoretical attack on political forms which prevented the free accumulation of private property. Cf. such terms as civil law, i.e., law which regulates the relations between individuals, as opposed to public law, which regulates the relations between the State and public bodies. The present context indicates the faultiness of the rendering "bourgeois society."

5

●

FROM
DEMOCRACY AND EDUCATION

John Dewey

EDUCATION AS A
NECESSITY OF LIFE

1. Renewal of Life by Transmission

The most notable distinction between living and inanimate things is that the former maintain themselves by renewal. A stone when struck resists. If its resistance is greater than the force of the blow struck, it remains outwardly unchanged. Otherwise, it is shattered into smaller bits. Never does the stone attempt to react in such a way that it may maintain itself against the blow, much less so as to render the blow a contributing factor to its own continued action. While the living thing may easily be crushed by superior force, it nonetheless tries to turn the energies which act upon it into means of its own further existence. If it cannot do so, it does not just split into smaller pieces (at least in the higher forms of life), but loses its identity as a living thing.

As long as it endures, it struggles to use surrounding energies in its own behalf. It uses light, air, moisture, and the material of soil. To say that it uses them is to say that it turns them into means of its own conservation. As long as

107

it is growing, the energy it expends in thus turning the environment to account is more than compensated for by the return it gets: it grows. Understanding the word "control" in this sense, it may be said that a living being is one that subjugates and controls for its own continued activity the energies that would otherwise use it up. Life is a self-renewing process through action upon the environment.

In all the higher forms this process cannot be kept up indefinitely. After a while they succumb; they die. The creature is not equal to the task of indefinite self-renewal. But continuity of the life process is not dependent upon the prolongation of the existence of any one individual. Reproduction of other forms of life goes on in continuous sequence. And though, as the geological record shows, not merely individuals but also species die out, the life process continues in increasingly complex forms. As some species die out, forms better adapted to utilize the obstacles against which they struggled in vain come into being. Continuity of life means continual readaptation of the environment to the needs of living organisms.

We have been speaking of life in its lowest terms—as a physical thing. But we use the word "life" to denote the whole range of experience, individual and racial. When we see a book called the *Life of Lincoln* we do not expect to find within its covers a treatise on physiology. We look for an account of social antecedents; a description of early surroundings, of the conditions and occupation of the family; of the chief episodes in the development of character; of signal struggles and achievements; of the individual's hopes, tastes, joys and sufferings. In precisely similar fashion we speak of the life of a savage tribe, of the Athenian people, of the American nation. "Life" covers customs, institutions, beliefs, victories and defeats, recreations and occupations.

We employ the word "experience" in the same pregnant sense. And to it, as well as to life in the bare physiological sense, the principle of continuity through renewal applies. With the renewal of physical existence goes, in the case of human beings, the re-creation of beliefs, ideals, hopes, happiness, misery, and practices. The continuity of any experience, through renewing of the social group, is a literal fact. Education, in its broadest sense, is the means of this social continuity of life. Every one of the constituent elements of a social group, in a modern city as in a savage tribe, is born immature, helpless, without language, beliefs, ideas, or social standards. Each individual, each unit who is the carrier of the life-experience of his group, in time passes away. Yet the life of the group goes on.

The primary ineluctable facts of the birth and death of each one of the constituent members in a social group determine the necessity of education. On one band, there is the contrast between the immaturity of the new-born members of the group—its future sole representatives—and the maturity of the adult members who possess the knowledge and customs of the group. On the other hand, there is the necessity that these immature members be not merely physically preserved in adequate numbers, but that they be initiated into the interests, purposes, information, skill, and practices of the mature members: otherwise the group will cease its characteristic life. Even in a savage tribe, the achievements of adults are far beyond what the immature members would be capable of if left to themselves. With the growth of civilization, the gap between the original capacities of the immature and the standards and customs of the elders increases. Mere physical growing up, mere mastery of the bare necessities of subsistence will not suffice to reproduce the life of the group. Deliberate effort and the taking of thoughtful pains are required. Beings who are born not only unaware of, but quite indifferent to, the aims and habits of the social group have to be rendered cognizant of them and actively interested. Education, and education alone, spans the gap.

Society exists through a process of transmission quite as much as biological life. This transmission occurs by means of communication of habits of doing, thinking, and feeling from the older to the younger. Without this communication of ideals, hopes, expectations, standards, opinions, from those members of society who are passing out of the group life to those who are coming into it, social life could not survive. If the members who compose a society lived on continuously, they might educate the new-born members, but it would be a task directed by personal interest rather than social need. Now it is a work of necessity.

If a plague carried off the members of a society all at once, it is obvious that the group would be permanently done for. Yet the death of each of its constituent members is as certain as if an epidemic took them all at once. But the graded difference in age, the fact that some are born as some die, makes possible through transmission of ideas and practices the constant reweaving of the social fabric. Yet this renewal is not automatic. Unless pains are taken to see that genuine and thorough transmission takes place, the most civilized group will relapse into barbarism and then into savagery. In fact, the human young are so immature that if they were left to themselves without the guidance and succor of others, they could not acquire the rudimentary abilities necessary for physical existence. The young of human beings compare so poorly in original efficiency with the young of many of the lower animals, that even the powers needed for physical sustentation have to be acquired under tuition. How much more, then, is this the case with respect to all the technological, artistic, scientific, and moral achievements of humanity!

2. *Education and Communication*

So obvious, indeed, is the necessity of teaching and learning for the continued existence of a society that we may seem to be dwelling unduly on a
truism. But justification is found in the fact that such emphasis is a means of
getting us away from an unduly scholastic and formal notion of education.
Schools are, indeed, one important method of the transmission which forms
the dispositions of the immature; but it is only one means, and, compared
with other agencies, a relatively superficial means. Only as we have grasped
the necessity of more fundamental and persistent modes of tuition can we
make sure of placing the scholastic methods in their true context.

Society not only continues to exist *by* transmission, *by* communication,
but it may fairly be said to exist *in* transmission, *in* communication. There
is more than a verbal tie between the words common, community, and
communication. Men live in a community in virtue of the things which they
have in common; and communication is the way in which they come to possess things in common. What they must have in common in order to form
a community or society are aims, beliefs, aspirations, knowledge–a common understanding–like-mindedness as the sociologists say. Such things
cannot be passed physically from one to another, like bricks; they cannot be
shared as persons would share a pie by dividing it into physical pieces. The
communication which insures participation in a common understanding is
one which secures similar emotional and intellectual dispositions–like ways
of responding to expectations and requirements.

Persons do not become a society by living in physical proximity, any
more than a man ceases to be socially influenced by being so many feet or
miles removed from others. A book or a letter may institute a more intimate
association between human beings separated thousands of miles from each
other than exists between dwellers under the same roof. Individuals do not
even compose a social group because they all work for a common end. The
parts of a machine work with a maximum of cooperativeness for a common
result, but they do not form a community. If, however, they were all cognizant of the common end and all interested in it so that they regulated their
specific activity in view of it, then they would form a community. But this
would involve communication. Each would have to know what the other
was about and would have to have some way of keeping the other informed
as to his own purpose and progress. Consensus demands communication.

We are thus compelled to recognize that within even the most social
group there are many relations which are not as yet social. A large number
of human relationships in any social group are still upon the machine-like
plane. Individuals use one another so as to get desired results, without reference to the emotional and intellectual disposition and consent of those

used. Such uses express physical superiority, or superiority of position, skill, technical ability, and command of tools, mechanical or fiscal. So far as the relations of parent and child, teacher and pupil, employer and employee, governor and governed, remain upon this level, they form no true social group, no matter how closely their respective activities touch one another. Giving and taking of orders modifies action and results, but does not of itself effect a sharing of purposes, a communication of interests.

Not only is social life identical with communication, but all communication (and hence all genuine social life) is educative. To be a recipient of a communication is to have an enlarged and changed experience. One shares in what another has thought and felt and insofar, meagerly or amply, has his own attitude modified. Nor is the one who communicates left unaffected. Try the experiment of communicating, with fullness and accuracy, some experience to another, especially if it be somewhat complicated, and you will find your own attitude toward your experience changing; otherwise you resort to expletives and ejaculations. The experience has to be formulated in order to be communicated. To formulate requires getting outside of it, seeing it as another would see it, considering what points of contact it has with the life of another so that it may be got into such form that he can appreciate its meaning. Except in dealing with commonplaces and catch phrases one has to assimilate, imaginatively, something of another's experience in order to tell him intelligently of one's own experience. All communication is like art. It may fairly be said, therefore, that any social arrangement that remains vitally social, or vitally shared, is educative to those who participate in it. Only when it becomes cast in a mold and runs in a routine way does it lose its educative power.

In final account, then, not only does social life demand teaching and learning for its own permanence, but the very process of living together educates. It enlarges and enlightens experience; it stimulates and enriches imagination; it creates responsibility for accuracy and vividness of statement and thought. A man really living alone (alone mentally as well as physically) would have little or no occasion to reflect upon his past experience to extract its net meaning. The inequality of achievement between the mature and the immature not only necessitates teaching the young, but the necessity of this teaching gives an immense stimulus to reducing experience to that order and form which will render it most easily communicable and hence most usable.

3. The Place of Formal Education

There is, accordingly, a marked difference between the education which every one gets from living with others, as long as he really lives instead of just continuing to subsist, and the deliberate educating of the young. In the former case the education is incidental; it is natural and important, but it is not the express reason of the association. While it may be said, without exaggeration, that the measure of the worth of any social institution, economic, domestic, political, legal, religious, is its effect in enlarging and improving experience; yet this effect is not a part of its original motive, which is limited and more immediately practical. Religious associations began, for example, in the desire to secure the favor of overruling powers and to ward off evil influences; family life in the desire to gratify appetites and secure family perpetuity; systematic labor, for the most part, because of enslavement to others, etc. Only gradually was the by-product of the institution, its effect upon the quality and extent of conscious life, noted, and only more gradually still was this effect considered as a directive factor in the conduct of the institution. Even today, in our industrial life, apart from certain values of industriousness and thrift, the intellectual and emotional reaction of the forms of human association under which the world's work is carried on receives little attention as compared with physical output.

But in dealing with the young, the fact of association itself as an immediate human fact, gains in importance. While it is easy to ignore in our contact with them the effect of our acts upon their disposition, or to subordinate that educative effect to some external and tangible result, it is not so easy as in dealing with adults. The need of training is too evident; the pressure to accomplish a change in their attitude and habits is too urgent to leave these consequences wholly out of account. Since our chief business with them is to enable them to share in a common life we cannot help considering whether or no we are forming the powers which will secure this ability. If humanity has made some headway in realizing that the ultimate value of every institution is its distinctively human effects—its effect upon conscious experience—we may well believe that this lesson has been learned largely through dealings with the young.

We are thus led to distinguish, within the broad educational process which we have been so far considering, a more formal kind of education—that of direct tuition or schooling. In undeveloped social groups, we find very little formal teaching and training. Savage groups mainly rely for instilling needed dispositions into the young upon the same sort of association which keeps adults loyal to their group. They have no special devices, material, or institutions for teaching save in connection with initiation ceremonies by which the youth are inducted into full social membership. For the most part, they depend upon children learning the customs of the adults, acquiring their emotional set and stock of ideas, by sharing in what the elders are doing. In part, this sharing is direct, taking part in the occupations of adults and thus serving an apprenticeship; in part, it is indirect, through the dramatic plays in which children reproduce the actions of grown-ups and thus learn to know what they are like. To savages it would seem preposterous to seek out a place where nothing but learning was going on in order that one might learn.

But as civilization advances, the gap between the capacities of the young and the concerns of adults widens. Learning by direct sharing in the pursuits of grown-ups becomes increasingly difficult except in the case of the less advanced occupations. Much of what adults do is so remote in space and in meaning that playful imitation is less and less adequate to reproduce its spirit. Ability to share effectively in adult activities thus depends upon a prior training given with this end in view. Intentional agencies—schools—and explicit material—studies—are devised. The task of teaching certain things is delegated to a special group of persons.

Without such formal education, it is not possible to transmit all the resources and achievements of a complex society. It also opens a way to a kind of experience which would not be accessible to the young, if they were left to pick up their training in informal association with others, since books and the symbols of knowledge are mastered.

But there are conspicuous dangers attendant upon the transition from indirect to formal education. Sharing in actual pursuit, whether directly or vicariously in play, is at least personal and vital. These qualities compensate, in some measure, for the narrowness of available opportunities. Formal instruction, on the contrary, easily becomes remote and dead—abstract and bookish, to use the ordinary words of depreciation. What accumulated knowledge exists in low grade societies is at least put into practice; it is transmuted into character; it exists with the depth of meaning that attaches to its coming within urgent daily interests.

But in an advanced culture much which has to be learned is stored in symbols. It is far from translation into familiar acts and objects. Such material is relatively technical and superficial. Taking the ordinary standard of reality as a measure, it is artificial. For this measure is connection with practical concerns. Such material exists in a world by itself, unassimilated to ordinary customs of thought and expression. There is the standing danger that the material of formal instruction will be merely the subject matter of the schools, isolated from the subject matter of life-experience. The permanent social interests are likely to be lost from view. Those which have not been carried over into the structure of social life, but which remain largely matters of technical information expressed in symbols, are made conspicuous in schools. Thus we reach the ordinary notion of education: the notion which ignores its social necessity and its identity with all human association that affects conscious life, and which identifies it with imparting information about remote matters and the conveying of learning through verbal signs: the acquisition of literacy.

Hence one of the weightiest problems with which the philosophy of education has to cope is the method of keeping a proper balance between the informal and the formal, the incidental and the intentional, modes of education. When the acquiring of information and of technical intellectual skill do not influence the formation of a social disposition, ordinary vital experience fails to gain in meaning, while schooling, insofar, creates only "sharps" in learning–that is, egoistic specialists. To avoid a split between what men consciously know because they are aware of having learned it by a specific job of learning–and what they unconsciously know because they have absorbed it in the formation of their characters by intercourse with others, becomes an increasingly delicate task with every development of special schooling.

EDUCATION AS A SOCIAL FUNCTION

1. The Nature and Meaning of Environment

We have seen that a community or social group sustains itself through continuous self-renewal, and that this renewal takes place by means of the educational growth of the immature members of the group. By various agencies, unintentional and designed, a society transforms uninitiated and seemingly alien beings into robust trustees of its own resources and ideals. Education is thus a fostering, a nurturing, a cultivating, process. All of these words mean that it implies attention to the conditions of growth. We also speak of rearing, raising, bringing up–words which express the difference of level which education aims to cover. Etymologically, the word education means just a process of leading or bringing up. When we have the outcome of the process in mind, we speak of education as shaping, forming, molding activity–that is, a shaping into the standard form of social activity. In this chapter we are concerned with the general features of the *way* in which a social group brings up its immature members into its own social form.

Since what is required is a transformation of the quality of experience till it partakes in the interests, purposes, and ideas current in the social group, the problem is evidently not one of mere physical forming. Things can be physically transported in space; they may be bodily conveyed. Beliefs and aspirations cannot be physically extracted and inserted. How then are they communicated? Given the impossibility of direct contagion or literal inculcation, our problem is to discover the method by which the young assimilate the point of view of the old, or the older bring the young into like-mindedness with themselves.

The answer, in general formulation, is: By means of the action of the environment in calling out certain responses. The required beliefs cannot be hammered in; the needed attitudes cannot be plastered on. But the particular medium in which an individual exists leads him to see and feel one thing rather than another; it leads him to have certain plans in order that be may act successfully with others; it strengthens some beliefs and weakens others as a condition of winning the approval of others. Thus it gradually produces in him a certain system of behavior, a certain disposition of action. The words "environment," "medium" denote something more than surroundings which encompass an individual. They denote the specific *continuity* of the surroundings with his own active tendencies. An inanimate being is, of course, continuous with its surroundings; but the environing circumstances do not, save metaphorically, constitute an environment. For the inorganic being is not *concerned* in the influences which affect it. On the other hand, some things which are remote in space and time from a living creature, especially a human creature, may form his environment even more truly than some of the things close to him. The things with which a man *varies* are his genuine environment. Thus the activities of the astronomer vary with the stars at which be gazes or about which he calculates. Of his immediate surroundings, his telescope is most intimately his environment. The environment of an antiquarian, as an antiquarian, consists of the remote epoch of human life with which he is concerned, and the relics, inscriptions, etc., by which he establishes connections with that period.

In brief, the environment consists of those conditions that promote or hinder, stimulate or inhibit, the *characteristic* activities of a living being. Water is the environment of a fish because it is necessary to the fish's activities—to its life. The north pole is a significant element in the environment of an arctic explorer, whether he succeeds in reaching it or not, because it defines his activities, makes them what they distinctively are. Just because life signifies not bare passive existence (supposing there is such a thing), but a way of acting, environment or medium signifies what enters into this activity as a sustaining or frustrating condition.

2. The Social Environment

A being whose activities are associated with others has a social environment. What he does and what he can do depend upon the expectations, demands, approvals, and condemnations of others. A being connected with other beings cannot perform his own activities without taking the activities of others into account. For they are the indispensable conditions of the realization of his tendencies. When he moves he stirs them and reciprocally. We might as well try to imagine a business man doing business, buying and selling, all by himself, as to conceive it possible to define the activities of an individual in terms of his isolated actions. The manufacturer moreover is as truly socially guided in his activities when he is laying plans in the privacy of his own countinghouse as when he is buying his raw material or selling his finished goods. Thinking and feeling that have to do with action in association with others is as much a social mode of behavior as is the most overt cooperative or hostile act.

What we have more especially to indicate is how the social medium nurtures its immature members. There is no great difficulty in seeing how it shapes the external habits of action. Even dogs and horses have their actions modified by association with human beings; they form different habits because human beings are concerned with what they do. Human beings control animals by controlling the natural stimuli which influence them; by creating a certain environment in other words. Food, bits and bridles, noises, vehicles, are used to direct the ways in which the natural or instinctive responses of horses occur. By operating steadily to call out certain acts, habits are formed which function with the same uniformity as the original stimuli. If a rat is put in a maze and finds food only by making a given number of turns in a given sequence, his activity is gradually modified till he habitually takes that course rather than another when he is hungry.

Human actions are modified in a like fashion. A burnt child dreads the fire; if a parent arranged conditions so that every time a child touched a certain toy he got burned, the child would learn to avoid that toy as automatically as he avoids touching fire. So far, however, we are dealing with what may be called training in distinction from educative teaching. The changes considered are in outer action rather than in mental and emotional dispositions of behavior. The distinction is not, however, a sharp one. The child might conceivably generate in time a violent antipathy, not only to that particular toy, but to the class of toys resembling it. The aversion might even persist after he had forgotten about the original burns; later on he might even invent some reason to account for his seemingly irrational antipathy. In some cases, altering the external habit of action by changing the environment to affect the stimuli to action will also alter the mental disposition concerned in the action. Yet this does not always happen; a person trained to dodge a threatening blow, dodges automatically with no corresponding thought or emotion. We have to find, then, some differentia of training from education.

A clew may be found in the fact that the horse does not really share in the social use to which his action is put. Some one else uses the horse to secure a result which is advantageous by making it advantageous to the horse to perform the act—he gets food, etc. But the horse, presumably, does not get any new interest. He remains interested in food, not in the service he is rendering. He is not a partner in a shared activity. Were he to become a copartner, he would, in engaging in the conjoint activity, have the same interest in its accomplishment which others have. He would share their ideas and emotions.

Now in many cases—too many cases—the activity of the immature human being is simply played upon to secure habits which are useful. He is trained like an animal rather than educated like a human being. His instincts remain attached to their original objects of pain or pleasure. But to get happiness or to avoid the pain of failure he has to act in a way agreeable to others. In other cases, he really shares or participates in the common activity. In this case, his original impulse is modified. He not merely acts in a way agreeing with the actions of others, but, in so acting, the same ideas and emotions are aroused in him that animate the others. A tribe, let us say, is warlike. The successes for which it strives, the achievements upon which it sets store, are connected with fighting and victory. The presence of this medium incites bellicose exhibitions in a boy, first in games, then in fact when he is strong enough. As he fights he wins approval and advancement; as he refrains, he is disliked, ridiculed, shut out from favorable recognition. It is not surprising that his original belligerent tendencies and emotions are strengthened at the expense of others, and that his ideas turn to things connected with war. Only in this way can he become fully a recognized member of his group. Thus his mental habitudes are gradually assimilated to those of his group.

If we formulate the principle involved in this illustration, we shall perceive that the social medium neither implants certain desires and ideas directly, nor yet merely establishes certain purely muscular habits of action, like "instinctively" winking or dodging a blow. Setting up conditions which stimulate certain visible and tangible ways of acting is the first step. Making the individual a sharer or partner in the associated activity so that he feels its success as his success, its failure as his failure, is the completing step. As soon as he is possessed by the emotional attitude of the group, he will be alert to recognize the special ends at which it aims and the means employed to secure success. His beliefs and ideas, in other words, will take a form similar to those of others in the group. He win also achieve pretty much the same stock of knowledge since that knowledge is an ingredient of his habitual pursuits.

The importance of language in gaining knowledge is doubtless the chief cause of the common notion that knowledge may be passed directly from one to another. It almost seems as if all we have to do to convey an idea into the mind of another is to convey a sound into his ear. Thus imparting knowledge gets assimilated to a purely physical process. But learning from language will be found, when analyzed, to confirm the principle just laid down. It would probably be admitted with little hesitation that a child gets the idea of, say, a hat by using it as other persons do; by covering the head with it, giving it to others to wear, having it put on by others when going out, etc.

But it may be asked how this principle of shared activity applies to getting through speech or reading the idea of, say, a Greek helmet, where no direct use of any kind enters in. What shared activity is there in learning from books about the discovery of America?

Since language tends to become the chief instrument of learning about many things, let us see how it works. The baby begins of course with mere sounds, noises, and tones having no meaning, expressing, that is, no idea. Sounds are just one kind of stimulus to direct response, some having a soothing effect, others tending to make one jump, and so on. The sound h-a-t would remain as meaningless as a sound in Choctaw, a seemingly inarticulate grunt, if it were not uttered in connection with an action which is participated in by a number of people. When the mother is taking the infant out of doors, she says "hat" as she puts something on the baby's head. Being taken out becomes an interest to the child; mother and child not only go out with each other physically, but both are *concerned* in the going out; they enjoy it in common. By conjunction with the other factors in activity the sound "hat" soon gets the same meaning for the child that it has for the parent; it becomes a sign of the activity into which it enters. The bare fact that language consists of sounds which are *mutually intelligible* is enough of itself to show that its meaning depends upon connection with a shared experience.

In short, the sound h-a-t gains meaning in precisely the same way that the thing "hat" gains it, by being used in a given way. And they acquire the same meaning with the child which they have with the adult because they are used in a common experience by both. The guarantee for the same manner of use is found in the fact that the thing and the sound are first employed in a *joint* activity, as a means of setting up an active connection between the child and a grown-up. Similar ideas or meanings spring up because both persons are engaged as partners in an action where what each does depends upon and influences what the other does. If two savages were engaged in a joint hunt for game, and a certain signal meant "move to the right" to the one who uttered it, and "move to the left" to the one who heard it, they obviously could not successfully carry on their hunt together. Understanding one another means that objects, including sounds, have the same value for both with respect to carrying on a common pursuit.

After sounds have got meaning through connection with other things employed in a joint undertaking, they can be used in connection with other like sounds to develop new meanings, precisely as the things for which they stand are combined. Thus the words in which a child learns about, say, the Greek helmet originally got a meaning (or were understood) by use in an action having a common interest and end. They now arouse a new meaning by inciting the one who hears or reads to rehearse imaginatively the activities in which the helmet has its use. For the time being, the one who understands the words "Greek helmet" becomes mentally a partner with those who used the helmet. He engages, through his imagination, in a shared activity. It is not easy to get the *full* meaning of words. Most persons probably stop with the idea that "helmet" denotes a queer kind of headgear a people called the Greeks once wore. We conclude, accordingly, that the use of language to convey and acquire ideas is an extension and refinement of the principle that things gain meaning by being used in a shared experience or joint action; in no sense does it contravene that principle. When words do not enter as factors into a shared situation, either overtly or imaginatively, they operate as pure physical stimuli, not as having a meaning or intellectual value. They set activity running in a given groove, but there is no accompanying conscious purpose or meaning. Thus, for example, the plus sign may be a stimulus to perform the act of writing one number under another and adding the numbers, but the person performing the act will operate much as an automaton would unless he realizes the meaning of what he does.

3. The Social Medium as Educative

Our net result thus far is that social environment forms the mental and emotional disposition of behavior in individuals by engaging them in activities that arouse and strengthen certain impulses, that have certain purposes and entail certain consequences. A child growing up in a family of musicians will inevitably have whatever capacities he has in music stimulated, and, relatively, stimulated more than other impulses which might have been awakened in another environment. Save as he takes an interest in music and gains a certain competency in it, he is "out of it"; he is unable to share in the life of the group to which he belongs. Some kinds of participation in the life of those with whom the individual is connected are inevitable; with respect to them, the social environment exercises an educative or formative influence unconsciously and apart from any set purpose.

   In savage and barbarian communities, such direct participation (constituting the indirect or incidental education of which we have spoken) furnishes almost the sole influence for rearing the young into the practices and beliefs of the group. Even in present-day societies, it furnishes the basic nurture of even the most insistently schooled youth. In accord with the interests and occupations of the group, certain things become objects of high esteem; others of aversion. Association does not create impulses or affection and dislike, but it furnishes the objects to which they attach themselves. The way our group or class does things tends to determine the proper objects of attention, and thus to prescribe the directions and limits of observation and memory. What is strange or foreign (that is to say outside the activities of the groups) tends to be morally forbidden and intellectually suspect. It seems almost incredible to us, for example, that things which we know very well could have escaped recognition in past ages. We incline to account for it by attributing congenital stupidity to out forerunners and by assuming superior native intelligence on our own part. But the explanation is that their modes of life did not call for attention to such facts, but held their minds riveted to other things. Just as the senses require sensible objects to stimulate them, so our powers of observation, recollection, and imagination do not work spontaneously, but are set in motion by the demands set up by current social occupations. The main texture of disposition is formed, independently of schooling, by such influences. What conscious, deliberate teaching can do is at most to free the capacities thus formed for fuller exercise, to purge them of some of their grossness, and to furnish objects which make their activity more productive of meaning.

While this "unconscious influence of the environment" is so subtle and pervasive that it affects every fiber of character and mind, it may be worth while to specify a few directions in which its effect is most marked. First, the habits of language. Fundamental modes of speech, the bulk of the vocabulary, are formed in the ordinary intercourse of life, carried on not as a set means of instruction but as a social necessity. The babe acquires, as we well say, the *mother* tongue. While speech habits thus contracted may be corrected or even displaced by conscious teaching, yet, in times of excitement, intentionally acquired modes of speech often fall away, and individuals relapse into their really native tongue. Secondly, manners. Example is notoriously more potent than precept. Good manners come, as we say, from good breeding or rather are good breeding; and breeding is acquired by habitual action, in response to habitual stimuli, not by conveying information. Despite the never ending play of conscious correction and instruction, the surrounding atmosphere and spirit is in the end the chief agent in forming manners. And manners are but minor morals. Moreover, in major morals, conscious instruction is likely to be efficacious only in the degree in which it falls in with the general "walk and conversation" of those who constitute the child's social environment. Thirdly, good taste and aesthetic appreciation. If the eye is constantly greeted by harmonious objects, having elegance of form and color, a standard of taste naturally grows up. The effect of a tawdry, unarranged, and overdecorated environment works for the deterioration of taste, just as meager and barren surroundings starve out the desire for beauty. Against such odds, conscious teaching can hardly do more than convey second-hand information as to what others think. Such taste never becomes spontaneous and personally engrained, but remains a labored reminder of what those think to whom one has been taught to look up. To say that the deeper standards of judgments of value are framed by the situations into which a person habitually enters is not so much to mention a fourth point, as it is to point out a fusion of those already mentioned. We rarely recognize the extent in which our conscious estimates of what is worth while and what is not, are due to standards of which we are not conscious at all. But in general it may be said that the things which we take for granted without inquiry or reflection are just the things which determine our conscious thinking and decide our conclusions. And these habitudes which lie below the level of reflection are just those which have been formed in the constant give and take of relationship with others.

4. The School as a Special Environment

The chief importance of this foregoing statement of the educative process which goes on willynilly is to lead us to note that the only way in which adults consciously control the kind of education which the immature get is by controlling the environment in which they act, and hence think and feel. We never educate directly, but indirectly by means of the environment. Whether we permit chance environments to do the work, or whether we design environments for the purpose makes a great difference. And any environment is a chance environment so far as its educative influence is concerned unless it has been deliberately regulated with reference to its educative effect. An intelligent home differs from an unintelligent one chiefly in that the habits of life and intercourse which prevail are chosen, or at least colored, by the thought of their bearing upon the development of children. But schools remain, of course, the typical instance of environments framed with express reference to influencing the mental and moral disposition of their members.

Roughly speaking, they come into existence when social traditions are so complex that a considerable part of the social store is committed to writing and transmitted through written symbols. Written symbols are even more artificial or conventional than spoken; they cannot be picked up in accidental intercourse with others. In addition, the written form tends to select and record matters which are comparatively foreign to everyday life. The achievements accumulated from generation to generation are deposited in it even though some of them have fallen temporarily out of use. Consequently as soon as a community depends to any considerable extent upon what lies beyond its own territory and its own immediate generation, it must rely upon the set agency of schools to insure adequate transmission of all its resources. To take an obvious illustration: The life of the ancient Greeks and Romans has profoundly influenced our own, and yet the ways in which they affect us do not present themselves on the surface of our ordinary experiences. In similar fashion, peoples still existing, but remote in space, British,

Germans, Italians, directly concern our own social affairs, but the nature of the interaction cannot be understood without explicit statement and attention. In precisely similar fashion, our daily associations cannot be trusted to make clear to the young the part played in our activities by remote physical energies, and by invisible structures. Hence a special mode of social intercourse is instituted, the school, to care for such matters.

This mode of association has three functions sufficiently specific, as compared with ordinary associations of life, to be noted. First, a complex civilization is too complex to be assimilated *in toto*. It has to be broken up into portions, as it were, and assimilated piecemeal, in a gradual and graded way. The relationships of our present social life are so numerous and so interwoven that a child placed in the most favorable position could not readily share in many of the most important of them. Not sharing in them, their meaning would not be communicated to him, would not become a part of his own mental disposition. There would be no seeing the trees because of the forest. Business, politics, art, science, religion, would make all at once a clamor for attention; confusion would be the outcome. The first office of the social organ we call the school is to provide a simplified environment. It selects the features which are fairly fundamental and capable of being responded to by the young. Then it establishes a progressive order, using the factors first acquired as means of gaining insight into what is more complicated.

In the second place, it is the business of the school environment to eliminate, so far as possible, the unworthy features of the existing environment from influence upon mental habitudes. It establishes a purified medium of action. Selection aims not only at simplifying but at weeding out what is undesirable. Every society gets encumbered with what is trivial, with dead wood from the past, and with what is positively perverse. The school has the duty of omitting such things from the environment which it supplies, and thereby doing what it can to counteract their influence in the ordinary social environment. By selecting the best for its exclusive use, it strives to reenforce the power of this best. As a society becomes more enlightened, it realizes that it is responsible *not* to transmit and conserve the whole of its existing achievements, but only such as make for a better future society. The school is its chief agency for the accomplishment of this end.

In the third place, it is the office of the school environment to balance the various elements in the social environment, and to see to it that each individual gets an opportunity to escape from the limitations of the social group in which he was born, and to come into living contact with a broader environment. Such words as "society" and "community" are likely to be misleading, for they have a tendency to make us think there is a single thing corresponding to the single word. As a matter of fact, a modern society is many societies more or less loosely connected. Each household with its immediate extension of friends makes a society; the village or street group of playmates is a community; each business group, each club, is another. Passing beyond these more intimate groups, there is in a country like our own a variety of races, religious affiliations, economic divisions. Inside the modern city, in spite of its nominal political unity, there are probably more communities, more differing customs, traditions, aspirations, and forms of government or control, than existed in an entire continent at an earlier epoch.

Each such group exercises a formative influence on the active dispositions of its members. A clique, a club, a gang, a Fagin's household of thieves, the prisoners in a jail, provide educative environments for those who enter into their collective or conjoint activities, as truly as a church, a labor union, a business partnership, or a political party. Each of them is a mode of associated or community life, quite as much as is a family, a town, or a state. There are also communities whose members have little or no direct contact with one another, like the guild of artists, the republic of letters, the members of the professional learned class scattered over the face of the earth. For they have aims in common, and the activity of each member is directly modified by knowledge of what others are doing.

In the olden times, the diversity of groups was largely a geographical matter. There were many societies, but each, within its own territory, was comparatively homogeneous. But with the development of commerce, transportation, intercommunication, and emigration, countries like the United States are composed of a combination of different groups with different traditional customs. It is this situation which has, perhaps more than any other one cause, forced the demand for an educational institution which shall provide something like a homogeneous and balanced environment for the young. Only in this way can the centrifugal forces set up by juxtaposition of different groups within one and the same political unit be counteracted. The intermingling in the school of youth of different races, differing religions, and unlike customs creates for all a new and broader environment. Common subject matter accustoms all to a unity of outlook upon a broader horizon than is visible to the members of any group while it is isolated. The assimilative force of the American public school is eloquent testimony to the efficacy of the common and balanced appeal.

The school has the function also of coordinating within the disposition of each individual the diverse influences of the various social environments into which he enters. One code prevails in the family; another, on the street; a third, in the workshop or store; a fourth, in the religious association. As a person passes from one of the environments to another, he is subjected to antagonistic pulls, and is in danger of being split into a being having different standards of judgment and emotion for different occasions. This danger imposes upon the school a steadying and integrating office.

THE DEMOCRATIC CONCEPTION IN EDUCATION

For the most part, save incidentally, we have hitherto been concerned with education as it may exist in any social group. We have now to make explicit the differences in the spirit, material, and method of education as it operates in different types of community life. To say that education is a social function, securing direction and development in the immature through their participation in the life of the group to which they belong, is to say in effect that education will vary with the quality of life which prevails in a group. Particularly is it true that a society which not only changes but which has the ideal of such change as will improve it, will have different standards and methods of education from one which aims simply at the perpetuation of its own customs. To make the general ideas set forth applicable to our own educational practice, it is, therefore, necessary to come to closer quarters with the nature of present social life.

1. The Implications of Human Association

Society is one word, but many things. Men associate together in all kinds of ways and for all kinds of purposes. One man is concerned in a multitude of diverse groups, in which his associates may be quite different. It often seems as if they had nothing in common except that they are modes of associated life. Within every larger social organization there are numerous minor groups: not only political subdivisions, but industrial, scientific, religious, associations. There are political parties with differing aims, social sets, cliques, gangs, corporations, partnerships, groups bound closely together by ties of blood, and so on in endless variety. In many modern states and in some ancient, there is great diversity of populations, of varying languages, religions, moral codes, and traditions. From this standpoint, many a minor political unit, one of our large cities, for example, is a congeries of loosely associated societies, rather than an inclusive and permeating community of action and thought.

The terms society, community, are thus ambiguous. They have both a eulogistic or normative sense, and a descriptive sense; a meaning *de jure* and a meaning *de facto*. In social philosophy, the former connotation is almost always uppermost. Society is conceived as one by its very nature. The qualities which accompany this unity, praiseworthy community of purpose and welfare, loyalty to public ends, mutuality of sympathy, are emphasized. But when we look at the facts which the term *denotes* instead of confining our attention to its intrinsic *connotation*, we find not unity, but a plurality of societies, good and bad. Men banded together in a criminal conspiracy, business aggregations that prey upon the public while serving it, political machines held together by the interest of plunder, are included. If it is said that such organizations are not societies because they do not meet the ideal requirements of the notion of society, the answer, in part, is that the conception of society is then made so "ideal" as to be of no use, having no reference to facts; and in part, that each of these organizations, no matter how opposed to the interests of other groups, has something of the praiseworthy qualities of "Society" which hold it together. There is honor among thieves, and a band of robbers has a common interest as respects its members. Gangs are marked by fraternal feeling, and narrow cliques by intense loyalty to their own codes. Family life may be marked by exclusiveness, suspicion, and jealousy as to those without, and yet be a model of amity and mutual aid within. Any education given by a group tends to socialize its members, but the quality and value of the socialization depends upon the habits and aims of the group.

Hence, once more, the need of a measure for the worth of any given mode of social life. In seeking this measure, we have to avoid two extremes. We cannot set up, out of our heads, something we regard as an ideal society. We must base our conception upon societies which actually exist, in order to have any assurance that our ideal is a practicable one. But, as we have just seen, the ideal cannot simply repeat the traits which are actually found. The problem is to extract the desirable traits of forms of community life which actually exist, and employ them to criticize undesirable features and suggest improvement. Now in any social group whatever, even in a gang of thieves, we find some interest held in common, and we find a certain amount of interaction and cooperative intercourse with other groups. From these two traits we derive our standard. How numerous and varied are the interests which are consciously shared? How full and free is the interplay with other forms of association? If we apply these considerations to, say, a criminal band, we find that the ties which consciously hold the members together are few in number, reducible almost to a common interest in plunder; and that they are of such a nature as to isolate the group from other groups with respect to give and take of the values of life. Hence, the education such a society gives is partial and distorted. If we take, on the other hand, the kind of family life which illustrates the standard, we find that there are material, intellectual, aesthetic interests in which all participate and that the progress of one member has worth for the experience of other members—it is readily communicable—and that the family is not an isolated whole, but enters intimately into relationships with business groups, with schools, with all the agencies of culture, as well as with other similar groups, and that it plays a due part in the political organization and in return receives support from it. In short, there are many interests consciously communicated and shared; and there are varied and free points of contact with other modes of association.

I. Let us apply the first element in this criterion to a despotically governed state. It is not true there is no common interest in such an organization between governed and governors. The authorities in command must
make some appeal to the native activities of the subjects, must call some of
their powers into play. Talleyrand said that a government could do everything with bayonets except sit on them. This cynical declaration is at least a
recognition that the bond of union is not merely one of coercive force. It
may be said, however, that the activities appealed to are themselves
unworthy and degrading–that such a government calls into functioning
activity simply capacity for fear. In a way, this statement is true. But it overlooks the fact that fear need not be an undesirable factor in experience. Caution, circumspection, prudence, desire to foresee future events so as to avert
what is harmful, these desirable traits are as much a product of calling the
impulse of fear into play as is cowardice and abject submission. The real difficulty is that the appeal to fear is *isolated.* In evoking dread and hope of specific tangible reward–say comfort and ease–many other capacities are left
untouched. Or rather, they are affected, but in such a way as to pervert
them. Instead of operating on their own account they are reduced to mere
servants of attaining pleasure and avoiding pain.

This is equivalent to saying that there is no extensive number of
common interests; there is no free play back and forth among the members
of the social group. Stimulation and response are exceedingly one-sided. In
order to have a large number of values in common, all the members of the
group must have an equable opportunity to receive and to take from others.
There must be a large variety of shared undertakings and experiences. Otherwise, the influences which educate some into masters, educate others into
slaves. And the experience of each party loses in meaning, when the free
interchange of varying modes of life-experience is arrested. A separation into
a privileged and a subject-class prevents social endosmosis. The evils thereby
affecting the superior class are less material and less perceptible, but equally
real. Their culture tends to be sterile, to be turned back to feed on itself; their
art becomes a showy display and artificial; their wealth luxurious; their
knowledge overspecialized; their manners fastidious rather than humane.

Lack of the free and equitable intercourse which springs from a variety
of shared interests makes intellectual stimulation unbalanced. Diversity of
stimulation means novelty, and novelty means challenge to thought. The
more activity is restricted to a few definite lines–as it is when there are rigid
class lines preventing adequate interplay of experiences–the more action
tends to become routine on the part of the class at a disadvantage, and capri-
cious, aimless, and explosive on the part of the class having the materially
fortunate position. Plato defined a slave as one who accepts from another the
purposes which control his conduct. This condition obtains even where there

is no slavery in the legal sense. It is found wherever men are engaged in activity which is socially serviceable, but whose service they do not understand and have no personal interest in. Much is said about scientific management of work. It is a narrow view which restricts the science which secures efficiency of operation to movements of the muscles. The chief opportunity for science is the discovery of the relations of a man to his work—including his relations to others who take part—which will enlist his intelligent interest in what he is doing. Efficiency in production often demands division of labor. But it is reduced to a mechanical routine unless workers see the technical, intellectual, and social relationships involved in what they do, and engage in their work because of the motivation furnished by such perceptions. The tendency to reduce such things as efficiency of activity and scientific management to purely technical externals is evidence of the one-sided stimulation of thought given to those in control of industry—those who supply its aims. Because of their lack of all-round and well-balanced social interest, there is not sufficient stimulus for attention to the human factors and relationships in industry. Intelligence is narrowed to the factors concerned with technical production and marketing of goods. No doubt, a very acute and intense intelligence in these narrow lines can be developed, but the failure to take into account the significant social factors means nonetheless an absence of mind, and a corresponding distortion of emotional life.

II. This illustration (whose point is to be extended to all associations lacking reciprocity of interest) brings us to our second point. The isolation and exclusiveness of a gang or clique brings its antisocial spirit into relief. But this same spirit is found wherever one group has interests "of its own" which shut it out from full interaction with other groups, so that its prevailing purpose is the protection of what it has got, instead of reorganization and progress through wider relationships. It marks nations in their isolation from one another; families which seclude their domestic concerns as if they had no connection with a larger life; schools when separated from the interest of home and community; the divisions of rich and poor; learned and unlearned. The essential point is that isolation makes for rigidity and formal institutionalizing of life, for static and selfish ideals within the group. That savage tribes regard aliens and enemies as synonymous is not accidental. It springs from the fact that they have identified their experience with rigid adherence to their past customs. On such a basis it is wholly logical to fear intercourse with others, for such contact might dissolve custom. It would certainly occasion reconstruction. It is a commonplace that an alert and expanding mental life depends upon an enlarging range of contact with the physical environment. But the principle applies even more significantly to the field where we are apt to ignore it—the sphere of social contacts.

Every expansive era in the history of mankind has coincided with the operation of factors which have tended to eliminate distance between peoples and classes previously hemmed off from one another. Even the alleged benefits of war, so far as more than alleged, spring from the fact that conflict of peoples at least enforces intercourse between them and thus accidentally enables them to learn from one another, and thereby to expand their horizons. Travel, economic and commercial tendencies, have at present gone far to break down external barriers; to bring peoples and classes into closer and more perceptible connection with one another. It remains for the most part to secure the intellectual and emotional significance of this physical annihilation of space.

2. The Democratic Ideal

The two elements in our criterion point to democracy. The first signifies not only more numerous and more varied points of shared common interest, but greater reliance upon the recognition of mutual interests as a factor in social control. The second means not only freer interaction between social groups (once isolated so far as intention could keep up a separation) but change in social habit—its continuous readjustment through meeting the new situations produced by varied intercourse. And these two traits are precisely what characterize the democratically constituted society.

Upon the educational side, we note first that the realization of a form of social life in which interests are mutually interpenetrating, and where progress, or readjustment, is an important consideration, makes a democratic community more interested than other communities have cause to be in deliberate and systematic education. The devotion of democracy to education is a familiar fact. The superficial explanation is that a government resting upon popular suffrage cannot be successful unless those who elect and who obey their governors are educated. Since a democratic society repudiates the principle of external authority, it must find a substitute in voluntary disposition and interest; these can be created only by education. But there is a deeper explanation. A democracy is more than a form of government; it is primarily a mode of associated living, of conjoint communicated experience. The extension in space of the number of individuals who participate in an interest so that each has to refer his own action to that of others, and to consider the action of others to give point and direction to his own, is equivalent to the breaking down of those barriers of class, race, and national territory which kept men from perceiving the full import of their activity. These more numerous and more varied points of contact denote a greater diversity of stimuli to which an individual has to respond; they consequently put a premium on variation in his action. They secure a liberation of powers which remain suppressed as long as the incitations to action are partial, as they must be in a group which in its exclusiveness shuts out many interests.

The widening of the area of shared concerns, and the liberation of a greater diversity of personal capacities which characterize a democracy, are not of course the product of deliberation and conscious effort. On the contrary, they were caused by the development of modes of manufacture and commerce, travel, migration, and intercommunication which flowed from the command of science over natural energy. But after greater individualization on one hand, and a broader community of interest on the other have come into existence, it is a matter of deliberate effort to sustain and extend them. Obviously a society to which stratification into separate classes would be fatal, must see to it that intellectual opportunities are accessible to all on equable and easy terms. A society marked off into classes need be specially attentive only to the education of its ruling elements. A society which is mobile, which is full of channels for the distribution of a change occurring anywhere, must see to it that its members are educated to personal initiative and adaptability. Otherwise, they will be overwhelmed by the changes in which they are caught and whose significance or connections they do not perceive. The result will be a confusion in which a few will appropriate to themselves the results of the blind and externally directed activities of others.

Part II

●

POLITICS AND EDUCATION

Introduction

Few people would deny that our educational system is in turmoil.[1] There is no longer agreement about how to approach education. As some of the selections below indicate, a single grand vision of educational purposes may no longer be appropriate. The main argument here is that those who would design and interpret a master plan would be products of their own social environments. As such, their approach could not do justice to the rich and varied cultural backgrounds of those who can contribute something to academia.

Until fairly recently, there were some common assumptions in higher education. There was a long established tradition that placed considerable importance on classic Western texts. Students were exposed to the wisdom of Plato, Aristotle, Locke, Mill and other giants of the Western intellectual tradition. However, in the last thirty years or so, the curriculum has begun to change.

We should not be surprised. With the social changes that began in the 1960s, including, among other things, the equal rights movement, the women's movement, and a general distrust of established social institutions, one should expect corresponding changes in education. Given the widespread focus on social and economic inequities between various social groups, and given the enormous scope of social problems such as environmental pollution and the threat of nuclear annihilation, it is no wonder that attention is given in every quarter to the concrete needs of the global community.

How will these important events influence higher education in our society? It is obvious that our curriculum will continue to shift toward political topics. Already a large percentage of courses in colleges and universities are designed to address today's burning issues: AIDS, environmental obligations, global politics, world hunger, the new reproductive technologies, and so on. There is, moreover, considerable incentive for colleges and universities to favor vocational courses at the expense of the humanities. Some even suggest that survival courses may eventually have first priority in our educational system.[2]

It is no wonder that educational institutions are reconsidering the value of classic Western texts. The urgency of this issue is demonstrated by the fact that schools, colleges, and universities do not have the resources to satisfy all interested groups. Even before our current social conflicts, it was a real chore to offer students an adequate sample of Western thought. There were so many different topics and areas of study that difficult choices had to be made. But, now, academicians are faced with the need to integrate their curriculum. There is a wide variety of classic Eastern texts, for example, and, in the future, there may be no presumption that Western texts deserve our primary attention. It is clear that educational institutions cannot simply offer everything on the menu. Even if such diverse interests could somehow be accommodated, it is doubtful that a given group would rest content with a token gesture in their direction.

Against the trend toward multiculturalism and moral relativism, Allan Bloom's *The Closing of the American Mind* emphasizes the continuity of the Western intellectual tradition. His main thesis is that the classics offer perennial lessons that are not diminished by cultural diversity and that offer insights about our own identity as a democratic society. He asks some hard questions about what our educational system is really trying to do. One of his responses is that it favors, correctly, in his estimation, the intellectual elite who possess great natural talents. Bloom believes that, in order to square this intellectual elitism with basic democratic principles, society must be taught the lessons of Plato, Locke, and others. He links relativism to license and argues that although relativists claim to accept the diversity of cultural values, they unwittingly embrace some of the universal rights acknowledged in the classic Western tradition.

Bloom goes on the offensive against what he feels are current trends in our institutions of higher learning. He dismisses the view that classic texts are the expressions of the unconscious class, race, or gender prejudices of their authors. There is, he says, a "common transcultural humanity."

Although the classics can be used for political purposes, he believes that their universal appeal has withstood the test of time.

Not surprisingly, Bloom's book has drawn an onslaught of critical responses, some of which appear to display more rhetoric than argument. Bloom complains that the language of what he calls the "new Left" is riddled with intolerance and "fascism." Sidney Hook grants Bloom that there have been many unreasoned attacks on his book and that the academic freedom of scholars has been limited by events such as the demonstrations on college campuses in the 1960s. Nevertheless, Hook maintains that Bloom's book makes basic conceptual blunders.

Hook argues that Bloom fails to distinguish subjectivism from objective relativism. The main problem with Bloom's book, as Hook sees it, is its assumption that if a claim's truth or falsity is determined in relation to cultural and other facts, that commits one to a subjectivist position. According to Hook, Bloom mistakenly labels every relativist as a subjectivist, despite the fact that a relativist can rightfully acknowledge the relational nature of truth without formulating truth conditions in terms of personal preference or other fanciful considerations.

Hook also rejects some of Bloom's Platonic assumptions. Plato maintained that the form of "the good" grounds all moral judgments and that this metaphysical entity can be recognized through self-reflection and reason. Hook objects that Bloom's book offers no arguments for such grand claims.[3]

Mortimer Adler's *The Paideia Proposal* is reminiscent of the pre-1960s approach to education. Adler not only advocates that pupils, K–12, be governed by the same educational objectives, but also insists that the same basic types of courses be offered to all students. Specialized courses and vocational courses are to be avoided. Adler argues that vocational courses are a wrongheaded attempt to offer a separate education to those incorrectly labelled as "uneducable." He reasons that all children, except for those with "irremediable brain damage," ought to be prepared by the schools for advanced learning. Adler thinks that democratic reform of our educational system is long overdue, but he believes these changes are to be organized around a common set of educational objectives. One of the main educational objectives is the preparation of children and young adults for responsible citizenship. Among others things, Adler feels that this requires students to be well versed in the Western classics. Works such as those of the Founding Fathers, which identify basic democratic principles, are said to be of particular importance here. The problem, as Adler sees it, is that our schools are not persistent when it comes to providing the fundamentals of education. He maintains that "the lack of coaching and drilling by itself accounts for the present deficiencies of many high school graduates in reading, writing, computing, and in following directions."[4]

The selections by Paulo Freire and Michael Apple can be viewed as responses to Adler's educational proposals. Both thinkers would object that Adler's approach is one-dimensional. Adler wants the schools to drill students on materials that ostensibly further common educational objectives. But, according to Freire and Apple, this is to ignore what the student has to offer the teacher and the rest of society. Freire and Apple believe that genuine education is a dynamic, interactive process and not, to use Nobuo Shimahara's phrase, a "unilateral monologue." Adler, in fact, appreciates this concern. Among other things, he proposes that some courses, at both the basic and college levels, be conducted through the Socratic method of dialogue, rather than through formal lecturing. According to this approach, teachers and students read a classic text carefully and engage in a question-and-answer session with each other.[5] Thus Adler believes that students are much more than mere passive receptors of information. Given Adler's position on the importance of the Socratic method in a respectable educational system, the differences between his approach to education and the educational proposals of Freire and Apple are not as deep as one might think—even though the proposals of Freire and Apple seem to involve an even more active role for the student.

Freire's main thesis is that even those who are illiterate and oppressed can become active participants in the quest for knowledge of self and environment. He would say that if education is to be successful, conservatives such as Adler and Bloom have to recognize that even the illiterate can offer something unique to the classroom.

Born into poverty in Recife, Brazil, Freire spent years teaching the impoverished and illiterate. His was one of the early voices for the inseparability of education and socieconomic conditions. Of course, Freire owes much of his approach to the writings of Marx and Dewey. Like Dewey, he adopts a problems approach to education. Education begins with the need to change something about ourselves and our environment. Students are products of their society, but they also help to shape society. Freire gives this Deweyan view of the world a contemporary political emphasis.

Apple attempts to debunk the view shared by Adler, Bloom, and other traditionalists that the school curriculum constitutes neutral or transcultural knowledge. Apple's point is that the values, ideals, and language of textbooks have been shaped by conservative economic and political forces, thereby slighting the experiences and contributions of less powerful social classes. Apple's debt to Marx is obvious. He wants to make us aware that for less powerful social classes schooling is a form of social control, an organized threat to their values and interests.

Apple's paper attempts to refute "democratic" reforms such as Adler's, which actually call for the centralization of authority over teaching and curriculum. Apple warns that although such plans are often cleverly disguised as democratic reforms, they exclude conceptions of the world that are central to other classes, races, and genders. Thus, what Adler welcomes, Apple dreads.

The next set of papers provides a detailed analysis of claims about neutrality in higher education. Like Marx, Dewey, Freire, and Apple, Nobuo Shimahara argues that the purpose of education should not be to preserve the perpetuating order of society. Shimahara's contribution is to point out that such a conservative policy of education is self-defeating, as educational institutions inevitably are shaped by the new experiences of students, faculty, and administrators. Universities do not operate in a vacuum. Shimahara wants us to acknowledge that, for example, the financial policies of an administration will influence what is being done in the classroom. If Shimahara and others of this Marxist-Deweyan bent are saying anything, it is that social theories are closely related to, and dependent upon, concrete social practices.

Against the view that a neutral university is not possible, Robert Simon argues that we must distinguish different types of neutrality; one type refers to the rules of critical inquiry (e.g. the rules of logic, the consideration of arguments, etc.), the other to total value freedom. Simon's point is that if a "neutral" university is one that does not commit itself to any values whatsoever, the claim that neutrality is impossible is all too obviously true. Educational institutions cannot function without some set of values. A more viable account, according to Simon, is that a neutral university is expected to commit itself to a certain set of values that requires procedures of evidence and argument. He says that the task of the university is to run partisan political preferences through the instruments of critical inquiry. A meaningful type of neutrality is thus said to be preserved by educational institutions.

Simon qualifies his thesis, however. We are told that sometimes it is permissible for a university to move beyond the forum of theoretical debate. He argues that sometimes the value of critical neutrality is overridden by other social values such as freedom. Here, he cites divestment from South Africa as an example.

Henry Aiken would say that Simon's concessions about divestment and other cases are indicative of the main problem with such an approach. Aiken would emphasize the close relation between a university's scholarly investigation of social duties and the actual social duties of a university that are reflected in that investigation. Aiken begins from the Aristotelian assumption that people are political beings with a natural tendency to improve society. According to Aiken, if the basic mission of the university is to promote the full intellectual, moral, and human development of all its members, then the university should not sever itself from social and political practices. Whereas Shimahara offers sociological grounds for the unity of educational theory and social practice, Aiken presents a moral case for it.[6]

NOTES

1. National Commission on Excellence in Education, *A Nation at Risk: The Imperative for Educational Reform* (Washington, D.C.: U.S. Department of Education, 1983).

2. James Herndon, *How to Survive in Your Native Land* (New York: Bantam Books, 1971).

3. In "Western Civ and Me: An Address at Harvard University," *Giants and Dwarfs* (New York: Simon & Schuster), Bloom claims that he did not defend the existence of "absolutes" in *The Closing of the American Mind.*

4. Mortimer Adler, *The Paideia Proposal* (New York: Macmillan, 1982), pp. 27–28.

5. Ibid., pp. 28–32. See also Mortimer J. Adler, "The Great Books, the Great Ideas, and a Lifetime of Learning," *Mortimer J. Adler Archives* [online], radicalacademy.com/adlerlowell/ec.htm.

6. I would like to acknowledge Howard Ozmon and Samuel Craver's book, *Philosophical Foundations of Education,* 4th ed. (New York: Macmillan, 1990). Their very fine book offered me my first glimpse of what would later come to be some of the selections for this section.

6

FROM *THE CLOSING* OF THE AMERICAN MIND

Allan Bloom

FROM SOCRATES'S *APOLOGY* TO HEIDEGGER'S *REKTORATSREDE*

I have included among the Enlightenment philosophers men like Machiavelli, Bacon, Montaigne, Hobbes, Descartes, Spinoza and Locke, along with the eighteenth-century thinkers like Montesquieu, Diderot and Voltaire, whose teachings are usually held to constitute the Enlightenment, because these latter were quite explicit about their debt to the originators of what the Enlightenment was in large measure only popularizing. The men of the Enlightenment proper were the first whose teachings were addressed not only, or primarily, to other philosophers or potential philosophers of the same rank, and who were concerned not only with those who understand but also with changing the opinions of mankind at large. Enlightenment was the first philosophically inspired "movement," a theoretical school that is a political force at the same time. The very word Enlightenment conveys this mixture of elements, as does Marxism, whereas Platonism and Epicureanism refer strictly to theories—which may have had this or that effect but whose essence is only theoretical. Although Plato and Aristotle had political philosophies, there is no regime to which one can point as a Platonic or an Aristotelian regime, in the sense that either thinker had founded the movement or party that actually established the regime. But Enlightenment is certainly responsible for liberal democracy, as is Marxism for communism. Intellectual historians have frequently been too impressed by these recent events in philosophy and politics to recognize how recent they are, that they constitute a new phenomenon in both domains, and that what is most profound and interesting about Enlightenment is its radical and self-conscious break with the philosophical tradition in the mode and degree of its political activity.

The Enlightenment thinkers understood themselves to be making a most daring innovation: according to Machiavelli, modern philosophy was to be politically effective, while Plato and Aristotle, and all the ancients who followed them since Socrates founded political philosophy were politically ineffective. Machiavelli claimed that he taught the effective truth, and he and practically all those who followed him endeavored to be politically effective. Machiavelli follows Callicles in Plato's *Gorgias*, who ridicules Socrates for being unable to defend himself, to avert insults or slaps in the face. The vulnerability of the philosopher would seem to be the starting place for the new reflection and the renewal of philosophy. This may seem trivial to many today, but the entire philosophic tradition, ancient and modern, took the relation of mind to society as the most fruitful beginning point for understanding the human situation. Certainly the first philosophy of which we have a full account begins with the trial and execution of the philosopher. And Machiavelli, the inspirer of the great philosophical systems of modernity, starts from this vulnerability of reason within the political order and makes it his business to correct it.

Some might say it was not concern with the fate of philosophers but the wish, in Bacon's phrase, to ease man's estate that motivated the modern thinkers. This, however, comes down to the same thing–a criticism of the ancient philosophers for their impotence, and a reflection on the relation of knowledge to civil society. The ancients were always praising virtue, but men were not made more virtuous as a result. Everywhere there were rotten regimes, tyrants persecuting peoples, rich exploiting poor, nobles keeping down commoners, men insufficiently protected by laws or arms, etc. Wise men saw clearly what was wrong in all this, but their wisdom did not generate power to do anything about it. The new philosophy claimed to have discovered the means to reform society and to secure the theoretical life. If the two purposes were not identical, they were intended to be complementary.

It must be remembered that this was a dispute within philosophy and that there was an agreement among the parties to it about what philosophy is. The moderns looked to and disagreed with the Greek philosophers and their heirs, the Roman philosophers. But they shared the view that philosophy, and with it what we call science, came to be in Greece and had never, so far as is known, come to be elsewhere. Philosophy is the rational account of the whole, or of nature. Nature is a notion that itself is of Greek origin and requisite to science. The principle of contradiction guided the discourse of all, and the moderns presented reasoned arguments against those of their predecessors with whom they disagreed. The moderns simply took over a large part of ancient astronomy and mathematics. And they, above all, agreed that the philosophic life is the highest life. Their quarrel is not like the differences between Moses and Socrates, or Jesus and Lucretius, where there is no common universe of discourse, but more like the differences between Newton and Einstein. It is a struggle for the possession of rationalism by rationalists. This fact is lost sight of, partly because scholasticism, the use of Aristotle by the Roman Catholic Church, was the phantom of philosophy within the old order that was violently attacked by the modern philosophers, more out of antitheological ire than by dislike of ancient philosophy. Another reason why the essential agreement between ancients and moderns is no longer clear is the modern science of intellectual history, which tends to see all differences of opinion as differences of "worldview," which blurs the distinction between disagreements founded on reason and those founded on faith.

The very term Enlightenment is connected with Plato's most powerful image about the relation between thinker and society, the cave. In the *Republic*, Socrates presents men as prisoners in a dark cave, bound and forced to look at a wall against which are projected images that they take to be the beings and that are for them the only reality. Freedom for man means escaping the bonds, civil society's conventions, leaving the cave and going up to where the sun illuminates the beings and seeing them as they really are. Contemplating them is at once freedom, truth and the greatest pleasure. Socrates's presentation is meant to show that we begin from deceptions, or myths, but that it is possible to aspire to a nonconventional world, to nature, by the use of reason. The false opinions can be corrected, and their inner contradictions impel thoughtful men to seek the truth. Education is the movement from darkness to light. Reason projected on to the beings about which at first we only darkly opine produces enlightenment.

The moderns accepted that reason can comprehend the beings, that there is a light to which science aspires. The entire difference between ancients and moderns concerns the cave, or nonmetaphorically, the relation between knowledge and civil society. Socrates never suggests that, even in the unlikely event that philosophers should be kings and possess absolute wisdom, the nature of the cave could be altered or that a civil society, a people, a *dēmos* could do without false opinions. The philosophers who returned to the cave would recognize that what others take to be reality is only image, but they could not make any but the happy few able to see the beings as they really are. They would guide the city reasonably, but in their absence the city would revert to unreason. Or to put it in another way, the unwise could not recognize the wise. Men like Bacon and Descartes, by contrast, thought that it was possible to make all men reasonable, to change what had always and everywhere been the case. Enlightenment meant to shine the light of being in the cave and forever to dim the images on the wall. Then there would be unity between the people and the philosopher. The whole issue turns on whether the cave is intractable, as Plato thought, or can be changed by a new kind of education, as the greatest philosophic figures of the seventeenth and eighteenth century taught.

As Plato tells us, Socrates was charged with impiety, of not holding the same gods the city held, and he was found guilty. Plato always presents Socrates as the archetypical philosopher. The events of Socrates's life, the problems be faced, represent what the philosopher as such must face. The *Apology* tells us that *the* political problem for the philosopher is the gods. It makes clear that the images on the wall of the cave about which men will not brook contradiction represent the gods. Socrates's reaction to the accusation is not to assert the right of academic freedom to pursue investigations into the things in the heavens and under the earth. He accepts the city's right to demand his belief. His defense, not very convincing, is that he is not a subversive. He asserts the great dignity of philosophy and tries as much as possible to reduce the gap between it and good citizenship. In other words, he temporizes or is insincere. His defense cannot be characterized as "intellectually honest" and is not quite to contemporary taste. He only wants to be left alone as much as possible, but is fully aware that a man who doubts what every good citizen is supposed to know and spends his life sitting around talking about virtue, rather than doing virtuous deeds, comes into conflict with the city. Characteristically, Socrates lives with the essential conflicts and illustrates them, rather than trying to abolish them. In the *Republic* he attempts to unite citizenship with philosophy. The only possible solution is for philosophers to rule, so there would be no opposition between the city's commands and what philosophy requires, or between power and wisdom. But this outline of a solution is ironic and impossible. It only serves to show what one must live with. The regime of philosopher-kings is usually ridiculed and regarded as totalitarian, but it contains much of what we really want. Practically everyone wants reason to rule, and no one thinks a man like Socrates should be ruled by inferiors or have to adjust what he thinks to them. What the *Republic* actually teaches is that none of this is possible and that our situation requires both much compromise and much intransigence, great risks and few hopes. The important thing is not speaking one's own mind, but finding a way to have one's own mind.

Contrary to common opinion, it is Enlightenment that was intent on philosophers' ruling, taking Socrates's ironies seriously. If they did not have the title of king, their political schemes were, all the same, designed to be put into practice. And they were put into practice, not by begging princes to listen to them but by philosophy's generating sufficient power to force princes to give way. The rule of philosophy is recognized in the insistence that regimes be constructed to protect the rights of man. The anger we experience on reading Socrates's censorship of the poets is unselfconscious, if we agree, as we willy-nilly do, that children must be taught the scientific method prior to any claims of the imagination on their belief or conduct. Enlightenment education really does what Socrates only tentatively proposes. Socrates, at least, tries to preserve poetry, whereas Enlightenment is almost indifferent to its fate. The fact that we think there should be poetry classes as well as education in reasoning helps us to miss the point: What happens to poetic imagination when the soul has been subjected to a rigorous discipline that resists poetry's greatest charms? The Enlightenment thinkers were very clear on this point. There is no discontinuity in the tradition about it. They were simply solving the problem to the advantage of reason, as Socrates wished it could be solved but thought it could not. Enlightenment is Socrates respected and free to study what he wants, and thereby it is civil society reconstituted. In the *Apology*, Socrates, who lives in thousandfold poverty because be neither works nor has inherited, proposes with ultimate insolence that he be fed at public expense at city hall. But what is the modern university, with its pay and tenure, other than a free lunch for philosophy and scientists?

Moreover, the Enlightenment's explicit effort to remove the religious passion from politics, resulting in distinctions like that between church and state, is motivated by the wish to prevent the highest principle in political life from being hostile to reason. This is the intention in the *Republic* of Socrates's reform of the stories about the gods told by the poets. Nothing that denies the principle of contradiction is allowed to be authoritative, for that is the reef against which Socrates foundered. But Socrates did not think that church and state could be separated. He would have treated both terms as artificial. The gods are believed to be the founders of every city and are its most important beings. He would not have dared to banish them in defense of himself.

The Enlightenment thinkers took on his case and carried on a war against the continuing threat to science posed by first causes that are irrational or beyond reason. The gradual but never perfect success of that war turns the desire to be reasonable into the right to be reasonable, into academic freedom. In the process, political life was rebuilt in ways that have proved intolerable to many statesmen and thinkers, and have gradually led to the reintroduction of religion and the irrational in new and often terrifying guises. This is what Socrates would have feared.

But here I am only indicating the unity of the tradition, that Enlightenment is an attempt to give political status to what Socrates represents. The academy and the university are the institutions that incorporate the Socratic spirit more or less well. Yet the existence of these institutions underlines at the same time how they differ from Socrates, who founded no institutions and had only friends.

THE STUDENT AND THE UNIVERSITY

What image does a first-rank college or university present today to a teenager leaving home for the first time, off to the adventure of a liberal education? He has four years of freedom to discover himself—a space between the intellectual wasteland he has left behind and the inevitable dreary professional training that awaits him after the baccalaureate. In this short time he must learn that there is a great world beyond the little one he knows, experience the exhilaration of it and digest enough of it to sustain himself in the intellectual deserts he is destined to traverse. He must do this, that is, if he is to have any hope of a higher life. These are the charmed years when he can, if he so chooses, become anything he wishes and when he has the opportunity to survey his alternatives, not merely those current in his time or provided by careers, but those available to him as a human being. The importance of these years for an American cannot be overestimated. They are civilization's only chance to get to him.

In looking at him we are forced to reflect on what he should learn if he is to be called educated; we must speculate on what the human potential to be fulfilled is. In the specialties we can avoid such speculation, and the avoidance of them is one of specialization's charms. But here it is a simple duty. What are we to teach this person? The answer may not be evident, but to attempt to answer the question is already to philosophize and to begin to educate. Such a concern in itself poses the question of the unity of man and the unity of the sciences. It is childishness to say, as some do, that everyone must be allowed to develop freely, that it is authoritarian to impose a point of view on the student. In that case, why have a university? If the response is "to provide an atmosphere for learning," we come back to our original questions at the second remove. Which atmosphere? Choices and reflection on the reasons for those choices are unavoidable. The university has to stand for something. The practical effects of unwillingness to think positively about the contents of a liberal education are, on the one hand, to ensure that all the vulgarities of the world outside the university will flourish within it, and, on the other, to impose a much harsher and more illiberal necessity on the student—the one given by the imperial and imperious demands of the specialized disciplines unfiltered by unifying thought.

The university now offers no distinctive visage to the young peon. He finds a democracy of the disciplines—which are there either because they are autochthonous or because they wandered in recently to perform some job that was demanded of the university. This democracy is really an anarchy, because there are no recognized rules for citizenship and no legitimate titles to rule. In short there is no vision, nor is there a set of competing visions, of what an educated human being is. The question has disappeared, for to pose it would be a threat to the peace. There is no organization of the sciences, no tree of knowledge. Out of chaos emerges dispiritedness, because it is impossible to make a reasonable choice. Better to give up on liberal education and get on with a specialty in which there is at least a prescribed curriculum and a prospective career. On the way the student can pick up in elective courses a little of whatever is thought to make one cultured. The student gets no intimation that great mysteries might be revealed to him, that new and higher motives of action might be discovered within him, that a different and more human way of life can be harmoniously constructed by what he is going to learn.

Simply, the university is not distinctive. Equality for us seems to culminate in the unwillingness and incapacity to make claims of superiority, particularly in the domains in which such claims have always been made—art, religion and philosophy. When Weber found that he could not choose between certain high opposites—reason versus revelation, Buddha versus Jesus—he did not conclude that all things are equally good, that the distinction between high and low disappears. As a matter of fact he intended to revitalize the consideration of these great alternatives in showing the gravity and danger involved in choosing among them; they were to be heightened in contrast to the trivial considerations of modern life that threatened to overgrow and render indistinguishable the profound problems the confrontation with which makes the bow of the soul taut. The serious intellectual life was for him the battleground of the great decisions, all of which are spiritual or "value" choices. One can no longer present this or that particular view of the educated or civilized man as authoritative; therefore one must say that education consists in knowing, really knowing, the small number of such views in their integrity. This distinction between profound and superficial—which takes the place of good and bad, true and false—provided a focus for serious study, but it hardly held out against the naturally relaxed democratic tendency to say, "Oh, what's the use?" The first university disruptions at Berkeley were explicitly directed against the multiversity smorgasbord and, I must confess, momentarily and partially engaged my sympathies. It may have even been the case that there was some small element of longing for an education in the motivation of those students. But nothing was done to guide or inform their energy, and the result was merely to add multilife-styles to multidisciplines, the diversity of perversity to the diversity of specialization. What we see so often happening in general happened here too; the insistent demand for greater community ended in greater isolation. Old agreements, old habits, old traditions were not so easily replaced.

Thus, when a student arrives at the university, he finds a bewildering variety of departments and a bewildering variety of courses. And there is no official guidance, no university-wide agreement, about what he *should* study. Nor does he usually find readily available examples, either among students or professors, of a unified use of the university's resources. It is easiest simply to make a career choice and go about getting prepared for that career. The programs designed for those having made such a choice render their students immune to charms that might lead them out of the conventionally respectable. The sirens sing *sotto voce* these days, and the young already have enough wax in their ears to pass them by without danger. These specialties can provide enough courses to take up most of their time for four years in preparation for the inevitable graduate study. With the few remaining courses they can do what they please, taking a bit of this and a bit of that. No public career these days—not doctor nor lawyer nor politician nor journalist nor businessman nor entertainer—has much to do with humane learning. An education, other than purely professional or technical, can even seem to be an impediment. That is why a countervailing atmosphere in the university would be necessary for the students to gain a taste for intellectual pleasures and learn that they are viable.

The real problem is those students who come hoping to find out what career they want to have, or are simply looking for an adventure with themselves. There are plenty of things for them to do—courses and disciplines enough to spend many a lifetime on. Each department or great division of the university makes a pitch for itself, and each offers a course of study that will make the student an initiate. But how to choose among them? How do they relate to one another? The fact is they do not address one another. They are competing and contradictory, without being aware of it. The problem of the whole is urgently indicated by the very existence of the specialties, but it is never systematically posed. The net effect of the student's encounter with the college catalogue is bewilderment and very often demoralization. It is just a matter of chance whether he finds one or two professors who can give him an insight into one of the great visions of education that have been the distinguishing part of every civilized nation. Most professors are specialists, concerned only with their own fields, interested in the advancement of those fields in their own terms, or in their own personal advancement in a world where all the rewards are on the side of professional distinction. They have been entirely emancipated from the old structure of the university, which at least helped to indicate that they are incomplete, only parts of an unexamined and undiscovered whole. So the student must navigate among a collection of carnival barkers, each trying to lure him into a particular sideshow. This undecided student is an embarrassment to most universities, because he seems to be saying, "I am a whole human being. Help me to form myself in my wholeness and let me develop my real potential," and he is the one to whom they have nothing to say.

Cornell was, as in so many other things, in advance of its time on this issue. The six-year Ph.D. program, richly supported by the Ford Foundation, was directed specifically to high school students who had already made "a firm career choice" and was intended to rush them through to the start of those careers. A sop was given to desolate humanists in the form of money to fund seminars that these young careerists could take on their way through the College of Arts and Sciences. For the rest, the educators could devote their energies to arranging and packaging the program without having to provide it with any substance. That kept them busy enough to avoid thinking about the nothingness of their endeavor. This has been the preferred mode of not looking the Beast in the Jungle in the face—structure, not content. The Cornell plan for dealing with the problem of liberal education was to suppress the students' longing for liberal education by encouraging their professionalism and their avarice, providing money and all the prestige the university had available to make careerism the centerpiece of the university.

The Cornell plan dared not state the radical truth, a well-kept secret: the colleges do not have enough to teach their students, not enough to justify keeping them four years, probably not even three years. If the focus is careers, there is hardly one specialty, outside the hardest of the hard natural sciences, which requires more than two years of preparatory training prior to graduate studies. The rest is just wasted time, or a period of ripening until the students are old enough for graduate studies. For many graduate careers, even less is really necessary. It is amazing how many undergraduates are poking around for courses to take, without any plan or question to ask, just filling up their college years. In fact, with rare exceptions, the courses are parts of specialties and not designed for general cultivation, or to investigate questions important for human beings as such. The so-called knowledge explosion and increasing specialization have not filled up the college years but emptied them. Those years are impediments; one wants to get beyond them. And in general the persons one finds in the professions need not have gone to college, if one is to judge by their tastes, their fund of learning or their interests. They might as well have spent their college years in the Peace

Corps or the like. These great universities—which can split the atom, find cures for the most terrible diseases, conduct surveys of whole populations and produce massive dictionaries of lost languages—cannot generate a modest program of general education for undergraduate students. This is a parable for our times.

There are attempts to fill the vacuum painlessly with various kinds of fancy packaging of what is already there—study abroad options, individualized majors, etc. Then there are Black Studies and Women's or Gender Studies, along with Learn Another Culture. Peace Studies are on their way to a similar prevalence. All this is designed to show that the university is with it and has something in addition to its traditional specialties. The latest item is computer literacy, the full cheapness of which is evident only to those who think a bit about what literacy might mean. It would make some sense to promote literacy literacy, inasmuch as most high school graduates nowadays have difficulty reading and writing. And some institutions are quietly undertaking this worthwhile task. But they do not trumpet the fact, because this is merely a high school function that our current sad state of educational affairs has thrust upon them, about which they are not inclined to boast.

Now that the distractions of the sixties are over, and undergraduate education has become more important again (because the graduate departments, aside from the professional schools, are in trouble due to the shortage of academic jobs), university officials have had somehow to deal with the undeniable fact that the students who enter are uncivilized, and that the universities have some responsibility for civilizing them. If one were to give a base interpretation of the schools' motives, one could allege that their concern stems from shame and self-interest. It is becoming all too evident that liberal education—which is what the small band of prestigious institutions are supposed to provide, in contrast to the big state schools, which are thought simply to prepare specialists to meet the practical demands of a complex society—has no content, that a certain kind of fraud is being perpetrated. For a time the great moral consciousness alleged to have been fostered in students by the great universities, especially their vocation as gladiators who fight war and racism, seemed to fulfill the demands of the collective university conscience. They were doing something other than offering preliminary training for doctors and lawyers. Concern and compassion were thought to be the indefinable X that pervaded all the parts of the Arts and Sciences campus. But when that evanescent mist dissipated during the seventies, and the faculties found themselves face to face with ill-educated young people with no intellectual tastes—unaware that there even are such things, obsessed with getting on with their careers before having looked at life—and the universities offered no counterpoise, no alternative goals, a reaction set in.

Liberal education—since it has for so long been ill-defined, has none of the crisp clarity or institutionalized prestige of the professions, but nevertheless perseveres and has money and respectability connected with it—has always been a battleground for those who are somewhat eccentric in relation to the specialties. It is in something like the condition of churches as opposed to, say, hospitals. Nobody is quite certain of what the religious institutions are supposed to do anymore, but they do have some kind of role either responding to a real human need or as the vestige of what was once a need, and they invite the exploitation of quacks, adventurers, cranks and fanatics. But they also solicit the warmest and most valiant efforts of persons of peculiar gravity and depth. In liberal education, too, the worst and the best fight it out, fakers versus authentics, sophists versus philosophers, for the favor of public opinion and for control over the study of man in our times. The most conspicuous participants in the struggle are administrators who are formally responsible for presenting some kind of public image of the education their colleges offer, persons with a political agenda or vulgarizers of what the specialties know, and real teachers of the humane disciplines who actually see their relation to the whole and urgently wish to preserve the awareness of it in their students' consciousness.

So, just as in the sixties universities were devoted to removing requirements, in the eighties they are busy with attempts to put them back in, a much more difficult task. The word of the day is "core." It is generally agreed that "we went a bit far in the sixties," and that a little fine-tuning has now become clearly necessary.

There are two typical responses to the problem. The easiest and most administratively satisfying solution is to make use of what is already there in the autonomous departments and simply force the students to cover the fields, i.e., take one or more courses in each of the general divisions of the university: natural science, social science and the humanities. The reigning ideology here is *breadth*, as was *openness* in the age of laxity. The courses are almost always the already existing introductory courses, which are of least interest to the major professors and merely assume the worth and reality of that which is to be studied. It is general education, in the sense in which a jack-of-all-trades is a generalist. He knows a bit of everything and is inferior to the specialist in each area. Students may wish to sample a variety of fields, and it may be good to encourage them to look around and see if there is something that attracts them in one of which they have no experience. But this is not a liberal education and does not satisfy any longing they have for one. It just teaches that there is no high-level generalism, and that what they are doing is preliminary to the real stuff and part of the childhood they are leaving behind. Thus they desire to get it over with and get on with what their professors do seriously. Without recognition of important questions of common concern, there cannot be serious liberal education, and attempts to establish it will be but failed gestures.

It is a more or less precise awareness of the inadequacy of this approach to core curricula that motivates the second approach, which consists of what one might call composite courses. These are constructions developed especially for general-education purposes and usually require collaboration of professors drawn from several departments. These courses have titles like "Man in Nature," "War and Moral Responsibility," "The Arts and Creativity," "Culture and the Individual." Everything, of course, depends upon who plans them and who teaches them. They have the clear advantage of requiring some reflection on the general needs of students and force specialized professors to broaden their perspectives, at least for a moment. The dangers are trendiness, mere popularization and lack of substantive rigor. In general, the natural scientists do not collaborate in such endeavors, and hence these courses tend to be unbalanced. In short, they do not point beyond themselves and do not provide the student with independent means to pursue permanent questions independently, as, for example, the study of Aristotle or Kant as wholes once did. They tend to be bits of this and that. Liberal education should give the student the sense that learning must and can be both synoptic and precise. For this, a very small, detailed problem can be the best way, if it is framed so as to open out on the whole. Unless the course has the specific intention to lead to the permanent questions, to make the student aware of them and give him some competence in the important works that treat of them, it tends to be a pleasant diversion and a dead end—because it has nothing to do with any program of further study he can imagine. If such programs engage the best energies of the best people in the university, they can be beneficial and provide some of the missing intellectual excitement for both professors and students. But they rarely do, and they are too cut off from the top, from what the various faculties see as their real business. Where the power is determines the life of the whole body. And the intellectual problems unresolved at the top cannot be resolved administratively below. The problem is the lack of any unity of the sciences and the loss of the will or the means even to discuss the issue. The illness above is the cause of the illness below, to which all the good-willed efforts of honest liberal educationists can at best be palliatives.

Of course, the only serious solution is the one that is almost universally rejected: the good old Great Books approach, in which a liberal education means reading certain generally recognized classic texts, just reading them, letting them dictate what the questions are and the method of approaching them—not forcing them into categories we make up, not treating them as historical products, but trying to read them as their authors wished them to be read. I am perfectly well aware of, and actually agree with, the objections to the Great Books cult. It is amateurish; it encourages an autodidact's self-assurance without competence; one cannot read all of the Great Books carefully; if one only reads Great Books, one can never know what a great, as opposed to an ordinary, book is; there is no way of determining who is to decide what a Great Book or what the canon is; books are made the ends and not the means; the whole movement has a certain coarse evangelistic tone that is the opposite of good taste; it engenders a spurious intimacy with greatness; and so forth. But one thing is certain: wherever the Great Books make up a central part of the curriculum, the students are excited and satisfied, feel they are doing something that is independent and fulfilling, getting something from the university they cannot get elsewhere. The very fact of this special experience, which leads nowhere beyond itself, provides them with a new alternative and a respect for study itself. The advantage they get is an awareness of the classic—particularly important for our innocents; an acquaintance with what big questions were when there were still big questions; models, at the very least, of how to go about answering them; and, perhaps most important of all, a fund of shared experiences and thoughts on which to ground their friendships with one another. Programs based upon judicious use of great texts provide the royal road to students' hearts. Their gratitude at learning of Achilles or the categorical imperative is boundless. Alexandre Koyré, the late historian of science, told me that his appreciation for America was great when—in the first course he taught at the University of Chicago, in 1940 at the beginning of his exile—a student spoke in his paper of Mr. Aristotle, unaware that be was not a contemporary. Koyré said that only an American could have the naive profundity to take Aristotle as living thought, unthinkable for most scholars. A good program of liberal education feeds the student's love of truth and passion to live a good life. It is the easiest thing in the world to devise courses of study, adapted to the particular conditions of each university, which thrill those who take them. The difficulty is in getting them accepted by the faculty.

None of the three great parts of the contemporary university is enthusiastic about the Great Books approach to education. The natural scientists are benevolent toward other fields and toward liberal education, if it does not steal away their students and does not take too much time from their preparatory studies. But they themselves are interested primarily in the solution of the questions now important in their disciplines and are not particularly concerned with discussions of their foundations, inasmuch as they are so evidently successful. They are indifferent to Newton's conception of time or his disputes with Leibniz about calculus; Aristotle's teleology is an absurdity beneath consideration. Scientific progress, they believe, no longer depends on the kind of comprehensive reflection given to the nature of science by men like Bacon, Descartes, Hume, Kant and Marx. This is merely historical study, and for a long time now, even the greatest scientists have given up thinking about Galileo and Newton. Progress is undoubted. The difficulties about the truth of science raised by positivism, and those about the goodness of science raised by Rousseau and Nietzsche, have not really penetrated to the center of scientific consciousness. Hence, no Great Books, but incremental progress, is the theme for them.

Social scientists are in general hostile, because the classic texts tend to deal with the human things the social sciences deal with, and they are very proud of having freed themselves from the shackles of such earlier thought to become truly scientific. And, unlike the natural scientists, they are insecure enough about their achievement to feel threatened by the works of earlier thinkers, perhaps a bit afraid that students will be seduced and fall back into the bad old ways. Moreover, with the possible exception of Weber and Freud, there are no social science books that can be said to be classic. This may be interpreted favorably to the social sciences by comparing them to the natural sciences, which can be said to be a living organism developing by the addition of little cells, a veritable body of knowledge proving itself to be such by the very fact of this almost unconscious growth, with thousands of parts oblivious to the whole, nevertheless contributing to it. This is in opposition to a work of imagination or of philosophy, where a single creator makes and surveys an artificial whole. But whether one interprets the absence of the classic in the social sciences in ways flattering or unflattering to them, the fact causes social scientists discomfort. I remember the professor who taught the introductory graduate courses in social science methodology, a famous historian, responding scornfully and angrily to a question I naively put to him about Thucydides with "Thucydides was a fool!"

More difficult to explain is the tepid reaction of humanists to Great Books education, inasmuch as these books now belong almost exclusively to what are called the humanities. One would think that high esteem for the classic would reinforce the spiritual power of the humanities, at a time when their temporal power is at its lowest. And it is true that the most active proponents of liberal education and the study of classic texts are indeed usually humanists. But there is division among them. Some humanities disciplines are just crusty specialties that, although they depend on the status of classic books for their existence, are not really interested in them in their natural state—much philology, for example, is concerned with the languages but not what is said in them—and will and can do nothing to support their own infrastructure. Some humanities disciplines are eager to join the real sciences and transcend their roots in the now overcome mythic past. Some humanists make the legitimate complaints about lack of competence in the teaching and learning of Great Books, although their criticism is frequently undermined by the fact that they are only defending recent scholarly interpretation of the classics rather than a vital, authentic understanding. In their reaction there is a strong element of specialist's jealousy and narrowness. Finally, a large part of the story is just the general debilitation of the humanities, which is both symptom and cause of our present condition.

To repeat, the crisis of liberal education is a reflection of a crisis at the peaks of learning, an incoherence and incompatibility among the first principles with which we interpret the world, an intellectual crisis of the greatest magnitude, which constitutes the crisis of our civilization. But perhaps it would be true to say that the crisis consists not so much in this incoherence but in our incapacity to discuss or even recognize it. Liberal education flourished when it prepared the way for the discussion of a unified view of nature and man's place in it, which the best minds debated on the highest level. It decayed when what lay beyond it were only specialties, the premises of which do not lead to any such vision. The highest is the partial intellect; there is no synopsis.

7

THE CLOSING OF THE AMERICAN MIND

An Intellectual Best-Seller Revisited

Sidney Hook

The phenomenal intellectual and commercial success of Allan Bloom's *The Closing of the American Mind* cannot be explained by the philosophical sophistication or political maturity of the American public. What it signifies is the widespread recognition that something is profoundly wrong with the American educational system. There is little agreement on what is wrong and why. But the dissatisfaction is periodically fed by government and foundation reports that are headlined in the press and become the subject of television programs. Despite increases in expenditures, the elementary schools seem unable to raise the level of functional literacy of those who complete their studies. Secondary education, especially in large metropolitan centers, is afflicted by increasing violence, drug addiction, and sexual promiscuity that contribute to a high dropout rate. Not only is there universal access to some form of higher—more accurately, tertiary—education but there is almost universal acceptance (except at Ivy League and a handful of other colleges), grade inflation, and declining standards, so that remedial courses in English and mathematics often make up a considerable portion of the curriculum for large numbers. It is unsafe to assume that those on whom degrees are bestowed possess the elements of what constituted a liberal arts education a generation or two ago. Whatever the specific reasons for the confusions and problems of the school system of the country–and the picture, granted, is certainly varied–every large section of the population has a grievance with some aspect of its operation.

Allan Bloom is convinced that he knows the reason for the failure of American education, particularly higher education–the headwaters of the system–whose products make their influence felt on all subordinate levels of instruction. He attributes the deficiences and troubles of higher education to its failure to grasp the central philosophical truths about human nature, and a consequent failure to devise a proper, ordered curriculum of studies that would transmit the perennial truths, problems, and aspirations of (in a term he often uses) "the human soul."

Any realistic conception of social causation would find rather naive Bloom's assumption that the social evils impinging on the school systems can be profoundly modified by curricular change or reorganization. On the other hand, given that the schools by themselves can neither reconstruct nor revolutionize society, it still remains true that they can gradually have *some* influence in modifying the attitudes and behavior of their students. They can do this not so much by the information they impart as by the values of appropriate conduct they stress, and especially the habits of mind (or mind-lessness) they teach their students. Although Bloom himself sometimes gives the impression that, as a seeker after the truth, he is indifferent to whether he influences or affects anyone or anything, like all educators from Plato to the present he really is trying to improve society or at least prevent it from going to the dogs. He certainly cannot be faulted on this score.

Before assessing the validity of Bloom's analysis of the current educational scene and his proposals for improving it, I must credit him with two indisputable achievements. The first is to have evoked the astonishing spectacle of the intellectual bankruptcy of the so-called political and cultural Left in its response to the positions he has developed in his book. With the exception of two reviews (one by Richard Rorty in the *New Republic*, the other by Richard Gambino in *Freedom at Issue*, both scholars of independent mind), nowhere is the thesis of Bloom's book adequately stated and criticized in the large array of attacks made against it. Most of the attacks on *The Closing of the American Mind* and its author do not even reach the level of argument. Bloom has simply become the target of abuse, accused of subverting democracy. One extreme radical young fogy, David Reiff, taxes Bloom with being, if not responsible for Lt. Colonel North and the Iran-Contra scandals, a philosophical apologist for actions of this sort. And of all places in the *Times Literary Supplement*, which, before its now-evident politicization, was thought to be one of the most disinterested intellectual journals in the English-speaking world.

The second and greater distinction of Bloom's book is his sober, brilliant, and really quite devastating account of the barbarous attack on American universities in the sixties—an attack from whose consequences they are still suffering. Bloom is not the first to draw the parallel between the riotous American students in the sixties and the behavior of the Nazi-infected students in German universities after Hitler came to power. Those who are too young to remember or who have tried to forget will find Bloom's account of what occurred at Cornell—which *mutatis mutandis* is what occurred at Harvard, NYU, Buffalo, San Francisco State, Berkeley, and other institutions—so galvanizing that it will overcome their initial incredulity. They will also find it shocking that he does not hold the riotous students themselves solely or even primarily responsible for the collapse of academic freedom and integrity during this period, but the faculties—their teachers. Students, Bloom writes, "discovered that the pompous teachers who catechized them about academic freedom could, with a little shove, be made into dancing bears." Most of the time only the threat of a shove sufficed, as it did in Nazi Germany, where distinguished intellectuals surprised the world by their servility. In mitigation to some extent of the German professors' behavior is that resistance required heroic conduct, since it invoked immediate dismissal, imprisonment, and worse. The American professors risked only unpopularity.

Much can be forgiven Bloom because of the story he tells, as distinct from his proposed remedy, all the more so because the memory of those violent days and the lessons that can be drawn from them have been largely ignored. It is striking that of the hundreds of millions of dollars expended on research projects by the great liberal educational foundations, not a single study can be found of the stormy period that transformed so many American universities into political battlefields. Someone has suggested that in part this can be explained by the fact that a considerable number of the university administrators of that era subsequently moved into positions of influence in the foundations as officers and board members.

This denial of the truth about the rampaging students of the sixties is reflected even in the most respectable of the critical reviews Bloom has received. Among the most disappointing of the reviews from a philosophical source is Martha Nussbaum's in the *New York Review of Books* (November 5, 1987). Through a pedantic display of classical learning she seeks to discredit Bloom's scholarship—scholarship that is not relevant to his central position. Her account of Bloom's criticism of the riotous behavior of the students of the sixties is a travesty. She pictures Bloom as a resolute defender of the political and social status quo, opposed to the improvement of society presumably because he was critical of the student demands. She refers to his "bitter account of the student movement of the sixties, during which Bloom, lonely opponent of corruption, attempted to stop various changes he deemed perni-

cious, such as changing the curriculum requirements and even of faculty ap-
pointment procedures in response to student demands. To this time of timidity
and lowering of standards he traces today's rootlessness and narcissism."

So this is what the arson, firebombs, and violence was about—curricular
disagreement. Extraordinary. The most charitable interpretation of anyone
capable of writing this way about the demands and behavior of the noting
students of the sixties is that Professor Nussbaum is too young to have any
memories of what occurred; or that for some odd reason she has not read the
literature of and about the sixties; or she is fearful of the hostile judgment of
those alumni of the sixties who, having escaped punishment at the hands of
the cowardly faculties they intimidated, are now teaching in the universities.
I don't know what explains Professor Nussbaum's case. She must have read
Bloom's book with ideological blinders on if she failed to understand that the
chief corruption Bloom was opposing was that of academic freedom. Despite
my fundamental differences with Allan Bloom—and we are separated by an
abyss—and despite the easy and frequent charges of his critics that his views
would lead to the curtailment of academic freedom, I have much more confidence that my academic freedom is safer in an institution governed by him
and his Straussian colleagues than in one governed by his critics.

Bloom indicts American students of the current generation for many
things: a lack of understanding of the perennial ideals of Western civilization, an absence of coherent intellectual outlook on the world, an addiction
to novelties in cultural life, a hypersensitivity to mind-numbing modern
music, the pursuit of sex as a kind of organized sport, a glorification of
freedom and an openness of mind whose consequences in fact close the student's mind to moral, metaphysical, and religious truths which constitute the
true legacy of liberal civilization. It would not be unfair to ask him for
empirical evidence of actual changes over the years in the basic beliefs of
the American student body. Certain student practices, of course, are new
and different—the vogue of new music, drugs, the flaunting of sexual promiscuity. But what seems to outrage Bloom most is what he calls the students'
moral and historical relativism. Sometimes he calls it "cultural relativism,"
sometimes "relativity," sometimes the belief that "truth is relative." His
opening sentence reads: "There is one thing a professor can be absolutely
certain of—almost every student entering the university believes, or says he
believes, that truth is relative." Students, he writes, "are unified only in their
relativism and in their allegiance to equality." Here we focus on his views
about relativity and disregard the fact that he is talking about students in our
elite universities and not the vast numbers still enrolled in religious and
church-related institutions.

It may be hard to believe, but Bloom's whole discussion of the theme
from the first page to the last is vitiated by a fundamental blunder. He con-

fuses subjectivism with moral relativity. He seems to be unaware of the difference between saying (1) all truth is relative, meaning nothing is true or false, good or bad, but that our saying so or feeling so makes it so, and saying (2) all truth is relational, depending upon a complex of things that determine its validity or objectivity. To Bloom the opposite of relational is absolute, not subjective. The subjectivist judgment is arbitrary: it does not call for reasons or evidence to buttress its claims. It does not make a cognitive claim at all. It merely declares a state of feeling. A relational or relativistic judgment, on the other hand, can be challenged to justify itself. Bloom seems not to have heard of the notion of objective relativism. Sometimes what a proposition is relational to is simple: "Milk is a nourishing food," in relation to the digestive systems of organisms of type x. This is perfectly compatible with the truth "Milk is not a nourishing food" in relation to the digestive systems of organisms of type y. No subjectivism here, only more specification. Bloom would recognize the point at once if someone were to ask him: "How far is Chicago?"

Often what makes a statement true or false, good or bad is much more complex, especially moral statements, since for the problem in hand they are related not only to facts but to shared values in that situation. The complexity of our moral statements depends on certain historical conditions and on the plurality of values always involved in a genuine moral problem. "What shall we do?" may be a technical problem merely concerning the best or most effective means to achieve a given end. But when it is a moral question, it always presupposes a conflict of ends that must be resolved here and now. No important policy issue is merely a technical problem of means. Bloom assumes that there exists one underlying good that can be grasped if we understand "the nature of man," and from which all moral judgments of good or bad can be ultimately derived in all situations. He also holds that there are a number of self-evident natural rights sufficient to answer all our questions of right and wrong.

Not only is this position false, but demonstrably false. He does not realize that our moral economy is one in which good often conflicts with good, and right with right. No matter what the particular good or right may be which we seek to absolutize, it may be overridden in the light of the possible consequences of our actions on other goods or rights to which we are committed in the particular historical situation we find ourselves.

Let us examine one of Bloom's own illustrations:

> The students, of course, cannot defend their opinion. It is something with which they have been indoctrinated. The best they can do is point out all the opinion and cultures there are and have been. What right, they ask, do I or anyone else have to say one is better than the others? If I pose the routine questions designed to confute them and make them think, such as, "If

you had been a British administrator in India, would you have let the natives under your governance burn the widow at the funeral of a man who had died," they either remain silent or reply that the British should never have been there in the first place. It is not that they know very much about other nations, or about their own. The purpose of their education is not to make them scholars but to provide them with a moral virtue-openness.

Well, the students Bloom taught at Chicago were very different apparently from those I taught at New York University. My students would have replied, "Of course the administrator should have tried to stamp out the barbarous practice . . . but not if the attempt was to result in communal riots and violence by fanatics resulting in widespread loss of life. The timing is important and it might be better to work through the Hindu religious authorities, not all of whom approved of the practice, even when it was really voluntary. As it is, it took the British almost fifty years before declaring the practice illegal." The students, in justifying their reply, probably would have brought up other historical instances in which an evil was tolerated for a time in order to avoid a greater evil. In passing, I doubt very much whether Bloom's students at Cornell, Toronto, or Chicago would have responded with the "openness" he reports if he had asked them about Hitler's racial laws, or the Holocaust.

The difference between Bloom and the objective relativists whose position he distorts is that, for him, good is good and right is right—and that's the end of it. To the objective relativist, however, morals are related to human weal and woe, to human and social needs, and to the feasible alternatives of action open to mankind at any historic time. But aren't there some practices that are intrinsically bad? Of course there are, as slavery is even when it has divine and religious institutional sanctions. But *intrinsic* does not mean *unrelated*—something utterly in itself. When the only alternative to enslaving prisoners of war was to slaughter them with their families, wouldn't Bloom have preferred the lesser evil of slavery, with its prospect of ultimate liberation? Would we not take it as a sign of some moral progress if a savage tribe were to enslave another defeated tribe, rather than to slaughter them, as was the custom?

Bloom, like his former colleague Harry Jaffa, glorifies Abraham Lincoln as a truly moral statesman inspired by the ideals of the Declaration of Independence. Hence it is surprising that Bloom does not recognize and appreciate Lincoln's pragmatic genius. Lincoln regarded slavery as a moral evil, yet he went to war not to abolish slavery but to save the Union. If the Union had not been preserved, there would have been no amendments to abolish slavery as an institution. It was the Thirteenth Amendment that outlawed slavery as an institution, not the Emancipation Proclamation, which emancipated slaves as a war measure. In the eyes of John Brown and other abolitionist fanatics, Lincoln would have been regarded as "a damned moral relativist," if the phrase had been in vogue in Bloom's sense. But Lincoln knew that prudence and a sense of timing were not only political virtues but moral ones. He feared the fanaticism of virtue, the idealisms focused only on one value or program pursued at *any* cost to other values violated by the means employed to achieve the ideal goal.

The facts of history, Bloom insists, have really nothing to do with the moral quality of an action. True, they have not *everything* to do with the moral judgment, because many of the qualities of human experience are transcultural, but sometimes the historic context is highly relevant. Both Bloom and his students, for example, would certainly be appalled if today horse thieves were subject to capital punishment. But had they lived centuries ago in regions where stealing a man's horse threatened his very survival, such punishment would not have been deemed cruel and unusual.

The conception of cultural and ethical relativism in American thought, as Bloom interprets it, leads to the view that "anything goes." The true conception, however, leads instead to a better understanding of the causes and conditions of the values and practices different groups hold, and the likely consequences of alternative policies in dealing with the conflicts that arise from such differences in order to discover the more reasonable and better way of preserving our democratic society. Bloom rejects this approach as "liberalism without natural rights"–rights, that is, enshrined in the Declaration of Independence and the Constitution, ultimately derivable from God and Nature. He makes no attempt to show how they can be derived from these theological and metaphysical notions. And he seems unaccountably indifferent to the obvious fact that the rights to life, liberty, and happiness in the Declaration are not always compatible with each other, and that the rights enumerated in the Constitution are often in direct conflict with each other. The right to due process and a fair trial may be threatened by the exercise of free speech. This makes it incoherent to regard all of them as inalienable, indefeasible, or absolute. The compulsions of an ordered society may make it necessary to override for a limited time any of the enumerated rights, hence none can be regarded as absolute. Only the use of intelligence or reason in making the decision can be deemed absolute.

To hold his view, Bloom is compelled to flagrantly distort history and to interpret the right to freedom of religion as belonging to the realm of knowledge rather than to practice. He must ignore also the fact that the practice is far from absolute, since a religion that practiced human sacrifice, or sacred prostitution, polygamy, or any other currently illegal action would not be tolerated under the constitutional right of freedom of religion. To cover up the glaring gaps in his argument–or rather the absence of argument–he charges that ethical relativism entails the lunatic doctrine that freedom, conceived as the right to do anything one pleases in the name of democracy, is absolute.

He taxes Oliver Wendell Holmes, as he does John Stuart Mill and John Dewey, with preparing the way to the present-day spurious openness he deplores. Holmes, he says, "renounced seeking for a principle to determine which speech is not tolerable in a democratic society and invoked instead an imprecise and practically meaningless standard, clear and present danger, which to all intents and purposes makes the preservation of public order the only common good."

The clear and present danger standard is imprecise because no one can foresee all the circumstances in which the consequences of speech, and even its modes, become problematic in a democracy. What is modifiably wrong with it is that some of Holmes's successors have made the declaration of what constitutes a clear and present danger—which is a *matter of fact* to be determined by a jury or Congress under certain safeguards—into a matter of law, as Judge Medina did. But Bloom's inference that to all intents and purposes the doctrine makes the preservation of public order under all circumstances an absolute desideratum is an arrant non sequitur. When it is properly invoked, it is best construed as an effort to preserve some of the other rights enumerated in the Constitution. The trouble with Holmes is that he was too optimistic and progressive, according to Bloom, and held that truth unaided by government "always triumphs in the market place of ideas. This optimism had not been shared by the Founders, who insisted that the principles of democratic government must be returned to and consulted, even though the consequences might be harsh for certain points of view—some merely tolerated and not respected, others forbidden outright. To their way of thinking, there should be no tolerance for the intolerant."

This is a strange reading both of Holmes and the Founding Fathers. What Bloom overlooks is that the Founders were intolerant only of the actively intolerant, otherwise they would not have tolerated Platonists, Catholics, fundamentalists of Protestant sects, Orthodox Jews, or philosophers like Bloom, whose theology (or constitutional theory in the case of Bloom) tolerated no heresy. Bloom is simply adapting to his own basic political theory the Augustinian dictum that error about first principles in theology has no rights. This is incompatible with the Jeffersonian legacy of the Founding Fathers developed by Holmes, Frankfurter, and Learned Hand. With respect to the most important issue that gave rise to the formulation of "the clear and present danger" doctrine, namely, the constitutional rights of members of the Communist party who are intolerant in both theory and practice, they held in effect that in a democratic polity communism may be tolerated as a heresy, but not as an active conspiracy. Communists (Leninists) are the true founders of twentieth-century totalitarian intolerance. In a democratic polity they can be tolerated as a heresy, but not as an *active* conspiracy.

Among the difficulties of Bloom's book is a certain lack of clarity in the use of his basic terms, chief among them "soul," "nature," and "reason." Is "soul," as Bloom uses it, a metaphor for the activity of an acculturated organism, or is he using it, in the Platonic and theological sense, as a substantial entity? When he speaks of "nature," is he speaking of the natural world, and of the human history or culture it supports, or of nature in some metaphysical sense, something over and above the quality and behavior patterns of things in their spatial and temporal dimensions? And when he speaks of "reason," is he speaking of a faculty or the capacity of intelligence? (In ordinary discourse when we say a person is intelligent, we mean, as a rule, that he or she is capable of giving adequate reasons or *grounds* for his or her judgments.)

The difficulty with Bloom's position is that, like Leo Strauss, he has not emancipated himself from the Greek notion that the cosmos is also an ethos, and that what is good and bad, right and wrong for man is essentially related to the cosmic order rather than to the reflective choices of men and women confronted by problems of what to do. Bloom speaks of "the rational quest for the good life according to nature." He tells us that "nature should be the standard by which we judge our own lives and the lives of people," but he does not tell us where we must go to find it. He certainly does not mean nature "red in tooth and claw" as a standard. Nor can the metaphysical or theological order be of any more help. We may hold that all men are biological brothers or brothers under the fatherhood of God. But this conviction does not clarify in the slightest why we believe it is wrong to act like Cain toward his brother Abel but right to act like Jonathan to David, who was not his brother. Nor does it follow from the theological doctrine that all men are equal in the sight of the Lord, that they are or should be equal in the sight of the Law, something well known both to the biblical Jews who petitioned the prophet Samuel to "appoint Thou a King over us," and to Charles I and the defenders of the divine right of kings.

Implicit in Bloom's analysis, and more explicit in the writings of his mentors, is his denial of the autonomy of the moral experiences. Without reference to the existence of God or to some metaphysical "order of the whole of things," we cannot, according to him, intelligibly determine what is right or wrong or rationally defend a belief in human rights conceived in Jeffersonian fashion as reasonable rights, not literally as natural rights. Bloom offers not a single plausible argument to defend his position but, to reassert it, falls back on pages upon pages about Nietzsche and relativity. He is strikingly and strangely sympathetic to Nietzsche under the twofold delusion that Nietzsche's declaration that "God is dead" left man not only bereft or in anguish but in terror without any compass to direct his life; and that the development of reason itself must lead to the rejection of reason.

All this is absurd. Hume long ago showed that there is no such thing as pure reason, that it always acts in the context of interest and passion. Thereafter a whole brigade of thinkers, including both Dewey and Freud (one of the few things they have in common) showed that the cultivation of reason or intelligence, by establishing new behavior or habit patterns, can modify and reorder the interests and passions to avoid self- and socially destructive consequences. Utopian fools believe that this can be done easily. It is just as foolish to believe that it is altogether impossible, that nothing can be done by intelligent nurture and education. Those who talk of "the bankruptcy of reason" or of science in virtue of the consequences of its development—which generates, of course, new problems and challenges—exhibit failure not only of nerve but of intelligence.

Let us finally return to the issue dividing Bloom from the pack of frenzied detractors of his book (among the latter, I note, are some of his ideological kinsmen, doubtless envious of his success)—that is, the issue of what the curriculum of a liberal arts college should be today. Bloom's approach rests upon the grasp and application of certain metaphysical truths about the nature of man and society. More comprehensive in its claim, and yet more detailed in its application, was the similar approach to higher education taken before him by Mortimer Adler and Robert Hutchins with an occasional assist from Alexander Meikeljohn as a justification of the curriculum of St. John's College. No protagonist of this approach has ever replied to my critical detailed evaluation of its program, an evaluation endorsed with respect to its scientific aspects by Richard Courant, Albert Einstein, and Bertrand Russell, and in whole by John Dewey. The book containing this critique, entitled *Education for Modern Man* (1946), presented an alternative required a program for the first two years of a liberal arts and science college education for all students before vocational specialization. It should also be noted that in the best critical review of Bloom's book so far published, that by Richard Rorty (which is really more critical of Strauss than of Bloom), Rorty, too, on empirical not metaphysical grounds, advocates a prescribed curriculum for "the first two years" of college life. Such a curriculum allows some adaptation to local conditions, but it includes the best features of the St. John's College curriculum. In range and depth, it covers much more ground than the recently emasculated course in Western Culture at Stanford University. The proposals deriving from this empirical approach, following Dewey's lead, are oriented to three reference points: first, the nature and needs of the students; second, the nature and needs of the society of which students are a part; and third, the subject matters, studies of which most effectively enable students to develop themselves as persons and live with mutual benefit among other persons in their society. I predict that Bloom will not be unhappy with what he finds in college curricula devised along these lines without benefit of any controlling metaphysics or theology.

Although written from an explicitly Deweyan standpoint, some of Rorty's formulations, however, may be misconstrued. He is quite right in saying that *with respect to the arena of public life,* "for Deweyans, the theoretical questions, 'Did Socrates answer Thrasymachus?' and 'Can we answer Hitler?' get replaced by practical questions like 'How can we arrange things so that people like Thrasymachus and Hitler will not come to power?' " But this should not be extended to Dewey's conception of the range of curricular questions open to consideration in the universities. "Did Socrates answer Thrasymachus?" is a perfectly legitimate, indeed, inescapable, question to any intelligent reader of Plato's *Republic,* and the answer seems to me obviously no. There are better answers to Thrasymachus. To the question "Can we answer Hitler?" the answer is "Easily, even if he is not likely to accept the answer." As for the practical questions on how to prevent people like Thrasymachus and Hitler from coming to power, universities may *discuss* all the proposals but *officially advocate* none. It is not likely in their present politicized state that their faculties are likely to have better ideas than the trade unions, churches, political parties, or any randomly selected group of literate citizens.

The specific details of any college curriculum are, of course, never fixed. They are affected by contingencies of national crises as well as by slow changes in the encompassing society of which the educational system is always a part. But it is possible to develop on empirical grounds, regardless of differences on first or last things, broad outlines for certain required areas of study appropriate for the liberal education of men and women in our time.

I attempted to do this in the midsixties when the tide of student activism swept away in most colleges the structure of required courses. It was in answer to the challenges of a fiery young rebel who concluded her tirade against the "class-angled and biased" required curriculum of the college with the following:

> Who are you, or anyone else, to tell me what my educational needs are? I, and I alone, am the best judge of what I want and what I need. What goes for me, goes for everybody. That's democracy in education.

This was a perfectly fair question, although some of my colleagues resented the tone and manner in which it was asked. I still regard my reply to her as valid and sufficient to make it possible to justify a course of study which Allan Bloom can approve and which, if he doesn't, can, I believe, withstand any criticism he can make of it.

Here is an abbreviated account of my answer to what students, men and women, need to know, whether they know they need it or not.

1. Every student has an objective need to be able to communicate clearly and effectively with his fellows, to grasp with comprehension

and accuracy the meaning of different types of discourse, and to express himself in a literate way.

2. Every student needs to have at least some rudimentary knowledge about his or her own body and mind, about the world of nature and its determining forces, about evolution and genetics, and allied matters that are central to a rational belief about the place of man in the universe. If they are to have any understanding of these things, they must possess more than the capacity to remember and parrot isolated facts. They must have some grasp of the principles that explain what they observe, some conception of the nature of scientific method. After all, the modern world is what it is in virtue of the influence of science and technology on nature and society. They cannot feel at home in the modern world ignorant of science.

3. Every student has a need to become intelligently aware of how his or her society functions, of the great historical, economic, and social forces shaping its future, of the alternatives of development still open to us, of the problems, predicaments, and programs they and their fellow citizens must face. Whether they want to revolutionize the world or save it from revolution, they must acquire a historical perspective, without which old evils may reappear under new faces and labels. Those who act as if they were born yesterday are the great simplifiers, who mistake their own audacity for objective readiness and often destroy the lives of others in the wreckage of their hopes.

4. Every student needs to be informed, not only of significant facts and theories about nature, society, and the human psyche, but also of the conflict of values and ideals in our time, of the great maps of life, the paths to salvation or damnation, under which human beings are enrolled. He or she must learn how to uncover the inescapable presence of values in every policy, how to relate them to their causes and consequences and costs in other values, and the difference between arbitrary and reasonable value judgments.

5. Every student needs to acquire some methodological sophistication that should sharpen his or her sense for evidence, relevance, and canons of validity. He or she should, at least in popular discourse and debate, be able to distinguish between disguised definitions and genuine empirical statements, between resolutions and generalizations, to nail the obvious statistical lie, and acquire an immunity to the rhetorical claptrap. . . .

6. Finally, every student has a need to be inducted into the cultural legacies of his civilization, its art, literature, and music. His sensibilities should be developed and disciplined, because they provide not only an unfailing occasion of delight and enjoyment in the present but also a source of enrichment of experience in the future.

A few months ago I had an interesting conversation with a bright young man who was on the dean's list at a prestigious eastern university. He had read my autobiography and complained with some justification that it didn't tell him enough about my personal life. "Aside from your political interests," he asked, "as students what were you and your friends really concerned with?" I thought back to the midtwenties and the students of my day, almost all of us came from lower-middle-class or working-class homes. "What made life exciting for us," I said, "were books, music—Haydn, Mozart, Beethoven—and love. What about your classmates?"

He hesitated for a moment and replied, "Well, I'm not speaking for myself, but I can safely say that the general run of my classmates are interested in sex, drugs, and rock 'n' roll. They say, after all, we live only once."

I heard myself reply, "You don't know what you're missing! Yes, you live only once, but these days you are likely to live an awfully long time, and you can't sustain yourself for long with sex, drugs, and rock 'n' roll. It will first degrade you, and then kill you. 'Today you live and tomorrow you die,' the wilder kids of my own generation used to say. If that were true, something could be said for it. But it is more often true that today you live and tomorrow you suffer, and for many long days after, too."

I relate this exchange not to show my readiness to deliver a homily, but to indicate that I felt the students he was describing were missing something, that they were radically mistaken—and not unregenerate or degenerate—that somehow or other an obvious truth had eluded them. I believe I felt at that moment something of what Allan Bloom must have felt as he wrote *The Closing of the American Mind*: a profound sadness at the prospect of thousands of young men and women missing out on a good thing and accepting in its place something altogether inferior.

Although I reject Allan Bloom's analysis of what is wrong with higher education in our day, and therefore I reject as well his remedies, I nonetheless wish to pay tribute to his good will and intellectual effort, which has succeeded in arousing the country to the necessity, at long last, of a serious debate on what a serious education for modern men and women should be. His noble failure will do more to enrich and uphold the quality of higher education in the United States than the recent vaunted reforms of curricular offerings that in the name of an unlimited, and therefore educationally meaningless, diversity seek to politicalize our universities.

8

FROM
THE PAIDEIA PROPOSAL:
AN EDUCATIONAL MANIFESTO

Mortimer J. Adler

To achieve the desired quality of democratic education, a one-track system of public schooling for twelve years must aim directly at three main objectives and make every effort to achieve them to a satisfactory degree.

These three objectives are determined by the vocations or callings common to all children when they grow up as citizens, earning their living and putting their free time to good use.

The first of these objectives has already been mentioned. It relates to that aspect of adult life which we call personal growth or self-improvement–mental, moral, and spiritual. Every child should be able to look forward not only to growing up but also to continued growth in all human dimensions throughout life. All should aspire to make as much of their powers as they can. Basic schooling should prepare them to take advantage of every opportunity for personal development that our society offers.

A second main objective has to do with another side of adult life–the individual's role as an enfranchised citizen of this republic. Citizens are the principal and permanent rulers of our society. Those elected to public office for a term of years are instrumental and transient rulers–in the service of the citizenry and responsible to the electorate.

The reason why universal suffrage in a true democracy calls for universal public schooling is that the former without the latter produces an ignorant electorate and amounts to a travesty of democratic institutions and processes. To avoid this danger, public schooling must be universal in more than its quantitative aspect. It must be universal also in its qualitative aspect. Hence, the second objective of basic schooling—an adequate preparation for discharging the duties and responsibilities of citizenship.

This requires not only the cultivation of the appropriate civic virtues, but also a sufficient understanding of the framework of our government and of its fundamental principles.

The third main objective takes account of the adult's need to earn a living in one or another occupation.

The twelve years of basic schooling must prepare them for this task, *not* by training them for one or another particular job in our industrial economy, but by giving them the basic skills that are common to all work in a society such as ours.

Here then are the three common callings to which all our children are destined: to earn a living in an intelligent and responsible fashion, to function as intelligent and responsible citizens, and to make both of these things serve the purpose of leading intelligent and responsible lives—to enjoy as fully as possible all the goods that make a human life as good as it can be.

To achieve these three goals, basic schooling must have for all a quality that can be best defined, *positively*, by saying that it must be general and liberal, and *negatively*, by saying that it must be nonspecialized and nonvocational.

Describing it as nonvocational may appear to be inconsistent with what has been said about its relation to earning a living. However, the schooling proposed is truly vocational in the sense that it aims to prepare children for the three vocations or callings common to all.

It is truly vocational in a further sense. It will prepare the young for earning a living by enabling them to understand the demands and workings of a technologically advanced society, and to become acquainted with its main occupations. It is nonvocational only in the sense that it does not narrowly train them for one or another particular job.

That kind of specialized or particularized job training at the level of basic schooling is in fact the reverse of something practical and effective in a society that is always changing and progressing. Anyone so trained will have to be retrained when he or she comes to his or her job. The techniques and technology will have moved on since the training in school took place,

Why, then, was such false vocationalism ever introduced into our schools? As the school population rapidly increased in the early decades of this century, educators and teachers turned to something that seemed more appropriate to do with that portion of the school population which they incorrectly and unjustly appraised as being uneducable—only trainable. In doing this, they violated the fundamental democratic maxim of equal educational opportunity.

As compared with narrow, specialized training for particular jobs, general schooling is of the greatest practical value. It is good not only because it is calculated to achieve two of the three main objectives at which basic schooling should aim—preparation for citizenship and for personal development and continued growth. It is also good practically because it will provide preparation for earning a living.

Of all the creatures on earth, human beings are the least specialized in anatomical equipment and in instinctive modes of behavior. They are, in consequence, more flexible than other creatures in their ability to adjust to the widest variety of environments and to rapidly changing external circumstances. They are adjustable to every clime and condition on earth and perpetually adjustable to the shock of change.

That is why general, nonspecialized schooling has the quality that most befits human nature. That is why, in terms of practicality and utility, it is better than any other kind of schooling.

But when we recognize that twelve years of general, nonspecialized schooling for all is the best policy—the most practical preparation for work—we should also realize that that is not its sole justification. It is not only the most expedient kind of schooling, but it is also best for the other reasons stated above: because it prepares our children to be good citizens and to lead good human lives.

To give the same quality of schooling to all requires a program of study that is both liberal and general, and that is, in several, crucial, overarching respects, one and the same for every child. All sidetracks, specialized courses, or elective choices must be eliminated. Allowing them will always lead a certain number of students to voluntarily downgrade their own education.

Elective choices are appropriate only in a curriculum that is intended for different avenues of specialization or different forms of preparation for the professions or technical careers. Electives and specialization are entirely proper at the level of advanced schooling—in our colleges, universities, and technical schools. They are wholly inappropriate at the level of basic schooling.

The course of study to be followed in the twelve years of basic schooling should, therefore, be completely required with only one exception. That exception is the choice of a second language. In addition to competence in the use of English as everyone's primary language, basic schooling should confer a certain degree of facility in the use of a second language. That second language should be open to elective choice.

The diagram below depicts in three columns three distinct modes of teaching and learning, rising in successive gradations of complexity and difficulty from the first to the twelfth year. All three modes are essential to the overall course of study.

These three columns are interconnected, as the diagram indicates. The different modes of learning on the part of the students and the different modes of teaching on the part of the teaching staff correspond to three different ways in which the mind can be improved–(1) by the acquisition of organized knowledge; (2) by the development of intellectual skills; and (3) by the enlargement of understanding, insight, and aesthetic appreciation.

In addition to the three main Columns of Learning, the required course of study also includes a group of auxiliary subjects, of which one is physical education and care of the body. This runs through all twelve years. Of the other two auxiliary subjects, instruction in a variety of manual arts occupies a number of years, but not all twelve; and the third consists of an introduction to the world of work and its range of occupations and careers. It is given in the last two of the twelve years.

	Column One	Column Two	Column Three
Goals	Acquisition of Organized Knowledge	Development of Intellectual Skills —Skills of Learning	Enlarged Understanding of Ideas and Values
	by means of	by means of	by means of
Means	Didactic Instruction Lectures and Responses Textbooks and Other Aids in three areas of subject-matter	Coaching, Exercises, and Supervised Practice in the operations of	Maieutic or Socratic Questioning and Active Participation in the
Areas Operations and Activities	Language, Literature and the Fine Arts	Reading, Writing, Speaking, Listening	Discussion of Books (Not Textbooks) and Other Works of Art and
	Mathematics and Natural Science	Calculating, Problem-Solving Observing, Measuring, Estimating	Involvement in Artistic Activities e.g., Music, Drama, Visual Arts
	History, Geography, and Social Studies	Exercising Critical Judgment	

The three columns do not correspond to separate courses, nor is one kind of teaching and learning necessarily confined to any one class.

9

FROM
PEDAGOGY OF THE OPPRESSED

Paulo Freire

CHAPTER 1

While the problem of humanization has always, from an axiological point of view, been man's central problem, it now takes on the character of an inescapable concern.[1] Concern for humanization leads at once to the recognition of dehumanization, not only as an ontological possibility but as a historical reality. And as man perceives the extent of dehumanization, he asks himself if humanization is a viable possibility. Within history, in concrete, objective contexts, both humanization and dehumanization are possibilities for man as an uncompleted being conscious of his incompletion.

But while both humanization and dehumanization are real alternatives, only the first is man's vocation. This vocation is constantly negated, yet it is affirmed by that very negation. It is thwarted by injustice, exploitation, oppression, and the violence of the oppressors; it is affirmed by the yearning of the oppressed for freedom and justice, and by their struggle to recover their lost humanity.

Dehumanization, which marks not only those whose humanity has been stolen, but also (though in a different way) those who have stolen it, is a *distortion* of the vocation of becoming more fully human. This distortion occurs within history; but it is not a historical vocation. Indeed, to admit of dehumanization as a historical vocation would lead either to cynicism or total despair. The struggle for humanization, for the emancipation of labor, for the overcoming of alienation, for the affirmation of men as persons would be meaningless. This struggle is possible only because dehumanization, although a concrete historical fact, is *not* a given destiny but the result of an unjust order that engenders violence in the oppressors, which in turn dehumanizes the oppressed.

Because it is a distortion of being more fully human, sooner or later being less human leads the oppressed to struggle against those who made them so. In order for this struggle to have meaning, the oppressed must not, in seeking to regain their humanity (which is a way to create it), become in turn oppressors of the oppressors, but rather restorers of the humanity of both.

This, then, is the great humanistic and historical task of the oppressed: to liberate themselves and their oppressors as well. The oppressors, who oppress, exploit, and rape by virtue of their power, cannot find in this power the strength to liberate either the oppressed or themselves. Only power that springs from the weakness of the oppressed will be sufficiently strong to free both. Any attempt to "soften" the power of the oppressor in deference to the weakness of the oppressed almost always manifests itself in the form of false generosity; indeed, the attempt never goes beyond this. In order to have the continued opportunity to express their "generosity," the oppressors must perpetuate injustice as well. An unjust social order is the permanent fount of this "generosity," which is nourished by death, despair, and poverty. That is why the dispensers of false generosity become desperate at the slightest threat to its source.

True generosity consists precisely in fighting to destroy the causes which nourish false charity. False charity constrains the fearful and subdued, the "rejects of life," to extend their trembling hands. True generosity lies in striving so that these hands—whether of individuals or entire peoples—need be extended less and less in supplication, so that more and more they become human bands which work and, working, transform the world.

This lesson and this apprenticeship must come, however, from the oppressed themselves and from those who are truly solidary with them. As individuals or as peoples, by fighting for the restoration of their humanity they will be attempting the restoration of true generosity. Who are better prepared than the oppressed to understand the terrible significance of an oppressive society? Who suffer the effects of oppression more than the oppressed? Who can better understand the necessity of liberation? They will not gain this liberation by chance but through the praxis of their quest for it, through their recognition of the necessity to fight for it. And this fight, because of the purpose given it by the oppressed, will actually constitute an act of love opposing the lovelessness which lies at the heart of the oppressors' violence, lovelessness even when clothed in false generosity.

But almost always, during the initial stage of the struggle, the oppressed, instead of striving for liberation, tend themselves to become oppressors, or "sub-oppressors." The very structure of their thought has been conditioned by the contradictions of the concrete, existential situation by which they were shaped. Their ideal is to be men; but for them, to be men is to be oppressors. This is their model of humanity. This phenomenon derives from the fact that the oppressed, at a certain moment of their existential experience, adopt an attitude of "adhesion" to the oppressor. Under these circumstances they cannot "consider" him sufficiently clearly to objectivize him—to discover him "outside" themselves. This does not necessarily mean that the oppressed are unaware that they are downtrodden. But their perception of themselves as oppressed is impaired by their submersion in the reality of oppression. At this level, their perception of themselves as opposites of the oppress or does not yet signify engagement in a struggle to overcome the contradiction;[2] the one pole aspires not to liberation, but to identification with its opposite pole.

In this situation the oppressed do not see the "new man" as the man to be born from the resolution of this contradiction, as oppression gives way to liberation. For them, the new man is themselves become oppressors. Their vision of the new man is individualistic; because of their identification with the oppressor, they have no consciousness of themselves as persons or as members of an oppressed class. It is not to become free men that they want agrarian reform, but in order to acquire land and thus become landowners— or, more precisely, bosses over other workers. It is a rare peasant who, once "promoted" to overseer, does not become more of a tyrant toward his former comrades than the owner himself. This is because the context of the peasant's situation, that is, oppression, remains unchanged. In this example, the overseer, in order to make sure of his job, must be as tough as the owner—and more so. Thus is illustrated our previous assertion that during the initial stage of their struggle the oppressed find in the oppressor their model of "manhood."

Even revolution, which transforms a concrete situation of oppression by establishing the process of liberation, must confront this phenomenon. Many of the oppressed who directly or indirectly participate in revolution intend—conditioned by the myths of the old order—to make it their private revolution. The shadow of their former oppressor is still cast over them.

The "fear of freedom" which afflicts the oppressed,[3] a fear which may equally well lead them to desire the role of oppressor or bind them to the role of oppressed, should be examined. One of the basic elements of the relationship between oppressor and oppressed is *prescription*. Every prescription represents the imposition of one man's choice upon another, transforming the consciousness of the man prescribed to into one that conforms with the prescriber's consciousness. Thus, the behavior of the oppressed is a prescribed behavior, following as it does the guidelines of the oppressor.

The oppressed, having internalized the image of the oppressor and adopted his guidelines, are fearful of freedom. Freedom would require them to eject this image and replace it with autonomy and responsibility. Freedom is acquired by conquest, not by gift. It must be pursued constantly and responsibly. Freedom is not an ideal located outside of man; nor is it an idea which becomes myth. It is rather the indispensable condition for the quest for human completion.

To surmount the situation of oppression, men must first critically recognize its causes, so that through transforming action they can create a new situation, one which makes possible the pursuit of a fuller humanity. But the struggle to be more fully human has already begun in the authentic struggle to transform the situation. Although the situation of oppression is a dehumanized and dehumanizing totality affecting both the oppressors and those whom they oppress, it is the latter who must, from their stifled humanity, wage for both the struggle for a fuller humanity; the oppressor, who is himself dehumanized because he dehumanizes others, is unable to lead this struggle.

However, the oppressed, who have adapted to the structure of domination in which they are immersed, and have become resigned to it, are inhibited from waging the struggle for freedom so long as they feel incapable of running the risks it requires. Moreover, their struggle for freedom threatens not only the oppressor, but also their own oppressed comrades who are fearful of still greater repression. When they discover within themselves the yearning to be free, they perceive that this yearning can be transformed into reality only when the same yearning is aroused in their comrades. But while dominated by the fear of freedom they refuse to appeal to others, or to listen to the appeals of others, or even to the appeals of their own conscience. They prefer gregariousness to authentic comradeship; they prefer the security of conformity with their state of unfreedom to the creative communion produced by freedom and even the very pursuit of freedom.

The oppressed suffer from the duality which has established itself in their innermost being. They discover that without freedom they cannot exist authentically. Yet, although they desire authentic existence, they fear it. They are at one and the same time themselves and the oppressor whose consciousness they have internalized. The conflict lies in the choice between being wholly themselves or being divided; between ejecting the oppressor within or not ejecting him; between human solidarity or alienation; between following prescriptions or having choices; between being spectators or actors; between acting or having the illusion of acting through the action of the oppressors; between speaking out or being silent, castrated in their power to create and re-create, in their power to transform the world. This is the tragic dilemma of the oppressed which their education must take into account.

This book will present some aspects of what the writer has termed the pedagogy of the oppressed, a pedagogy which must be forged *with*, not *for*, the oppressed (whether individuals or peoples) in the incessant struggle to regain their humanity. This pedagogy makes oppression and its causes objects of reflection by the oppressed, and from that reflection will come their necessary engagement in the struggle for their liberation. And in the struggle this pedagogy will be made and remade.

The central problem is this: How can the oppressed, as divided, unauthentic beings, participate in developing the pedagogy of their liberation? Only as they discover themselves to be "hosts" of the oppressor can they contribute to the midwifery of their liberating pedagogy. As long as they live in the duality in which *to be* is *to be like*, and *to be like* is *to be like the oppressor*, this contribution is impossible. The pedagogy of the oppressed is an instrument for their critical discovery that both they and their oppressors are manifestations of dehumanization.

Liberation is thus a childbirth, and a painful one. The man who emerges is a new man, viable only as the oppressor-oppressed contradiction is superseded by the humanization of all men. Or to put it another way, the solution of this contradiction is born in the labor which brings into the world this new man: no longer oppressor nor longer oppressed, but man in the process of achieving freedom.

This solution cannot be achieved in idealistic terms. In order for the oppressed to be able to wage the struggle for their liberation, they must perceive the reality of oppression not as a closed world from which there is no exit, but as a limiting situation which they can transform. This perception is a necessary but not a sufficient condition for liberation; it must become the motivating force for liberating action. Nor does the discovery by the oppressed that they exist in dialectical relationship to the oppressor, as his antithesis—that without them the oppressor could not exist[4]—in itself constitute liberation. The oppressed can overcome the contradiction in which they are caught only when this perception enlists them in the struggle to free themselves.

The same is true with respect to the individual oppressor as a person. Discovering himself to be an oppressor may cause considerable anguish, but it does not necessarily lead to solidarity with the oppressed. Rationalizing his guilt through paternalistic treatment of the oppressed, all the while holding them fast in a position of dependence, will not do. Solidarity requires that one enter into the situation of those with whom one is solidary; it is a radical posture. If what characterizes the oppressed is their subordination to the consciousness of the master, as Hegel affirms,[5] true solidarity with the oppressed means fighting at their side to transform the objective reality which has made them these "beings for another." The oppressor is solidary with the oppressed only when he stops regarding the oppressed as an abstract category and sees them as persons who have been unjustly dealt with, deprived of their voice, cheated in the sale of their labor—when he stops making pious, sentimental, and individualistic gestures and risks an act of love. True solidarity is found only in the plenitude of this act of love, in its existentiality, in its praxis. To affirm that men are persons and as persons should be free, and yet to do nothing tangible to make this affirmation a reality, is a farce.

Since it is in a concrete situation that the oppressor-oppressed contradiction is established, the resolution of this contradiction must be *objectively* verifiable. Hence, the radical requirement—both for the man who discovers himself to be an oppressor and for the oppressed—that the concrete situation which begets oppression must be transformed.

To present this radical demand for the objective transformation of reality, to combat subjectivist immobility which would divert the recognition of oppression into patient waiting for oppression to disappear by itself, is not to dismiss the role of subjectivity in the struggle to change structures. On the contrary, one cannot conceive of objectivity without subjectivity. Neither can exist without the other, nor can they be dichotomized. The separation of objectivity from subjectivity, the denial of the latter when analyzing reality or acting upon it, is objectivism. On the other hand, the denial of objectivity in analysis or action, resulting in a subjectivism which leads to solipsistic positions, denies action itself by denying objective reality. Neither objectivism nor subjectivism, nor yet psychologism. is propounded here, but rather subjectivity and objectivity in constant dialectical relationship.

To deny the importance of subjectivity in the process of transforming the world and history is naive and simplistic. It is to admit the impossible: a world without men. This objectivistic position is as ingenuous as that of subjectivism, which postulates men without a world. World and men do not exist apart from each other, they exist in constant interaction. Marx does not espouse such a dichotomy, nor does any other critical, realistic thinker. What Marx criticized and scientifically destroyed was not subjectivity, but subjectivism and psychologism. Just as objective social reality exists not by chance, but as the product of human action, so it is not transformed by chance. If men produce social reality (which in the "inversion of the praxis" turns back upon them and conditions them), then transforming that reality is a historical task, a task for men.

CHAPTER 2

A careful analysis of the teacher-student relationship at any level, inside or outside the school, reveals its fundamentally *narrative* character. This relationship involves a narrating Subject (the teacher) and patient, listening objects (the students). The contents, whether values or empirical dimensions of reality, tend in the process of being narrated to become lifeless and petrified. Education is suffering from narration sickness.

The teacher talks about reality as if it were motionless, static, compartmentalized, and predictable. Or else he expounds on a topic completely alien to the existential experience of the students. His task is to "fill" the students with the contents of his narration—contents which are detached from reality, disconnected from the totality that engendered them and could give them significance. Words are emptied of their concreteness and become a hollow, alienated, and alienating verbosity.

The outstanding characteristic of this narrative education, then, is the sonority of words, not their transforming power. "Four times four is sixteen; the capital of Pará is Belém." The student records, memorizes, and repeats these phrases without perceiving what four times four really means, or realizing the true significance of "capital" in the affirmation "the capital of Pará is Belém," that is, what Belém means for Pará and what Pará means for Brazil.

Narration (with the teacher as narrator) leads the students to memorize mechanically the narrated content. Worse yet, it turns them into "containers," into "receptacles" to be "filled" by the teacher. The more completely he fills the receptacles, the better a teacher he is. The more meekly the receptacles permit themselves to be filled, the better students they are.

Education thus becomes an act of depositing, in which the students are the depositories and the teacher is the depositor. Instead of communicating, the teacher issues communiques and makes deposits which the students patiently receive, memorize, and repeat. This is the "banking" concept of education, in which the scope of action allowed to the students extends only as far as receiving, filing, and storing the deposits. They do, it is true, have the opportunity to become collectors or cataloguers of the things they store. But in the last analysis, it is men themselves who are filed away through the lack of creativity, transformation, and knowledge in this (at best) misguided system. For apart from inquiry, apart from the praxis, men cannot be truly human. Knowledge emerges only through invention and reinvention, through the restless, impatient, continuing, hopeful inquiry men pursue in the world, with the world, and with each other.

In the banking concept of education, knowledge is a gift bestowed by those who consider themselves knowledgeable upon those whom they consider to know nothing. Projecting an absolute ignorance onto others, a characteristic of the ideology of oppression, negates education and knowledge as processes of inquiry. The teacher presents himself to his students as their necessary opposite; by considering their ignorance absolute, he justifies his own existence. The students, alienated like the slave in the Hegelian dialectic, accept their ignorance as justifying the teacher's existence—but, unlike the slave, they never discover that they educate the teacher.

The raison d'être of libertarian education, on the other hand, lies in its drive toward reconciliation. Education must begin with the solution of the teacher-student contradiction, by reconciling the poles of the contradiction so that both are simultaneously teachers *and* students.

This solution is not (nor can it be) found in the banking concept. On the contrary, banking education maintains and even stimulates the contradiction through the following attitudes and practices, which mirror oppressive society as a whole:

(a) the teacher teaches and the students are taught;

(b) the teacher knows everything and the students know nothing;

(c) the teacher thinks and the students are thought about;

(d) the teacher talks and the students listen—meekly;

(e) the teacher disciplines and the students are disciplined;

(f) the teacher chooses and enforces his choice, and the students comply;

(g) the teacher acts and the students have the illusion of acting through the action of the teacher;

(h) the teacher chooses the program content, and the students (who were not consulted) adapt to it;

(i) the teacher confuses the authority of knowledge with his own professional authority, which he sets in opposition to the freedom of the students;

(j) the teacher is the Subject of the learning process, while the pupils are mere objects.

It is not surprising that the banking concept of education regards men as adaptable, manageable beings. The more students work at storing the deposits entrusted to them, the less they develop the critical consciousness which would result from their intervention in the world as transformers of that world. The more completely they accept the passive role imposed on them, the more they tend simply to adapt to the world as it is and to the fragmented view of reality deposited in them.

The capability of banking education to minimize or annul the students' creative power and to stimulate their credulity serves the interests of the oppressors, who care neither to have the world revealed nor to see it transformed. The oppressors use their "humanitarianism" to preserve a profitable situation. Thus they react almost instinctively against any experiment in education which stimulates the critical faculties and is not content with a partial view of reality but always seeks out the ties which link one point to another and one problem to another.

Indeed, the interests of the oppressors lie in "changing the consciousness of the oppressed, not the situation which oppresses them";[6] for the more the oppressed can be led to adapt to that situation, the more easily they can be dominated. To achieve this end, the oppressors use the banking concept of education in conjunction with a paternalistic social action apparatus, within which the oppressed receive the euphemistic title of "welfare recipients." They are treated as individual cases, as marginal men who deviate from the general configuration of a "good, organized, and just" society. The oppressed are regarded as the pathology of the healthy society, which must therefore adjust these "incompetent and lazy" folk to its own patterns by changing their mentality. These marginals need to be "integrated," "incorporated" into the healthy society that they have "forsaken."

The truth is, however, that the oppressed are not "marginals," are not men living "outside" society. They have always been "inside"—inside the structure which made them "beings for others." The solution is not to "integrate" them into the structure of oppression, but to transform that structure so that they can become "beings for themselves." Such transformation, of course, would undermine the oppressors' purposes; hence their utilization of the banking concept of education to avoid the threat of student *conscientização.**

The banking approach to adult education, for example, will never propose to students that they critically consider reality. It will deal instead with such vital questions as whether Roger gave green grass to the goat, and insist upon the importance of learning that, on the contrary, *R*oger gave green grass to the *r*abbit. The "humanism" of the banking approach masks the effort to turn men into automatons—the very negation of their ontological vocation to be more fully human.

Those who use the banking approach, knowingly or unknowingly (for there are innumerable well-intentioned bank-clerk teachers who do not realize that they are serving only to dehumanize), fail to perceive that the deposits themselves contain contradictions about reality. But, sooner or later, these contradictions may lead formerly passive students to turn against their domestication and the attempt to domesticate reality. They may discover through existential experience that their present way of life is irreconcilable with their vocation to become fully human. They may perceive through their relations with reality that reality is really a *process*, undergoing constant transformation. If men are searchers and their ontological vocation

---

*The term *conscientização* refers to learning to perceive social, political, and economic contradictions, and to take action against the oppressive elements of reality—translator's note.

is humanization, sooner or later they may perceive the contradiction in which banking education seeks to maintain them, and then engage themselves in the struggle for their liberation.

But the humanist, revolutionary educator cannot wait for this possibility to materialize. From the outset, his efforts must coincide with those of the students to engage in critical thinking and the quest for mutual humanization. His efforts must be imbued with a profound trust in men and their creative power. To achieve this, he must be a partner of the students in his relations with them.

The banking concept does not admit to such partnership—and necessarily so. To resolve the teacher-student contradiction, to exchange the role of depositor, prescriber, domesticator, for the role of student among students would be to undermine the power of oppression and serve the cause of liberation.

Implicit in the banking concept is the assumption of a dichotomy between man and the world: man is merely *in* the world, not *with* the world or with others; man is spectator, not re-creator. In this view, man is not a conscious being (*corpo consciente*); he is rather the possessor of a consciousness: an empty "mind" passively open to the reception of deposits of reality from the world outside. For example, my desk, my books, my coffee cup, all the objects before me—as bits of the world which surrounds me—would be "inside" me, exactly as I am inside my study right now. This view makes no distinction between being accessible to consciousness and entering consciousness. The distinction, however, is essential: the objects which surround me are simply accessible to my consciousness, not located within it. I am aware of them, but they are not inside me.

It follows logically from the banking notion of consciousness that the educator's role is to regulate the way the world "enters into" the students. His task is to organize a process which already occurs spontaneously, to "fill" the students by making deposits of information which he considers to constitute true knowledge.[7] And since men "receive" the world as passive entities, education should make them more passive still, and adapt them to the world. The educated man is the adapted man, because he is better "fit" for the world. Translated into practice, this concept is well suited to the purposes of the oppressors, whose tranquility rests on how well men fit the world the oppressors have created, and how little they question it.

The more completely the majority adapt to the purposes which the dominant minority prescribe for them (thereby depriving them of the right to their own purposes), the more easily the minority can continue to prescribe. The theory and practice of banking education serve this end quite efficiently. Verbalistic lessons, reading requirements,[8] the methods for evaluating "knowledge," the distance between the teacher and the taught, the criteria for promotion: everything in this ready-to-wear approach serves to obviate thinking.

The bank-clerk educator does not realize that there is no true security in his hypertrophied role, that one must seek to live *with* others in solidarity. One cannot impose oneself, nor even merely coexist with one's students. Solidarity requires true communication, and the concept by which such an educator is guided fears and proscribes communication.

Yet only through communication can human life hold meaning. The teacher's thinking is authenticated only by the authenticity of the students' thinking. The teacher cannot think for his students, nor can he impose his thought on them. Authentic thinking, thinking that is concerned about *reality*, does not take place in ivory tower isolation, but only in communication. If it is true that thought has meaning only when generated by action upon the world, the subordination of students to teachers becomes impossible.

Because banking education begins with a false understanding of men as objects, it cannot promote the development of what Fromm calls "biophily," but instead produces its opposite: "necrophily."

> While life is characterized by growth in a structured, functional manner, the necrophilous person loves all that does not grow, all that is mechanical. The necrophilous person is driven by the desire to transform the organic into the inorganic, to approach life mechanically, as if all living persons were things. . . . Memory, rather than experience; having, rather than being, is what counts. The necrophilous person can relate to an object—a flower or a person—only if he possesses it; hence a threat to his possession is a threat to himself; if he loses possession he loses contact with the world. . . . He loves control, and in the act of controlling he kills life.[9]

Oppression—overwhelming control—is necrophilic; it is nourished by love of death, not life. The banking concept of education, which serves the interests of oppression, is also necrophilic. Based on a mechanistic, static, naturalistic, spatialized view of consciousness, it transforms students into receiving objects. It attempts to control thinking and action, leads men to adjust to the world, and inhibits their creative power.

When their efforts to act responsibly are frustrated, when they find themselves unable to use their faculties, men suffer. "This suffering due to impotence is rooted in the very fact that the human equilibrium has been disturbed."[10] But the inability to act which causes men's anguish also causes them to reject their impotence, by attempting

> . . . to restore [their] capacity to act. But can [they], and how? One way is to submit to and identify with a person or group having power. By this symbolic participation in another person's life, [men have] the illusion of

acting, when in reality [they] only submit to and become a part of those who act.[11]

Populist manifestations perhaps best exemplify this type of behavior by the oppressed, who, by identifying with charismatic leaders, come to feel that they themselves are active and effective. The rebellion they express as they emerge in the historical process is motivated by that desire to act effectively. The dominant elites consider the remedy to be more domination and repression, carried out in the name of freedom, order, and social peace (that is, the peace of the elites). Thus they can condemn–logically, from their point of view–"the violence of a strike by workers and [can] call upon the state in the same breath to use violence in putting down the strike."[12]

Education as the exercise of domination stimulates the credulity of students, with the ideological intent (often not perceived by educators) of indoctrinating them to adapt to the world of oppression. This accusation is not made in the naive hope that the dominant elites will thereby simply abandon the practice. Its objective is to call the attention of true humanists to the fact that they cannot use banking educational methods in the pursuit of liberation, for they would only negate that very pursuit. Nor may a revolutionary society inherit these methods from an oppressor society. The revolutionary society which practices banking education is either misguided or mistrusting of men. In either event, it is threatened by the specter of reaction.

Unfortunately, those who espouse the cause of liberation are themselves surrounded and influenced by the climate which generates the banking concept, and often do not perceive its true significance or its dehumanizing power. Paradoxically, then, they utilize this same instrument of alienation in what they consider an effort to liberate. Indeed, some "revolutionaries" brand as "innocents," "dreamers," or even "reactionaries" those who would challenge this educational practice. But one does not liberate men by alienating them. Authentic liberation–the process of humanization–is not another deposit to be made in men. Liberation is a praxis: the action and reflection of men upon their world in order to transform it. Those truly committed to the cause of liberation can accept neither the mechanistic concept of consciousness as an empty vessel to be filled, nor the use of banking methods of domination (propaganda, slogans–deposits) in the name of liberation.

Those truly committed to liberation must reject the banking concept in its entirety, adopting instead a concept of men as conscious beings, and consciousness as consciousness intent upon the world. They must abandon the educational goal of deposit making and replace it with the posing of the problems of men in their relations, with the world. "Problem-posing" education, responding to the essence of consciousness–*intentionality*–rejects communiques and embodies communication. It epitomizes the special characteristic of consciousness: being *conscious of,* not only as intent on objects but as turned in upon itself in a Jasperian "split"—consciousness as consciousness *of* consciousness.

Liberating education consists in acts of cognition, not transferrals of information. It is a learning situation in which the cognizable object (far from being the end of the cognitive act) intermediates the cognitive actors—teacher on the one hand and students on the other. Accordingly, the practice of problem-posing education entails at the outset that the teacher-student contradiction be resolved. Dialogical relations—indispensable to the capacity of cognitive actors to cooperate in perceiving the same cognizable object—are otherwise impossible.

Indeed, problem-posing education, which breaks with the vertical patterns characteristic of banking education, can fulfill its function as the practice of freedom only if it can overcome the above contradiction. Through dialogue, the teacher-of-the-students and the students-of-the-teacher cease to exist and a new term emerges: teacher-student with students-teachers. The teacher is no longer merely the-one-who-teaches, but one who is himself taught in dialogue with the students, who in turn while being taught also teach. They become jointly responsible for a process in which all grow. In this process, arguments based on "authority" are no longer valid; in order to function, authority must be *on the side of* freedom, not *against* it. Here, no one teaches another, nor is anyone self-taught. Men teach each other, mediated by the world, by the cognizable objects which in banking education are "owned" by the teacher.

The banking concept (with its tendency to dichotomize everything) distinguishes two stages in the action of the educator. During the first, he cognizes a cognizable object while he prepares his lessons in his study or his laboratory; during the second, he expounds to his students about that object. The students are not called upon to know, but to memorize the contents narrated by the teacher. Nor do the students practice any act of cognition, since the object toward which that act should be directed is the property of the teacher rather than a medium evoking the critical reflection of both teacher and students. Hence in the name of the "preservation of culture and knowledge" we have a system which achieves neither true knowledge nor true culture.

The problem-posing method does not dichotomize the activity of the teacher-student: he is not "cognitive" at one point and "narrative" at another. He is always "cognitive," whether preparing a project or engaging in dialogue with the students. He does not regard cognizable objects as his private property, but as the object of reflection by himself and the students. In this way, the problemposing educator constantly re-forms his reflections in the reflection of the students. The students—no longer docile listeners—are now critical coinvestigators in dialogue with the teacher. The teacher presents the material to the students for their consideration, and reconsiders his earlier considerations as the students express their own. The role of the problem-posing educator is to create, together with the students, the conditions under which knowledge at the level of the *doxa* is superseded by true knowledge, at the level of the *logos.*

Whereas banking education anesthetizes and inhibits creative power, problem-posing education involves a constant unveiling of reality. The former attempts to maintain the *submersion* of consciousness; the latter strives for the *emergence* of consciousness and *critical intervention* in reality.

Students, as they are increasingly posed with problems relating to themselves in the world and with the world, will feel increasingly challenged and obliged to respond to that challenge. Because they apprehend the challenge as interrelated to other problems within a total context, not as a theoretical question, the resulting comprehension tends to be increasingly critical and thus constantly less alienated. Their response to the challenge evokes new challenges, followed by new understandings; and gradually the students come to regard themselves as committed.

Education as the practice of freedom—as opposed to education as the practice of domination—denies that man is abstract, isolated, independent, and unattached to the world; it also denies that the world exists as a reality apart from men. Authentic reflection considers neither abstract man nor the world without men, but men in their relations with the world. In these relations consciousness and world are simultaneous: consciousness neither precedes the world nor follows it.

> La conscience et le monde sont dormés d'un même coup: extérieur par essence à la conscience, le monde est, par essence relatif à elle.[13]

In one of our culture circles in Chile, the group was discussing the anthropological concept of culture. In the midst of the discussion, a peasant who by banking standards was completely ignorant said: "Now I see that without man there is no world." When the educator responded: "Let's say, for the sake of argument, that all the men on earth were to die, but that the earth itself remained, together with trees, birds, animals, rivers, seas, the stars . . . wouldn't all this be a world?" "Oh no," the peasant replied emphatically. "There would be no one to say: 'This is a world.' "

The peasant wished to express the idea that there would be lacking the consciousness of the world which necessarily implies the world of consciousness. *I* cannot exist without a *not-I.* In turn, the *not-I* depends on that existence. The world which brings consciousness into existence becomes the world of that consciousness. Hence, the previously cited affirmation of Sartre: "La conscience et le monde sont dormés d'un même coup."

As men, simultaneously reflecting on themselves and on the world, increase the scope of their perception, they begin to direct their observations toward previously inconspicuous phenomena:

> In perception properly so-called, as an explicit awareness [*Gewahren*], I am turned towards the object, to the paper, for instance. I apprehend it as being this here and now. The apprehension is a singling out, every object having a background in experience. Around and about the paper lie books, pencils, ink-well, and so forth, and these in a certain sense are also "perceived," perceptually there, in the "field of intuition"; but whilst I was turned towards the paper there was no turning in their direction, nor any apprehending of them, not even in a secondary sense. They appeared and yet were not singled out, were not posited on their own account. Every perception of a thing has such a zone of background intuitions or background awareness, if "intuiting" already includes the state of being turned towards, and this also is a "conscious experience," or more briefly a "consciousness of" all indeed that in point of fact lies in the co-perceived objective background.[14]

That which had existed objectively but had not been perceived in its deeper implications (if indeed it was perceived at all) begins to "stand out," assuming the character of a problem and therefore of challenge. Thus, men begin to single out elements from their "background awarenesses" and to reflect upon them. These elements are now objects of men's consideration, and, as such, objects of their action and cognition.

In problem-posing education, men develop their power to perceive critically *the way they exist* in the world *with which* and *in which* they find themselves; they come to see the world not as a static reality, but as a reality in process, in transformation. Although the dialectical relations of men with the world exist independently of how these relations are perceived (or whether or not they are perceived at all), it is also true that the form of action men adopt is to a large extent a function of how they perceive themselves in the world. Hence, the teacher-student and the students-teachers reflect simultaneously on themselves and the world without dichotomizing this reflection from action, and thus establish an authentic form of thought and action.

Once again, the two educational concepts and practices under analysis come into conflict. Banking education (for obvious reasons) attempts, by mythicizing reality, to conceal certain facts which explain the way men exist in the world; problem-posing education sets itself the task of demythologizing. Banking education resists dialogue; problem-posing education regards dialogue as indispensable to the act of cognition which unveils reality. Banking education treats students as objects of assistance; problem-posing education makes them critical thinkers. Banking education inhibits creativity and domesticates (although it cannot completely destroy) the *intentionality* of consciousness by isolating consciousness from the world, thereby denying men the their ontological and historical vocation of

becoming more fully human. Problem-posing education bases itself on creativity and stimulates true reflection and action upon reality, thereby
responding to the vocation of men as beings who are authentic only when
engaged in inquiry and creative transformation. In sum: banking theory and
practice, as immobilizing and fixating forces, fail to acknowledge men as
historical beings; problem-posing theory and practice take man's historicity
as their starting point.

Problem-posing education affirms men as beings in the process of
becoming–as unfinished, uncompleted beings in and with a likewise unfinished reality. Indeed, in contrast to other animals who are unfinished, but
not historical, men know themselves to be unfinished; they are aware of
their incompletion. In this incompletion and this awareness lie the very
roots of education as an exclusively human manifestation. The unfinished
character of men and the transformational character of reality necessitate
that education be an ongoing activity.

Education is thus constantly remade in the praxis. In order to *be*, it must
become. Its "duration" (in the Bergsonian meaning of the word) is found in
the interplay of the opposites *permanence* and *change*. The banking method
emphasizes permanence and becomes reactionary; problem-posing education–which accepts neither a "well-behaved" present nor a predetermined
future–roots itself in the dynamic present and becomes revolutionary.

Problem-posing education is revolutionary futurity. Hence it is
prophetic (and, as such, hopeful). Hence, it corresponds to the historical
nature of man. Hence, it affirms men as beings who transcend themselves,
who move forward and look ahead, for whom immobility represents a fatal
threat, for whom looking at the past must only be a means of understanding
more clearly what and who they are so that they can more wisely build the
future. Hence, it identifies with the movement which engages men as beings
aware of their incompletion–a historical movement which has its point of
departure, its Subjects and its objective.

The point of departure of the movement lies in men themselves. But
since men do not exist apart from the world, apart from reality, the movement must begin with the men-world relationship. Accordingly, the point of
departure must always be with men in the "here and now," which constitutes the situation within which they are submerged, from which they
emerge, and in which they intervene. Only by starting from this situation–
which determines their perception of it–can they begin to move. To do this
authentically they must perceive their state not as fated and unalterable, but
merely as limiting–and therefore challenging.

Whereas the banking method directly or indirectly reinforces men's
fatalistic perception of their situation, the problem-posing method presents
this very situation to them as a problem. As the situation becomes the object

of their cognition, the naive or magical perception which produced their fatalism gives way to perception which is able to perceive itself even as it perceives reality, and can thus be critically objective about that reality.

A deepened consciousness of their situation leads men to apprehend that situation as a historical reality susceptible of transformation. Resignation gives way to the drive for transformation and inquiry, over which men feel themselves to be in control. If men, as historical beings necessarily engaged with other men in a movement of inquiry, did not control that movement, it would be (and is) a violation of men's humanity. Any situation in which some men prevent others from engaging in the process of inquiry is one of violence. The means used are not important; to alienate men from their own decision making is to change them into objects.

This movement of inquiry must be directed toward humanization—man's historical vocation. The pursuit of full humanity, however, cannot be carried out in isolation or individualism, but only in fellowship and solidarity; therefore it cannot unfold in the antagonistic relations between oppressors and oppressed. No one can be authentically human while he prevents others from being so. Attempting *to be more* human, individualistically, leads to *having more*, egotistically: a form of dehumanization. Not that it is not fundamental *to have* in order *to be* human. Precisely because it is necessary, some men's *having* must not be allowed to constitute an obstacle to others' *having*, must not consolidate the power of the former to crush the latter.

Problem-posing education, as a humanist and liberating praxis, posits as fundamental that men subjected to domination must fight for their emancipation. To that end, it enables teachers and students to become Subjects of the educational process by overcoming authoritarianism and an alienating intellectualism; it also enables men to overcome their false perception of reality. The world—no longer something to be described with deceptive words—becomes the object of that transforming action by men which results in their humanization.

Problem-posing education does not and cannot serve the interests of the oppressor. No oppressive order could permit the oppressed to begin to question: Why? While only a revolutionary society can carry out this education in systematic terms, the revolutionary leaders need not take full power before they can employ the method. In the revolutionary process, the leaders cannot utilize the banking method as an interim measure, justified on grounds of expediency, with the intention of *later* behaving in a genuinely revolutionary fashion. They must be revolutionary—that is to say, dialogical—from the outset.

NOTES

1. The current movements of rebellion, especially those of youth, while they necessarily reflect the peculiarities of their respective settings, manifest in their essence this preoccupation with man and men as beings in the world and with the world—preoccupation with thwat and how they are "being." As they place consumer civilization in judgment, denounce bureaucracies of all types, demand the transformation of the universities (changing the rigid nature of the teacher-student relationship and placing that relationship within the context of reality), propose the transformation of reality itself so that universities can be renewed, attack old orders and established institutions in the attempt to affirm men as the Subjects of decision, all these movements reflect the style of our age, which is more anthropological than anthropocentric.

2. As used throughout this book, the term "contradiction" denotes the dialectical conflict between opposing social forces—translator's note. Translator: Myra Bergman Ramos.

3. This fear of freedom is also to be found in the oppressors, though, obviously, in a different form. The oppressed are afraid to embrace freedom; the oppressors are afraid of losing the "freedom" to oppress.

4. See Georg Hegel, *The Phenomenology of Mind* (New York, 1967), pp. 236–37.

5. Analyzing the dialectical relationship between the consciousness of the master and the consciousness of the oppressed, Hegel states: "The one is independent, and its essential nature is to be for itself; the other is dependent, and its essence is life or existence for another. The former is the Master, or Lord, the latter the Bondsman." Ibid., p. 234.

6. Simone de Beauvoir, *La Pensee de Droite, Aujord'hui* (Paris); ST, *El Pensamiento politico de la Derecha* (Buenos Aires, 1963), p. 34.

7. This concept corresponds to what Sartre calls the "digestive" or "nutritive" concept of education, in which knowledge is "fed" by the teacher to the students to "fill them out." See Jean-Paul Sarte, "Une idée fundamentale de la phénomenologie de Husserl: L'intentionalité," *Situations I* (Paris, 1947).

8. For example, some professors specify in their reading lists that a book should be read from pages 10 to 15—and do this to "help" their students!

9. Eric Fromm, *The Heart of Man* (New York, 1966), p. 41.

10. Ibid., p. 31.

11. Ibid.

12. Reinhold Niebuhr, *Moral Man and Immoral Soceity* (New York, 1960), p. 130.

13. Sartre, "Une idée fundamentale."

14. Edmund Husserl, *Ideas—General Introduction to Pure Phenomenology* (London, 1969), pp. 105–106.

10

•

THE TEXT AND CULTURAL POLITICS

Michael W. Apple

This paper analyzes the politics of the textbook as part of the social construction of reality, knowledge. education, and schooling. The textbook becomes a site of struggle against the myth of the school curriculum as a neutral form of knowledge. It legitimates selective forms of knowledge and culture underlying supposedly democratic reforms heavily influenced by conservative economic and political forces, eclipsing the historical experiences and cultural expression of the less powerful. Though textbooks are cultural artifacts participating in the social organization of knowledge, they are not simply products consumed by an unwitting, passive readership on whom their content is imposed. Response to a text may be that of domination, negotiation, or opposition. Countering the hegemony of the " selective tradition" of authoritarian conceptions and uses of school knowledge entails politicized, multiple readings of the various contexts of textbooks, through which both the positive and negative power relations surrounding the text work themselves out.

WHOSE KNOWLEDGE IS OF MOST WORTH?

Reality doesn't stalk around with a label. What something is, what it does, one's evaluation of it, all this is not naturally preordained. It is socially constructed. This is the case even when we talk about the institutions that organize a good deal of our lives. Take schools, for example. For some groups of people, schooling is seen as a vast engine of democracy—opening horizons, ensuring mobility, and so on. For others, the reality of schooling is strikingly different. It is seen as a form of social control, or, perhaps, as the embodiment of cultural dangers, institutions whose curricula and teaching practices threaten the moral universe of the students who attend them.

While not all of us may agree with this diagnosis of what schools do, this latter position contains a very important insight. It recognizes that behind Spencer's famous question about "What knowledge is of most worth?" there lies another even more contentious question, "Whose knowledge is of most worth?"

During the past two decades, a good deal of progress has been made on answering the question of whose knowledge becomes socially legitimate in schools.[1] While much still remains to be understood, we are now much closer to having an adequate understanding of the relationship between school knowledge and the larger society than before. Yet, little attention has actually been paid to that one artifact that plays such a major role in defining whose culture is taught—*the textbook.*

Of course, there have been literally thousands of studies of textbooks over the years.[2] But, by and large, until relatively recently, most of these remained unconcerned with the politics of culture. All too many researchers could still be characterized by the phrase coined years ago by C. Wright Mills, "abstract empiricists." These "hunters and gatherers of social numbers"[3] remain unconnected to the relations of inequality that surround them.

This is a distinct problem since texts are not simply "delivery systems" of "facts." They are at once the results of political, economic, and cultural activities, battles, and compromises. They are conceived, designed, and authored by people with real interests. They are published within the political and economic constraints of markets, resources, and power.[4] And what texts mean and how they are used are fought over by communities with distinctly different commitments and by teachers and students as well.

As I have argued in a series of volumes, it is naive to think of the school curriculum as neutral knowledge.[5] Rather, what counts as legitimate knowledge is the result of complex power relations and struggles among identifiable class, race, gender, and religious groups. Thus, education and power are terms of an indissoluble couplet. It is at times of social upheaval that this relationship between education and power becomes most visible. Such a relationship was and continues to be made manifest in the struggles by women, people of color, and others to have their history and knowledge included in the curriculum. Driven by an economic crisis and a crisis in ideology and authority relations, it has become even more visible in the past decade or so in the resurgent conservative attacks on schooling. "Authoritarian populism" is in the air and the New Right has been more than a little successful in bringing its own power to bear on the goals, content, and process of schooling.[6]

The movement to the right has not stopped outside the schoolroom door, as you well know. Current plans for the centralization of authority over teaching and curriculum, often cleverly disguised as "democratic" reforms, are hardly off the drawing board before new management proposals or privatization initiatives are introduced. In the United States, evidence for such offensives abounds with the introduction of mandatory competency testing for students and teachers, the calls for a return to a (romanticized) common curriculum, the reduction of educational goals to those primarily of business and industry, the proposals for voucher or "choice" plans, the pressure to legislate morality and values from the right, and the introduction of state-mandated content on "free enterprise" and the like. Similar tendencies are more than a little evident in Britain and in some cases are even more advanced.

All of this has brought about countervailing movements in the schools. The slower but still interesting growth of more democratically run schools, of practices and policies that give community groups and teachers considerably more authority in text selection and curriculum determination, in teaching strategy, in the use of funds, in administration, and in developing more flexible and less authoritarian evaluation schemes is providing some cause for optimism in the midst of the conservative restoration.[7]

Even with these positive signs, however, it is clear that the New Right has been able to rearticulate traditional political and cultural themes. In so doing, it has often effectively mobilized a mass base of adherents. Among its most powerful causes and effects has been the growing feeling of disaffection about public schooling among conservative groups. Large numbers of parents and other people no longer trust either the institutions or the teachers and administrators in them to make "correct" decisions about what should be taught and how to teach it. The rapid growth of evangelical schooling, of censorship, of textbook controversies, and the emerging tendency of many parents to teach their children at home rather than send them to state-supported schools are clear indications of this loss of legitimacy.[8]

The ideology that stands behind this is often very complex. It combines a commitment to both the "traditional family" and clear gender roles with the commitment to "traditional values" and literal religiosity. Also often packed into this is a defense of capitalist economics, patriotism, the

"Western tradition," anticommunism, and a deep mistrust of the "welfare state."[9] When this ideology is applied to schooling, the result can be as simple as dissatisfaction with an occasional book or assignment. On the other hand, the result can be a major conflict that threatens to go well beyond the boundaries of our usual debates about schooling.

Few places in the United States are more well known in this latter context than Kanawha County, West Virginia. In the mid-1970s, it became the scene of one of the most explosive controversies over what schools should teach, who should decide, and what beliefs should guide our educational programs. What began as a protest by a small group of conservative parents, religious leaders, and businesspeople over the content and design of the textbooks that had been approved for use in local schools soon spread to include school boycotts, violence, and a wrenching split within the community that in many ways has yet to heal.

There were a number of important contributing factors that heightened tensions in West Virginia. Schools in rural areas had been recently consolidated. Class relations and relations between the county and the city were increasingly tense. The lack of participation by rural parents (or many parents at all, for that matter) in text selection or in educational decision making in general also led to increasing alienation. Furthermore, the cultural history of the region, with its fierce independence, its fundamentalist religious traditions, and its history of economic depression helped create conditions for serious unrest. Finally, Kanawha County became a cause célèbre for national right-wing groups who offered moral, legal, and organizational support to the conservative activists there.[10]

It is important to realize, then, that controversies over "official knowledge" that usually center around what is included and excluded in textbooks really signify more profound political, economic, and cultural relations and histories. Conflicts over texts are often proxies for wider questions of power relations. They involve what people hold most dear. And, as in the case of Kanawha County, they can quickly escalate into conflicts over these deeper issues.

Yet, textbooks are surely important in and of themselves. They signify—through their content and form—particular constructions of reality, particular ways of selecting and organizing that vast universe of possible knowledge. They embody what Raymond Williams called the selective tradition—someone's selection, someone's vision of legitimate knowledge and culture, one that in the process of enfranchising one group's cultural capital disenfranchises another's.[11]

Texts are really messages to and about the future. As part of a curriculum, they participate in no less than the organized knowledge system of society. They participate in creating what a society has recognized as legitimate and truthful. They help set the canons of truthfulness and, as such, also help recreate a major reference point for what knowledge, culture, belief, and morality really *are*.[12]

Yet such a statement—even with its recognition that texts participate in constructing ideologies and ontologies—is basically misleading in many important ways. For it is not a "society" that has created such texts, but specific groups of people. "We" haven't built such curriculum artifacts in the simple sense that there is universal agreement among all of us and this is what gets to be official knowledge. In fact, the very use of the pronoun "we" simplifies matters all too much.

As Fred Inglis so cogently argues, the pronoun "we"

> smooths over the deep corrugations and ruptures caused precisely by struggle over how that authoritative and editorial "we" is going to be used The [text], it is not melodramatic to declare, really is the battleground for an intellectual civil war, and the battle for cultural authority is a wayward, intermittingly fierce, always protracted and fervent one.[13]

Let me give one example. In the 1930s, conservative groups in the United States mounted a campaign against one of the more progressive textbook series in use in schools. *Man and His Changing World*, by Harold Rugg and his colleagues, became the subject of a concerted attack by the National Association of Manufacturers, the American Legion, the Advertising Federation of America, and other "neutral" groups. They charged that Rugg's books were socialist, anti-American, antibusiness, and so forth. The conservative campaign was more than a little successful in forcing school districts to withdraw Rugg's series from classrooms and libraries. So successful were they that sales fell from nearly 300,000 copies in 1938 to only approximately 20,000 in 1944.[14]

We, of course, may have reservations about such texts today, not least of which would be the sexist title. But, one thing that the Rugg case makes clear is that the politics of the textbook is not something new by any means. Current issues surrounding texts—their ideology, their very status as central definers of what we should teach, even their very effectiveness and their design—echo the past moments of these concerns that have had such a long history in so many countries.

Few aspects of schooling currently have been subject to more intense scrutiny and criticism than the text. Perhaps one of the most graphic descriptions is provided by A. Graham Down of the Council for Basic Education:

> Textbooks, for better or worse, dominate what students learn. They set the curriculum, and often the facts learned, in most subjects. For many students, textbooks are their first and sometimes only early exposure to books

and to reading. The public regards textbooks as authoritative, accurate, and necessary. And teachers rely on them to organize lessons and structure subject matter. But the current system of textbook adoption has filled our schools with Trojan horses–glossily covered blocks of paper whose words emerge to deaden the minds of our nation's youth, and make them enemies of learning.[15]

This statement is made just as powerfully by the author of a recent study of what she has called "America's textbook fiasco":

Imagine a public policy system that is perfectly designed to produce textbooks that confuse, mislead, and profoundly bore students, while at the same time making all of the adults involved in the process look good, not only in their own eyes, but in the eyes of others. Although there are some good textbooks on the market, publishers and editors are virtually compelled by public policies and practices to create textbooks that confuse students with non sequiturs, that mislead them with misinformation. and that profoundly bore them with pointlessly arid writing.[16]

REGULATION OR LIBERATION AND THE TEXT

In order to understand these criticisms and to understand both some of the reasons why texts look the way they do and why they contain some groups' perspectives and not others', we also need to realize that the world of the book has not been cut off from the world of commerce. Books are not only cultural artifacts. They are economic commodities as well. Even though texts may be vehicles of ideas, they still have to be "peddled on a market."[17] This is a market, however, that–especially in the national and international world of textbook publishing–is politically volatile, as the Kanawha County experience so clearly documented.

Texts are caught up in a complicated set of political and economic dynamics. Text publishing often is highly competitive. In the United States, where text production is a commercial enterprise situated within the vicissitudes of a capitalist market, decisions about the "bottom line" determine what books are published and for how long. Yet, this situation is not just controlled by the "invisible hand" of the market. It is also largely determined by the highly visible "political" hand of state textbook adoption policies.[18]

Nearly half of the states–most of them in the southern tier and the "sun belt"–have state textbook adoption committees that by and large choose what texts will be purchased by the schools in that state. The economics of profit and loss of this situation makes it imperative that publishers devote nearly all of their efforts to guaranteeing a place on these lists of approved texts. Because of this, the texts made available to the entire nation, and the knowledge considered legitimate in them, are determined by what will sell in Texas, California, Florida, and so forth. There can be no doubt that the political and ideological controversies over content in these states, controversies that were often very similar to those that surfaced in Kanawha County, have had a very real impact on what and whose knowledge is made available. It is also clear that Kanawha County was affected by and had an impact on these larger battles over legitimate knowledge.

Economic and political realities structure text publishing not only internally, however. On an international level, the major text-publishing conglomerates control the market of much of the material not only in the capitalist centers, but in many other nations as well. Cultural domination is a fact of life for millions of students throughout the world, in part because of the economic control of communication and publishing by multinational firms, in part because of the ideologies and systems of political and cultural control of new elites within former colonial countries.[19] All of this, too, has led to complicated relations and struggles over official knowledge and the text between "center" and "periphery" and within these areas as well.

I want to stress that all of this is not simply—as in the case of newly emerging nations, Kanawha County, or the Rugg textbooks—of historical interest. The controversies over the form and content of the textbook have not diminished. In fact, they have become even more heated in the United States in particular. The changing ideological climate has had a major impact on debates over what should be taught in schools and on how it should be taught and evaluated. There is considerable pressure to raise the standards of texts; make them more "difficult"; standardize their content; make certain that the texts place more stress on "American" themes of patriotism, free enterprise, and the "Western tradition"; and link their content to statewide and national tests of educational achievement.

These kinds of pressures are not felt only in the United States. The text has become the center of ideological and educational conflict in a number of other countries as well. In Japan, for instance, the government approval of a right-wing history textbook that retold the story of the brutal Japanese invasion and occupation of China and Korea in a more positive light has stimulated widespread international antagonism and has led to considerable controversy in Japan as well.

Along these same lines, at the very time that the text has become a source of contention for conservative movements, it has stood at the center of controversy for not being progressive enough. Class, gender, and race bias has been widespread in the materials. All too often, "legitimate" knowledge does not include the historical experiences and cultural expressions of labor, women, people of color, and others who have been less powerful.[20]

All of these controversies are not "simply" about the content of the books students find—or don't find—in their schools, though obviously they are about that as well. The issues also involve profoundly different definitions of the common good,[21] about our society and where it should be heading, about cultural visions, and about our children's future. To quote from Inglis again, the entire curriculum, in which the text plays so large a part, is "both the text and context in which production and values intersect: it is the twistpoint of imagination and power."[22] In the context of the politics of the textbook, it is the issue of power that should concern us the most.

The concept of power merely connotes the capacity to act and to do so effectively. However, in the ways we use the idea of power in our daily discourse, "the word comes on strongly and menacingly, and its presence is duly fearful."[23] This "dark side" of power is, of course, complemented by a more positive vision. Here, power is seen as connected to a people acting democratically and collectively, in the open, for the best ideals.[24] It is this dual concept of power that concerns us here, both at the level of theory (how we think about the relationship between legitimate knowledge and power) and practice (how texts actually embody this relationship). Both the positive and the negative senses of power are essential for us to understand these relationships. Taken together, they signify that arguments about textbooks are really a form of *cultural politics*. They involve the very nature of the connections between cultural visions and differential power.

This, of course, is not new to anyone who has been interested in the history of the relationship among books, literacy, and popular movements. Books—and one's ability to read them—have themselves been inherently caught up in cultural politics. Take the case of Voltaire, that leader of the Enlightenment who a wanted to become a member of the nobility. For him, the Enlightenment should begin with the "grands." Only when it had captured the hearts and minds of society's commanding heights, only then could it concern itself with the masses below. But, for Voltaire and many of his followers, one caution should be taken very seriously: One should take care to prevent the masses from learning to read.[25]

For others, teaching the masses to read could have a more "beneficial effect." It enables a "civilizing" process, in which dominated groups would be made more moral, more obedient, more influenced by "real culture."[26] And for still others, such literacy could bring social transformation in its wake. It could lead to a "critical literacy," one that would be part of larger movements for a more democratic culture, economy, and polity.[27] The dual sense of the power of the text emerges clearly here.

Thus, activities that we now ask students to engage in every day, activities as "simple" and basic as reading and writing, can be at one and the same time forms of regulation and exploitation and potential modes of resistance, celebration, and solidarity. Here, I am reminded of Caliban's cry, "You taught me language; and my profit on't is, I know how to curse."[28]

This contradictory sense of the politics of the book is made clearer if we go into the classrooms of the past. For example, texts have often been related to forms of bureaucratic regulation both of teachers' lives and those of students. Thus, one teacher in Boston in 1899 relates a story of what happened in her first year of teaching during an observation by the school principal. As the teacher rather proudly watched one of her children read aloud an assigned lesson from the text, the principal was less than pleased with the performance of the teacher or her pupil. In the words of the teacher:

> The proper way to read in the public school in 1899 was to say, "page 35, chapter 4" and holding the book in the right hand, with the toes pointing at an angle of forty-five degrees, the head held straight and high, the eyes looking directly ahead, the pupil would lift up his voice and struggle in loud, unnatural tones. Now, I had attended to the position of the toes, the right arm, and the nose, but had failed to enforce the mentioning of page and chapter.[29]

Here, the text participates in both bodily and ideological regulation. The textbook in this instance is part of a system of enforcing a sense of duty, morality, and cultural correctness. Yet, historically, the standardized text was struggled for as well as against by many teachers. Faced with large classes, difficult working conditions, insufficient training, and, even more importantly, little time to prepare lessons for the vast array of subjects and students they were responsible for, teachers often looked upon texts not necessarily as impositions but as essential tools. For young women elementary school teachers, the text helped prevent exploitation.[30] It solved a multitude of practical problems. It led not only to deskilling, but to time to become more skilled as a teacher as well.[31] Thus, there were demands for standardized texts by teachers even in the face of what happened to that teacher in Boston and to so many others.

This struggle over texts was linked to broader concerns about who should control the curriculum in schools. Teachers, especially those most politically active, constantly sought to have a say in what they taught. This was seen as part of a larger fight for democratic rights. Margaret Haley, for instance, one of the leaders of the first teachers' union in the United States, saw a great need for teachers to work against the tendency toward making the teacher "a mere factory hand, whose duty it is to carry out mechanically and unquestioningly the ideas and orders of those clothed with authority of position."[32] Teachers had to fight against the deskilling or, as she called it, "factoryizing" methods of control being sponsored by administrative and industrial leaders. One of the reasons she was so strongly in favor of teachers' councils as mechanisms of control of schools was that this would reduce considerably the immense power over teaching and texts that administrators then possessed. Quoting John Dewey approvingly, Haley wrote, "If there is a single public-school system in the United States where there is official and constitutional provision made for submitting questions of methods, of discipline and teaching, and the questions of curriculum, textbooks, etc. to the discussion of those actually engaged in the work of teaching, that fact has escaped my notice."[33]

In this instance, teacher control over the choice of textbooks and how they were to be used was part of a more extensive movement to enhance the democratic rights of teachers on the job. Without such teacher control, teachers would be the equivalent of factory workers whose every move was determined by management.

These points about the contradictory relationships teachers have had with texts and the way such books depower and empower at different moments (and perhaps at the same time) documents something of importance. It is too easy to see a cultural practice or a book as totally carrying its politics around with it, "as if written on its brow for ever and a day." Rather, its political functioning "depends on the network of social and ideological relations" it participates in.[34] Text writing, reading, and use can be retrogressive or progressive (and sometimes some combination of both) depending on the social context. Textbooks can be fought against because they are part of a system of moral regulation. They can be fought for both as providing essential assistance in the labor of teaching or as part of a larger strategy of democratization.

What textbooks do, the social roles they play for different groups, is then *very complicated.* This has important implications not only for the politics of how and by whom textbooks are used, but for the politics of the internal qualities, the content, and organization of the text. Just as crucially, it also has an immense bearing on how people actually read and interpret the text. It is to these issues that I now want to turn.

THE POLITICS OF CULTURAL INCORPORATION

We cannot assume that because so much of education has been linked to processes of class, gender, and race stratification[35] that all of the knowledge chosen to be included in texts simply represents relations of, say, cultural domination or only includes the knowledge of dominant groups. This point requires that I speak theoretically and politically in this section of my argument, for all too many critical analyses of school knowledge—of what is included and excluded in the overt and hidden curricula of the school—take the easy way out. Reductive analysis comes cheap. Reality, however, is complex. Let us look at this in more detail.

It has been argued in considerable detail elsewhere that the selection and organization of knowledge for schools is an ideological process, one that serves the interests of particular classes and social groups.[36] However, as I just noted, this does not mean that the entire corpus of school knowledge is "a mirror reflection of ruling class ideas, imposed in an unmediated and coercive manner." Instead, "the processes of cultural incorporation are dynamic, reflecting both continuities and contradictions of that dominant culture and the continual remaking and relegitimation of that culture's plausibility system."[37] Curricula are not imposed in countries like the United States. Rather, they are the products of often intense conflicts, negotiations, and attempts at rebuilding hegemonic control by actually incorporating the knowledge and perspectives of the less powerful under the umbrella of the discourse of dominant groups.

This is clear in the case of the textbook. As disenfranchised groups have fought to have their knowledge take center stage in the debates over cultural legitimacy, one trend has dominated in text production. In essence, little is usually dropped from textbooks. Major ideological frameworks do not get markedly changed. Textbook publishers are under considerable and constant pressure to include more in their books. Progressive items are perhaps mentioned, then, but not developed in depth.[38] Dominance is partly maintained here through compromise and the process of "mentioning."

Tony Bennett's discussion of the process by which dominant cultures actually become dominant is worth quoting at length here:

> Dominant culture gains a purchase not in being imposed, as an alien external force, on to the cultures of subordinate groups, but by reaching into these cultures, reshaping them, hooking them and, with them, the people whose consciousness and experience is defined in their terms, into an association with the values and ideologies of the ruling groups in society. Such processes neither erase the cultures of subordinate groups, nor do they rob "the people" of their "true culture": what they do do is shuffle those cultures on to an ideological and cultural terrain in which they can be disconnected from whatever radical impulses which may (but need not) have fuelled them and be connected to more conservative or, often, downright reactionary cultural and ideological tendencies.[39]

In some cases, "mentioning" may operate in exactly this way, integrate selective elements into the dominant tradition by bringing them into close association with the values of powerful groups. There will be times, however, when such a strategy will not be successful. Oppositional cultures may at times use elements of the dominant culture against such groups. Bennett goes on, describing how oppositional cultures operate, as well:

Similarly, resistance to the dominant culture does not take the form of launching against it a ready-formed, constantly simmering oppositional culture–always there, but in need of being turned up from time to time. Oppositional cultural values are formed and take shape only in the context of their struggle with the dominant culture, a struggle which may borrow some of its resources from that culture and which must concede some ground to it if it is to be able to connect with it–and thereby with those whose consciousness and experience is partly shaped by it–in order, by turning it back upon itself, to peel it away, to create a space within and against it in which contradictory values can echo, reverberate and be heard.[40]

Some texts may, in fact, have such progressive "echoes" within them. Then are victories in the politics of official knowledge, not only defeats.

Sometimes, of course, not only are people successful in creating some space where such contradictory values can indeed "echo, reverberate, and be heard," but they transform the entire social space. They create entirely new kinds of governments, new possibilities for democratic political, economic, and cultural arrangements. In these situations, the role of education takes on even more importance, since new knowledge, new ethics, and a new reality seek to replace the old. This is one of the reasons that those of us committed to more participatory and democratic cultures inside and outside of schools must give serious attention to changes in official knowledge in those nations that have sought to overthrow their colonial or elitist heritage. Here, the politics of the text takes on special importance, since the textbook often represents an overt attempt to help create a new cultural reality.

New social contexts, new processes of text creation, a new cultural politics, the transformation of authority relations, and new ways of reading texts– all of this can evolve and help usher in a positive rather than a negative sense of the power of the text. Less regulatory and more emancipatory relations of texts to real people can begin to evolve, a possibility made real in many of the programs of critical literacy that have had such a positive impact in nations throughout the world. Here people help create their own "texts," ones that signify their emerging power in the control of their own destinies.

However, we should not be overly romantic here. Such transformations of cultural authority and mechanisms of control and incorporation will not be easy. For example, certainly, the ideas and values of a people are not directly prescribed by the conceptions of the world of dominant groups and, just as certain, there will be many instances where people have been successful in creating realistic and workable alternatives to the culture and texts in dominance. Yet, we do need to acknowledge that the social distribution of what is considered legitimate knowledge *is* skewed in many nations. The social institutions directly concerned with the "transmission" of this knowledge, such as schools and the media, are grounded in and structured by the class, gender, and race inequalities that organize the society in which we live. The area of symbolic production is not divorced from the unequal relations of power that structure other spheres.[41]

Speaking only of class relations (but much the same could be said about race and gender), Stuart Hall, one of the most insightful analysts of cultural politics, puts it this way:

> Ruling or dominant conceptions of the world do not directly prescribe the mental content of the illusions that supposedly fill the heads of dominated classes. But the circle of dominant ideas does accumulate the symbolic power to map or classify the world for others; its classifications do acquire not only the constraining power of dominance over other modes of thought but also the initial authority of habit and instinct. It becomes the horizon of the taken-for-granted: what the world is and how it works, for all practical purposes. Ruling ideas may dominate other conceptions of the social world by setting the limit on what will appear as rational, reasonable, credible, indeed sayable or thinkable within the given vocabularies of motive and action available to us. Their dominance lies precisely in the power they have to contain within their limits, to frame within their circumference of thought, the reasoning and calculation of other social groups.[42]

In the United States, there has been a movement of exactly this kind. Dominant groups—really a coalition of economic modernizers, what has been called the old humanists, and neoconservative intellectuals—have attempted to create an ideological consensus around the return to traditional knowledge. The "great books" and "great ideas" of the "Western tradition" will preserve democracy. By returning to the common culture that has made this nation great, schools will increase student achievement and discipline, increase our international competitiveness, and ultimately reduce unemployment and poverty.

Mirrored in the problematic educational and cultural visions of volumes such as Bloom's *The Closing of the American Mind* and Hirsch's *Cultural Literacy*, this position is probably best represented in quotes from former Secretary of Education William Bennett. In his view, we are finally emerging out of a crisis in which "we neglected and denied much of the best in education." For a period, "we simply stopped doing the right things [and] allowed an assault on intellectual and moral standards." This assault on the current state of education has led schools to fall away from "the principles of our tradition."[43]

Yet, for Bennett, "the people" have now risen up. "The 1980s gave birth to a grass roots movement for educational reform that has generated a renewed commitment to excellence, character, and fundamentals." Because of this, "we have reason for optimism." Why? Because the national debate on education is now focused on truly important matters: mastering the basics; . . . insisting on high standards and expectations; ensuring discipline in the classroom; conveying a grasp of our moral and political principles; and nurturing the character of our young.[44]

Notice the use of "we," "the people," here. Notice as well the assumed consensus on "basics" and "fundamentals" and the romanticization of the past both in schools and the larger society. The use of these terms, the attempt to bring people in under the ideological umbrella of the conservative restoration, is very clever rhetorically. As many people in the United States, Britain, and elsewhere—where rightist governments have been very active in transforming what education is about—have begun to realize, however, this ideological incorporation is having no small measure of success at the level of policy and at the level of whose knowledge and values are to be taught.[45]

If this movement has its way, the texts made available and the knowledge included in them will surely represent a major loss for many of the groups who have had successes in bringing their knowledge and culture more directly into the body of legitimate content in schools. Just as surely, the ideologies that will dominate the official knowledge will represent a considerably more elitist orientation than what we have now.

Yet, perhaps surely is not the correct word here. The situation is actually more complex than that, something we have learned from many of the newer methods of interpreting how social messages are actually "found" in texts.

Allan Luke has dealt with such issues very persuasively. It would be best to quote him at length here:

A major pitfall of research in the sociology of curriculum has been its willingness to accept text form as a mere adjunct means for the delivery of ideological content: the former described in terms of dominant metaphors, images, or key ideas: the latter described in terms of the sum total of values, beliefs, and ideas which might be seen to constitute a false consciousness. For much content analysis presumes that text mirrors or reflects a particular ideological position, which in turn can be connected to specific class interests. . . . It is predicated on the possibility of a one-to-one identification of school knowledge with textually represented ideas of the dominant classes. Even those critics who have recognized that the ideology encoded in curricular texts may reflect the internally contradictory character of a dominant culture have tended to neglect the need for a more complex model of text analysis, one that does not suppose that texts are simply readable, literal representations of "someone else's" version of social reality, objective knowledge and human relations. For texts do not always mean or communicate what they say.[46]

These are important points, for they imply that we need more sophisticated and nuanced models of textual analysis. While we should certainly not be at all sanguine about the effects of the conservative restoration on texts and the curriculum, if texts do not simply represent dominant beliefs in some straightforward way, and if dominant cultures contain contradictions, fissures, and even elements of the culture of popular groups, then our readings of what knowledge is "in" texts cannot be done by the application of a simple formula.

We can claim, for instance, that the meaning of a text is not necessarily intrinsic to it. As poststructuralist theories would have it, meaning is "the product of a system of differences into which the text is articulated." Thus, there is not "one text," but many. Any text is open to multiple readings. This puts into doubt any claim that one can determine the meanings and politics of a text "by a straightforward encounter with the text itself." It also raises serious questions About whether one can fully understand the text by mechanically applying any interpretive procedure. Meanings, then, can be and are multiple and contradictory and we must always be willing to "read" our own readings of a text, to interpret our own interpretations of what it means.[47] Answering the question of "whose knowledge" is in a text is not at all simple it seems, though clearly the right would very much like to reduce the range of meanings one might find.

This is true of our own interpretations of what is in textbooks. But it is also just as true for the students who sit in schools and at home and read (or in many cases do not read) their texts. I want to stress this point, not only at the level of theory and politics as I have been stressing here, but at the level of practice.

We cannot assume that what is "in" the text is actually taught. Nor can we assume that what is taught is actually learned. Teachers have a long history of mediating and transforming text material when they employ it in classrooms. Students bring their own classed, raced, and gendered biographies with them, as well. They, too, accept, reinterpret, and reject what counts as legitimate knowledge selectively. As critical ethnographies of schools have shown, students (and teachers) are not empty vessels into which knowledge is poured. Rather than what Freire has called "banking" education,[48] students are active constructors of the meanings of the education they encounter.[49]

We can talk about three ways in which people can potentially respond to a text: dominated, negotiated, and oppositional. In the dominant reading of a text, one accepts the messages at face value. In a negotiated response, the reader may dispute a particular claim, but accept the overall tendencies or interpretations of a text. Finally, an oppositional response rejects these dominant tendencies and interpretations. The reader "repositions" herself or himself in relation to the text and takes on the position of the oppressed.[50] These are, of course, no more than ideal types and many responses will be a contradictory combination of all three. But the point is that not only do texts themselves have contradictory elements, audiences *construct* their own responses to texts. They do not passively receive texts, but actually read them based on their own class, race, gender, and religious experiences.

An immense amount of work needs to be done on student acceptance, interpretation, reinterpretation, or partial and/or total rejection of texts. While there is a tradition of such research, much of it quite good, most of this in education is done in an overly psychologized manner. It is more concerned with questions of learning and achievement than it is with the equally important and prior issues of whose knowledge it is that students are learning, negotiating, or opposing and what the sociocultural roots and effects are of such processes. Yet we simply cannot fully understand the power of the text, what it does ideologically and politically (or educationally, for that matter) unless we take very seriously the way students actually read them—not only as individuals but as members of, social groups with their own particular cultures and histories.[51] For every textbook, then, there are multiple texts—contradictions within it, multiple readings of it, and different uses to which it will be put. Texts—be they the standardized, grade-level specific books so beloved by school systems or the novels, trade books, and alternative materials that teachers use either to supplement these books or simply to replace them—are part of a complex story of cultural politics. They can signify authority (not always legitimate) or freedom.

To recognize this, then, is also to recognize that our task as critically and democratically minded educators is itself a political one. We must acknowledge and understand the tremendous capacity of dominant institutions to regenerate themselves "not only in their material foundations and structures but in that hearts and minds of people." Yet, at the very same time, we need never to lose sight of the power of popular organizations, of real people, to struggle, resist, and transform them.[52] Cultural authority, what counts as legitimate knowledge, what norms and values are represented in the officially sponsored curriculum of the school, all of these serve as important arenas in which the positive and negative relations of power surrounding the text will work themselves out. And all of them involve the hopes and dreams of real people in real institutions, in real relations of inequality.

From all that I have said here, it should be clear that I oppose the idea that there can be one textual authority, one definitive set of "facts" that is divorced from its context of power relations. A "common culture" can never be an extension to everyone of what a minority mean and believe. Rather, and crucially, it requires not the stipulation and incorporation within textbooks of lists and concepts that make us all "culturally literate," *but the cre-*

ation of the conditions necessary for all people to participate in the creation and re-creation of meanings and values. It requires a democratic process in which all people–not simply those who see themselves as the intellectual guardians of the "Western tradition"–can be involved in the deliberation of what is important.[53] It should go without saying that this necessitates the removal of the very real material obstacles–unequal power, wealth, time for reflection–that stand in the way of such participation.[54]

The very idea that there is one set of values that must guide the "selective tradition" can be a great danger, especially in contexts of differential power. Take, as one example, a famous line that was printed on an equally famous public building. It read, "There is one road to freedom. Its milestones are obedience, diligence, honesty, order, cleanliness, temperance, truth, sacrifice, and love of country." Many people may perhaps agree with much of the sentiment represented by these words. It may be of some interest that the building on which they appeared was in the administration block of the concentration camp at Dachau.[55]

We must ask, then, are we in the business of creating dead texts and dead minds? If we accept the title of educator–with all of the ethical and political commitments this entails–I think we already know what our answer should be.

A more extensive version of this essay appears in Michael W. Apple and Linda Christian-Smith, The Politics of the Textbook. *(New York: Routledge, 1991).*

NOTES

1. See, for example, M. W. Apple and L. Weis, eds., *Ideology and Practice in Schooling* (Philadelphia: Temple University Press, 1983).

2. A. Woodward, D. L. Elliot, and K. Carter Negel, eds., *Textbooks in School and Society* (New York: Garland, 1988).

3. F. Inglis, *Popular Culture and Political Power* (New York: St. Martin's Press, 1988), p. 9.

4. A. Luke, *Literacy, Textbooks, and Ideology* (Philadelphia: Falmer Press, 1988), pp. 27–29.

5. M. W. Apple, *Education and Power* (New York: Routledge, 1985); *Ideology and Curriculum,* 2d ed. (New York: Routledge, 1990).

6. M. W. Apple, "Redefining Equality: Authoritarian Populism and the Conservative Restoration," *Teachers College Record* 90 (winter 1988): 167–84.

7. A. Bastian et al., *Choosing Equality: The Case for Democratic Schooling* (Philadelphia: Temple University Press, 1986).

8. See, for example, S. Rose, *Keeping Them out of the Hands of Satan* (New York: Routledge, 1988).

9. A. Hunter, *Children in the Service of Conservatism* (Madison: University of Wisconsin Institute for Legal Studies, 1988).

10. J. Moffett, *Storm in the Mountains* (Carbondale: Southern Illinois University Press, 1988).

11. R. Williams, *The Long Revolution* (London: Chatto and Windus, 1961). See also Apple, *Ideology and Curriculum*.

12. F. Inglis, *The Management of Ignorance: A Political Theory of the Curriculum* (New York: Basil Blackwell, 1985), pp. 22–23.

13. Ibid., p. 23.

14. M. Schipper, "Textbook Controversy: Past and Present," *New York University Education Quarterly* 14 (spring/summer 1983): 31–36.

15. A. G. Down, "Preface," in H. Tyson-Bernstein, *A Conspiracy of Good Intentions: America's Textbook Fiasco* (Washington: Council for Basic Education, 1988), p. viii.

16. Tyson-Bernstein, *A Conspiracy of Good Intensions*.

17. R. Darnton, *The Literary Underground of the Old Regime* (Cambridge: Harvard University Press, 1982), p. 199.

18. M. W. Apple, "Regulating the Text: The Socio/Historical Roots of State Control," *Educational Policy* 3 (1989): 107–23.

19. P. Altbach, *The Knowledge Context* (Albany: State University of New York Press, 1988); P. Altbach and G. Kelly, eds., *Education and the Colonial Experience* (New Brunswick, N.J.: Transaction, 1984).

20. L. Roman, L. Christian-Smith, and E. Ellsworth, *Becoming Feminine: The Politics of Popular Culture* (Philadelphia: Falmer Press, 1988).

21. M. Raskin, *The Common Good* (New York: Routledge, 1986).

22. Inglis, *The Management of Ignorance*, p. 142.

23. Inglis, *Popular Culture and Political Power*, p. 4.

24. Ibid.

25. Darnton, *The Literary Underground of the Old Regime*, p. 13.

26. J. Batsleer et al., *Rewriting English: Cultural Politics of Gender and Class* (New York: Methuen, 1985).

27. C. Lankshear and M. Lawler, *Literacy, Schooling, and Revolution* (Philadelphia: Falmer Press, 1987).

28. Batsleer et al., *Rewriting English*.

29. Quoted in J. W. Fraser, "Agents of Democracy: Urban Elementary School teachers and the Conditions of Teaching," in *American Teachers: Histories of a Profession at Work*, ed. D. Warren (New York: Macmillan, 1989), p. 128.

30. M. W. Apple, *Teachers and Texts: A Political Economy of Class and Gender Relations in Education* (New York: Routledge, 1986).

31. Ibid.

32. Quoted in Fraser, "Agents of Democracy," p. 128.

33. Ibid., p. 138.

34. T. Bennett, "Introduction: Popular Culture and 'The Turn to Gramsci,'" in *Popular Culture and Social Relations*, eds., T. Bennett, C. Mercer, and J. Woollacott (Philadelphia: Open University Press, 1986), p. xvi.

35. Apple, *Education and Power*, Apple and Weis, *Ideology and Practice in Schooling*.

36. Apple, *Education and Power*, L. Christian-Smith, *Becoming a Woman through Romance* (New York: Routledge, 1991).

37. Luke, *Literacy, Textbooks, and Ideology*, p. 24.

38. Tyson-Bernstein, *A Conspiracy of Good Intentions*, p. 18.

39. T. Bennett, "The Politics of the 'Popular' and Popular Culture," in *Popular Culture and Social Relations*, p. 19.

40. Ibid.

41. S. Hall, "The Toad in the Garden: Thatcherism among the Tourists," in *Marxism and the Interpretation of Culture*, eds. C. Nelson and L. Grossberg (Urbana: University of Illinois Press, 1988), p. 44.

42. Ibid.

43. W. Bennett, *Our Children and Our Country* (New York: Simon & Schuster, 1988), p. 9.

44. Ibid., p.10.

45. Apple, "Redefining Equality."

46. Luke, *Literacy, Textbooks, and Ideology*, pp. 29–30.

47. L. Grossberg and C. Nelson, "Introduction: The Territory of Marxism," in *Marxism and the Interpretation of Culture*, p. 8.

48. P. Freire, *Pedagogy of the Oppressed* (New York: Herder and Herder, 1973).

49. R. Everhart, *Reading, Writing, and Resistance* (Boston: Routledge & Kegan Paul, 1983); A. McRobbie, "Working-Class Girls and the Culture of Femininity," in *Women Take Issue*, ed. Women's Studies Group (London: Hutchison, 1978); L. Weis, *Between Two Worlds* (Boston: Routledge & Kegan Paul, 1985); P. Willis, *Learning to Labor* (New York: Columbia University Press, 1981).

50. T. Modleski, *Studies in Entertainment* (Bloomington: Indiana University Press, 1986), p. xi.

51. Christian-Smith, *Becoming a Woman through Romance*; E. Ellsworth, "Illicit Pleasures: Feminist Spectators and *Personal Best*," in *Becoming Feminine*, eds. Roman, Christian-Smith, and Ellsworth; E. Ellsworth, "Why Doesn't This Feel Empowering? Working through the Repressive Myths of Critical Pedagogy," *Harvard Educational Review* 59 (1989): 297–324.

52. Batsleer et al., *Rewriting English*, p. 5.

53. Apple, *Ideology and Curriculum*.

54. R. Williams, *Resources of Hope* (New York: Verso, 1989), pp. 37–38.

55. D. Horne, *The Public Culture* (Dover, N.H.: Pluto Press, 1986), p. 76.

11

●

THE OBSOLETE NEUTRALITY OF HIGHER EDUCATION

Nobuo Shimahara

Τhe problem of neutrality of education has been a thorny one and also will be a vital one in the future. According to conservatism, education is a force which maintains the perpetuating order of society intact against the impact of new forces. Those subscribing to a "radical" view, on the other hand, contend that the schools should contribute to social construction by helping youth develop critical attitudes and habits of action. Dewey, as one of the persuasive proponents of the latter position, argued that the former view generates a negative social effect with its acquiescence in the perpetuation of social and moral disorder created by the development of cultural complexity. The clarity of the social emphasis of the school, he further contended, is demanded urgently.[1] His view, nonetheless, points to abstinence and futility in a conservative perspective.

This discussion aims to provide an alternative to Richard Hofstadter's renewed appeal for neutrality in higher education. By no means is it limited to any single university in trouble, but rather widely related to dilemmas, with different degrees of intensity, that a number of institutions of higher education have confronted where student unrest exists.

Columbia University is one of the campuses in this

nation where explosive student power burst out. Hofstadter, a distinguished Columbia historian, delivered the commencement address at his university in the face of student unrest.

He called for neutrality on the part of the university: "... neutrality should continue to define our aim, and we should resist the demand that the university espouse the political commitments of any of its members."[2] He emphasized that the central function of the university is to develop "free inquiry," "free forum," and "free criticism." One of the major roles is "to examine, critically and without stint, the assumptions that prevail" in our society. Thus, "to realize its essential character, the university has to be dependent upon something less precarious than the momentary balance of forces in society."[3] But it is impressed now by its grave fragility: a major evil causing this fragility is "politicizing" attempts by students. The needed ethical mandate, thus, is self-restraints and self-criticisms. Hofstadter further argued that to assault academic centers of study and thought as a way of changing social order is to show a complete disregard for the intrinsic character of the university.

The appeal to neutrality as an attempt to resolve the dilemmas is futile and obsolete. First, our colleges are politically influenced to a significant degree and occasionally adulterated by politicians. The research patterns of an advanced university, for example, are determined, more or less, by the structure of investments of private industries and the order of political priorities of the federal government. Moreover, university trustees and alumni, who usually control either local or national political and economic power, strongly influence university direction and basic policies. The university inevitably reflects the national political and economic structures. This realism should not be concealed.

Free inquiry is meaningful and beneficial when it relates itself to social life, including political realms. Although Hofstadter emphasized the essential status of free inquiry, he did not provide a practical reference to its relevance for the wide horizon of human life involving man's struggles to improve his culture by the use of scientific and humanistic inquiry; nor did he give any reference to the use of examined assumptions of our society. Should inquiry of higher education be an isolated laboratory process? Ought it be a monologue entirely detached from a dialogue with social life?

Human life is characterized by the principle of continuum. It operates in all processes of evolution, including the psychocultural. Free inquiry and forum, which examine the basic assumptions of a society and which produce new concepts and methodology, on the one hand, and social action, on the other, are on the same evolutionary continuum of human enterprise to create man's culture; theory and action are not self-determinative entities. Instead, they constitute complementary relations. The foregoing view is supported further by Whyte's renunciation of the neutrality of science as a manifestation of the illusion of "dissociated man" and a separation of science from inner human conflicts.[4]

A widely prevailing notion on educational management has been that the administration of higher education is endowed with unilateral authority to determine the structure and course of the educational institution. Students are computed numbers existing outside the processes of decision making. It is essential to admit honestly the rigidified and politicized structure of the administration of higher education which is responsible for forcing students to political action.

Intellectual youth now are awakened and more perceptive than ever. Sartre's dictum, "Existence precedes essence," now is being translated into sociological and political terms—Process precedes structure. The rise of the French unrest, the civil rights movement, and student activism are illustrative historic events. Political, economic, and educational institutions have failed to meet students' needs and aspirations, and subsequent individual frustrations have given a rise to a process directed against the status quo, as well as an impetus to their struggles to restructure the present social reality. What is often absent in the orientative framework of higher education is an appreciable recognition of deep concern of intellectual youth with critical problems of the nation and the international situation.

Can we resolve the disturbing academic upheavals by preaching educational neutrality and ethical self-restraints? Can we do this by accusing students of, and banning, their politicizing attempts when the authorities of their universities rationalize their own politicizing? My answer is negative. Therefore, I submit that neutrality for the university is dangerous because it is a disguised form of unilateral monologue. It discourages students' sensitivity and commitments to their society. Student political action must be cared for, and canalized into a constructive form where free dialogue has the possibility of resolving frustrations, anxieties, and revolts against authority. Universities and colleges should establish "chairs for the future and human crises"[5] that will canalize students' energy into proper action-oriented inquiry.

The collaboration between action and theory is urgent in our contemporary crises. Whyte aptly suggests that "presidents of universities should require of their heads of departments a statement of the direct or indirect relevance of their subject to the human situation today."[6] Inquiry makes a great service to men and women when it inquires into alternatives of human life and possibilities of human promise by carrying the thoughts and research of the campus directly to the heart of the human community.

Professors should serve as an ethical center for student activities, whether they are academic or political. They should be a vital agent directing their students through the adequate understanding of students' needs, hopes, and frustrations, instead of creating a monolithic, authoritarian setup for various types of students.

A meaningful dialogue should be created between administration and students, and between professors and students. The unilateral monologue practiced by administrators and professors should be converted to bilateral participation and dialogue so that students may engage in meaningful interplay with them through the implementation of effective communication channels.

As Whyte, Bertrand Russell, and other thinkers asserted, it is a pressing task of sciences and human struggles to identify a "formative process" toward a unitary, global order of human community. The effort to achieve this goal anticipates the development of what Whyte called the concepts of "unitary man" and "global thought. Polarization is most dangerous to the fulfillment of these concepts. Thus, it also is dangerous to separate completely political from academic commitments since they are internal ingredients of unitary man. To develop a formative process and a unitary order, men and women should foster social and political sensitivity and commitments. Here free inquiry and forum, if meaningful at all, must play a significant role to work out effective methodology for political participation in the community embracing academic microcommunities.

The university will become a creative force if explosive energy of intellectual youth is canalized into constructive, responsible, and democratic forms by encouraging it to find effective channels of communication and by authentic and enthusiastic responses of university authorities to it.

NOTES

1. John Dewey, "Educational and Social Change," *Social Frontier* (May 1936): 238.

2. *New York Times,* June 5, 1968.

3. Ibid.

4. Lancelot Whyte, *The Next Development in Man* (New York: Holt, 1948), pp. 276–77.

5. This was suggested in Julian Huxley, *The Human Crisis* (Seattle: University of Washington Press, 1963).

6. Lancelot Whyte, "The End of the Age of Separatism," *Saturday Review*, May 18, 1968, p. 65.

12

A DEFENSE OF THE NEUTRAL UNIVERSITY

Robert L. Simon

I n times of major social controversy, should colleges and universities function as political agents on behalf of particular causes? Although this issue is often forgotten in times of political quiescence, it rises to the surface again during times of political conflict. Protests against the Vietnam War, as well as concern in the 1980s over divestment of university investments in corporations doing business in South Africa, have generated criticism of the view that universities should be politically neutral. Can academic institutions justifiably remain silent in the face of such events as genocide, the waging of unjust wars, systematic and pervasive racial discrimination, political oppression, and world hunger? On the other hand, if a university or college becomes a partisan political agent, can it fulfill other functions, including the academic ones that are its very reason for being? Are there moral reasons, based on academic functions, for the university to refrain from partisan political action?

Questions such as these have at least two important characteristics. First, they are normative in that they concern the principles or norms that *ought* to guide the behavior of institutions of higher learning in the political arena. Their focus is not what the behavior of such institutions is but what it should be. Second, they concern the behavior of colleges and universities as *institutions*, not the behavior of the individuals, such as faculty members and students, who may attend or be employed there.

Consider the claim that colleges and universities as institutions should be politically neutral. Before examining substantive arguments for and against it, it is important to realize that much of the controversy over the neutrality thesis is conceptual rather than moral. That is, what looks like heated moral disagreement over whether universities should be neutral will often, upon analysis, rest on divergent conceptions of the nature of neutrality itself. If different parties to an argument mean different things by neutrality, they may not be disagreeing about the same issue in the first place. It is important not to assume that the meaning of *neutrality* is clear or understood the same by all of us, in considering the issue with which I will begin: whether it is even possible for colleges and universities to be neutral.

SKEPTICISM AND THE CONCEPT OF NEUTRALITY

Many critics of the ideal of a politically neutral university would deny that the central issue at stake is whether colleges and universities *should* be politically neutral. On their view, since it makes sense to say universities ought to act a certain way only if they can act in that way, the fundamental issue is whether neutrality is even possible. In the view of many, it is not. Thus, Robert Paul Wolff argues in an acute critique of the university from the point of view of radicalism of the 1960s that

> as a prescription for institutional behavior, the doctrine of value neutrality suffers from the worst disability which can afflict a norm: what it prescribes is not wrong; it is impossible. A large university in America simply cannot adopt a value-neutral stance, either externally or internally, no matter how hard it tries.[1]

However, we need to be careful before accepting such a conclusion too quickly. Perhaps, as John Searle has suggested, skeptics about the very possibility of neutrality are like certain sorts of epistemological skeptics who question whether knowledge is possible. The kind of skeptic Searle has in mind simply defines knowledge in such a way that it can never be attained.[2] But of course, just because knowledge in the skeptic's sense is unattainable, it does not follow that knowledge in some other significant sense is unattainable as well. Similarly, perhaps the skeptic can show that neutrality, conceived in some particular way, is impossible. It does not follow, however, that neutrality conceived in some other way is necessarily impossible or worthless.

For example, one popular argument is that no university can be value neutral, because the principle that the university *ought* to be value neutral is itself a normative claim that expresses a value. A second argument points out that a university by its very nature is committed to values such as knowledge, truth, and rational discourse.

Such arguments do show that no university can be strictly value free. They bring out the salutary point that the commitment to be neutral, like other value commitments, requires a rational defense. However, they undermine the ideal of the politically neutral university only if political neutrality and total value freedom are equivalent. But as we will see, there are some significant senses of value neutrality that are not equivalent to total value freedom. Hence, even if the university cannot (and should not) be value free, that is irrelevant to the evaluation of at least some significant versions of the neutrality thesis.

Other skeptics point out that the university's action (or inaction) must have political consequences. Therefore, they conclude that neutrality is impossible, for on their view, even the failure to take a stand on significant issues has causal implications. Therefore, no matter what the university does, it has political consequences. At the very least, the status quo is left unchanged. As Wolff argues in *The Ideal of the University,*

> Omissions are frequently even more significant politically than commissions in American politics, for those in positions of decision usually rule by default rather than by consent. Hence, acquiescence in governmental acts, under the guise of impartiality, actually strengthens the established forces and makes successful opposition all the harder.[3]

The skeptic makes a number of strong points here. Clearly, in at least some contexts, the failure to act can be of moral significance and require moral justification. Thus, if I learn that a killer will attempt to murder you at a particular place and time, and I can warn you at little cost to myself, my failure to do so is morally culpable.

However, from my moral responsibility for acts of omission as well as acts of commission, it does not follow that I automatically fail to be neutral. All that follows is that neutrality requires a defense, not that it is a myth.

This is an important point and is perhaps best illustrated by the constitutional prohibition in the United States against an establishment of religion. This clause requires at least that the government be neutral toward particular religions and is minimally satisfied if the government does nothing to favor one religion over another. Of course, the decision to be neutral in such a way requires a moral defense. It is not necessarily value free. Nevertheless, the government is neutral toward particular religions.

The skeptic might protest that by not actively favoring a minority religion, the government is covertly preserving the status quo and so is not really neutral after all. But all the situation amounts to is that the government is leaving things as they otherwise would be. It is keeping its nose out of religion. That is just what proponents of governmental neutrality toward religion *mean* by governmental neutrality. So the skeptic's legitimate point that the decision to be neutral requires a moral justification does not establish that neutrality is a myth but only that neutrality itself is hardly uncontroversial or value free.

Let us consider further the logic of "you are either with us or against us." The argument, when exposed to the light of day, seems to go as follows:

1. Failure to actually support me has the consequence of making my opponents' position better off than it would have been had you supported me.
2. Hence, your failure to support me has the consequence of making my opponents better off.
3. Hence, you have actually supported my opponents.
4. Clearly, you are not neutral but rather are my opponent as well.

One point worth considering is that premise 1 is not more plausible than position 1:

1'. Failure to support my opponents has the consequence of making my position better off than it would have been had you supported them.

By substituting 1' for 1 and then making the same inferences, one can with equal plausibility conclude that you have chosen my side rather than that of my opponents. It is of course true that failure to take a stand deprives one side of an issue of support. But the point is that it does so as well for the other side! That is exactly why it is neutral, not in the sense of being consequence free but in the sense of being nonpartisan, of not interfering on behalf of any one religion.

The fallacy involved in the assertion that "you are either with me or against me" is that it can be said by *either side* to third parties. The implications are logically devastating. Both sides could regard the third party as an opponent (since if it is not with us it is against us) or, with equal plausibility, as an ally (since it is not for our opponent, it must be with us). Surely, any formula that implies such blatant contradictions must be rejected as logically incoherent.

However, if, in spite of this point, the skeptic still wants to stipulate that the failure to actively support one side aids the other, then it follows trivially (by definition) that *any* decision, including the decision not to make a decision, has political consequences and is not neutral. Let us call an act or policy that has no effect, from either action or inaction, on a political controversy consequentially neutral. Given the skeptic's assumptions, no agent can be consequentially neutral. However, even if we ignore the logical incoherence already pointed out, the skeptic's victory is a hollow one. Even if consequential neutrality is unattainable, many other kinds of neutrality may be quite feasible. Thus, even if the government fails to be consequentially neutral with respect to religion, it can be neutral in some other sense. For example, it can provide no active support for any particular religion over any other, and it may be important that it does not. Similarly, although it is doubtful if a university can avoid performing any act that would have political consequences—a conceptual impossibility once we define failure to aid one side as aiding the other—the university can still avoid becoming a partisan on many issues. It can also avoid acting with political motive or intent.

Accordingly, it is doubtful if the skeptical arguments I have considered show that neutrality is impossible. Moreover, even if they do show that some kinds of neutrality, such as absolute value freedom or consequential neutrality, are impossible, they leave open whether other significant forms of neutrality are possible. Skeptical arguments do remind us that the decision to be neutral is itself a morally significant one for which the agent may be held morally responsible. Whether or not we ought to be neutral is itself an ethical issue. Be that as it may, the skeptic's premises that universities cannot be value free, that the stance of neutrality itself is value laden, and that inaction as well as action has political consequences, do not imply that all kinds of neutrality are conceptually incoherent or logically beyond our grasp.

NEUTRALITY AND PROFESSORIAL ETHICS

I recently came across an article on the teaching of ethics in which a philosophy professor declared that his goal as a teacher was to "save students from their parents."[4] I would have agreed with that statement when I started my teaching career, but as my children grew I started to have doubts. Now that my eldest son has just entered college, I'm sure it is false.

Be that as it may, the author's claim raises a number of important general issues. Should a professor in an ethics course attempt to get students to question their own values? Should the professor go further and aim at having the students reject a particular set of traditional norms? May such a professor permissibly aim at having students adopt the specific values deemed most acceptable by the instructor? Is there any sense in which the individual instructor in the college classroom should be neutral with respect to ethical or political values?

Let me begin by considering two admittedly extreme responses to this question. According to the first, which we can call the model of partisanship, the professor should try, using whatever means of persuasion will prove most effective, to get students to adopt the values the instructor thinks are most important.

Clearly, this model will have few if any adherents. It has little if anything to do with education but in effect views the professor as someone whose role it is to indoctrinate students. Students are not treated as persons in their own right but as things to be manipulated by whatever persuasive techniques work best. In effect, the veneer of education is employed to cloak what is really going on, namely, indoctrination of the less powerful by the more powerful. Indeed, using one's status as a professor to impose one's values on students through nonrational means is a form of harassment, ethically on par with sexual harassment, in which a person in a position of power uses it to coerce or to manipulate others.

If there are adherents of the extreme partisan view, they may retort that the alternative is nonexistent, since there really are no rules of rational inquiry that are ideologically neutral. According to this retort, even to adopt ground rules of inquiry is a political act that has covert ideological implications. Now, in a trivial sense, this reply is correct, if only because, as we have seen, rationality is itself a value. Moreover, the decision to adopt rational procedures may have as a consequence that certain political positions receive more support than others, since they appear more reasonable to rational investigators. It does not follow, however, that the rules fail to be neutral in a significant sense; they may have intellectual warrant or standing apart from the political preferences of those who hold them.

Thus, if the model of partisanship is to be defended in public discourse and not just imposed upon us by manipulative techniques or coercion, its adherents themselves must appeal to rules of rational inquiry. If no such rules had any warrant or justification, apart from the political preferences of those who employ them, the whole institution of public rational discourse and critical inquiry would be an illusion. Not only would the university itself be a fraud, but no partisan advocate of any position could show it to be more justified than any other. The very process of justification would be nothing more than a manifestation of the very political commitment to be justified. This is a very high price to be paid for the model of partisanship. Indeed, since the model implies that its advocates can give us no good reason for accepting it, since "good reasons" themselves are a fiction, we cannot both accept the model and conduct a rational inquiry into the nature of neutrality. Accordingly, the model of partisanship, at least in its extreme form, must be rejected by all those committed to the university as a center of rational inquiry and critical discussion.

This point does not necessarily presuppose that totally value-free or uncontroversial principles of inquiry and discussion can be justified. It does imply, rather, that the instructor is committed to employing some standards of inquiry and evaluation that are regarded as at least provisionally warranted, and not simply because their use supports the ideology or partisan value commitments of the user. Such warrant may be broadly pragmatic, and far from value free, but it must constitute an independent test of the positions the user attempts to justify within inquiry itself. Thus, even the Rawlsian method of reflective equilibrium, which requires us to test our considered judgments of particular cases against our principles so as to promote overall systematic coherence in our moral conceptual scheme, allows the possibility that some of our most cherished beliefs may be undermined by the weight of overall systematic considerations with which they might clash.[5]

Consider now the second model of professorial ethics, which I can call the model of absolute neutrality. According to this model, the professor must be absolutely value neutral in the classroom. The instructor's job, on this view, is just to present information, not to evaluate it. Where there is controversy in a discipline, different positions are to be explained, but the professor is not to take a stand on which is most plausible. While it might be permissible for the professor to take the position of an advocate of each important viewpoint as it is presented to the student, no special preference or weight is to be given for the viewpoint the professor favors. Thereby, respect is shown for the autonomy of students, since no one attempts to impose a position upon them, and instructors refrain from using their superior knowledge or the prestige of their position to influence students by nonrational means.

While the respect for individual autonomy underlying the model of absolute neutrality is admirable, it is far from clear that the model itself is even coherent. Surely an instructor *must* make at least some value judgments, for example, judgments about what material ought to be included in the course, what controversies are worth exploring, and what arguments are significant enough to explore in depth. Moreover, the instructor's commitment to respecting the autonomy of students is itself a fundamental moral value.

Accordingly, neither the model of neutrality nor that of partisanship is fully acceptable, at least in their extreme forms. Of course, the extreme versions of each model may be modified to escape the sort of objections I have considered. For example, an advocate of neutrality might attempt to distinguish between *professional* value judgments, such as judgments about the relative importance of various issues for the discipline, which cannot be avoided by the instructor, and personal *moral or political* value judgments, which can be avoided. An advocate of partisanship might acknowledge rational constraints on discourse but maintain that instructors should defend their moral and political convictions within the universe of critical discourse demarcated by such criteria of rationality.

Rather than pursue questions raised by various modifications of the different models, the important point for my purpose is that both kinds of modifications limit the *partisanship* of the instructor. Both presuppose that the instructor is a scholar first and a partisan second. More precisely, partisanship is governed by rules of scholarship and critical inquiry. Thus, on the revised model of neutrality, it is acknowledged that value judgments must be made, but they are to be based on the professional judgment of the scholar and presumably can be defended by appeal to commonly accepted professional standards. Similarly, advocates of a modified model of partisanship concede that advocacy must be limited by such canons of critical inquiry as respect for the evidence, rules of logical argumentation, openness to objection, and the like. Students are to be persuaded by rational discourse or not persuaded at all. Manipulation by persuasive but nonrational techniques is prohibited.

There is a sense, then, in which proponents of both models should concede that the professor is to be *neutral.* Proponents of both models should acknowledge that classroom discussion must take place within a framework of rules of critical inquiry. Adherence to those rules is neutral in the sense that adherence by itself does not dictate the substantive position that emerges. On the contrary, substantive positions that prove unsatisfactory within such a framework must either be revised or replaced when a more satisfactory competitor is available.

Let us call this kind of neutrality *critical neutrality* because it requires adherence to rules of critical inquiry that do not by themselves determine which substantive positions will prove most satisfactory within the realm of inquiry they govern. Such rules need not themselves be value free or neutral in any other sense. They are neutral only in the sense that they constitute a court of appeal independent of the personal preferences of the investigators.

Adherence to critical neutrality does not require neutrality in any of the senses that the skeptic has found incoherent. In particular, it does not require value freedom. Neither does it require consequential neutrality. On the contrary, adherence to canons of critical neutrality may have profound effects on students and on other professionals working in the discipline. Neither does it require that the teacher avoid advocacy of substantive positions. As long as advocacy is carried out within the critical framework, it may well be educationally desirable, so long as students are sufficiently mature and possess sufficient critical tools to be able to form reasonably independent judgments of their own.

Before turning to this last constraint, consider whether critical neutrality really is possible. If possible, is it desirable? Whether critical neutrality is possible depends upon whether rules of critical inquiry exist for various disciplines independently of internal substantive positions as specified. This is not the place to argue that such rules do exist. However, it certainly is possible that they do. More important, their existence seems to be a presupposition of critical inquiry itself. Indeed, it is hard to see how the skeptic could rationally maintain that there are no such rules without implicitly appealing to them in the course of the argument. Thus, at the very least, the burden of proof is on the skeptic why skepticism about critical neutrality is not itself incoherent, since it undermines the very framework within which justification takes place.

Assuming, then, that critical neutrality is possible, I can ask if it is also desirable. In fact, two sorts of arguments can be given for showing not only that critical neutrality is desirable but that adherence to the framework of critical neutrality is morally required for instructors in higher education.

The first is based on rights or entitlements generated by the autonomy of students and colleagues. As autonomous agents, such individuals are wronged if they are manipulated by the intentional presentation of misinformation or by persuasive use of nonrational emotive techniques designed to distort inquiry so as promote acceptance of the instructor's own views. In such a case, the offending instructor is subject to the same criticism as one who misuses professorial authority or prestige to secure sexual favors from students. In each case, power is being wrongly used to manipulate others to one's own advantage, thereby limiting the other's possibilities for autonomous choice.

Second, violation of critical neutrality is a violation of the canons of inquiry that govern the central educational function of the college or university. Respect for critical inquiry can be seen as intrinsically valuable, for an atmosphere where different points of view can be freely debated and examined best promotes free and informed choice by us all. Even if there are extreme cases in which it seems defensible to violate critical neutrality, general conformity surely is desirable. Moreover, given the moral weight of the reasons supporting conformity, only countervailing moral considerations of the weightiest kind could justify overriding the ethics of critical inquiry in specific cases.

We can conclude, then, that individual instructors should be committed neither to the extreme model of neutrality nor to the extreme model of partisanship. Rather, regardless of their other values or positions, they should be committed to a general policy of adherence to the ethics of critical inquiry. Because of the especially significant values underlying such an ethic, it can be outweighed only when even more significant considerations count in favor of making an exception.

NEUTRALITY AND THE UNIVERSITY

Although the university cannot be value neutral in the sense of being totally value free, my discussion so far suggests that there may be other senses of neutrality worth considering. In particular, it can be argued that just as the individual instructor is obligated to respect the rules and canons of rational inquiry in the classroom, so the university is morally required to maintain an institutional climate in which such rules govern discourse and inquiry. If so, it can be argued that the university as an institution must be neutral in a sense similar to the way an umpire in baseball must be neutral. Just as the umpire has an ethical obligation to be a neutral arbiter rather than a partisan of one team or another, the university also may have an ethical obligation not to become just another partisan with an interest in defeating opponents.

Perhaps, then, the kind of neutrality appropriate for colleges and universities may be *institutional critical neutrality*, namely, adherence to the values, rules, and principles of critical inquiry and discussion regardless of which substantive positions are thereby advanced.

Clearly, institutional critical neutrality is not an uncontroversial notion. To begin with, critics may argue that to support rules of rational discourse is itself to take a substantive position in opposition to opponents of rationality or adherents of faith over reason. But since proponents of institutional critical neutrality need not claim that the university can or should be value neutral, the objection in this form need not bother them. Their point is not that neutrality requires total suspension of values. On the contrary, as we have seen, institutional critical neutrality is itself a value posture that requires an ethical defense. What such neutrality requires is not total value freedom but rather adherence to and protection of those values and norms that are constituents of critical inquiry and promotion of conditions under which critical inquiry can flourish.

A more troublesome form of the objection is the denial that there is any neutral set of rules or norms constitutive of critical inquiry, Rather, critical inquiry itself is arguably an essentially contested concept, conceived of in different ways by proponents of different ideological positions.[6] Thus, the kind of norms of critical inquiry supported by a Marxist or a pragmatist may differ from those favored by an ethical emotivist, who relies on the epistemology of classical empiricism. Indeed, it is at least arguable that the values we hold influence the kind of norms of critical inquiry we think most warranted. Thus, a pragmatist might maintain that evaluation of scientific theories, and hence of what count as facts, properly takes into account value-laden judgments concerning the overall satisfactoriness of the theory and its rivals.[7] If so, there may be no favored conception of "the canons" of critical inquiry that is value free.

While these points surely have force, it is far from clear that institutional critical neutrality requires the university to take a stand on such controversial epistemological questions. Rather, the commitment is to an institution within which such controversies can be pursued, where positions are defended by argument rather than force and debate is open to those qualified to participate in it. This commitment does not require the university to decide between, say, Quine and Popper, but only to ensure that the parties to the debate have a fair opportunity to present their arguments.

But aren't proponents of different ideological views all too likely to disagree over what counts as a fair opportunity to participate in debate? When debate is open or closed and what counts as defending a position by reason can be equally controversial. Neutral accounts of such notions, we may be told, are not to be found.

Important disputes can arise over the nature of free inquiry, but they arguably concern borderline cases. Arguably, there is a common core of principles that all constituents of a university community must accept, including the commitment to consider evidence, even evidence against one's own position, on its merits and the rejection of coercion as a means of silencing opposition. Without allegiance to these core elements of rational inquiry, no rational debate seems possible to begin with.

However, even if we ignore the case for core elements of rational inquiry, it doesn't necessarily follow that institutional critical neutrality is undermined. Even if the nature of critical inquiry is itself inherently controversial, it doesn't follow that the values at stake in debate among various conceptions of critical inquiry are political values, let alone the same political values at stake in currently controversial issues. Thus, canons of critical inquiry are still neutral in the sense that the position one takes in epistemological debate need not determine or be determined by one's partisan political stance. For example, parties who disagree on divestment can still agree that different sides should be heard in debate on each side of the issue. Similarly, commitment to divestment does not necessarily imply commitment to acceptance of the legitimacy of specific forms of protest against universities that do not divest. Thus, even if there are no inherently uncontroversial principles of critical inquiry, it still may be the case that for every dispute, there are some higher-order principles of inquiry accepted by all sides.[8]

But doesn't the university itself restrict debate in favor of already established positions? Aren't proponents of many "eccentric" epistemological positions excluded from the university community? Thus, there are no departments of astrology on campus, nor is creationism often defended, let alone given equal footing with evolutionary biology.

Clearly, not all epistemological positions or worldviews are represented in the university. But it does not follow that institutional critical neutrality is a fraud. To see why, consider again the constitutional requirement that prohibits the establishment of religion in America. As interpreted by the courts, the establishment clause does not require government hostility toward religion. Rather, it requires the separation of religion from public life and prohibits the active government support of one religion over others.

Now it would be absurd to argue that neutrality has been violated simply because some religions have no adherents. If commitment to particular religions is based on the decisions of the citizens themselves, rather than government intervention, neutrality is preserved. The point of neutrality is not to ensure that every religion has some supporters but rather to ensure that government policy does not officially sanction some religions and suppress others.

A related point can be made about institutional critical neutrality in the university. Just as individual citizens themselves have the right to make their own religious commitments, so scholars have the right (and obligation) to determine what views to explore and defend within their areas of professional competency. If such scholars, as a result of their inquiries, determine that some views are not worth examining, or are different in kind from those that can be examined within critical inquiry, then that decision does not violate the institution's neutrality. Rather, a major purpose served by institutional critical neutrality is to promote an atmosphere in which various hypotheses can be evaluated, whether they are metahypotheses about the rules for critical inquiry or first-order hypotheses within particular disciplines.

It is important to keep in mind here the distinction between limitations on debate *within* a field and limitations on metadebate *about* the limitations within a particular field.[9] Thus, no respectable scientific department would offer courses in astrology, but debate on whether there is a justifiable difference between science and astrology might take place in a course on philosophy of science. Thus, I would suggest that limits on debate within the university, and on views that may be represented, are justified when (1) the limitations are supportable by appeal to the publicly accessible results of critical inquiry; (2) the limitations are proportional in force to the degree of support in their favor; and (3) the limitations are debatable in metainquiry about the discipline in question. These conditions allow inquirers to concentrate on areas of examination they consider significant, while containing checks against dogmatism and intolerance.

My discussion suggests that institutional critical neutrality is ultimately grounded on the values of personal autonomy and critical investigation. Such a justification of neutrality can now be examined more closely.

IS THE NEUTRAL UNIVERSITY DESIRABLE?

Perhaps enough has been said to show that common skeptical arguments against the very possibility of a neutral university face serious problems. At the very least, the burden of proof is on the skeptic either to show how the objections can be avoided or to construct new skeptical arguments.

However, to say that neutrality is possible is one thing; to show that it also is morally defensible is another. Perhaps a beginning has been made in that direction by suggesting a connection between institutional critical neutrality and respect for the autonomy of individual members of the university community. The key idea here is that if the university becomes a political agent, individual members of the university community will be in a less favorable position to make decisions on the basis of the very kind of critical inquiry it is the university's first obligation to protect.

Although no knock-down proof of this thesis can be supplied here, perhaps the following considerations are sufficient to create a presumptive case in favor of the importance of institutional critical neutrality. As we will see, the argument for it is multifaceted. A variety of factors each lends some weight to the justification of neutrality. The argument gains force as the weight of the different factors is aggregated.

To begin with, when the university takes a partisan political stand in an area outside the sphere of values bound up with critical inquiry, it at least implicitly lends its authority, prestige, and power to a particular side. The university then becomes vulnerable to conflicts of interest between its duty to maintain the framework of political inquiry and its new political obligations. For example, if the university *qua* takes the position that aid to the Nicaraguan Contras is immoral and should not be supported, what policy implications follow for issuing invitations to speakers who support the Contras, appointing professors who are sympathetic to the Contras, donating funds to groups opposing the Contras, reacting to pro-Contra demonstrations, and the like? While it may be possible for the university to simply take a stand, yet take no other action, it is likely that if the stand is genuine, the very act of taking it may have negative implications for critical inquiry. Indeed, the same argument supporting the taking of a stand is also likely to support more direct and forceful action in favor of political goals as well.

Even if the university is still willing to appoint instructors who dissent from its political stands, to invite speakers representing a diversity of views, and so on, is it as likely that such people will be attracted to an institution where their views have been officially rejected, perhaps even designated as immoral, or at least placed in an initially subordinate position? Even if some are attracted or remain, they have been labeled as dissenters from an official position and must argue under an imposed handicap that arises not from consideration or evaluation of evidence but from a political act by the institution that employs them. Loss of neutrality may result in the emergence of the partisan university, which stands for a set of political and ideological principles and is far too intellectually homogeneous as a result. The diversity so essential for critical inquiry would be absent or, at best, be at serious risk.

Moreover, once the university is identified in the broader society as a (perhaps powerful) political agent, it can expect to be on the receiving as well as the giving end of political battles. The privileges and immunities extended to it because of its nonpartisan character surely are likely to come under fire. Why should opponents of the university's political stance allow it tax exemptions because of its educational status when more and more of its resources and energies are devoted to support of political positions contrary to their own? Why not treat it like any other political opponent instead? Why not try to weaken it? And as still more of the university's resources are devoted to fighting off such attacks, greater conflict with the needs of and support for critical inquiry can be expected.

Most important, in the partisan university would each individual be as free as we would wish to pursue inquiry where it led, to dissent from prevailing views, to follow independent paths? If not, individuals themselves would have less of an opportunity to develop autonomously, and critical inquiry itself would be harmed. All of us would be impoverished in the same way we are impoverished whenever any view becomes orthodox not because of its merits as established in open inquiry but because it has been artificially protected from the challenges such inquiry generates.

But hasn't it already been conceded that at the individual level, the classroom instructor under certain conditions may argue for substantive positions without undermining the autonomy of students? Why doesn't a similar conclusion follow about the taking of substantive political stands by the university itself?

This objection would be decisive if the roles of the individual teacher and the college or university were logically parallel. However, consider whether the two are relevantly different. Classroom instructors are individuals whose primary professional obligation is to engage in inquiry and disseminate the results. The scholar's findings, in other words, should reflect judicious evaluation of evidence, and evaluation that can be criticized in appropriate professional and public forums. The university, however, were it to take overt political stands, is likely to do so not as a result of evaluation of evidence but because of compromise or consensus among its various factions. It follows, then, that the university's taking of a political stance is not a contribution to inquiry in the same way as is the taking of a substantive position by a trained scholar.

More important, the individual does not play the same institutional role as the university with respect to critical inquiry. The latter, but not the former, is the institutional protector of the values essential to critical inquiry. For the very institution designed to umpire the critical process also to become a player within the process raises the problems I have already discussed. Accordingly, it is at best far from clear whether my earlier analysis of the right and obligations of the individual instructor can be applied without modification to the institution as well. To assume the two are parallel is as dangerous as assuming that because individuals may adopt particular religious perspectives, the state may permissibly do so as well.

To summarize, for the university to become a partisan political agent would create inherent conflicts of interest between different kinds of goals. Thus, the prestige and power of the university would be placed on one side of various political debates; yet the university would also have the obligation to encourage independent thinking on these issues and not to load the dice in favor of particular positions in advance of inquiry. Not only would decisions favoring particular sides to political conflicts appear biased, they might actually be biased. The very institution charged with the responsibility of protecting the values of open, rational inquiry becomes committed to a second set of values, which, on occasion, may call for subverting open, rational inquiry or at least diverting substantial attention (and sometimes resources) from it. It would be as if the state were held to be the partisan of particular religious perspective and, at one and the same time, charged with protecting religious freedom and tolerance. Because the potential for conflict of interest is so great and the danger to religious liberty so serious, we require state neutrality toward religion. Is the case for university neutrality any different?

I do not mean to say that universities generally *are* neutral or that they generally *do* uphold the canons of critical inquiry. Rather, violations of neutrality may occur, but their existence does not refute the neutrality thesis. Violations of institutional critical neutrality are grounds for criticism in the same of neutrality, not reasons for rejecting neutrality itself.

My discussion suggests, then, that an important case can be made for institutional critical neutrality. That is, just as state neutrality toward religion is a significant protection for the freedom of individuals to make their own religious choices, so institutional critical neutrality provides similar protection for individuals to make their own choices within critical inquiry. The case parallels that for state neutrality toward religion. If neutrality in one area is justifiable, so too is a similar kind of neutrality in the other.

However, adherence to institutional critical neutrality may have its limits. Critics of neutrality may point to hard cases in which it is far from clear not only that colleges and universities are or have been neutral but also that they *should* be neutral to begin with.

HARD CASES FOR THE NEUTRALITY THESIS

One set of hard cases concerns university regulation of student behavior. The claim here is that the university enforces a set of socially approved values, or values deemed desirable by the university itself, which imply the taking of substantive moral positions. Although the passing of *in loco parentis* may have reduced the degree to which institutions of higher learning regulate student social life, some core values often are enforced or supported. While these vary from institution to institution, even the most liberal colleges and universities frequently regulate consumption of alcohol and drugs, assign roommates only of the same gender, and in light of the AIDS epidemic, adopt value-laden policies (either by making condoms available or by urging sexual abstinence) on what might otherwise be appropriate sexual behavior.

Consider first whether policies regulating the use of drugs necessarily violate neutrality. Normally, university regulations in such areas follow legal requirements but they may also sometimes reflect nonneutral values about the nature of the good life. However, at least some form of regulation may also be justifiable without such appeal. In particular, since the university's commitment is to rational inquiry, it can promulgate rules designed to protect rational discourse without violation of the requirement of critical neutrality. Drug abuse can undermine critical inquiry either by harming the health of users, generating addiction (which undermines autonomy), or creating a climate hostile to intellectual endeavor. Accordingly, drug and alcohol regulations need not be inconsistent with neutrality but, at least in some forms, can be justified by appeal to the very values central to the university's intellectual mission.

While this kind of argument does have force, it raises serious questions if pushed too far. Can appeal to the need for an intellectually healthy institutional climate be used to silence disturbing views? For example, can offensive speech be regulated on the grounds that it promotes such disharmony within the community that inquiry itself is threatened? What if the expression of some views is so offensive to minority groups that they feel harassed and even threatened? Should the expression of the offending viewpoints be forbidden on the grounds of preserving the kind of diverse community in which intellectual inquiry is best carried on? Or should free expression carry the day, since, without it, opinions that any sufficiently powerful or vocal group finds offensive will be excluded a priori from rational debate and discussion.

The problem arises because institutional critical neutrality encompasses a cluster of related values that are normally mutually reinforcing but can conflict in unusual circumstances. Thus, critical inquiry requires free and open debate but also requires a diverse community so that issues can be examined from a variety of perspectives. The problem is that in pursuing one of these values, we may sometimes be faced with hard choices about limiting pursuit of the others. Free and open debate, for example, may permit the expression of opinion that some groups find intimidating and may lead to their withdrawal from the university community.[10]

While I doubt if there are any easy formulas for reconciling such conflicts, two general points at least deserve consideration. The first is that the possible conflict of values at issue does not undermine the case for university neutrality, because the conflict is not between neutrality and some other value, such as partisanship, but rather over how neutrality itself is to be understood. In the kind of example I have cited, both open debate and a diverse community are essential for significant critical discussion; the issue is a conflict between two aspects of institutional critical neutrality itself.

Second, while there may be cases in which free speech should be limited in the name of preserving community, it is plausible to think that the burden of proof should be on those who would set limits in particular cases. Surely, when one enters the university, one is in effect consenting to engage in that activity for which the university exists: critical investigation of difficult and significant questions. It is unlikely that many people can seriously engage in such an activity without sometimes encountering views that offend them or that they find threatening. In a sense, the risk of being offended is one we expect members of the university community to bear, just as the risk of being hit by an errant shot is one golfers assume when they enter the golf course. Both are part of the normal context of the activity in question. Therefore, a special case must be made if inquiry is to be silenced on the grounds of potential disruption of the intellectual community. The speech in question must not be merely offensive to some group or individuals. It must amount to a threat or a form of harassment that undermines the rights of the victims to engage in inquiry as full members of the university community.

Keeping these points in mind, consider university regulations that bear on sexual morality. They also raise difficulties for the neutrality thesis, but perhaps they can be handled in ways already suggested. For example, a university might react to the threat of AIDS in different ways. Suppose it were argued that any response will reflect a particular view of sexual morality and so will fail to be neutral. Thus, if the university urges sexual abstinence as the first line of defense, it seems to be reflecting one moral perspective, whereas if it distributes condoms, it seems to be reflecting quite another. Either way, the critic will argue, the university has taken a partisan stand on a controversial moral and political issue.

Remember, however, that neutrality as defended here is not value free. It is not the refusal to endorse any set of values whatsoever. Rather, institutional critical neutrality encompasses a particular set of values, namely, those necessary for the university to carry out its mission as a center of critical inquiry and discussion. With this proviso in mind, a neutral policy does seem possible. That is, the university should inform students of alternatives, indicating that sexual abstinence clearly will enable one to avoid AIDS but adding that if individuals choose not be sexually abstinent, the use of condoms makes sex considerably safer than would otherwise be the case. Making condoms actually available can be justified along lines similar to those justifying policies on drugs and alcohol: lowering risk to other members of the university community and promoting a climate in which intellectual inquiry can flourish.

By adopting such a policy, the university shows respect for the rationality and autonomy of its students, faculty, and staff. There is no one official position that the institution endorses. Rather, it makes information available and supports individuals in the choices they themselves make.

But isn't this stance itself value laden, inconsistent with other ethical positions? In particular, doesn't it rest on a particular conception of the good that is widely accepted within what might broadly be called the Western liberal individualist tradition but that would be rejected from many alternative political and social perspectives? In particular, hasn't the university embraced as a normative ideal the conception of the individual as rational and autonomous? The good life is identified as the life of the rational autonomous individual. While this may be a defensible conception of the good, the critic win argue that it is hardly a neutral one.[11]

This point has considerable force. Indeed, I believe it should be accepted, once its implications are properly understood. That is, although this point has force when directed against a certain conception of neutrality—neutrality as value freedom—it does not have force against the conception defended in this essay. If the kind of neutrality proper to the university is not value freedom or even neutrality with respect to the good, then the objection loses force.

My suggestion has been that the kind of neutrality proper to the university is institutional critical neutrality. That is, it is the kind of neutrality presupposed by regard for critical inquiry and rational discussion. Critical inquiry and rational discussion are defensible, in turn, because of their role in the search for truth and in the development of free, autonomous individuals. Moreover, these ultimate values of the university are not merely arbitrary, just one set of culturally bound variables among others. Rather, they are presupposed by *any* attempt to arrive at *justified* or *defensible* answers to problems. For example, anyone who seriously discusses whether the university should be politically neutral attempts to come to an autonomous decision based on truths, or at least justified beliefs. Therefore, the university's mission is presupposed by the very attempt to ask what its mission should be.

Neutrality of the limited kind defended in this essay is far from value free. In fact, it is founded on values so fundamental that they can reasonably be regarded as presuppositions of any further inquiry, including inquiry into the nature of value itself. Hence, they cannot be lightly disregarded by any civilization worthy of the name.

Accordingly, although all counterexamples cannot be discussed here, we have seen that there are strategies available for dealing with some especially difficult cases. Some of the alleged counterexamples will be seen upon analysis not to involve a conflict between neutrality and an overriding value, but to be between two aspects of neutrality itself. Others assume that neutrality requires value freedom, ignoring the point that the university may legitimately enforce values central to its function as a guardian of critical inquiry. Still other conflicts may be resolved without violation of neutrality by presenting autonomous individuals with the options available to them and letting them make their own decisions. Finally, as we have seen in an earlier section, some value judgments may be enforced, subject to expressed limitations, if sufficient support is found within critical inquiry itself (for example, astrology may be excluded from the curriculum). Such strategies may not be adequate to deal with all counterexamples, as we will see in the next section. However, they may at least suggest that genuine counterexamples may be far harder to come by than at first might be thought and that sufficient reason exists for the burden of proof in particular cases to be on opponents of neutrality, not supporters.

The university, however is not only a refuge from society in which critical reflection takes place; it is also an actor or agent in that society as well. In our own time, considerable controversy has arisen over the university's attempts to raise the funds needed for its operation. In particular, does neutrality allow the university to use any efficient means necessary to carry out its mission, regardless of the morality of the means involved? For example, should universities invest in companies doing business in oppressive societies? In particular, does a commitment to university neutrality imply that colleges and universities need not even consider the morality of investing in companies that do business in South Africa, thus, according to critics, indirectly supporting the systematic, pervasive, and oppressive racist system that is dominant there?

DIVESTMENT: A COUNTEREXAMPLE TO NEUTRALITY?

Is a neutral policy with respect to university investments even possible? Isn't investing in a business supporting it? Indeed, don't universities fail to be neutral in investing in businesses and corporations, for by so doing, are they not part and parcel of the Western capitalist system?

Some of these questions raise issues discussed earlier, Clearly, there is a sense in which investment precludes a certain kind of neutrality. Investments have consequences, and these consequences might be politically significant. However, they do not preclude neutrality in all significant senses. Thus, my decision to order a certain textbook for my course might have the consequence of supporting a particular publisher and harming a rival publisher of a competing text, but that need not have been my intent. My intent was only to order the best available text, not to favor one publisher over another. Similarly, a university's intent in investing may not be to favor one regime over another, one corporation over another, or one economic system over another. It may simply be to help carry out the mission of the university as effectively as possible.[12]

But isn't this neutrality of intent merely trivial? After all, if our action has terrible consequences, isn't it simple bad faith to say that we intended to be neutral? In any case, isn't it at least possible that the obligation to refrain from doing evil sometimes overrides the obligation to be neutral?

I think the answer is sometimes yes. However, before turning to such exceptional cases, something needs to be said for a general policy of neutrality of intent in making investments. In particular, consider whether universities would be more justified in following a neutral investment policy, aimed at maximizing financial return, over one in which all major investment decisions were made so as to maximize some moral value—for example, good consequences, social justice, or equality.

There are at least four arguments against the second alternative that are worth considering. First, it is often unclear just what investment will promote the moral value in question. Since university officials (as well as faculty) have no special moral insight into what is the truly moral investment and since the university's own educational function is especially worth supporting, priority should be given to maximizing profit—profit that benefits education.

Second, unless the university makes clear in advance just what its moral values are, it will be using contributions of donors, fees obtained from students, and taxpayers' dollars for reasons that were not knowable at the time the funds were provided. Indeed, donors might be morally opposed to some of the uses (either positive investments in a particular enterprise or diversion of funds away from an enterprise) to which money was put. In a sense, the donors would be used as mere means for implementing the moral sensibilities of others. Such a policy would not only tend to have the effect of drastically lowering support for education, it would wrong individuals whose contributions were obtained under false pretenses.

Third, how is the university to decide which investments are the truly moral ones? Who speaks for the university? Surely, it is not just the majority of the faculty who should make such a decision. At best, it is simply unclear in most cases who has the authority to make moral decisions of the kind in question for the institution.

Finally, and most important, the consequent politicization of the university is all too likely to threaten institutional critical neutrality in the ways outlined earlier. If all or even most investment decisions were made in part on moral grounds, the university would have to take official positions on a large number of significant moral and political issues. Taking such positions not only might undermine support for higher education within the larger society; it would create the kinds of conflicts between educational and political values discussed in section 2.

However, even if there are good reasons for a *general* policy of neutrality of intent in investment policy, there still may be specific exceptions. In some cases, an injustice may be so gross, so uncontroversial in character that all reasonable people recognize it for what it is. Moreover, it may be that for the university to invest in a way that helps perpetuate the injustice or to illegitimately profit from it, is to commit a great wrong.[13] Whereas its purposes may be noble, the university has no more right than any other agent or institution to actually commit gross injustice or to violate the rights of others. For example, if a university in a large urban setting owns property it rents to tenants, it surely has the same obligation as any other landlord to treat its tenants justly and not to exploit them. That is, although the university arguably may not have an obligation to do good, or even to avoid doing *any* evil, however small, it surely has an obligation not to commit gross injustice; especially not to engage or participate in what a colleague has called a moral catastrophe.[14] Moreover, even if investment decisions made for the purpose of avoiding the commission of serious injustice do involve some unfairness to donors, the donors themselves have no right to contribute to promotion of injustice. In such special cases, moral concerns may override neutrality of intent.

Thus, proponents of divestment seem to me to have a sound case when they argue that the university should not be neutral where a moral catastrophe, such as the present oppression of people of color in South Africa, is concerned. On the other hand, it is far from clear to me that opponents of divestment actually appeal, or need to appeal, to neutrality either. As a matter of fact, most colleges and universities that have not fully divested endorse the Sullivan Principles, which sanction investment in companies doing business in South Africa only if those companies meet specific standards of nondiscriminatory treatment of workers. By accepting the Sullivan Principles, which set moral limits on investment policy, institutions have already ceased to be neutral.

The real debate between proponents and opponents of divestment, it seems to me, is not and should not be over neutrality. Rather, it is whether divestment is required to prevent the university from participating in or illegitimately making a profit from gross, systematic, and blatant injustice and oppression. I suggest that both proponents and opponents of divestment should accept this ground rule. Both should acknowledge that divestment is required if otherwise the university would cause, be an agent of, or profit in a morally illegitimate way from moral catastrophe. This principle is neutral with respect to both positions: an opponent of divestment can accept the principle but oppose divestment by rejecting its application to the actual situation of the university.

In fact, the most sensitive and thoughtful opponents of divestment always have argued that the university would be committing an injustice *by divesting*.[15] According to such a view, divesting would lead to withdrawal of American companies from South Africa, which would in turn place greater control of the South African economy in the hands of white South Africans, the very group most resistant to reform and most likely to mistreat black and colored workers. My point is not that such a highly controversial view is correct, for it clearly is debatable on a variety of grounds, but rather to suggest that the real argument in this area is not over neutrality but over what is the truly moral policy. Opponents of divestment do themselves a disservice when they hide behind the banner of neutrality, which I suggest cannot be stretched so far as to cover the actual committing of or participation in gross and blatant injustice and oppression. On the other hand, proponents of divestment may distort the true issue when they speak as if all their critics care about is profits, as if there were no moral concerns that might lead people to disagree in this area.[16] Moreover, they do a great disservice to the university itself when they jump from the premise that neutrality does not shield the university from moral examination of the divestment issue, to the conclusion that neutrality itself is but a sham and illusion.

CONCLUSIONS

What I have tried to show in this essay is that a case can be made for the claim that universities ought to be politically neutral. In order to make this case, however, different conceptions of neutrality need to be distinguished. Not all kinds of neutrality are either possible or defensible. Perhaps enough has been said, however, to show that the skeptical claim that neutrality is impossible rests either on dubious conceptual maneuvers or where successful, rules out only certain conceptions of neutrality but not others.

I have tried to show that one conception, institutional critical neutrality, is both possible and defensible. I have also argued that it supports a general policy of neutrality of intent in investments. Such a policy, as we have seen, need not be absolute or without exception, However, given the arguments in its favor, the burden of proof properly rests on those who want the exception made. Thus, the argument of this essay supports a general policy of neutrality but suggests principles that allow for rare exceptions, of which the case for divestment may well be most prominent.

Much of the case for university neutrality, as we have seen, is *indirect.* The neutral university is as defensible as state neutrality toward religion. Accordingly, if I have pointed to genuine parallels between the two kinds of neutrality, those committed to state neutrality toward religion may find there is more to be said for university neutrality—at least when construed in the limited way suggested here—than they might otherwise have thought.

None of this explication denies that the university fulfills useful social functions and that many of these functions serve the interests of powerful groups in society (although it is also true that much—perhaps most—criticism of existing institutions comes from the university as well).[17] Thus, the consequences of university behavior often have political implications, as does state neutrality toward religion, However, the kind of neutrality defended here is not consequentialist neutrality but institutional critical neutrality, which is morally defensible because of its connection with free inquiry and respect for the autonomy of persons. Moreover, it does not follow because the skills universities impart are socially useful that universities are *conservative,* since those skills may be just as applicable to social criticism (and may even engender it) as to preservation of existing injustice.

In any case, the argument for neutrality should not be confused with a plea for a value-free university. Instead, like state neutrality with respect to religion, for which a parallel case can be made, the kind of neutrality defended here is deeply value laden. It requires respect for individual autonomy and for the values implicit in critical inquiry. Although such neutrality may sometimes be outweighed by competing moral values, it itself rests on moral considerations of great force. Therefore, it should never be overridden lightly. The burden of proof is properly placed on those who want to violate it. Institutional neutrality, then, is not the all-purpose shield that some proponents have used to preclude even the possibility of the moral critique of institutional policy. On the other hand, neither is it the sham that critics have dismissed as conceptually incoherent. Instead, it is an especially important value that we disregard only at our own peril, and at the peril of the intellectual life itself.

My work on this paper was supported by a Hamilton College Faculty Fellowship. I am very grateful for this support. I am also grateful for helpful suggestions for revision made by a reviewer for Temple University Press.

I addressed the topic of the neutral university sixteen years ago in a paper titled "The Concept of a Politically Neutral University," which appeared in Philosophy and Political Action, *eds. Virginia Held, Kai Nielson, and Charles Parsons (New York: Oxford University Press, 1972), pp. 217–33. Although I still think many of the themes of that article are defensible—and try to develop them more fully and defend them here—I hope this paper remedies what I now see as defects of the earlier one.*

NOTES

1. Robert Paul Wolff, *The Ideal of the University* (Boston: Beacon Press, 1969), p. 70.

2. John Searle, *The Campus War: A Sympathetic Look at the University in Agony* (New York: World, 1971), pp. 199–200.

3. Wolff, *Ideal of the University*, p. 71.

4. Richard Mohr, "Teaching as Politics," *Report from the Center for Philosophy and Public Policy* 6 (summer 1986), 8.

5. John Rawls, *A Theory of Justice* (Cambridge: Harvard University Press, 1971), pp. 46–53. For appeal to "wide" reflective equilibrium in favor of a more radical form of egalitarianism than Rawls supports, see Kai Nielson, *Equality and Liberty* (Totowa, N.J.: Rowman and Allanheld, 1985), pp. 13–44

6. Thus, there may be different conceptions of critical inquiry just as there can be different conceptions of justice, equality, or liberty.

7. However, even within pragmatism, "satisfactoriness" need not be construed to include political and moral value judgments. Rather, justification may depend on "systematic virtues," such as coherence and consistency, which need not be at issue in partisan political debates. See, for example, W. V. Quine and J. S. Ullian, *The Web of Belief* (New York: Random House, 1978), pp. 64–82, for an account of scientific justification in terms of the epistemic (but not necessarily political) virtues of systems of thought.

8. If not, it is unclear whether critical inquiry is even possible as a rational activity. That is, if there are no ground rules that different sides of a debate find acceptable, the debate has no rational resolution. If all or even most issues were like that, it is far from clear that an institution devoted to the pursuit of truth and rational inquiry would even be possible. Universities might still exist, but they would perform other functions, e.g., professional training. Accordingly, the belief that there are general ground rules of critical inquiry available for adjudication of particular disputes within disciplines is a presupposition of the institution of the university, as conceived in this paper.

9. I borrow this point from my earlier paper, "The Concept of a Politically Neutral University," p. 231.

10. Alternatively, some forms of affirmative action may be justified, consistent with institutional critical neutrality, as means of promoting needed diversity within the university.

11. I owe this point to discussions with Patrick Neal and to his paper, "A Liberal Theory of the Good?" *Canadian Journal of Philosophy* 17, no. 3 (1987): 567–82.

12. I stated this point in "The Concept of a Politically Neutral University," p. 226, in terms of a distinction between overt and covert neutrality.

13. The question of whether it is wrong to accept profits from injustice is more complex than many parties to the divestment debate may acknowledge. To begin with, a sensitive opponent of divestment would deny that universities that invest in certain corporations doing business in South Africa actually do profit from injustice. For such a person surely would argue that if the corporations treat their employees equally, regardless of race, they are not contributing to injustice but opposing it. Such an argument may be incorrect, but that needs to be shown and not just assumed.

More important, we need to beware of double standards in this area. Just as opponents of divestment are often too quick to hide uncritically behind the banner of neutrality, so too are proponents sometimes too quick to impose on others moral standards that they seem reluctant to apply to themselves. Thus, if it is wrong for the university to profit from injustice in South Africa, is it also equally wrong for individuals? If one's college does not divest, is one morally required to "divest" from it? If a college divests from corporations doing business in South Africa, can it accept gifts from them? If not, can students legitimately accept employment from such companies? What about scholarships, financial aid, or grants offered by such corporations?

Finally, is it wrong or morally prohibited to profit in any way from injustice, however small the profit or however indirectly it is obtained? If so, isn't such wrongdoing virtually unavoidable in a complex, interdependent world? If not, we need to be careful about where we draw the line. It is all too easy to do so in what may be a biased way; the university's profits from injustice are grossly immoral, but the individual benefits we ourselves do not choose to forgo are simply the necessary by-products of living in a complex society.

Because such issues cannot be addressed here, I accept the principle that the university should not profit from injustice in morally illegitimate ways, leaving open which specific ways of profiting from injustice are morally illegitimate.

For a useful discussion of the double standard, from the point of view of a critic of the divestment movement, see Robert L. Payton, "Tainted Money: The Ethics and Rhetoric of Divestment," *Change* 19 (May–June 1987): 55–60.

14. I owe this way of putting the point to Rick Werner.

15. See, for example, Payton, "Tainted Money," esp. p. 58.

16. Thus, even given total moral agreement about the gross immorality of apartheid in South Africa, the morality of divestment as a means for ending apartheid or of divorcing the university from it is a separate issue of significant complexity.

17. For an argument that the university's social functions in our actual society make it an agent of the status quo, see Michael Parenti, *Power and the Powerless* (New York: St. Martin's Press, 1978), pp. 158–63. A proponent of institutional critical neutrality could respond in a variety of ways. For example, if the university's functions compromise institutional critical neutrality, the proponent of neutrality would reject them. Proponents of neutrality also, as we have seen, can consistently reject university commission of serious injustice. On the other hand, it is no more a violation of institutional critical neutrality if schools and colleges reward certain virtues (such as the disposition to complete assignments on time) that are also useful for corporate employees than it is a failure of state neutrality toward religion if some organized religions advocate certain socially useful virtues (such as compassion and altruism).

13

CAN AMERICAN
UNIVERSITIES
BE DEPOLITICIZED?

Henry David Aiken

In his inaugural address a year ago last autumn, Morris Abram, the second president of my own university, Brandeis, called for a general "depoliticizing" of our universities and colleges. Many others, both inside the universities and out, are making similar appeals. The hope, it seems, is for a return to a golden age of higher education when professors professed, and administrators, delighted to leave well enough alone, spent their time passing the hat, balancing budgets, acting as substitute parents, and performing such ceremonial acts as presiding at faculty meetings and commencement exercises. Of course such a golden age is long gone. It hasn't existed at private colleges for generations; at public colleges and universities, many of which evolved out of the old land-grant colleges, it never existed. In fact, another university president (or rather ex-president), James Perkins of Cornell, has argued approvingly that American institutions of higher learning generally have combined in a unique way the three "missions" of teaching, research, and service. By "service," however, Perkins seems originally to have had in mind primarily service to the state and to the national society over which the state presides. In times past, such services have often grudgingly been performed; indeed, faculties and students alike have frequently debated whether they do not compromise the integrity of the American scholar. And even when members of the university have accepted the principle that the college should also include a service station, they have rarely agreed among themselves as to the proper nature or extent of the services to be rendered. But such disagreements, like the services themselves, are inescapably political.

For example, long before the Vietnam War made the ROTC such a bone of contention on our campuses, many academicians, old as well as young, insisted that this conspicuous tie between the academy and the military be severed. Occasionally, moreover, they prevailed, thereby saving their colleges' energies for better ways of showing patriotism. Another example may be mentioned which is more interesting and important. As some of you may recall, it was during the First World War, at Columbia, and during the Second, at Harvard, that programs which now go by the name of General Education were respectively initiated at those distinguished universities where recently there has been so much turmoil. At the outset, the purpose of such programs was undisguisedly political: their function, quite simply, was to awaken the minds of hitherto indifferent or misguided students to the transcendental virtues of our American system and to the wickedness of all systems that oppose it. To be sure, this great awakening should be accomplished in a suitably genteel and roundabout way, by searching out the fountainheads of freedom in the works of such ancient masters as Plato (the greatest of all exponents of the aristocratic ideal who reserved the higher forms of learning for the guardians of his ideal Republic) and Aristotle (the first pragmatist who preferred a mixed polity in which nonetheless some men, being slaves by nature, cannot be allowed to participate since they are unable to grasp the meaning of political obligation). From the beginning, of course, General Education was widely opposed. Some opposed it on the grounds that so obviously politicized an educational venture demeans the university, whose modes of political indoctrination should be less conspicious; others (in their own way perhaps anticipating educationist such as President Abram) opposed it on the ground that any form of politicking on the campus should be excluded since it diverts institutions of higher learning from their proper business, which is advancement and dissemination of learning. Were they consistent, such purists, who do not pause to examine the varieties of human learning, would have to go much further. In America, however, where even purists are pragmatists, few have questioned the prerogatives of established departments of political science and sociology, in which much time and energy are spent in ideological and hence political controversy.

Several lessons may be drawn from this example: one is that politicized activity on the part of the members of the so-called academic community is generally acceptable if it is sufficiently concealed, indirect, learned, and firmly established; it is below the salt only when it becomes open and direct, formally unlearned and boldly innovative. But another and happier lesson may be learned from the example of General Education. For it was through the efforts of highly politicized academic patriots that a great educational movement was launched whose function has been to revive the spirit of what used to be called liberal education in an age of rampant specialism, professionalism, and scientism. The failures of the movement, alas, are all too plain. But in nearly all cases they are owing to the fact that its exponents have been too timid and too concessive, too limited in their demands for educational reform, too conventional in their conception of the forms of education that are necessary for free men in a really free society.

Here it should be emphasized that purists who oppose such existing politically oriented educational programs as the ROTC or General Education are politicized by the very act of opposing them. In fact, the only way a scholar can avoid the trap of politics is by shutting the door to his study, pulling down the shades, and sticking, despite hell and high water, to his own neutral researches and to courses of instruction related exclusively to them. President Abram's presidential address, whether he realized it or not, was a political act, in the same way that the actions of committed anarchists, who yearn to dispense altogether with politics, employ political means to achieve their postpolitical ends. The state, as we have learned, never does its own withering away. But of course the depoliticizers (if "depoliticize" is a word then so is "depoliticizer"), like the anarchists, cannot succeed. History, human nature, not to mention existing versions of the American dream, all conspire against them. In one direction, the Pentagon and the great scientific-technological establishments that are themselves so closely intertwined with government, will continue to find their way into the universities and colleges, in part because they have an insatiable need for the products of the "knowledge factory." In the opposite direction, even the most servile university, in bringing together exceptionally lively and imaginative individuals, also brings into existence what I call a "shadow university" where free men find ways of instructing, and advising one another about the social and political conditions of a more fully human life. In Russia, in Spain, in Czechoslovakia, and in the United States, the university has always served in spite of itself as a breeding ground for the education of political dissenters, reformers, and revolutionists. The only way to disperse such dissidents, and so to prevent them from enlightening one another, would be to disband the universities. But this is precisely what the state and its functionaries, academic and otherwise, cannot afford to do. Hence, since politics, like nature, abhors a vacuum, the educationally absorbing question is not whether the universities and colleges can be depoliticized, but rather what forms of political activity they may properly encourage or tolerate. And it is to this question that we must presently address ourselves.

Still, granted that efforts to depoliticize the academy are, to put the point least offensively, quixotic, it is an instructive exercise in the philosophy of higher education to perform the imaginative experiment of considering what the educational as well as human results would be, were our colleges actually to succeed in eliminating every form of political activity from the academy.

In the first place, liberal education would disappear. For liberal education is intended by definition for free men, and free men, by definition, are political beings, concerned not with their own self-government only, but with the liberation of all their kind from every form of human bondage, including those forms of bondage by which men in societies enslave one another. Clearly, liberal education is committed from the outset of the study of institutions, including the state, and this not merely as they have been and are, but as they ought or ought not to be. In a word, to depoliticize the university would require the exclusion of all normative social and political studies. But it would also entail the abandonment of ethics, since, as Aristotle long ago pointed out, ethics and politics are ultimately inseparable. And since ethics, broadly conceived, is the heartland of philosophy, it would have to exclude philosophy too, or at least those parts of it that are not purely analytical. Neither Aristotle nor Plato—nor, above all, Socrates—could get a job in the depoliticized academy.

Indeed, as we ponder the matter we are driven to the conclusion that a depoliticized academy could not tolerate any educational program nor any sort of sustained speculation and criticism aimed at the radical reformation of human personality. "Know thyself," said the oracle. But what would be the point of trying to know oneself, with the help of enlightened teachers, unless one were determined to change one's life? And how could one think of undertaking such a task if one were not prepared to entertain the possibility or necessity of actions which, if they succeeded, might revolutionize all our social institutions, including of course the colleges and the state themselves?

I am bound to say also that a fully depoliticized academy could not permit any form of religious study which aimed at something more than the external examination of historical religions, their creeds and rituals, and churchly paraphernalia. For active religious reflection, as Paul Tillich used to say, has to do with matters of ultimate concern to us as human beings, with what is worthy of our profoundest loyalty and love. But the awakened religious consciousness, as all great religious leaders, from the Prophets and Jesus to Gandhi and Pope John XXIII, have demonstrated both in their teachings and in their lives, is always a threat to the established order, including the political order. Indeed, great religious geniuses, like great philosophers, and artists—*by their very existence*—endanger the established orders, and the dominations and obsessions of their governing elites.

What, then would be left to the higher learning were all significant political thought and activity excluded from the university? We are driven, I think, to the conclusions that if our academies were systematically depoliticized, many traditional and humanly important parts of the humanities and the so-called social sciences, even in their present-day confused and emasculated forms, would have to be dropped from the curriculum. Moreover, many researches now conducted under the more austere auspices of natural science departments would have to be abandoned, since their results, devoid of theoretical interest, have value only for governments committed to the deadly business of power politics. To be more concrete (and I shall continue to play our little game as even-handedly as possible), one cannot imagine that cathedrals of pure scholarship would tolerate such political activists as Professor Marcuse or (at the other extreme) Professor Sidney Hook; no doubt Chomsky would have to go, but so too would Professors Schlesinger and Galbraith, to say nothing of such eminent newcomers to the academic scene as Professors Humphrey and Johnson. But these are not all. For thousands of indentured technological scientists, along with their multitudes of graduate assistants, would also have to find new jobs in the great industrial laboratories where there is no quibbling about the aims of higher education.

What about the student activists, who are currently such burrs in the saddles of our academic administrators? Surely there would be no place for them, even if they stopped carrying arms and rifling the files of deans of the faculty. For they would still be politicized. So it would be necessary to proscribe such student organizations as the SDS and (were the authorities consistent) the Young Republican Clubs. And if the reply were made, which is not without merit, that one can get an education of sorts by engaging in such extracurricular political activities, the reply, in this instance, would fall, for a political education is still a part of the political life of men in societies.

Nor have I forgotten here the distinction between forms of political education that are topical and directly activistic and those concerned more abstractly with the critique and formation of general ideological principles which serve their political ends more indirectly. And to those who concede that the higher learning *should* have a place for studies of the latter sort (and I fully agree with them) the reply must be that they are forgetting the game we are playing. I cannot see how an academy, depoliticized in any depth, could tolerate a William James, a John Dewey, or a Bertrand Russell, and any more than it could tolerate a Marcuse. For again, all forms of political reasoning, whether abstractly ideological like Plato's *Republic* and Rousseau's *Social Contract,* or concrete and topical, like the *Declaration of Independence,* the *Emancipation Proclamation,* or the *Communist Manifesto,* have a practical intention: that is to say, they are aimed, whether for the longer or shorter run, at the modification of active political-social attitudes. In fact, they defeat their own purposes if, when the time is ripe, they fail to move us to action designed to reform or, if necessary, revolutionize the existing order.

In sum, a thoroughly depoliticized academy, were it ever actualized, would not be an institute for all the forms of advanced study necessary to the progressive enlightenment of mature human beings, but instead would be learned mandarins lost finally both to the world and to themselves. No doubt an affluent society like our own, which presumably can afford anything that takes its fancy, could afford such an institution, and for a time at least it might even be willing to tolerate it, just as it now tolerates religious retreats and sanctuaries. What is more doubtful is that the internal purity of the academy could be maintained. How could it make certain that a few whole men—whether students or professors—might not get into it by mistake? And how could it guarantee that such impure spirits, like our own campus rebels, would not in the end become so alienated from it that, despairing of further argument with their uncomprehending superiors, they would not be disposed at last, like all other alienists, to take matters into their own hands? Surely it is not hard to imagine in these troubled times that beginning with teach-ins and sit-ins, they might be tempted to seize the administration building by main force and hold the president and his deans incommunicado until their "non-negotiable" demands for a more liberal conception of higher education were met.

Suppose they did. In such an event, we may well imagine, a depoliticized college president or board of trustees would be exceedingly reluctant to make use of the strong arm of the state. For in so doing they would of course be responding in kind—that is to say, politically—to the actions of the rebels. Still, one must suppose that in the end they would feel obliged, necessarily in uneasy conscience, to call in the police in order to protect the integrity and the freedom of the academy. But what sort of freedom would this be? Not, surely, the freedom to discuss in a critical spirit the nature and limits of science, whithersoever the argument might lead. For anyone who starts asking limiting questions about the proper aims and functions of scientific inquiries may well find that such limits are extremely unclear or else that they are in need of radical revision in an age like our own in which governments, with the indispensable help of scientists, can destroy mankind. No matter how paradoxically, it is doubtful whether a depoliticized academy could tolerate active and open debates about the aims of the higher learning as a whole, since these would almost certainly result in disagreements whose implications are inescapably political. Indeed, the whole problem of academic freedom would become so stylized, so touchy, that discussions of it would be permitted only in cases of specific violations, and then only by safe men who have accepted in advance the ground rules established by academic authorities who understand the limitations of a politicized academy.

Suppose, however, that some overly conscientious professor raised questions about the wisdom or the good faith of his superiors? Would he not also have to be put down in one way or another, thus further compromising the purity of the guardians of the depoliticized academy? What then? Here plainly the road becomes exceedingly slippery. But compromise, as usual, leads to compromise. And one may as well be hung for a sheep as for a lamb. In the real world, as Plato himself foretold, intelligent purists must also be realists, and even the depoliticized academy needs guardians who are willing and able to sustain it. Physicists and mathematicians, as well as poets, must eat and their studies and laboratories must be decently provided for. Hence donors must be solicited, foundations appealed to, legislatures and governors of states placated and cajoled, congressmen begged, and presidents of state exhorted. Thus in practice even the purest institutions of advanced study and higher learning require their front men, who know how to wheedle funds from those who possess or control them: lobbyists, public-relations men, and sober-sided presidents like Mr. Pusey, who know how to talk to congressional committees that might otherwise not be able to understand the nonpolitical aspirations of the academies. But this is not all. For academicians, no matter how chaste their intentions, are invariably misunderstood by the hoi polloi that live in the slums that surround the precincts of the academy, and in many cases are owned—in trust of course—by the academies for purposes of future expansion and for the housing of their own less affluent members. Let us face it. The hoi polloi do not understand, nor care to understand, the purposes of the academy; what they see are oppressive landlords, indifferent and condescending professors, students who raise hell on Saturday night. So the academy must either maintain its own praetorian guards, which invariably prove inadequate to the demands made upon them, or else be willing to call upon the armed services of the city or the state in order to protect its privacy and its property against intruders who mean harm to the members of its community. Extraterritorial rights are not honored save at a price. And the price, as we may as well recognize, is a price whose name is politics.

Is this picture overdrawn? Then merely by an inch. Does it also ring a bell? I believe it must. Can the deep inconsistencies which it involves be overcome? Short of utopia, I am sure they cannot. The conclusion is inescapable: The managers of our academic establishments, like their allies in our legislatures and state houses, in the congress, and the White House, who tell us that the proper business of the universities and colleges is not with politics but only with the advancement of neutral learning, are either disingenuous and hence guilty of bad faith or else so self-deceived that they are incompetent and deserve to be removed from office.

These, I realize, are harsh terms; nor do I use them lightly. Let me explain. Such men act in bad faith, or else are self-deceived to the point of madness when they invoke the image of the academy as a haven and repository of pure learning, itself completely at variance with the actual practices of their own institutions, and then condemn, or else—as the English put it—send down obstreperous student activists who give them the lie direct and the countercheck quarrelsome. They act in bad faith, or are self-deluded, when they accept government or foundation money, which commonly has political strings attached, yet pretend that they are free, and are outraged when dissident students and faculty members point this out to them and then, in their own turn, take steps, not at ways genteel, to see that those strings are cut. They are disingenuous when they represent themselves as agents of law and order, yet never raise deep questions about the justice of that law or order, nor acknowledge that there can be no law or order without government and hence politics.

They are particularly disingenuous, let me add, when they argue, as McGeorge Bundy and others do, that university administrations and governing boards possess merely formal power and that the actual power and authority in the academy resides in the faculty, when they know that our faculties are chock full of careerists who have no interest in its governance so long as they themselves are left alone to do their work according to their own flickering lights. As they very well know, faculties are nearly always self-divided and usually incapable of independent and decisive action to rectify either educational wrongs or administrative malpractices. They also know how clever and determined administrators, with their own informal ties to government, industry, and business, can and do manipulate their faculties to secure their own frequently political ends. Finally, these apologists for faculty authority cannot fail to know, especially in this time of troubles, that formal power can always be reconverted into actual power by university presidents and by the governing boards at whose pleasure all presidents enjoy their tenure.

They speak and act in bad faith when they pretend to be votaries of reasonableness, yet reserve for themselves the peremptory authority to determine for students and faculty members alike the standards and limits of reasonableness, and times and places where their critics may foregather to present their reasons for opposing existing academic practices and policies. Above all, they are either appallingly naive or again are guilty of bad faith when they angrily condemn those dissidents who, disillusioned by arguments that get them nowhere, resort to force, yet in the clutch react—and overreact—in kind.

But here I myself may have been a bit disingenuous. For I concede that gentlemen like the presidents of universities such as Columbia and Harvard do not react in kind to students who unceremoniously eject academic deans from their offices, occupy administrative buildings, rifle files, and sip presidential sherry in order to quiet their nerves. For as they well know, the force employed by the students is informal, personal, and usually intramural and poorly organized, whereas the force upon which they themselves rely is extramural, highly skilled, well armed, and sublimely confident in the assurance of its constituted authority. Of course such administrators know full well that when the chips are down, as they have so often been of late, this majesterial power is always incomparably greater than that of their youthful opponents, with their obscenities, sticks and stones, pop bottles, their occasional pistols (for we must be fair), most of them unused, and their bare hands and unshielded bodies.

These last comments may be misleading. Let me then emphasize that it is not part of my own argument to condone acts of gross violence, whether on the part of the university authorities and the governments that offer their moral and military support, or on the part of misguided students—black as well as white—that jeopardize the very existence of *liberal* learning (and mind you, I emphasize the word "liberal"). Cowardly arsonists who come in the night to burn books and manuscripts, studies, libraries, are not exponents of freedom, their own included. On the contrary, from the point of view which I defend, the destruction of any constructive and liberating work of the human mind is always appalling. But if a burned book or study is something forever to be grieved over, broken heads or backs are far more lamentable, especially when they are the heads and backs of innocents who are always sacrificed when men in groups resort to violence.

But this is not the place to undertake a general discussion of violence and its legitimate (or illegitimate) issues. It is my conviction that in most situations, thoughtful but sparing use by academic administrators of the legal device of injunction is justified in order to protect scholars and students, as well as the legitimate fruits of their labors, against marauding hordes whose only purpose is to terrorize the academy and to destroy the materials and records necessary to its proper work. This conviction commits me, accordingly, to the view that the university as a corporate body is entitled to perform legal and political acts in its own defense. By the same token, however, I am obliged to consider whether the university, as such, may also be entitled to take other political positions when its own integrity is threatened.

As it happens, Professor Hook and I found ourselves in at least partial agreement some years ago when a number of distinguished colleagues proposed, at a business meeting of the American Philosophical Association, that the association, as a corporate body, condemn the government's policies in Vietnam. And I, for my part, contended that a purely professional organization, concerned exclusively with its own professional business and ends, was not entitled to take political stands not closely germane to that business and those ends. This, so I argued, in no way denied the right of members of our association, speaking not only as private persons but also, if they wished, as individual members of the group, to condemn the Vietnam War (which I myself have always heartily opposed). And I agreed to sign any sensible memorandum or petition deploring the war, not only in my own person but also as a member of the association. (I should add in passing that the American Philosophical Association, if one could judge by its annual programs, seems to me to have long since given up any common concern with the pursuit of wisdom and has become as narrowly specialized and professionalized as, say, the American Association of Morticians.)

The fact is that I am less certain now than I was then of this position. For I now see that even a fairly narrow professional association, dedicated to a small part of the advancement of learning, may find its own work undermined, or even rendered impossible, by policies and actions of the state. However, I shall waive this question here. For the sake of argument, I am prepared to reaffirm the position I took in 1967 regarding the provenance of the American Philosophical Association, viewed simply as a professional society. And I do so because I want to free myself for independent scrutiny of the situation of the university in matters of this sort.

Now, most academicians, including not only students and professors but also administrators, generally agree that the university is not and cannot be understood as a mere galaxy of professional associations. To be sure, its task includes the advancement of learning, by research and teaching, in a wide variety of subjects. And this task has its important professional side, which includes the granting of degrees to student apprentices that will qualify them for more advanced work in particular fields, as well as the creation and maintenance of conditions necessary to the researches of established professional scholars. But the university is much more than an institute for the training of preprofessionals and the support of professional scholars. It is also the great unifying institution of higher learning whose difficult task, above all, includes the education of free men. Because of this, the educational heart of the university is, or should be, its college, not its professional graduate schools.

Thus, unlike the professional society, the university has educational responsibilities which cannot be defined in purely professional terms. As we know, professional societies can sometimes function tolerably well under governments which are repressive and warlike. The university, however, by its nature is threatened by any social or political policy which diminishes the freedom of ordinary citizens. More positively, because the university bears such a heavy responsibility for the full intellectual, moral, and human development of all its members, professors as well as students, it has a corporate obligation to protest, and in some circumstances even to defy or obstruct, social practices or political policies which undermine or constrict its comprehensive educational purposes.

Given the organizational principles which at present obtain in the American university, I for one am loathe to support, without qualification, any and all corporate decisions affecting the relations of the academy to the national society or its government, which the university's existing governing boards and administrative officers may come to. Many such boards and officers lack a clear notion of the extensive freedom necessary to the university. But the faculties and student bodies of the university whose primary concerns are educational, in the wide sense I have here in mind, do seem to me to have the right, after full and open debate, to speak and act against certain social and governmental policies and practices as corporate bodies. Thus, I should argue, the faculties of universities in the South have the right, and perhaps the obligation, to adopt corporate principles and to express corporate attitudes which are at variance with the segregationalist and racist policies of existing state governments. I should also argue, in the same vein, that faculties, perhaps in concert with students, have the right and at times the obligation to condemn, and on occasion to obstruct, policies and practices of the federal government which are inimical to their own educational purposes.

I am not a formalist. Student bodies and faculties, as well as university presidents and boards of trustees, are liable to error and confusion. Indeed, I can imagine circumstances in which wise administrators may be obliged to make decisions at variance with those adopted by their faculties and students. In every institution, in my judgment, no man or group of men is, or should be, sovereign. Yet this does not, I think, affect the point at issue. Universities, and especially their faculties and students, have rights and responsibilities which entitle or indeed require them to make corporate decisions of a political nature when national or state governments adopt policies which undermine the conditions of liberal learning. Of course such decisions should be thoughtfully made, and even when thoughtfully made they may still be mistaken. And it is the duty of minority groups within the university to point out such errors when they occur. Indeed they themselves may be obliged to obstruct or to defy decisions which, in their view, are academically as well as politically unwise. But these qualifications do not impugn the principle: the university, and especially its faculty and students, have the right to take corporate political action when such action is necessary in order to protect the wide and deep aims of higher education.

In bringing this part of my paper to a close, let me emphasize that every institution, if only in its own defense, is involved in politics. The church-state problem, for example, necessarily involved the churches in corporate political action. The same holds, as Leslie Fielder has discovered, even of the family. Politics is an inescapable dimension of every form of institutional activity. And those who refuse to involve themselves in it must, if they are responsible, foreswear participation in every form of institutional life. To my mind, however, this is platitudinous. The great and ineluctable fact is that no institution, given its ends, is more profoundly involved in problems of politics and government than the university.

Thus, as I have tried to show, the question before us is not whether the university can be depoilticized. Rather it is the question of how and to what ends the university should engage in political activity, and what forms of political activity are proper to it.

To this question my answers must be brief. I shall proceed from those problems which are more topical and hence debatable to those that are more enduring.

To begin with, the university must be free to call in question and, on occasion, oppose any form of service to the nation-state designed primarily to enhance the state's military power. Here I have in mind not only such forms of military instruction as are conducted by the ROTC, but, far more important, research projects supported by federal grants-in-aid whose basic purpose is to increase our national capacity for nuclear warfare. Beyond this, the university is entirely within its rights if it refuses to countenance forms of research designed to explore means of degrading or maiming human beings or of destroying natural resources upon which they are dependent for life. For the university, as an institution of higher learning dedicated to the religious, moral, and political enlightenment, defeats its own ends and undermines the conditions of its own existence when it, or the members of its faculties, engage in such activities as a matter of course. Moreover, the forms of enlightenment fostered by the university are by their very nature public. Hence the university is entitled to deny, and in my judgment should deny, the use of its facilities to academicians involved in the work of such secret governmental services as the CIA and the FBI. And of course the same applies to similar services to industry or other social institutions or societies. In a word, academicians cannot also be secret agents. Finally, the university must be free to criticize, or on occasion actively oppose, both particular public policies and private practices which create an ambience inimical to its own broad educational purposes. And it must make available the use of its facilities to members of the academic community who are concerned to criticize and to oppose such policies and practices.

At the level of ideology, I should deny no member of the academy the right, in the proper circumstances and under proper auspices, to defend any form of thought, religious, ethical, or political, no matter how heterodox, so long as he does so in a manner which is appropriate to it. It is sometimes argued that the only forms of inquiry which are proper to the university as the primary institution of higher learning are those that aim at scientific truth. In another way, it is argued that the only studies which a university should support, or tolerate, are those which are "neutral" or "value free." As I have already suggested, such a principle is educationally pernicious, since, among other things, it precludes the possibility of philosophical investigations whose task is to provide critiques of all forms of putative knowledge. Without begging basic philosophical questions, it simply cannot be assumed that the scientific method is the one and only method of achieving human understanding. A philosopher, not to mention a theologian, a moralist, a literary critic, or an artist, must be free not merely to consider what forms of study are proper to his activity, but also to employ the methods and procedures which upon reflection he deems appropriate. If he is mistaken, then it is the business of his colleagues and students to expose his errors.

What concerns me here, above all, are these pervasive but frequently unformulated philosophies, or ideologies of higher learning, that regard liberal education, which is concerned with the development and enlargement of the whole life of the mind, to be a dispensable or peripheral luxury. On another level, such philosophies are deeply suspicious, or even fearful, of liberal education precisely because it is not and cannot be neutral in the scientific sense. From the latter point of view, liberal education, owing to its active concern not merely with scientific study but also with the appraisal and advocacy of religious, ethical, and political attitudes and institutions, automatically involves the teacher and his students in controversial issues which can and do create an atmosphere of dissension which is inimical to that basic congeniality of mind which a community of scholars seems to require.

In reply I must take the bit in my teeth: liberal education does indeed lead to controversy, and undoubtedly its exponents and participants are given forms of dissension that frequently go very deep. The liberal mind is inherently nonconformist, and nonconformity usually has a political aspect. In my view, however, controversy, dissension, and nonconformity are indispensable to intellectual and hence educational development. Accordingly, the price in terms of conflict, both within the faculty and the student body, simply has to be paid. And if this reduces the sense of community among the members of the university, we must make the best of it. The business of higher education is not to make those engaged in it comfortable with one another, but to advance all the basic forms of human understanding. In short, I do not deplore conflict on the university campus, I applaud it. Nor in saying this do I commit myself to an uncritical or flaccid acquiescence in all the forms of turmoil which now beset our universities. Physical violence on the campus is nearly always to be deplored. And the same holds not only for student "revolutionaries" but also for administrative "reactionaries."

Let me close by making some positive proposals which, if adopted, would greatly reduce the wrong sort of tension which has now become endemic to the contemporary American university. A great part of this tension, which reflects analogous tensions within the wider society, is owing to the obsolete organization of the academy. I do not deplore academic leadership, and certainly such leadership must come, in some part, from the university administration. But this requires that university administrators and, behind them, the governing boards, be educators and not merely arbiters and fund-raisers. And they cannot be, or remain, educators unless they also study, teach, and go to school. To this end, I propose a principle of rotation that will close the profound intellectual, moral, and political gaps that presently divide the various academic classes. Administrators must be given, or obliged to take, leave from time to time so that they may renew, in a more concrete and intimate way, their understanding of the work, the attitudes, and the problems of their faculties and students. They must be obliged in a more-than-ceremonial way to participate in the life and work of both faculties and students. Administration, in short, must no longer be treated as a full-time job, and, again, if we all will have to pay a certain price for the change, then so be it. Faculty members must be enabled to participate fully in the governance of the university. Thus, faculty members should be elected by the governing boards in whose hands, as we have learned, to our sorrow, great actual as well as formal power still resides. In some degree the same holds with respect to students. For example, able and enlightened students must not only be permitted but encouraged to participate in the instruction of their classmates and in the formation and revision of departmental curricula. And, in sum, through these and other entirely practicable changes, actions can and must be taken to convert what is now merely an institution into a truer community of self-respecting and mutually understanding scholars.

Beyond this, valuable forms of educational and political activity that are now conducted exclusively within the shadow university should be encouraged to come out of the shadow and to be recognized, not as extracurricular alternatives to football or Saturday night parties, but as relevant educational activities designed for the improvement of the understanding of all members of the university community. Specifically, dissident and radical groups, whose aim is the reconstruction of the whole society, must not merely be tolerated with a grimace, but invited to meet in the light of day with those who disagree with them so that meaningful and continuous dialogues may be established concerning the problems and jobs of work to be done in our confused and faltering social system.

Nor is this all. More enlightened head-start, upward- and outward-bound programs should be established in order to bring into, and so to enrich, the intellectual life of the academic community, many more gifted but disadvantaged students whose deprivation, real as well as imagined, are owing to poverty, inadequate secondary school education, and racial prejudice. These students must be provided with ample scholarships that may enable them to live and to study on equal terms with their classmates. Further, the colleges and universities must be prepared to invite to the campus, whether on a full or part-time basis, knowledgeable and enlightened laymen who have so much to tell us about the possibilities, educational and otherwise, of reform and reconstruction throughout the national society. And sustained programs of adult education need to be established which are no longer marginal and conducted by disadvantaged professors in need of another honest buck.

But all these, of course, are no more than approach shots. What is necessary, above all, is a massive return to the ideals and practices of liberal education itself, properly updated for contemporary men and women who have something more to do in the world than acquire forms of professional and vocational training that may enable them to move upward in the social and economic hierarchy. These ideals and practices must also be reintroduced into the graduate and professional schools. We need and must have forms of liberal education that are relevant to the lives of human beings in an age of unprecedented social and cultural crisis, in an age in which there are problems of life which human beings have never had to face before: the massive consolidation of power in the hands of elites responsible in practice to no one but themselves; the contests for ideological and political control by great states, all of them, including our own, increasingly repressive and totalistic; and, most important of all, the uncontrolled employment of weapons of destruction that, in an instant, can convert this planet into a scene of lunar desolation where the life and work of civilized human beings is completely blotted out.

This is the great and difficult work that lies before us. In an era in which as never before the academy is the state's most important institutional auxiliary, we must again make sure that what we call higher education is an education, not for technicians and specialists only, but for autonomous men, enlightened and unafraid. Ours is the responsibility to make certain that the advancement of learning includes the improvement of our understanding of what it means to be a human being. And this task, once again, imposes responsibilities whose meanings are through and through political.

Part III

•

FREE SPEECH ON CAMPUS

Introduction

Perhaps nothing is valued by academicians as highly as a free environment that encourages originality and exceptional achievements. Of course, such freedom is not absolute. Academic institutions must formulate rules that are designed to protect the rights and well-being of each of its members. Simply put, if an individual utilizes his or her freedom irresponsibly, this may threaten the freedom and well-being of others in the community. Therein lies the fundamental conflict that grounds the debate in this section.

The basic problems arising from the tension between "freedom" and "security" are hardly novel items to philosophers, politicians, and social theorists. The Founding Fathers focused considerable attention on this very problem when they were deciding how to construct a successful representative government. They relied, in part, on the notion of freedom defended by John Locke. As indicated in the selections in part 1, Plato and Locke were well aware of the tension between freedom and security.

As we have already seen, Plato's *Republic* advocates censorship, manipulation, and outright prevarication, as long as such techniques are used to further the legitimate interests of the state. These "legitimate interests" are to be determined by a Philosopher-Ruler who is obligated by "reason" to follow standards of eternal truth. These standards, referred to as the "forms," obligate a ruler no less than they do the rest of his kingdom. However, the Philosopher-Ruler is the only person truly capable of learning what people should be doing. According to Plato, the masses are to be prompted to follow the dictates of reason through the ruler's regulation of literature, poetry, music, and other activities.

Plato's social and political system requires extensive state control. Plato realizes that his master plan would allow citizens little freedom, and it is interesting that his notion of freedom is to be understood in purely negative terms. "Freedom" is the absence of constraints. The extent of one's freedom depends upon the extent to which one's circumstances, legal obligations, and other external factors limit one's freedom of action. Plato believes that the conflict between freedom and security is irreconcilable. He, of course, opts for security at the expense of freedom.

John Locke's notion of freedom differs considerably from Plato's. As the selections from the *Second Treatise* indicated, Locke maintains that freedom is much more than the absence of constraints. Its positive aspects hinge on what Locke takes to be the intimate connection between freedom and the "law of nature" (i.e., reason). Locke insists that individual freedom is the ability of the individual to act and order his life according to reason. An individual's freedom rests upon the ability of reason to reduce arbitrary social and political factors that would otherwise direct his life. He is "free" to construct a representative government for his own security, one that is based upon his consent. By means of this social contract an individual's freedom (both negative and positive) is protected. In this way, Locke attempts a reconciliation between freedom and security. Unlike Plato, Locke maintains that security can preserve and even enhance freedom.

This attempt to reconcile freedom and security is central to John Dewey's *Democracy and Education*. Dewey maintains that individual development is compatible with social progress and a community's shared purposes. Indeed, he insists that individual development requires them. For Dewey, there can be no genuine individuality apart from supportive democratic social institutions. Without the security, education, and encouragement that society offers an individual, freedom is meaningless. Dewey's emphasis on the interplay between individual creativity and a supportive social environment has led to curious results. On the one hand, his approach has been criticized for its purported antidemocratic elements. Here Dewey's account is said to stifle individual freedom in the name of scientific progress and social harmony. Yet, at the other extreme, it is said that his account portrays society as a playground for the individual.

Perhaps more than any other major philosopher John Stuart Mill sought to demonstrate the importance of individual freedom. For Mill, as the selections from *On Liberty* indicate, the fundamental task of society is to retain as much freedom for the individual as possible. His general thesis is that social restrictions on individual liberties are only justified if such restrictions are essential to the protection or self-development of others. Aside from this restriction, Mill maintains that no verbal or written expression, however distasteful or odious, is to be prohibited by law. It would seem, therefore, that Mill would not have approved of legal prohibitions on racist speech. For one thing, Mill was greatly concerned about the general tendency of institutions to become more and more authoritative. But Mill's objection to institutional prohibitions on free speech is not merely based upon his desire to limit social control over the individual. Mill places enormous importance on the value of freedom itself. According to him, freedom is an intrinsic component of happiness, and, as such, is an essential measure of the health and success of any society.

In her essay "Democratic Education in Difficult Times," Amy Gutman objects that Mill's approach to educational institutions is extremist. It glorifies the freedom of individuals at the expense of the cultivation of virtue—a disastrous prescription according to Gutman. At the other extreme is Plato's system of education, which Gutman also rejects. She objects to Plato's proposal to sacrifice individual freedom for the sake of his standards of civic virtue. According to Gutman, Plato mistakenly seeks one correct conception of education when there is no such privileged point of view. Indeed, she maintains that the diversity of educational approaches within a democratic society is vital to the advancement of knowledge.

Against Mill, Gutman argues that students need protection from repressive and discriminatory institutional policies. She says that Mill rejects any institutional policy or curriculum designed to teach moral and social values to students. Alternatively, Mill wants such institutions merely to provide students with factual descriptions along with the tools of scientific and factual inquiry. Gutman believes that Mill's advice is unrealistic. She finds that, invariably, any curriculum is going to reflect the social and political values of the group that designed it. Gutman suggests that educational institutions should encourage diversity in conceptions of education and morality, rather than engage in a futile attempt to design a value-free curriculum. (The discussions of neutrality in the previous part would be particularly helpful here.)

Gutman believes that her democratic conception of education strikes a balance between freedom and security. Her emphasis on diversity of perspectives and public debate is designed to avoid Plato's prescription for stifling individual freedom, while her suggestion to protect students against discrimination is aimed at avoiding the perils of Mill's laissez-faire approach.

Gutman's interpretation of Mill's theory as an uncompromising defense of freedom in academia is open to debate—after all, as we can see here, Mill's theory supports legal prohibitions for actions that damage the freedom or *well-being* of others—but she offers important advice for managing the tension between freedom and security. Gutman refers to the necessity of protecting students from indoctrination, and thereby supports restrictions on discriminatory institutional practices. However, Gutman's essay does not specifically address the issue of racist speech on college campuses. Indeed, her suggestions are meant to be general and to emphasize both the advantages of free discussion as well as the need to protect students from discriminatory practices.

The transition from the thought of Plato, Mill, and other historical thinkers to contemporary discussions is anything but smooth. What is very different about the free speech debates in our own time is their central focus on the protection of certain classes in our society. The historical figures, especially Locke and the Founding Fathers, would have been very uncomfortable with today's emphasis on protecting minorities. Let us not confuse their use of the term "minority" with today's usage. For them, a "minority" referred to a relatively small group of people united by circumstance or by some common passion or interest. To us, the term usually refers to an ethnic group. Ethnicity, race, and gender occupy our thoughts in a way that would have been quite foreign to these philosophers. Whether or not this is a positive change is the subject of contemporary debate.

In the selection by Thomas Grey, "Discriminatory Harassment and Free Speech," we are warned that minorities need special protection against racial slurs and other types of hate speech. Because of basic social inequalities, Grey feels that certain ethnic and racial groups are especially vulnerable to hate speech. He argues that even if university policies offer unequal protections in favor of minorities, this is necessary given their special circumstances. Alan Keyes, who was a candidate for the Republican nomination for president in 2000, strongly disagrees. In "Freedom Through Moral Education," he argues that offering minority students special protection against verbal harassment not only patronizes them, but also inhibits their moral education.

Obviously, the fact that Locke and the Founding Fathers would have sided with Keyes is not going to decide this debate. For the very fact that a James Madison did not stress race is seen by many people today to reflect a national tragedy. Charles Lawrence III, in "If He Hollers, Let Him Go: Regulating Racist Speech on Campus," wants decisive steps taken to protect black students from racist speech. He does not believe that his position is in any way extreme, and he tries to establish an acceptable line between constitutionally protected and regulable racist speech. Nadine Strossen, now president of the American Civil Liberties Union, objects to Lawrence's justification for drawing the line as he does. She argues that Lawrence's reasoning would pave the way for the prohibition of all racist speech on campus, thereby transgressing First Amendment guarantees.

What would Dewey have said about the debate between Lawrence and Strossen? How would he have reconciled the importance of free expression with the need to protect students from verbal harassment? Dewey's emphasis on the need for a safe, nurturing, learning environment certainly adds impetus to Lawrence's point of view. However, the stress that Dewey places on individuality, freedom, and educating the ignorant seems to point in Strossen's direction. We are reminded that in offering a middle ground for the free speech debate on our campuses, Dewey's work will not decide these policy debates for us.

One thing is clear, however. Debates such as these between Charles Lawrence and Nadine Strossen, and between Thomas Grey and Alan Keyes are more than mere theoretical contests. The way that academicians, students, and administrators relate to each other is shaped, to a large extent, by such debates.

14

FROM *ON LIBERTY*

John Stuart Mill

Let us suppose, therefore, that the government is entirely at one with the people, and never thinks of exerting any power of coercion unless in agreement with what it conceives to be their voice. But I deny the right of the people to exercise such coercion, either by themselves or by their government. The power itself is illegitimate. The best government has no more title to it than the worst. It is as noxious, or more noxious, when exerted in accordance with public opinion, than when in opposition to it. If all mankind minus one, were of one opinion, and only one person were of the contrary opinion, mankind would be no more justified in silencing that one person, than he, if he had the power, would be justified in silencing mankind. Were an opinion a personal possession of no value except to the owner; if to be obstructed in the enjoyment of it were simply a private injury, it would make some difference whether the injury was inflicted only on a few persons or on many. But the peculiar evil of silencing the expression of an opinion is, that it is robbing the human race; posterity as well as the existing generation; those who dissent from the opinion, still more than those who hold it. If the opinion is right, they are deprived of the opportunity of exchanging error for truth: if wrong, they lose, what is almost as great a benefit, the clearer perception and livelier impression of truth, produced by its collision with error.

It is necessary to consider separately these two hypotheses, each of which has a distinct branch of the argument corresponding to it. We can never be sure that the opinion we are endeavoring to stifle is a false opinion; and if we were sure, stifling it would be an evil still.

First: the opinion which it is attempted to suppress by authority may possibly be true. Those who desire to suppress it, of course deny its truth; but they are not infallible. They have no authority to decide the question for all mankind, and exclude every other person from the means of judging. To refuse a hearing to an opinion, because they are sure that it is false, is to assume that *their* certainty is the same thing as *absolute* certainty. All silencing of discussion is an assumption of infallibility. Its condemnation may be allowed to rest on this common argument, not the worse for being common.

Unfortunately for the good sense of mankind, the fact of their fallibility is far from carrying the weight in their practical judgment, which is always allowed to it in theory; for while every one well knows himself to be fallible, few think it necessary to take any precautions against their own fallibility, or admit the supposition that any opinion, of which they feel very certain, may be one of the examples of the error to which they acknowledge themselves to be liable. Absolute princes, or others who are accustomed to unlimited deference, usually feel this complete confidence in their own opinions on nearly all subjects. People more happily situated, who sometimes hear their opinions disputed, and are not wholly unused to be set right when they are wrong, place the same unbounded reliance only on such of their opinions as are shared by all who surround them, or to whom they habitually defer: for in proportion to a man's want of confidence in his own solitary judgment, does he usually repose, with implicit trust, on the infallibility of "the world" in general. And the world, to each individual, means the part of it with which he comes in contact; his party, his sect, his church, his class of society: the man may be called, by comparison, almost liberal and large-minded to whom it means anything so comprehensive as his own country or his own age. Nor is his faith in this collective authority at all shaken by his being aware that other ages, countries, sects, churches, classes, and parties have thought, and even now think, the exact reverse. He devolves upon his own world the responsibility of being in the right against the dissentient worlds of other people; and it never troubles him that mere accident has decided which of these numerous worlds is the object of his reliance, and that the same causes which make him a Churchman in London, would have made him a Buddhist or a Confucian in Pekin. Yet it is as evident in itself, as any amount of argument can make it, that ages are no more infallible than individuals; every age having held many opinions which subsequent ages have deemed not only false but absurd; and it is as certain that many opinions, now general, will be rejected by future ages, as it is that many, once general, are rejected by the present.

The objection likely to be made to this argument would probably take some such form as the following. There is no greater assumption of infallibility in forbidding the propagation of error, than in any other thing which is done by public authority on its own judgment and responsibility. Judgment is given to men that they may use it. Because it may be used erroneously, are men to be told that they ought not to use it at all? To prohibit what they think pernicious, is not claiming exemption from error, but fulfilling the duty incumbent on them, although fallible, of acting on their conscientious conviction. If we were never to act on our opinions, because those opinions may be wrong, we should leave all our interests uncared for, and all our duties unperformed. An objection which applies to all conduct, can be no valid objection to any conduct in particular. It is the duty of governments, and of individuals, to form the truest opinions they can; to form them carefully, and never impose them upon others unless they are quite sure of being right. But when they are sure (such reasoners may say), it is not conscientiousness but cowardice to shrink from acting on their opinions, and allow doctrines which they honestly think dangerous to the welfare of mankind, either in this life or in another, to be scattered abroad without restraint, because other people, in less enlightened times, have persecuted opinions now believed to be true. Let us take care, it may be said, not to make the same mistake: but governments and nations have made mistakes in other things, which are not denied to be fit subjects for the exercise of authority: they have laid on bad taxes, made unjust wars. Ought we therefore to lay on no taxes, and, under whatever provocation, make no wars? Men, and governments, must act to the best of their ability. There is no such thing as absolute certainty, but there is assurance sufficient for the purposes of human life. We may, and must, assume our opinion to be true for the guidance of our own conduct: and it is assuming no more when we forbid bad men to pervert society by the propagation of opinions which we regard as false and pernicious.

I answer, that it is assuming very much more. There is the greatest difference between presuming an opinion to be true, because, with every opportunity for contesting it, it has not been refuted, and assuming its truth for the purpose of not permitting its refutation. Complete liberty of contradicting and disproving our opinion, is the very condition which justifies us in assuming its truth for purposes of action; and on no other terms can a being with human faculties have any rational assurance of being right.

Let us now pass to the second division of the argument, and dismissing the supposition that any of the received opinions may be false, let us assume them to be true, and examine into the worth of the manner in which they are likely to be held, when their truth is not freely and openly canvassed. However unwillingly a person who has a strong opinion may admit the possibility that his opinion may be false, he ought to be moved by the consideration that however true it may be, if it is not fully, frequently, and fearlessly discussed, it will be held as a dead dogma, not a living truth.

There is a class of persons (happily not quite so numerous as formerly) who think it enough if a person assents undoubtingly to what they think true, though he has no knowledge whatever of the grounds of the opinion, and could not make a tenable defense of it against the most superficial objections. Such persons, if they can once get their creed taught from authority, naturally think that no good, and some harm, comes of its being allowed to be questioned. Where their influence prevails, they make it nearly impossible for the received opinion to be rejected wisely and considerately, though it may still be rejected rashly and ignorantly; for to shut out discussion entirely is seldom possible, and when it once gets in, beliefs not grounded on conviction are apt to give way before the slightest semblance of an argument. Waiving, however, this possibility—assuming that the true opinion abides in the mind, but abides as a prejudice, a belief independent of, and proof against, argument—this is not the way in which truth ought to be held by a rational being. This is not knowing the truth. Truth, thus held, is but one superstition the more accidentally clinging to the words which enunciate a truth.

If the intellect and judgment of mankind ought to be cultivated, a thing which Protestants at least do not deny, on what can these faculties be more appropriately exercised by any one, than on the things which concern him so much that it is considered necessary for him to hold opinions on them? If the cultivation of the understanding consists in one thing more than in another, it is surely in learning the grounds of one's own opinions. Whatever people believe, on subjects on which it is of the first importance to believe rightly, they ought to be able to defend against at least the common objections. But, some one may say, "Let them be *taught* the grounds of their opinions. It does not follow that opinions must be merely parroted because they are never heard controverted. Persons who learn geometry do not simply commit the theorems to memory, but understand and learn likewise the demonstrations; and it would be absurd to say that they remain ignorant of the grounds of geometrical truths, because they never hear any one deny, and attempt to disprove them." Undoubtedly: and such teaching suffices on a subject like mathematics, where there is nothing at all to be said on the wrong side of the question. The peculiarity of the evidence of mathematical truths is, that all the argument is on one side. There are no objections, and no answers to objections. But on every subject on which difference of opinion is possible, the truth depends on a balance to be struck between two sets of conflicting reasons. Even in natural philosophy, there is always some other explanation possible of the same facts; some geocentric theory instead of heliocentric, some phlogiston instead of oxygen; and it has to be shown why that other theory cannot be the true one: and until this is shown, and until we know how it is shown, we do not understand the grounds of our opinion. But when we turn to subjects infinitely more complicated, to morals, religion, politics, social relations, and the business of life, three-fourths of the arguments for every disputed opinion consist in dispelling the appearances which favor some opinion different from it. The greatest orator, save one, of antiquity, has left it on record that he always studied his adversary's case with as great, if not with still greater, intensity than even his own. What Cicero practiced as the means of forensic success, requires to be imitated by all who study any subject in order to arrive at the truth. He who knows only his own side of the case, knows little of that. His reasons may be good, and no one may have been able to refute them. But if he is equally unable to refute the reasons on the opposite side; if he does not so much as know what they are, he has no ground for preferring either opinion. The rational position for him would be suspension of judgment, and unless he contents himself with that, he is either led by authority, or adopts, like the generality of the world, the side to which he feels most inclination. Nor is it enough that he should hear the arguments of adversaries from his own teachers, presented as they state them, and accompanied by what they offer as refutations. That is not the way to do justice to the arguments, or bring them into real contact with his own mind. He must be able to hear them from persons who actually believe them; who defend them in earnest, and do their very utmost for them. He must know them in their most plausible and persuasive form; he must feel the whole force of the difficulty which the true view of the subject has to encounter and dispose of; else he will never really possess himself of the portion of truth which meets and removes that difficulty. Ninety-nine in a hundred of what are called educated men are in this condition; even of those who can argue fluently for their opinions. Their conclusion may be true, but it might be false for anything they know: they have never thrown themselves into the mental position of those who think differently from them, and considered what such persons may have to say; and consequently they do not, in any proper sense of the word, know the doctrine which they themselves profess. They do not know those parts of it which explain and justify the remainder; the considerations which show that a fact which seemingly conflicts with another is reconcilable with it, or that, of two apparently strong reasons, one and not the other ought to be preferred. All that part of the truth which turns the scale, and decides the judgment of a completely informed mind, they are strangers to; nor is it ever really known, but to those who have attended equally and impartially to both sides, and endeavored to see the reasons of both in the strongest light. So essential is this discipline to a real understanding of moral and human subjects, that if opponents of all important truths do not exist, it is indispensable to imagine them, and supply them with the strongest arguments which the most skilful devil's advocate can conjure up.

To abate the force of these considerations, an enemy of free discussion may be supposed to say, that there is no necessity for mankind in general to know and understand all that can be said against or for their opinions by philosophers and theologians. That it is not needful for common men to be able to expose all the misstatements or fallacies of an ingenious opponent. That it is enough if there is always somebody capable of answering them, so that nothing likely to mislead uninstructed persons remains unrefuted. That simple minds, having been taught the obvious grounds of the truths inculcated in them, may trust to authority for the rest, and being aware that they have neither knowledge nor talent to resolve every difficulty which can be raised, may repose in the assurance that all those which have been raised have been or can be answered, by those who are specially trained to the task.

Conceding to this view of the subject the utmost that can be claimed for it by those most easily satisfied with the amount of understanding of truth which ought to accompany the belief of it; even so, the argument for free discussion is no way weakened. For even this doctrine acknowledges that mankind ought to have a rational assurance that all objections have been satisfactorily answered; and how are they to be answered if that which requires to be answered is not spoken? or how can the answer be known to be satisfactory, if the objectors have no opportunity of showing that it is unsatisfactory? If not the public, at least the philosophers and theologians who are to resolve the difficulties, must make themselves familiar with those difficulties in their most puzzling form; and this cannot be accomplished unless they are freely stated, and placed in the most advantageous light which they admit of.

It still remains to speak of one of the principal causes which make diversity of opinion advantageous, and will continue to do so until mankind shall have entered a stage of intellectual advancement which at present seems at an incalculable distance. We have hitherto considered only two possibilities: that the received opinion may be false, and some other opinion, consequently, true; or that, the received opinion being true, a conflict with the opposite error is essential to a clear apprehension and deep feeling of its truth. But there is a commoner case than either of these; when the conflicting doctrines, instead of being one true and the other false, share the truth between them; and the nonconforming opinion is needed to supply the remainder of the truth, of which the received doctrine embodies only a part. Popular opinions, on subjects not palpable to sense, are often true, but seldom or never the whole truth. They are a part of the truth; sometimes a greater, sometimes a smaller part, but exaggerated, distorted, and disjoined from the truths by which they ought to be accompanied and limited. Heretical opinions, on the other hand, are generally some of these suppressed and neglected truths, bursting the bonds which kept them down, and either seeking reconciliation with the truth contained in the common opinion, or fronting it as enemies, and setting themselves up, with similar exclusiveness, as the whole truth. The latter case is hitherto the most frequent, as, in the human mind, one-sidedness has always been the rule, and many-sidedness the exception. Hence, even in revolutions of opinion, one part of the truth usually sets while another rises. Even progress, which ought to superadd, for the most part only substitutes, one partial and incomplete truth for another; improvement consisting chiefly in this, that the new fragment of truth is more wanted, more adapted to the needs of the time, than that which it displaces.

I have already observed that, owing to the absence of any recognized general principles, liberty is often granted where it should be withheld, as well as withheld where it should be granted; and one of the cases in which, in the modern European world, the sentiment of liberty is the strongest, is a case where, in my view, it is altogether misplaced. A person should be free to do as he likes in his own concerns; but he ought not to be free to do as he likes in acting for another, under the pretext that the affairs of the other are his own affairs. The State, while it respects the liberty of each in what specially regards himself, is bound to maintain a vigilant control over his exercise of any power which it allows him to possess over others. This obligation is almost entirely disregarded in the case of the family relations, a case, in its direct influence on human happiness, more important than all others taken together. The almost despotic power of husbands over wives needs not be enlarged upon here, because nothing more is needed for the complete removal of the evil, than that wives should have the same rights, and should receive the protection of law in the same manner, as all other persons; and because, on this subject, the defenders of established injustice do not avail themselves of the plea of liberty, but stand forth openly as the champions of power. It is in the case of children, that misapplied notions of liberty are a real obstacle to the fulfillment by the State of its duties. One would almost think that a man's children were supposed to be literally, and not metaphorically, a part of himself, so jealous is opinion of the smallest interference of law with his absolute and exclusive control over them; more jealous than of almost any interference with his own freedom of action: so much less do the generality of mankind value liberty than power. Consider, for example, the case of education. Is it not almost a self-evident axiom, that the State should require and compel the education, up to a certain standard, of every human being who is born its citizen? Yet who is there that is not afraid to recognize and assert this truth? Hardly any one indeed will deny that it is one of the most sacred duties of the parents (or, as law and usage now stand, the father), after summoning a human being into the world, to give to that being an education fitting him to perform his part well in life towards others and towards himself. But while this is unanimously declared to be the father's duty, scarcely anybody, in this country, will bear to hear of obliging him to perform it. Instead of his being required to make any exertion or sacrifice for securing education to the child, it is left to his choice to accept it or not when it is provided gratis! It still remains unrecognized, that to bring a child into existence without a fair prospect of being able, not only to provide food for its body, but instruction and training for its mind, is a moral crime, both against the unfortunate offspring and against society; and that if the parent does not fulfill this obligation, the State ought to see it fulfilled, at the charge, as far as possible, of the parent.

Were the duty of enforcing universal education once admitted, there would be an end to the difficulties about what the State should teach, and how it should teach, which now convert the subject into a mere battle-field for sects and parties, causing the time and labor which should have been spent in educating, to be wasted in quarreling about education. If the government would make up its mind to *require* for every child a good education, it might save itself the trouble of *providing* one. It might leave to parents to obtain the education where and how they pleased, and content itself with helping to pay the school fees of the poorer classes of children, and defraying the entire school expenses of those who have no one else pay for them. The objections which are urged with reason against State education, do not apply to the enforcement of education by the State, but to the State's taking upon itself to direct that education: which is a totally different thing. That the whole or any large part of the education of the people should be in State hands, I go as far as any one in deprecating. All that has been said of the importance of individuality of character, and diversity in opinions and modes of conduct, involves, as of the same unspeakable importance, diversity of education. A general State education is a mere contrivance for molding people to be exactly like one another: and as the mold in which it casts them is that which pleases the predominant power in the government, whether this be a monarch, a priesthood, an aristocracy, or the majority of the existing generation in proportion as it is efficient and successful, it establishes a despotism over the mind, leading by natural tendency to one over the body. An education established and controlled by the State should only exist, if it exist at all, as one among many competing experiments, carried on for the purpose of example and stimulus, to keep the others up to a certain standard of excellence. Unless, indeed, when society in general is in so backward a state that it could not or would not provide for itself any proper institutions of education, unless the government undertook the task: then, indeed, the government may, as the less of two great evils, take upon itself the business of schools and universities, as it may that of joint-stock companies, when private enterprise, in a shape fitted for undertaking great works of industry, does not exist in the country. But in general, if the country contains a sufficient number of persons qualified to provide education under government auspices, the same persons would be able and willing to give an equally good education on the voluntary principle, under the assurance of remuneration afforded by a law rendering education compulsory, combined with the State aid to those unable to defray the expense.

The instrument for enforcing the law could be no other than public examinations, extending to all children, and beginning at an early age. An age might be fixed at which every child must be examined, to ascertain if he (or she) is able to read. If a child proves unable, the father, unless he has some sufficient ground of excuse, might be subjected to a moderate fine, to be worked out, if necessary, by his labor, and the child might be put to school at his expense. Once in every year the examination should be renewed, with a gradually extending range of subjects, so as to make the universal acquisition, and what is more, retention, of a certain minimum of general knowledge, virtually compulsory. Beyond that minimum, there should be voluntary examinations on all subjects, at which all who come up to a certain standard of proficiency might claim a certificate. To prevent the State from exercising, through these arrangements, an improper influence over opinion, the knowledge required for passing an examination (beyond the merely instrumental parts of knowledge, such as languages and their use) should, even in the higher classes of examinations, be confined to facts and positive science exclusively. The examinations on religion, politics, or other disputed topics, should not turn on the truth or falsehood of opinions, but on the matter of fact that such and such an opinion is held, on such grounds, by such authors, or schools, or churches. Under this system, the rising generation would be no worse off in regard to all disputed truths, than they are at present; they would be brought up either churchmen or dissenters as they now are, the State merely taking care that they should be instructed churchmen, or instructed dissenters. There would be nothing to hinder them from being taught religion, if their parents chose, at the same schools where they were taught other things. All attempts by the State to bias the conclusions of its citizens on disputed subjects, are evil; but it may very properly offer to ascertain and certify that a person possesses the knowledge, requisite to make his conclusions, on any given subject, worth attending to. A student of philosophy would be the better for being able to stand an examination both in Locke and in Kant, whichever of the two he takes up with, or even if with neither: and there is no reasonable objection to examining an atheist in the evidences of Christianity, provided he is not required to profess a belief a them. The examinations, however, in the higher branches of knowledge should, I conceive, be entirely voluntary. It would be giving too dangerous a power to governmentes, were they allowed to exclude any one from professions, even from the profession of teacher, for alleged deficiency of qualifications: and I think, with Wilhelm von Humboldt, that degrees, or other public certificates of scientific or professional acquirements, should be given to all who present themselves for examination, and stand the test; but that such certificates should confer no advantage over competitors, other than the weight which may be attached to their testimony by public opinion.

15

DEMOCRATIC EDUCATION IN DIFFICULT TIMES

Amy Gutman

These are difficult times because we are difficult people. There are undoubtedly other, less "personal" reasons that make these difficult times and also other, more "structural" reasons that help explain why we are difficult people, but I want to begin by focusing on the fact that we *are*–for whatever simple or complicatcd reasons–difficult people.

When I say we are difficult people, I have something very simple in mind. Most Americans value freedom of speech and also value protection from falsehood, deceit, and defamation. Yet it is impossible to provide complete freedom of speech and still prevent the widespread dissemination of falsehoods, deceits, and defamations. Most Americans value freedom of religion, and also want governments to shape the social environment so that people are predisposed to believe in "good" religions (or philosophies of life) rather than "bad" ones. Yet a society that grants complete freedom of religion cannot shape an environment resistant to repugnant religions.

Most Americans value living and working where we like, and also value stable, friendly, and familiar places in which to live and work. We value the freedom to choose our sexual partners and rechoose them, and we also place a high value on stable nuclear families. Most Americans want to use their market freedom to secure a standard of living that is staggeringly high by any historical perspective, yet we are also sensitive to the plight of other people's children, which threatens this expectation. Most Americans would like to see our freedoms extended to other people, but we fear that by opening our borders, we decrease the chances of our own (and our children's) educational and economic improvement.

The tension within each set of values–between individual freedom and civic virtue–poses a challenge for educating Americans. It is impossible to educate children to maximize both their freedom and their civic virtue. Yet Americans want both–although some people seem willing to settle for freedom for themselves and civic virtue for others. This formula obviously will not work. Far from obvious, however, is how our educational institutions should come to terms with the tension between individual freedom and civic virtue. Should they try to reconcile these seemingly unreconcilable values? Or give priority to one value over the other? Or find the one, morally best way of coping with each of these tensions? Or should we continue to muddle through much as we have done in the past? Rarely do Americans turn to philosophy for help, except in those rare times when the consequences of muddling through seem unbearable. We then reconcile ourselves to philosophizing; we make a necessity out of a virtue.

While these times are undoubtedly difficult in many ways, philosophy is probably not necessary for getting us through them (and philosophy will certainly not be sufficient). Our nation's political ideals–liberty *and* justice *for all*–remain at risk, but the risks to economically and educationally advantaged Americans are not so great that we have no practical alternative to muddling through. Philosophizing still seems to be a practical luxury. Some of us may be able to withstand the practical risks of politics and education as usual. But, as a society we would do better, both morally and practically, to be more philosophically guided in our educational politics.

By what philosophy should we be guided? The several philosophies that compete for our allegiance suggest radically different ways of dealing with the tensions that make us difficult people. Despite their differences, they all try to *dissolve* the tension between individual freedom and civic virtue in a potent philosophical solution, and thereby avoid the political problems that flow from the tension. Perhaps the most distinctive feature of a democratic theory of education is its simultaneous refusal to dissolve these tensions philosophically and its insistence on finding a principled, rather than simply a pragmatic, way of living with the tensions. Living with the tensions will never be easy, but the alternatives to democratic education that promise to make us easier people are far worse. One of the strongest arguments for democratic education–as for democracy itself–is that the alternatives are worse. So let us consider the two most philosophically potent and politically influential alternatives to a democratic state of education: a Platonic family state and a liberal state of individuals.

THE FAMILY STATE AND THE LIBERAL STATE

One of the greatest treatises on education ever written, Plato's *Republic*, offers a way of dissolving the tensions between individual freedom and virtue: Subsume all that is valuable with regard to individual freedom into civic virtue. The means of subsumption is education: Teach children that they cannot realize their own good except by contributing to the social good. Not just any social good will do: Children must be taught the true good, the one that rightly orders their souls, the one consonant with their varying natures. Unless children learn to associate their own good with the social good, a peaceful and prosperous society will be impossible. Unless the social good that they are taught is consonant with their nature and worthy of their pursuit, they will grow to be unfulfilled and dissatisfied with the society that miseducated them. All education that is not guided by *the* social good and the *truth* in human nature is miseducation. All such societies will degenerate because of internal disharmony.

Peculiarly enough, the Platonic family state provides the philosophical underpinnings of an ongoing American search for "the one best system." The system tries to dissolve the tensions between individual freedom and civic virtue by educating all children to identify their interests with the social good. In practice, the moral costs of dissolving the tension are great: Catholic children were once whipped for refusing to read the ("right") King James version of the Bible; college students today are ridiculed (or dismissed as uneducable) for reading Plato's *Phaedrus* in the wrong way. (So Allan Bloom asks rhetorically: "How does a youngster who sees sublimation where Plato saw divination learn from Plato, let alone think Plato can speak to him?")[1]

Repression of reasonable points of view is half the problem of the family state. The other half is political tyranny justified in the name of educational enlightenment. In the *Republic*, Socrates tells Glaucon that "it's better for all to he ruled by what is divine and prudent, especially when one has it as his own within himself; but, if not, *set over one from outside*, so that insofar as possible all will be alike and friends, piloted by the same thing."[2] Children must not be set free until the right regime—the "divine and prudent" one—is established within their souls.

Who holds the key to the right regime? Not the Socrates who boasts of being the only Athenian wise enough to know his own ignorance. Socrates imagines that there may be someone wiser even than he, someone who has left the cave, and seen the light, someone who therefore knows the right regime for all souls. To create a family state, that philosopher must return to the cave, become "king," and wipe the social slate clean by exiling "all those in the city who happen to be older than ten: and taking over their children . . . rear them—far away from those dispositions they now have from their parents."[3] This is not a small price to pay for dissolving the tensions with which we now live. Socrates himself recoils from the idea on behalf of his imaginary philosopher-king, suggesting that he "won't be willing to mind the political things . . . unless some divine chance coincidentally comes to pass."[4]

This problem with the family state is not a purely practical one—pointing to the impossibility of finding someone wiser than Socrates who could educate well-ordered souls in a poorly ordered society. Even if there were someone wiser than Socrates in our midst, he or she still could not claim the right to order the souls of all citizens. A good life must be one that a person recognizes as such, lived from the inside, according to one's own best lights. The neo-Platonic quest for the one best system, which subsumes individual freedom into the social good, denies this insight of individualism. Even if Plato were right about the objectively good life, we would still have to look past the *Republic* for a politically legitimate way of associating individual freedom and civic virtue, through governing.

Radically opposed to the family state is what I call the state of individuals or the liberal state as it is commonly but misleadingly called. The state of individuals overcomes the tensions between freedom and virtue in a way precisely the opposite of that in the family state: It actively supports only those institutions instrumental to individual freedom of choice. The principled neutrality of the state of individuals aims to maximize the freedom of individuals to pursue their diverse conceptions of the private good. If the Platonic family state strives for the unity of a traditional family, the state of individuals strives for the diversity of a modern shopping mall. To paraphrase John Stuart Mill: All attempts by the state to bias the conclusions of its citizens, including its children, on disputed subjects are evil, as are all unnecessary restrictions on their choices. This is the contemporary liberal credo of neutrality for the sake of opportunity and choice.

Just as the family state provides the philosophical underpinnings for "the one best system," the state of individuals provides philosophical inspiration for "child-centered" education. Of course, proponents of the state of individuals recognize that all educators must limit children's choices, but only for the sake of developing their capacity for rational choice or for the sake of cultural coherence. American schoolchildren are taught English rather than Bengali or Spanish, not by choice but by cultural determination. This culturally determined curriculum, contemporary liberals like Bruce Ackerman tell us, legitimately limits the range of their future choices insofar as such limitation is necessary for cultural coherence. Other limits on children's choices—whether for the sake of moral development or the shaping of democratic character—are unjustified, for these would be based on what Ackerman calls "adult pretensions to moral superiority."[5]

The horticultural imagery so prevalent in Plato—pruning and weeding children's desires, shaping their character—has no place in the state of individuals: "We have no right to look upon future citizens as if we were master gardeners who can tell the difference between a pernicious weed and a beautiful flower."[6] We do have a right, according to Ackerman, perhaps even a duty, to shape the character and bias the choices of children for the sake of cultural coherence. Education in the state of individuals builds on our cultural but not our moral biases. We educate children to be Americans who are free to choose but we do not bias their choices (or shape their character) for the sake of moral goodness. We educate rational shoppers but not good people or virtuous citizens.

Why say that parents and teachers should be free to guide children's choices for the sake of cultural coherence but not for the sake of cultivating good character or choosing a morally good life? After all, sometimes the claim on the part of parents and teachers that they know the difference between morally good and bad, or better and worse, is not a *pretension* to moral superiority, but a reflection of their greater moral understanding. Honesty is better than deceitfulness, industriousness better than sloth, insight better than insensitivity, kindness better than cruelty—and not just because honest, industrious, insightful, and kind people have more freedom of choice. They may have less freedom of choice precisely because they are constrained by these virtues. We nonetheless value these virtues because there is more to a good life and to a good society than freedom; that is one good reason why we are likely to remain difficult people, torn between freedom and other virtues that are not mere means to or by-products of freedom.

The "neutrality" premise (no authority has a right to act on a belief that one conception of the good life is better than any other) simplifies life for some contemporary liberals, allowing them to defend freedom of choice singlemindedly, but the lameness of the defense is particularly evident in American education. Consumer choice is a reasonable guiding principle for designing a shopping mall, but it is an irresponsible and incomplete principle for designing a high school. Educators must limit students' freedom of choice on some ground; otherwise education simply ceases. Cultural prejudice may seem like the politically safest guide to limiting choice, but it is not a satisfactory substitute for moral principle. Nor is it politically safe: Teaching cultural prejudices is no less politically controversial than teaching moral principles, as recent battles over bilingualism and the content of core curricula indicate.

The family state and the state of individuals offer us the following choice: Either we must educate children so that they are free to choose among the widest range of lives because freedom of choice is the paramount good, or we must educate children so that they will choose *the* life that is best because a rightly ordered soul is the paramount good. Let children define their own identity or define it for them. Give children liberty or give them virtue. This is a morally false choice. Cultivating character and intellect through education constrains children's future choices, but it does not uniquely determine them. There need be nothing illegitimate about such constraints, although some constraints surely are illegitimate. The question we must therefore ask is not whether to maximize freedom or to inculcate virtue, but how to combine freedom with virtue. This creates a new question: which freedoms and what virtues? We must focus not just on the future freedom of children but also the present freedom of parents, not just on the virtues necessary for a good life but also those necessary for a just society.

This reformulation does not resolve but at least it comprehends the problem of associating individual freedom and civic virtue that Americans face today: Citizens of a religiously and ethnically diverse society disagree on the relative value of freedom and virtue; we disagree on the nature of a good life and good character. No political philosophy can authoritatively resolve all our disagreements–not only because no one is smart enough to comprehend a comprehensive good, but because no mortal, no matter how wise, can legitimately impose a good life on people who cannot live that life from the inside. Nor can anyone legitimately impose liberal neutrality on people who value virtue as well as freedom. We stand at a philosophical and political impasse unless we can defend another alternative.

A DEMOCRATIC ALTERNATIVE: PUBLIC DEBATE

The alternative I want to defend is democratic in several significant respects. First, it does not tyrannize over common sense, either by subsuming individual freedom into the common social good or by collapsing civic virtue (or social justice) into individual freedom. Second, a democratic theory of education provides principled criticism of all educational authorities (including parents) who tyrannize children in any way, whether by depriving them of an education adequate to citizenship or by repressing reasonable challenges to popular ideas. Third, a democratic theory supports educational institutions that are conducive to democratic deliberation, institutions that make a democratic virtue out of our inevitable disagreements over educational problems. The virtue, too simply stated, is that we can publicly debate educational problems in a way much more likely to increase our understanding of education and each other than if we were to leave the management of schools, as Kant suggested, "to depend entirely upon the judgment of the most enlightened experts."[7] The policies that result from our democratic deliberations will not always be the right ones, but they will be more enlightened–by the values and concerns of the many communities that constitute a democracy–than those that would have been made by unaccountable experts.

This understanding of democratic education is, however, incomplete. The threat of repression and discrimination remains. Democratic processes can be used to destroy democratic education. They can be used to undermine the intellectual foundations of future democratic deliberations by repressing unpopular ways of thinking or excluding some future citizens from an education adequate for participating in democratic politics. A democratic society must not be constrained to legislate what the wisest parent or philosopher wants for his or her child, but it must be constrained not to legislate policies that render democracy repressive or discriminatory. A democratic theory of education recognizes the importance of empowering citizens to make educational policy and also of constraining their choices to a broad range of policies that are nonrepressive and nondiscriminatory, so as to preserve the intellectual and social foundations of democracy. Democracy must be understood not merely (or primarily) as a *process* of majority rule, but rather as an *ideal* of a society whose adults members are, and continue to be, equipped by their education and authorized by political structures to share in ruling. A democratic society must educate all educable children to be capable of participating in collectively shaping their society.

Democracy makes no claim to being an uncontroversial standard. Not all societies or all citizens in our society are committed to democracy (although all, according to this argument, should be). Those who are not committed to democracy are stuck at the impasse I characterized earlier: They assert their commitment to civic virtue or to individual freedom always at the expenses of denying the legitimacy of the other value. The practical consequence of this thinking is that basic freedoms are sacrificed to communal virtue or freedom is expanded so far as to forgo the virtues essential to a just society. The legitimating claim of democracy is therefore not that it will be accepted by all citizens (let alone all philosophers)–no political philosophy can sensibly claim such a Panglossian future. Its legitimating claim is one of political morality: A state of democratic education is minimally objectionable insofar as it leaves maximum moral room for citizens deliberately to shape their society, not in their own image, but in an image that they can legitimately identify with their informed, moral choices.

You cannot govern unless you have first been governed. You must govern after you have been governed. These twin maxims, not Platonic but

Aristotelian in origin, are at the root of a democratic understanding of both politics and education: being governed and governing in turn, where governing includes the nurturing of children by parents, their formal instruction by professionals, the structuring of public instruction by public officials accountable to citizens, and the shaping of culture by both private and public authorities—constrained or ideally informed by the principles of nonrepression and nondiscrimination.

There are many ways that this democratic understanding (were it more fully elaborated) could make a difference in the way we think about education and practice it. I offer here one small but significant example.

EVOLUTION OR CREATIONISM: A TEST CASE

In October 1986, a federal district court ruled that the public schools of Hawkins County, Tennessee, must exempt the children of a group of fundamentalist Christian parents from basic reading classes. Those classes assigned Holt, Rinehart, & Winston texts, texts that had been unanimously approved by the Hawkins County Board of Education on recommendation of their textbook selection committee. The content of the Holt, Rinehart series offended the religious views of these parents, who had joined together as Citizens Organized for Better Schools (COBS) and unsuccessfully petitioned the school board to have their children taught from unoffensive texts. The parents objected to, among other things: a story depicting a young boy having fun while cooking on grounds that the story "denigrates the differences between the sexes" that the Bible endorses; a story entitled "A Visit to Mars" on grounds that it encourages children to use their imaginations in ways incompatible with fundamentalist faith, a story entitled "Hunchback Madonna," which describes the religious and social practices of an Indian settlement in New Mexico, on grounds that the story teaches Catholicism; an excerpt from Anne Frank's *Diary of a Young Girl* on grounds that it suggests that nonorthodox belief in God is better than no belief at all. The principal and school board both refused to exempt the children from using the Holt, Rinehart readers. The parents took the Hawkins County Public School District to court.

District Court Judge Thomas Hull found nothing wrong with the Holt, Rinehart series, and said so. Yet he concluded that the children must be exempted from reading the series and therefore from their readikng classes because, in his words,

> plaintiffs [the parents of the children] sincerely believe that the affirmation
> of these philosophical viewpoints is repulsive to their Christian faith, so
> repulsive that they must not allow their children to be exposed to the Holt

series. This is their religious belief. They have drawn a line, and it is not for us to say that the line they drew was an unreasonable one.[8]

Why is it not for us to say?

Not because the parents of those children should have ultimate authority over their education. If that were the case, it would not be for us (or Judge Hull) to say that they must be educated at all. Yet Judge Hull ruled that the children take standardized tests in reading rather than read standardized texts. If standardized tests are justified, then there must be something that all children should learn independently of what their parents want them to learn.

Not because democratic education is compatible with the fundamentalist view that forbids exposure to knowledge about religions, cultures, and convictions that differ from their own, on grounds that such knowledge corrupts the soul. The parents in this case claimed that their children would be corrupted by exposure to beliefs and values that contradict their own religious views unless it was explained that the other views are incorrect and that their views are the correct ones. Democratic education is surely incompatible with this fundamentalist view of knowledge and morality.

Not because democratic education rests on a conception of the good society that threatens the fundamentalist view of a good life and must defer to fundamentalism for the sake of neutrality. Any defensible political understanding of education depends on some conception of a good society, and every conception worth defending threatens some way of life.

It is a sad fact of democracy in the United States that some citizens still hold religious beliefs that reject teaching children the democratic values of mutual respect for reasonable differences of opinion and rational deliberation among differing ways of life. A rejection of democratic values does not, however, constitute a criticism of democracy any more than the rejection by a committed misogynist of the rights of women constitutes a critique of feminism. Both the parents and the misogynists of course have a right to voice their opinions, but in neither case do they have a right to insist that a democratic state teach or sanction their opinions.

Another argument sometimes offered in defense of the claims of fundamentalist parents is that democratic education consists solely of teaching certain facts, not certain values or virtues, to future citizens. This position is superficially similar to John Stuart Mill's conclusion that the state limit its educational authority to public examinations "confined to facts and positive science exclusively."[9] If this is what we should say about public education, it cannot be because knowing facts is more crucial to a good life or good citizenship than being virtuous. Nor can it be because facts are neutral, while values are not. Might it be because citizens can more easily agree on a body of facts than on a set of values or virtues to be taught to all children? Perhaps this argument was soundly prudential when Mill made it, but its premise is surely very shaky today. The political controversies that have raged in recent years over the biases of testing and the claims of creationism against evolution amply demonstrate how controversial the teaching and testing of facts can be. This is no more or less controversial, however, than the teaching (or not teaching) of civic virtue. If it is political controversy that we wish the state above all else to avoid, our only alternative is to advocate repression, in its most thoroughgoing and insidious form.

NEITHER DISCRIMINATION NOR REPRESSION

There is no defensible political understanding of education that is not tied to some conception of a good society, and there is no conception that is not controversial. Which conception should we therefore defend? Judge Hull hinted at a conception of liberal neutrality: Secular texts must not be imposed on fundamentalist children because they are not neutral among all competing conceptions of the good life. The Holt, Rinehart readers surely are not neutral between fundmentalist Christianity and secular humanism. Nor, as Judge Hull recognized, could any readers be neutral between defer-ence to God's will as literally revealed in the Bible or authoritatively inter-preted by a fundamentalist church, and critical inquiry or mutual respect among persons. Liberal individualists think of themselves as committed only to the latter set of virtues—critical inquiry and mutual respect—but the logic of liberal neutrality does not support their commitment in politics except as a morally lame expression of personal opinion. This expression is insufficient to justify any form of public schooling. The content of public schooling cannot be neutral among competing conceptions of the good life, and if it could, we would not and should not care to support it.

It is not for us to deny fundamentalist parents the right to draw the wrong line for their children in their homes and churches. Parental freedom entails this limited right.[10] It *is* for us to say that parents do not have a right to veto a line drawn by public schools unless that line is repressive or dis-criminatory. If parents, judges, or philosopher-kings are allowed to veto lines drawn by public schools when those lines are neither repressive nor discrminatory, then democratic institutions are denied their legitimate role in shaping the character of citizens.

Is democracy not also repressive if it denies the teaching of Christian fundmentalist convictions within public schools, or, what amounts to the same thing, if it requires the teaching of views inimical to fundamentalist convictions? This challenge to democratic education rests on a serious mis-understanding that a policy is repressive simply because it requires publicly funded or subsidized schools to teach views that are inimical to the sincerely held beliefs of some parents. Nonrepression requires the prevention of repressive practices, that is, practices that stifle rational understanding and inquiry. It is a reductio ad absurdum to claim that preventing such prevention itself constitutes repression.

To defend public schools against the charge of repression by fundamentalist parents does not, however, entail defending the status quo in American public education—far from it. We must criticize schools that fall short of the democratic ideal by, for example, being overly centralized and bureaucratized, and therefore unconducive to the exercise of both democratic deliberation by citizens and democratic professionalism by teachers. (Simply summarized, democratic professionalism authorizes teachers, at the same time that it obligates them, to uphold the principle of nonrepression, for example, by cultivating in future citizens the capacity for critical reflection on their culture. The ideal of democratic professionalism also obligates public officials to create the working conditions that make possible the exercise of democratic professionalism.) These comments can only begin to touch on the problems that plague our schools, judged from the perspective of a democratic ideal of education.

A democratic society cedes to citizens, parents, teachers, and public officials authority over education, but that authority is limited by the very democratic ideal that supports it. Not even an overwhelming majority has the authority to maintain separate schools for blacks, to ban sex education from schools, to teach creationism as science, or to ban politically unpopular books from school libraries. The first two practices are discriminatory, the second two are repressive. The defense of these judgments concerning our educational practices requires interpretation and application of the democratic standards of nonrepression and nondiscrimination. Because the standards are not merely formal, there is no way of mechanically applying them to cases. We cannot, for example, simply ask whether teaching evolution (or creationism) conflicts with some parents' convictions and if it does, conclude that the practice is repressive. The test of nonrepression and nondiscrimination is not popularity among citizens, parents, teachers, or public officials. Repression entails restriction of rational inquiry, not conflict with personal beliefs, however deeply held those beliefs. For every educational practice or institution, we must therefore ask whether the practice or institution in its actual context restricts (or impedes) rational inquiry and therefore is repressive, or whether it excludes some children from educational goods for reasons unrelated to the legitimate social purposes of those goods and therefore is discriminatory.

Some judgments will be relatively easy: Forcing teachers to teach creationism instead of evolution restricts rational inquiry for the sake of furthering sectarian religion and therefore is repressive. Other judgments require more extended argument: Is it repressive to teach evolution but to require equal time for creationism? If equal time for creationism entails teaching that it is as reasonable to believe that the world with all its creatures was created in seven clays as it is to believe that it took *much* longer, then the demand for equal time is indirectly repressive: It undermines the secular standards of reasoning that make democratic education possible in this country. If public schools are permitted to teach the reasonableness of creationism, then the same principle will allow them to teach the reasonableness of divine punishment for the sins of non-Christians or any other minority that happens not to control the school curriculum. On the other hand, if teachers may subject creationist ideas to the same standards of reasoning to which other views presented in their classrooms are subjected, then the demand for equal time may be benign—or even conducive to democratic education. Of course, this is not the interpretation of equal time that proponents of creationism have in mind.

EDUCATION AND POLITICS

Democratic standards often do not yield either simple or single answers to questions—such as how much money schools should allocate for educating the handicapped, the gifted, and the average student. That democratic standars do not yield simple answers is a necessity, given the complexity of our collective life; that they do not yield single answers is a virtue, which underscores the democratic critique of "the one best system." Democracy is valuable for far more than its capacity to achieve correct outcomes. It is also valuable for enabling societies to govern themselves, rather than to be governed by an intelligence unrelated to their nature. If democratic societies are to be self-governing, they must remain free to make mistakes in educating children, so long as those mistakes do not discriminate against some children or prevent others from governing themselves freely in the future. The promise of a democratic education is to support self-government without sanctioning majority tyranny or sacrificing future self-government.

It is not for me to say whether my theoretical understanding of democratic education fulfills this promise, but I am sure that the practical promise of any decent theory of democratic education is far from fulfilled in the United States today. I believe that the burden of a democratic theory of education is to show how, with the proper will, we could restructure American society to approach the democratic ideal, even if we never realize it entirely. As a democrat, the most I can consistently offer is criticism of our dominant educational ideas and institutions, and constructive suggestions for democratic directions of change. The possibility of constructive change depends on the will of those who wield political and economic power in this country. In a better society, that will would be more democratic.

These are therefore difficult times for democratic education not only because we are difficult people who must find a principled way of accommodating both individual freedom and civic virtue, but also (and as importantly) because our political and economic institutions are so far from being democratic that they discriminate against the very people who would benefit most directly from a more democratic education and therefore would be most likely to support it. Democratic education is unlikely to succeed if these institutions remain significantly undemocratic. We cannot conclude from this that political or economic reform must precede educational reform. Our choices are not so stark, nor so easy. To improve significantly the working conditions, the political opportunities, or the schooling of poor Americans requires political pressure from the poor themselves, yet they are the citizens most likely to have been educated in highly authoritarian schools (and families) and least likely to participate in politics (or to be effective when they do).

To realize democratic education in this country, political and economic institutions must become more democratic. For these institutions to become more democratic, education must be democratized. It would be foolish to focus solely on a single sphere, whether politics, economics, or education: first, because the prospects of success in any sphere are limited, and second, because the spheres are interdependent. Small but significant changes in one often bring small but significant changes in the others.

Democratic education does not simplify our outlook on education, but it reorients it away from conventional goals (such as educating every child for the appropriate occupation or for choice among the widest range of occupations) toward a more political understanding of educational ends. The cultivation of the virtues, knowledge, and skills necessary for democratic deliberation should have primacy over other ends of public education in a democratic society because such political education prepares citizens to share as equals in *consciously* reproducing (not replicating) their own society, rather than being subject to external forces of reproduction beyond their collective control. Conscious social reproduction is the ideal not only of democratic education but of democratic politics as well.

At the level of primary schooling, the primacy of political education supplies a principled argument against tracking, sexist education, racial segregation, and narrowly vocational education. Even when these practices improve the academic achievement of students, they neglect the virtues of citizenship, cultivated by a common education characterized by respect for racial, religious, intellectual, and sexual differences among students. The moral primacy of political education also supports a presumption in favor of more participatory and deliberative over more disciplinary methods of teaching. Even when student participation threatens to produce some degree of disorder within schools, it may be defended on democratic grounds for cultivating political skills and social commitments. Conversely, even when a principal succeeds in bringing order to an unruly student body, as has Joe Clark of Eastside High School in Paterson, New Jersey, he may be criticized on democratic grounds for intimidating students rather than reasoning with them, for not tolerating peaceful dissent among teachers, and for expelling problem students in unprecedented numbers (over a three-year period, more than 1,900 students dropped out of Eastside High, many of them expelled by Clark).

Democratic education aims at the empowerment of free and equal citizens, people who are willing and able to share together in shaping their own society. Democratic education therefore constrains public policies by the principles of nonrepression and nondiscrimination for the sake of securing democratic self-government. Within these constraints, democratic education makes a virtue out of the disagreements that inevitably flow from ethnic, religious, sexual, and intellectual diversity.

Above all, democratic education accepts the fact that we are difficult people. Whereas the Platonic family state denies this fact by subsuming individual freedom into civic virtue and the state of individuals denies it by elevating freedom above virtue, democratic education empowers citizens to make their own decisions on how to combine freedom with virtue. Democratic education thereby authorizes people to direct their individual and collective destinies. Fully recognizing that the aims of democratic education may never be fully realized, difficult people should demand no more of our political and educational institutions, and should settle for no less.

NOTES

1. Allan Bloom, *The Closing of the American Mind* (New York: Simon & Schuster, 1987), p. 238.

2. Socrates, *Republic of Plato*, trans. Allan Bloom (New York: Basic Books, 1968), p. 273 (590D).

3. Ibid., p. 220 (541A).

4. Ibid., p. 274 (592A).

5. Bruce Ackerman, *Social Justice in the Liberal State* (New Haven: Yale University Press, 1980), p. 148.

6. Ibid., p. 139.

7. Immanuel Kant, *Kant on Education*, trans. Annette Churton (Boston: D. C. Heath, 1900), p. 17.

8. *Bob Mozart et al.* v *Hawkins County Public Schools* et al., U.S. District Court for

the Eastern District of Tennessee, Northeastern Division, No. CIV-2-83-401 (October 24, 1986), p. 12. The United States Court of Appeals (Sixth Circuit) reversed the decision of the district court and remanded with directions to dismiss the complaint (827 F. 2d. 1058 [6th Cir. 1987]).

9. John Stuart Mill, "On Liberty," in *Utilitarianism, On Liberty, Essays on Bentham* (New York: New American Library, 1962), p. 241 (chap. 5, par. 14).

10. The right is limited not by virtue of being weak, but by virtue of leaving room for other educational authorities.

16

DISCRIMINATORY HARASSMENT AND FREE SPEECH

Thomas C. Grey

I want to say a few words on the problem of discriminatory verbal abuse on the American campus. This problem has engaged me in a practical way at Stanford University for the last few years. I was faculty cochair of the campus disciplinary council when we had a serious racial insult incident. The problem might have come before our council, but ultimately no charges were brought. The incident led others on campus to formulate a set of regulations meant to handle these problems, and I later drafted my own version of such a proposal, which provided the basis for the regulation that the university finally adopted in June 1990.[1]

The title for this panel seems to capture the three clusters of values that overlap on this problem: values of civility, of civil liberty or free expression, and of civil fights or antidiscrimination. I want to start by largely setting the issue of civility to one side. Civility is an important value for universities, and civility and courtesy in manner of speech can be required in the classroom from teachers and students alike. But in my view, this value is not best pursued by coercive disciplinary regulations of campuswide application.

That brings me to the clash between civil liberties and civil rights on the question of verbal harassment. Liberals of my sort are not used to having these two clusters of values collide with each other; we think of ourselves as supporting both equally. We are uncomfortable when they collide, and our natural impulse is to try and wish (or pretend to reason) the conflict away. Nevertheless, I believe that conflict is inescapable here.

The civil libertarian purist will tolerate no disciplinary regulation whatever of abusive or harassing speech on campus. A more moderate and common civil libertarian position, though, would call for prohibiting the most egregious forms of verbal abuse, as long as this is carried out by some narrowly defined, content-neutral and viewpoint-neutral restriction of traditionally recognized exceptions to full First Amendment protection like "defamation,"[2] "fighting words,"[3] or speech that constitutes "intentional infliction of emotional distress."[4]

The civil rights approach to harassment regulation starts with the concept of "hostile environment discrimination" that has become familiar in employment law. The basic idea is that a private-sector employer violates Title VII of the Civil Rights Act of 1964[5] (and a public-sector employer violates the Fourteenth Amendment) if it fails to take reasonable steps to remedy a workplace environment that is differentially hostile to women[6] or minority employees.[7] If a woman or black employee is faced by a barrage of sexist or racist insults from fellow workers, the employer is not free to take a hands-off attitude.[8] The work environment, insofar as it is reasonably within the employer's control, is part of the terms and conditions of employment. If those terms and conditions are worse for black or women employees than for white or male employees doing the same work at the same pay, this constitutes illegal employment discrimination.[9] The hostile-environment doctrine is not a controversial innovation of liberal judges; a unanimous Supreme Court has endorsed it,[10] and Judge Posner has written an interesting opinion applying the idea to hold a public employer liable.[11] It is well-established civil rights law.

Should this doctrine be applied to the campus? The notion is that students are deprived of equal educational opportunity if discriminatory harassment is prevalent and university administrators fail to take reasonable remedial steps. But direct transfer of the hostile-environment discrimination concept to the campus, without any civil liberties check, can readily produce the kind of regulation that was enacted at the University of Michigan, and subsequently struck down by a federal district court, properly in my mind, as a violation of the First Amendment.[12]

The Michigan regulation simply prohibited conduct or speech that foreseeably contributed to an unequally hostile environment for racial minorities, women, gay and lesbian students, and the other groups already protected under the university's general antidiscrimination policy.[13] This rule is a classic example of the "bad tendency" test that modern First Amendment analysis so strongly disfavors.[14] Administrators straightforwardly applying this regulation could plausibly charge students with disciplinary violations for saying such things as that women are not naturally suited to the hard sciences, or that black people are genetically less intelligent than whites, or that homosexuality is a disease or a sin.

Statements like these, frequently repeated in the presence of members of the groups in question, simply *do* as a matter of common sense make the atmosphere more difficult for these individuals on a campus and hence deny them a level educational playing field with students not so stigmatized. At the same time, such statements are core examples of what the First Amendment is meant to protect. There can hardly be a free university, or a free society generally, without open public debate of such central issues of science, public policy, and social organization.

So we do have a conflict between civil rights and civil liberties, as both have come to be commonly (and relatively uncontroversially) understood. The Stanford harassment regulation offers a mediation of this clash. The basic idea is not original (though the regulation does differ from others in some of its details); the University of California at Berkeley has adopted a regulation roughly along these lines,[15] and a similar regulation has been adopted at the University of Texas at Austin.[16] What all these proposals share in common is the idea of *intersecting* one or more of the established exceptions to full First Amendment protection with the civil rights doctrine of hostile-environment discrimination. The proposals prohibit speech that both amounts to "fighting words" or "intentional infliction of emotional distress" on the one hand, and discriminates on an otherwise prohibited basis on the other.

The Stanford regulation establishes a campus offense with three elements. First, the speaker must intend to insult or degrade an individual or small group of individuals on the basis of their race, sex, or other characteristic mentioned in the university's general antidiscrimination policy. This predicate protects insensitive but unintentional slurs, and also protects "group defamation" (as traditionally understood) from punishment as harassment. Second, the speech must be directly addressed to the individual or individuals. This caveat restricts the offense to the face-to-face or "I-thou" situation. Third, the speech must use "insulting or 'fighting' words," a requirement that quotes the Supreme Court's language from *Chaplinsky*.[17] In the context of antidiscrimination policy, these words are defined as those that are "commonly understood to convey direct and visceral hatred or contempt for human beings on the basis of their sex, race,"[18] and so on.

This formula is a lawyerly attempt to define a concept everyone intuitively understands: the basic gutter epithets of racism, sexism, homophobia, and the like. That requirement very much narrows the regulation. What might be called the speech of polite bigotry is not covered, even when it is addressed directly to the victim. And by virtue of the requirement of individual address, even gutter epithets, used with degrading intent, can be uttered with impunity in a general publication or a speech to a general rally; Klan speech, neo-Nazi speech, and Farrakhan-style speech do not violate the regulation.

The prohibition is thus quite narrow from a civil rights perspective and it is narrow for civil libertarian reasons. But even moderate civil libertarians may not be satisfied because the regulation seems to violate *neutrality*. It is certainly not content neutral. It addresses only speech that is discriminatory, that insults people on the basis of their race, sex, and the other "suspect classifications" of antidiscrimination law. You can say something horrible to someone's face about his or her mother without violating the campus disciplinary code.

An additional and still more difficult point, from many civil libertarians' perspective, is that the rule appears to lack viewpoint neutrality, and so to violate one of the core principles of free-speech law. The rule covers only speech using terms or other symbols that are "commonly understood" as viscerally insulting on the basis of sex, race, and so on.[19] As I understand this requirement, it will be asymmetrical in practice because there are just no terms that are "commonly understood" to be viscerally insulting to white people as such, to men as such, or to straight people as such.

As a "framer" of the Stanford regulation, I do not claim any particular interpretive privilege for my understanding of its meaning. A judicial officer will have to apply the ordinance to the facts of a case and interpret it in that context. But if I were that judicial officer, I would not regard a term to be "commonly understood" as viscerally insulting to people having the trait to which the term refers in the absence of a widely shared, deeply felt, and historically rooted social prejudice against people with that trait. I do not even know what terms are current among blacks, Latinos, or gays to refer in a derogatory way to whites, Anglos, or straights. No sentient black, Latino, or gay person is in similar doubt about the standard gutter epithets that refer to their groups.

The result is asymmetrical in the following sense. In those unhappy moments when the contemporary campus becomes a multicultural armed camp, the Stanford regulation would prevent me from firing my most powerful verbal assault weapons across racial, sexual, or sexual preference lines. By contrast, people of color, women, and gays and lesbians can use all the words they have at their disposal against me. This result seems an impermissible failure of viewpoint neutrality to some civil libertarians.

In my view, the asymmetry revealed here already exists in the social world in which we live and is neither created nor enhanced, but rather combatted, by the harassment ordinance. My point is not original; I am merely applying the basic doctrine animating civil rights law from *Brown* v *Board of Education*[20] onward. That doctrine makes the concept of stigma or insult central to civil rights analysis. *Plessy* v *Ferguson*[21] stood for the proposition that so far as the law was concerned, the racial insult of separate-but-equal segregation did not exist except in the oversensitive imaginations of black people. *Brown* settled the issue that Jim Crow's legal impact did *not* fall equally on blacks and whites.[22] In the same spirit, and on the same basis of knowledge of our society, we should recognize that the insults "nigger" and "whitey" are not equivalent.

Yet we still hear *Plessy*'s doctrine preached. Today it takes the form of the claim that asymmetrical restrictions of racial insults are patronizing to students of color.[23] Such restrictions imply, it is said, that whites can take care of themselves in verbal rough-and-tumble, while blacks as a "protected group" are weaker and need official protection. *Brown*'s answer to *Plessy* is also the answer to this argument. American society and its history have created the asymmetry; a regulation cannot attempt to redress that asymmetry without taking it into account.

On the issue of patronization, I should add that in my experience, most students of color support discriminatory harassment restrictions of the Stanford type or stronger ones. If these restrictions are somehow insulting to them, why do they not see it? Are they too dumb? Is it not patronizing to suppose that they do not see their true interests on this question?

The limitation of the harassment prohibition to *discriminatory* insults is actually supported by civil liberties considerations as well. It is constitutional to punish other (nondiscriminatory) fighting words, but the policy of keeping restrictions on free speech as narrow as possible counsels against doing so. Fitting the prohibition to the civil rights enforcement model justifies the restriction on its scope.

A number of students and colleagues have urged to me that if hurtful fighting words are to be banned, an evenhanded approach requires restrictions against using terms like "racist" against white conservatives when, for instance, they oppose affirmative action. These are, in current conditions on our campuses, said to be fighting words or words that inflict emotional distress.

I do not dispute the premise. The reason for not extending prohibition to such utterances again sounds in civil libertarian values. It can be hurtful and enraging to be called a racist, a Nazi, a terrorist, or a Stalinist when one is not. But these are legitimate terms applied, sometimes appropriately, in political debate. There *are* real racists, Nazis, terrorists, and Stalinists. The proper extension of these terms is an endlessly disputable political question, and I would prefer not to involve the disciplinary adjudicative process in deciding when the terms are applied appropriately and when not. The questions are too political to be settled in a judicial hearing.

By distinction, no one is appropriately called one of the gutter insults of discrimination. No one is ever a "nigger" or a "faggot." The connotation of these terms is that persons of a certain race or a certain sexual orientation are less than human. To say that is what the terms are there for—it is all they are there for. When they are used against a fellow human being, face to face, in the posture of I to thou, these words can inflict injury worse than many a physical assault. To treat them as such is the minimum that a decent code of conduct can do.

NOTES

1. Stanford University is a private university not technically subject to First Amendment restrictions. The draft proposal recommends that Stanford's "Fundamental Standard" for speech on campus be interpreted under the "fighting words" doctrine.

2. See e.g. *Curtis Publishing Co.* v *Butts*, 388 U.S. 130 (1967); *New York Times Co.* v *Sullivan*, 376 U.S. 254 (1964); *Beauharnais* v *Illinois*, 343 U.S. 250 (1952).

3. See, e.g., *Chaplinsky* v *New Hampshire*, 315 U.S. 568 (1942).

4. See, e.g., *Hustler Magazine* v *Falwell*, 485 U.S. 46 (1988).

5. Civil Rights Act of 1964, Title VII, 42 U.S.C. § 2000c to 2000e-17 (1988).

6. See *Broderick* v *Ruder*, 685 F. Supp. 1269, 1277 (D.D.C. 1988): "A hostile work environment claim is actionable under Title VII if unwelcomed sexual advances, requests for sexual favors, and other verbal or physical conduct of a sexual nature are so pervasive that it can reasonably be said that they create a hostile or offensive work environment."

7. See *Gilbert* v *City of Little Rock, Ark.*, 722 F.2d 1390, 1394 (8th Cir. 1983): "An employer violates Title VII simply by creating or condoning an environment at the work place which significantly and adversely affects the psychological well-being of an employee because of his or her race."

8. See *Ways* v *City of Lincoln*, 705 F. Supp. 1420. 1422 (D. Neb. 1988), *aff'd in part and rev'd in part.* 871 F 2d 750 (8th Civ 1999): "An employer may not . . . allow an employee to be subjected to a course of racial harassment by co-workers. Once an employer has knowledge of a racially hostile atmosphere in a place of employment, the employer has an affirmative duty to take reasonable steps to eliminate that hostile atmosphere."

9. See 42 U.S.C. § 2000e-2 (1988); *Bohen* v *City of East Chicago, Ind.*, 799 F.2d 1190 (7th Cir. 1986).

10. See *Meritor Savings Bank* v *Vinson*, 477 U.S. 57. 65–67 (1985).

11. See *Bohen* v *City of Fast Chicago, Ind.*

12. See *Doe* v *University of Mich.*, 721 F. Supp. 852, 863 (E.D. Mich. 1989): a public university may not "establish an anti-discrimination policy which had the effect of prohibiting certain speech because it disagreed with ideas or messages

sought to be conveyed," and may not "proscribe speech simply because it was found to be offensive, even gravely so, by large numbers of people."

13. Under the Michigan rule, persons were subject to discipline for "any behavior, verbal or physical, that stigmatizes or victimizes an individual on the basis of race, ethnicity, religion, sex, sexual orientation, creed, national origin, ancestry, age, marital status, handicap or Vietnam-era veteran status." Ibid. at 856.

14. For the modern position that discredits the *Whitney* v *California*, 274 U.S. 357 (1927), "bad tendency" test, see *Brandenburg* v *Ohio*. 395 U.S. 444 (1969).

15. See Office of the President, University of California at Berkeley, Addition to Section 51.00, Student Conduct, Policies Applying to Campus Activities, Organizations. and Students (Part A) (September 21, 1989) (utilizing "fighting words" approach) (available in office of *Harvard Journal of Law & Public Policy*).

16. See Office of the President. Univ. of Texas at Austin, Policy Memorandum 4.120. Prohibition of Racial Harassment of Students (August 1, 1990) (utilizing "intentional infliction of emotional distress" approach) (available in office of *Harvard Journal of Law & Public Policy*).

17. See *Chaplinsky* v *New Hampshire*, 315 U.S. 568 573 (1942).

18. Stanford University, Fundamental Standard Interpretation, Free Expression and Discriminatory Harassment 1 (June 1990) (available in office of *Harvard Journal of Law & Public Policy*).

19. Ibid.

20. 347 U.S. 483 (1954).

21. 163 U.S. 537 (1896).

22. See *Brown*, 347 U. S. at 494: "Segregation of white and colored children in public schools has a detrimental effect upon the colored children. The impact is greater when it has the sanction of the law; for the policy of separating the races is usually interpreted as denoting the inferiority of the negro group."

23. See Alan L. Keyes, "Freedom Through Moral Education," *Harvard Journal of Law & Public Policy* 14 (1991): 165 [299, this volume]. Reprinted in this volume, pp. 295–300.

17

FREEDOM THROUGH MORAL EDUCATION

Alan L. Keyes

The debate over the regulation of speech at universities often becomes a conflict between civil libertarians and civil rights advocates. Unfortunately, this conflict obscures the real issue and becomes an excuse to ignore what is really at stake. It does so, in part, because some participants in the debate like to think that knowledge can be conveyed in a value-neutral manner. Nevertheless, the debate is really about moral education—about how we establish, encourage, and maintain moral behavior.

The most intriguing aspect of seeing the problem in this light is that the very conduct restricted by campus speech regulation lies at the foundation of serious moral education. Moral education involves apportioning praise and blame to guide our conduct. It is not education of the mind, accomplished by sitting down and reading ethics. Rather, because personal sentiments are necessary to translate moral precepts into moral actions, moral education requires what might have been called at one time "sentimental education." We believe that some things are repugnant, nasty, or unacceptable, and thus we would not do them. Likewise, we believe that some things are attractive, wonderful, or acceptable, and thus we would do them. Therefore, to instill moral feelings we must be able to use the vocabulary of praise and blame, appreciation and opprobrium.

In this regard, insult is actually a very useful tool. Insults can attack immoral behavior by exposing it, by ripping off its mask and allowing us to see the corrupt for what they really are. As a result, we should not banish the vocabulary of insult from our society as long as it is effective in fighting emotionally those who engage in immoral conduct.

The distinction between using the tools of praise and blame, appreciation and opprobrium on the one hand, and using coercion on the other, may reflect the distinction between enforcing mores and enforcing laws. For example, in determining what constitutes an acceptable romantic overture, we do not have a formal code of conduct to prescribe acceptable and unacceptable behavior. Instead, this code develops largely on its own. Approach a person of the opposite sex in a certain way, and that person may respond favorably. Approach the same person in a different way, and that person may laugh or use derogatory names.

The second category of response has reduced many an inept lover to despair. Repeated often enough, it may even amount to a form of personal abuse. Still, we do not subject this sort of invidious discrimination to formal regulation. And yet, if the argument for campus speech restrictions depends on the harmful effects of certain words, why are inept lovers not a protected class? There are probably students wandering this very campus who are in the process of being emotionally destroyed. They will carry wounds with them for the rest of their lives. Despite this, however, most people would find my question humorous or ask how anyone could seriously propose to limit this sort of discrimination.

Similarly, we do not regulate the significant prejudice endured by the ugly. Society denies them many important things, including the chance of ever being ravishing movie stars or of engaging in many similar occupations. Yet, because the relevant distinctions do not appear to involve moral judgments on the order of "you are a bad person," few think that this discrimination should be regulated. Someone might be ugly, but that does not make him a bad person. Clearly, the debate over speech restrictions cannot turn solely on the discriminatory use of judgmental language or even on the effects of such language.

There is little disagreement that conduct, and even speech to a certain extent, should be regulated to maintain an acceptable moral atmosphere. This regulation occurs all the time, both in society at large and on college campuses. For instance, public fornication is illegal in most places. It is unacceptable, indecent behavior, and those who engage in it are punished in various ways. Now, for believers in sexual liberation, public fornication is arguably a type of free speech. It makes a statement about the acceptability, and even the beauty, of a particular human behavior. Society proscribes it nevertheless. Not even Charles Lawrence could convince us that public fornication is a message that should be protected under the First Amendment.[1]

Therefore, reducing the debate to civil liberties versus civil rights misses the point. The debate is really about which moral standards we should enforce coercively, which moral standards we should not enforce coercively, and, ultimately, what these moral standards should be.

Although these questions are today most often raised and debated at universities, they are probably more easily resolved in society at large. There, a very easy principle emerges: the principle of politeness. Under ordinary circumstances we can set up rules that determine what kinds of conduct are becoming to citizens and what kinds of conduct are not. As long as we apply these rules without making invidious distinctions, we are reasonably safe.

Although couched in more lawyerly verbiage, courts apply an essentially similar principle when they consider fighting words and breaches of peace.[2] In permitting some degree of regulation, they look at the impact of disruptive speech or behavior on what is arguably a public good requiring protection: civility.

Universities face a harder problem because moral education, the real crux of this dispute, plays a different role in the context of campus life. Education prepares students for citizenship in a free society. Accordingly, politeness takes on a different meaning under these special circumstances–just as being polite in the court of the king is not the same thing as being polite in a democratic context. Yet, the suggested university codes of conduct go beyond the mere regulation of politeness. Instead, these regulations represent an effort to establish and teach new moral standards to replace older moral standards. Moreover, in their dependence on coercion, the new standards may run directly counter to the older ones.

The treatment of homosexuality is a very good illustration of this phenomenon. Homosexuality was, until recently, a taboo word on campuses and elsewhere. Parents taught their children that it was ugly and dirty. They did so in order to turn their moral conviction that homosexual conduct was bad into moral actions by their children. Repugnance at homosexual behavior was seen as necessary to defend against whatever temptation it might present.

Some may claim that this method of teaching was discriminatory. Nonetheless, as I have argued earlier, this method has been commonly used to translate moral precepts into moral actions throughout human history. People point a finger at certain conduct and call it bad, ugly, shameful, dirty, or repugnant. They ridicule and revile it. Many books of the Bible, for instance, contain pages filled with invectives against the wicked.[3]

Significantly, however, we no longer think that invectives used in biblical times constitute fighting words. For example, if we singled out those people in this room who have engaged in any form of premarital sexual activity and called them fornicators and whoremongers, they would probably shrug off or pay no attention to the attack. Over time, then, fighting words may change along with our sense of what constitutes acceptable and unacceptable behavior.

At the same time, if we singled out people who engaged in homosexual acts and called them sodomites or other names, these would still be fighting words. Homosexual rights advocates argue that the use of such words is cause for the intervention of coercive force.[4] In fact, what they are really arguing for is the protection of a still-controversial moral judgment about homosexuality. Because heterosexual promiscuity is generally acceptable, it requires no such formal defense. We do not establish rules to punish its opponents. Homosexuality, by contrast, has not yet achieved the same accepted status. Nonetheless, its defenders seek to create rules to stigmatize its critics. They have even invented a word to convey this stigma: homophobia.

Actually, homophobia is not a good word for this purpose. If homophobia is a true phobia, then it is a neurosis for which people are not responsible. If this is the case, why punish them for it? After all, the fear of immoral behavior is, in many, an uncontrollable impulse. Such people reflexively remove themselves from the presence of what they believe to be evil. They involuntarily try to oppose and destroy immorality.

Furthermore, in some instances, we think such instincts are wonderful. For example, we would approve of the uncontrollable desire to prevent, by whatever means, a murder in our presence. Likewise, we would approve of the innate impulse to flee from the scene of a human sacrifice considered ugly and revolting. We think such instincts are normal and desirable because they reflect standards that are, in some sense, commonly agreed-upon.

By contrast, while everyone understands the general meaning of the term "sexual orientation," the fact remains that people have all kinds of odd sexual tastes. As a society, we are in basic agreement that some of these tastes, such as bestiality, are repugnant. Consequently, we should have the right to raise our children to regard certain behavior as worthy of opprobrium. Those who engage in bestiality, therefore, are rightly ridiculed and scorned in order to support the moral feelings we try to inculcate in our young. Yet, by broadly protecting "sexual orientation," are we not suppressing all forms of praise and blame directed at any sexual behavior whatsoever? Do we not thereby undermine the ability to impart any kind of moral education based on this or other standards?

This is just a general aspect of the problem, but we can only start dealing with it when we face the reality that the issue here is not one of minority rights versus free speech. Instead, the issue is one of identifying both the correct moral standards for universities to uphold and the proper methods for upholding these standards. In this regard, the question becomes whether rules against harassment on the basis of race, gender, or sexual orientation are desirable or justified.

Civil libertarians commonly approach this question, particularly with respect to universities, by talking about the need to preserve free speech as a marketplace of ideas.[5] In a way, this approach is good because it considers the impact of speech restrictions on the pursuit of truth. Yet, the interesting thing about truth is that, although we may seek it for a long time, we are not likely to find it. Nevertheless, the pursuit of truth, as Socrates argued long ago, should be an end in itself, to be valued in and of itself.[6] Consequently, the ability to engage in this pursuit, and to engage in it with strength and courage, is also a benefit. It is, in fact, the chief benefit that should result from a liberal education. The results of liberal education are not nec- essarily measured by what goes into a student's mind in the form of information, but rather by what remains in a student's character in the form of the ability to seek and pursue truth despite difficulties. Thus, the basic problem with the speech restrictions meant to protect various minorities, including blacks, is that they weaken students' ability to seek and pursue truth.

These restrictions are, at the outset, based on patronizing and paternalistic assumptions. Telling blacks that whites have the moral character to shrug off epithets, and they do not, is an insult. Saying that whites have the innate capacity to defend themselves against verbal attack, and blacks do not, compounds the insult. Finally, building this imputed genetic weakness into codes of conduct for the protection of blacks makes perhaps the most insulting, most invidious, most racist statement of all.

These codes are more than insulting; they are ultimately incapacitating. Students come to a university to learn how to engage in the pursuit of truth, in the battle of ideas. This battle is like any other; it requires effective training. For example, the army does not teach soldiers how to fight by establishing rules that prevent stronger conscripts from assaulting weaker ones with certain weapons. To be sure, such rules would permit weaker soldiers to complete their course of training comfortably insulated from certain forms of attack. Such soldiers may volunteer to go to war on the basis of such training, but they would surely be among the first to die.

In calling for speech restrictions, Charles Lawrence argues that certain insults scar or lead to debilitating anxiety.[7] Similarly, when a black student is called a racial epithet, all thoughts are supposedly removed from his mind and he immediately becomes unable to act.[8] Yet, isn't education supposed to prepare students to seek truth, to pursue it, and to persist in this endeavor despite the obstacles? Should students really be protected from these obstacles instead of preparing for them? If a black student steps out of Stanford University into his first argument with a gutter fighter over an important issue, gets called a racial epithet, and loses his mind, should he not go back to Stanford and seek a refund?

The most fundamental problem with campus speech restrictions is that in protecting certain students they ultimately make these students weaker. The restrictions institutionalize victimization by leaving the victimized unprepared to fight against it. This effect might be tolerable as long as minorities live underneath the paternalistic wing of universities such as Stanford. But it is likely to be devastating when they go into a world where no protection exists. That world is the real world, regardless of the laws we make.

Education must offer something more, particularly to those who wish to be free. Freedom is in essence the ability to defend oneself. It does not consist of seeking champions for one's defense—that is not freedom, but feudalism. Therefore, instead of looking for rulers and laws to defend us, we must be able to rule ourselves and make our own laws. This ability must be inside every individual. It should be the result of a liberal education that, true to its name, strengthens people and prepares them to be free.

NOTES

1. See e.g., Charles Lawrence III, "If He Hollers Let Him Go: Regulating Racist Speech on Campus," *Duke Law Journal* (1990): 431. Reprinted in this volume, pp. 301–32.

2. See e.g., *Cox* v *Louisiana*, 379 U.S. 536 (1965); *Edwards* v *South Carolina*, 372 U.S. 229 (1963); *Feiner* v *New York*, 340 U.S. 315 (1951); *Terminiello* v *Chicago*, 337 U.S. 1 (1949); *Chaplinsky* v *New Hampshire*, 315 U.S. 568 (1942).

3. See, e.g., Isa. 1:21–23. 19:11–15, 57:3-5; Jer. 5:7–9, 23:10–14; Matt. 23:1–33.

4. See, e.g., Lawrence, "If He Hollers," pp. 452–56 [309–11, this volume].

5. See, e.g., J. S. Mill, *On Liberty*, pp. 18–52 (D. Spitz, ed., 1975). See also *Abrams* v *United States*, 250 U.S. 616, 630 (Holmes J., dissenting).

6. See, e.g., Plato, *Gorgias* (W. Hamilton, trans. and ed. 1960).

7. See Gunther and Lawrence, "Good Speech, Bad Speech," *Stanford Law Review* (spring 1990): 4, 6, 8.

8. See Lawrence, "If He Hollers," pp. 452–53 [309–10, this volume].

18

FROM "IF HE HOLLERS, LET HIM GO: REGULATING RACIST SPEECH ON CAMPUS"

Charles R. Lawrence III

BROWN V *BOARD OF EDUCATION*: A CASE ABOUT REGULATING RACIST SPEECH

The landmark case of *Brown* v *Board of Education* is not a case we normally think of as a case about speech. As read most narrowly, the case is about the rights of black children to equal educational opportunity. But *Brown* can also be read more broadly to articulate a principle central to any substantive understanding of the equal protection clause, the foundation on which all antidiscrimination law rests. This is the principle of equal citizenship. Under that principle "every individual is presumptively entitled to be treated by the organized society as a respected, responsible, and participating member."[1] Furthermore, it requires the affirmative disestablishment of societal practices that treat people as members of an inferior or dependent caste, as unworthy to participate in the larger community. The holding in *Brown*–that racially segregated schools violate the equal protection clause–reflects the fact that segregation amounts to a demeaning, caste-creating practice.[2]

The key to this understanding of *Brown* is that the practice of segregation, the practice the Court held inherently unconstitutional, was *speech.*
Brown held that segregation is unconstitutional not simply because the physical separation of black and white children is bad,[3] or because resources
were distributed unequally among black and white schools.[4] *Brown* held that
segregated schools were unconstitutional primarily because of the *message*
segregation conveys–the message that black children are an untouchable
caste, unfit to be educated with white children.[5] Segregation serves its purpose by conveying an idea. It stamps a badge of inferiority upon blacks, and
this badge communicates a message to others in the community, as well as
to blacks wearing the badge, that is injurious to blacks. Therefore, *Brown*
may be read as regulating the content of racist speech. As a regulation of
racist speech, the decision is an exception to the usual rule that regulation
of speech content is presumed unconstitutional.[6]

The Conduct/Speech Distinction

Some civil libertarians argue that my analysis of *Brown* conflates speech and
conduct. They maintain that the segregation outlawed in *Brown* was discriminatory conduct, not speech, and the defamatory message conveyed by
segregation simply was an incidental by-product of that conduct. This position is often stated as follows: "Of course segregation conveys a message but
this could be said of almost all conduct. To take an extreme example, a murderer conveys a message of hatred for his victim. [But], we would not argue
that we can't punish the murder–the primary conduct–merely because of
this message which is its secondary by-product.[7] This objection to my
reading of *Brown* misperceives the central point of the argument. I have not
ignored the distinction between the speech and conduct elements of segregation by mistake. Rather, my analysis turns on that distinction. It asks the
question whether there is a purpose for outlawing segregation that is unrelated to its message,[8] and it concludes the answer is "no."

If, for example, John W. Davis, counsel for the Board of Education of
Topeka, Kansas, had been asked during oral argument in *Brown* to state the
board's purpose in educating black and white children in separate schools,
he would have been hard pressed to answer in a way unrelated to the purpose of designating black children as inferior.[9] If segregation's primary goal
is to convey the message of white supremacy, then *Brown*'s declaration that
segregation is unconstitutional amounts to a regulation of the message of
white supremacy.[10] Properly understood, *Brown* and its progeny require that
the systematic group defamation of segregation be disestablished.[11]
Although the exclusion of black children from white schools and the denial
of educational resources and association that accompany exclusion can be

characterized as conduct, these particular instances of conduct are concerned primarily with communicating the idea of white supremacy. The nonspeech elements are by-products of the main message rather than the message simply a by-product of unlawful conduct.[12]

The public accommodations provisions of the Civil Rights Act of 1964[13] provide another example illuminating why laws against discrimination are also regulation of racist speech. The legislative history and the Supreme Court's opinions upholding the act establish that Congress was concerned that blacks have access to public accommodations to eliminate impediments to the free flow of interstate commerce,[14] but this purpose could have been achieved through a regime of separate-but-equal accommodations. Title II goes further; it incorporates the principle of the inherent inequality of segregation, and prohibits restaurant owners from providing separate places at the lunch counter for "whites" and "coloreds." Even if the same food and the same service are provided, separate-but-equal facilities are unlawful. If the signs indicating separate facilities remain in place, then the statute is violated despite proof that restaurant patrons are free to disregard the signs.[15] Outlawing these signs graphically illustrates my point that antidiscrimination laws are primarily regulations of the content of racist speech.

Another way to understand the inseparability of racist speech and discriminatory conduct is to view individual racist acts as part of a totality. When viewed in this manner, white supremacists' conduct or speech is forbidden by the equal protection clause.[16] The goal of white supremacy is not achieved by individual acts or even by the cumulative acts of a group, but rather it is achieved by the institutionalization of the ideas of white supremacy. The institutionalization of white supremacy within our culture has created conduct on the societal level that is greater than the sum of individual racist acts. The racist acts of millions of individuals are mutually reinforcing and cumulative because the status quo of institutionalized white supremacy remains long after deliberate racist actions subside.[17]

It is difficult to recognize the institutional significance of white supremacy or how it *acts* to harm, partially because of its ubiquity. We simply do not see most racist conduct because we experience a world in which whites are supreme as simply "the world." Much racist conduct is considered unrelated to race or regarded as neutral because racist conduct maintains the status quo, the status quo of the world as we have known it. Catharine MacKinnon has observed that "to the extent that pornography succeeds in constructing social reality, it becomes invisible as harm."[18] Thus, pornography "is more act-like than thought-like."[19] This truth about gender discrimination is equally true of racism.

Just because one can express the idea or message embodied by a practice such as white supremacy does not necessarily equate that practice with the idea.[20] Slavery was an idea as well as a practice, but the Court recognized the inseparability of idea and practice in the institution of slavery when it held the enabling clause of the Thirteenth Amendment clothed Congress with the power to pass "all laws necessary and proper for abolishing all badges and incidents of slavery in the United States.[21] This understanding also informs the regulation of speech/conduct in the public accommodations provisions of the Civil Rights Act of 1964 discussed above. When the racist restaurant or hotel owner puts a "whites only" sign in his window, his sign is more than speech. Putting up the sign is more than an act excluding black patrons who see the sign. The sign is part of the larger practice of segregation and white supremacy that constructs and maintains a culture in which nonwhites are excluded from full citizenship.[22] The inseparability of the idea and practice of racism is central to *Brown's* holding that segregation is inherently unconstitutional.

Racism is both 100 percent speech and 100 percent conduct.[23] Discriminatory conduct is not racist unless it also conveys the message of white supremacy—unless it is interpreted within the culture to advance the structure and ideology of white supremacy.[24] Likewise, all racist speech constructs the social reality that constrains the liberty of nonwhites because of their race. By limiting the life opportunities of others, this act of constructing meaning also makes racist speech conduct.

The Public/Private Distinction

There are critics who would contend that *Brown* is inapposite because the equal protection clause only restricts government behavior, whereas the First Amendment protects the speech of private persons. They say, "Of course we want to prevent the state from defaming blacks, but we must continue to be vigilant about protecting the speech rights, even of racist individuals, from the government. In both cases our concern must be protecting the individual from the unjust power of the state."

At first blush, this position seems persuasive, but its persuasiveness relies upon the mystifying properties of constitutional ideology. In particular, I refer to the state action doctrine.[25] By restricting the application of the Fourteenth Amendment to discrimination implicating the government, the state action rule immunizes private discriminators from constitutional scrutiny. In so doing, it leaves untouched the largest part of the vast system of segregation in the United States. The *Civil Rights Cases*, in which this doctrine was firmly established, stands as a monument preserving American racial discrimination. Although the origin of state action is textual, countervailing values of privacy, freedom of association, and free speech all have been used to justify the rule's exculpation of private racism.[26]

In the abstract, the right to make decisions about how we will educate our children or with whom we will associate is an important value in American society. But when we decontextualize by viewing this privacy value in the abstract, we ignore the way it operates in the real world.[27] We do not ask ourselves, for example, whether it is a value to which all persons have equal access. And we do not inquire about who has the resources to send their children to private school or move to an exclusive suburb.[28] The privacy value, when presented as an ideal, seems an appropriate limitation on racial justice because we naively believe that everyone has an equal stake in this value.

The argument that distinguishes private racist speech from the government speech outlawed by *Brown* suffers from the same decontextualizing ideology. If the government is involved in a joint venture with private contractors to engage in the business of defaming blacks, should it be able to escape the constitutional mandate that makes that business illegal simply by handing over the copyright and the printing presses to its partners in crime? I think not. And yet this is the essence of the position that espouses First Amendment protection for those partners.

In an insightful article considering the constitutional implications of government regulation of pornography, Frank Michelman has observed that the idea of state action plays a crucial, if unspoken, role for judges and civil libertarians who favor an absolute rule against government regulation of private pornographic publications (or racist speech), even when that expression is causative "of effects fairly describable . . . as deprivations of liberty and denials of equal protection of the laws."[29] He notes that judges and civil libertarians would not balance the evils of private subversions of liberty and equal protection against the evils of government censorship because "the Constitution, through the state action doctrine, in effect tells them not to."[30] Michelman suggests that the state action doctrine, by directing us to the text of the Fourteenth Amendment, diverts our attention from the underlying issue—whether we should balance the evils of private deprivations of liberty against the government deprivations of liberty that may arise out of state regulations designed to avert those private deprivations.

When a person responds to the argument that *Brown* mandates the abolition of racist speech by reciting the state action doctrine, she fails to consider that the alternative to regulating racist speech is infringement of the claims of blacks to liberty and equal protection.[31] The best way to constitutionally protect these competing interests is to balance them directly. To invoke the state action doctrine is to circumvent our value judgment as to how these competing interests should be balanced.[32]

The deference usually given to the First Amendment values in this balance is justified using the argument that racist speech is unpopular speech, that, like the speech of civil rights activists, pacifists, and religious and political dissenters, it is in need of special protection from majoritarian censorship. But for over three hundred years, racist speech has been the liturgy of America's leading established religion, the religion of racism. Racist speech remains a vital and regrettably popular characteristic of the American vernacular.[33] It must be noted that there has not yet been satisfactory retraction of the government-sponsored defamation of the in the slavery clauses,[34] the Dred Scott decision,[35] the black codes, the segregation statutes, and countless other group libels. The injury to blacks is hardly redressed by deciding the government must no longer injure our reputation if one then invokes the First Amendment to ensure that racist speech continues to thrive in an unregulated private market.[36]

Consider, for example, the case of *McLaurin* v *Oklahoma State Regents*,[37] where the University of Oklahoma graduate school, under order by a federal court to admit McLaurin, a black student, designated a special seat, roped off from other seats, in each classroom, the library, and the cafeteria. The Supreme Court held that this arrangement was unconstitutional because McLaurin could not have had an equal opportunity to learn and participate if he were humiliated and symbolically stigmatized as an untouchable. Would it be any less injurious if all McLaurin's classmates had shown up at the class wearing blackface? Should this symbolic speech be protected by the constitution? Yet, according to a *Time* magazine report, last fall at the University of Wisconsin "members of the Zeta Beta Tau fraternity staged a mock slave auction, complete with some pledges in blackface."[38] More recently, at the same university, white male students trailed black female students shouting, "I've never tried a nigger before."[39] These young women were no less severely injured than was Mr. McLaurin simply because the university did not directly sponsor their assault. If the university fails to protect them in their right to pursue their education free from this kind of degradation and humiliation, then surely there are constitutional values at stake.

It is a very sad irony that the first instinct of many civil libertarians has been to express concern for possible infringement of the assailants' liberties while barely noticing the constitutional rights of the assailed. Shortly after *Brown*, many Southern communities tried to escape the mandate of desegregation by closing public schools and opening private (white) academies. These attempts to avoid the Fourteenth Amendment through the privatization of discrimination consistently were invalidated by the courts.[40] In essence, the Supreme Court held that the defamatory message of segregation would not be insulated from constitutional proscription simply because the speaker was a nongovernment entity.

The Supreme Court also has indicated that Congress may enact legislation regulating private racist speech. In upholding the public accommodations provisions of Title II of the Civil Rights Act of 1964[41] in *Heart of Atlanta Motel* v *United States,* the Court implicitly rejected the argument that the absence of state action meant that private discriminators were protected by First Amendment free speech and associational rights.[42] Likewise in *Bob Jones University* v *United States,*[43] the court sustained the Internal Revenue Service's decision to discontinue tax exempt status for a college with a policy against interracial dating and marriage. The college framed its objection in terms of the free exercise of religion, since their policy was religiously motivated, but the Supreme Court found that the government had "a fundamental, overriding interest in eradicating racial discrimination in education" that "substantially outweighs whatever burden denial of tax benefits"[44] placed on the college's exercise of its religious beliefs. It is difficult to believe that the university would have fared any better under free speech analysis or if the policy had been merely a statement of principle rather than an enforceable disciplinary regulation.[45] Regulation of private racist speech also has been held constitutional in the context of prohibition of race-designated advertisements for employees, home sales, and rentals.[46]

Thus *Brown* and the antidiscrimination law it spawned provide precedent for my position that the content regulation of racist speech is not only permissible but may be required by the Constitution in certain circumstances. This precedent may not mean that we should advocate the government regulation of all racist speech, but it should give us pause in assuming absolutist positions about regulations aimed at the message or idea such speech conveys. If we understand *Brown*–the cornerstone of the civil rights movement and equal protection doctrine–correctly, and if we understand the necessity of disestablishing the system of signs and symbols that signal blacks' inferiority, then we should not proclaim that all racist speech that stops short of physical violence must be defended.

RACIST SPEECH AS THE FUNCTIONAL EQUIVALENT OF FIGHTING WORDS

Much recent debate over the efficacy of regulating racist speech has focused on the efforts by colleges and universities to respond to the burgeoning incidents of racial harassment on their campuses. At Stanford, where I teach, there has been considerable controversy over the questions whether racist and other discriminatory verbal harassment should be regulated and what form that regulation should take. Proponents of regulation have been sensitive to the danger of inhibiting expression, and the current regulation (which was drafted by my colleague Tom Grey) manifests that sensitivity. It is drafted somewhat more narrowly than I would have preferred, leaving unregulated hate speech that occurs in settings where there is a captive audience, speech that I would regulate. But I largely agree with this regulation's substance and approach.[47] I include it here as one example of a regulation of racist speech that I would argue violates neither First Amendment precedent nor principle. The regulation reads as follows:

> Fundamental Standard Interpretation: Free Expression and Discriminatory Harassment
>
> 1. Stanford is committed to the principles of free inquiry and free expression. Students have the right to hold and vigorously defend and promote their opinions, thus entering them into the life of the University. there to flourish or wither according to their merits. Respect for this right requires that students tolerate even expression of opinions which they find abhorrent. Intimidation of students by other students in their exercise of this right, by violence or threat of violence, is therefore considered to be a violation of the Fundamental Standard.
>
> 2. Stanford is also committed to principles of equal opportunity and non-discrimination. Each student has the right to equal access to a Stanford education, without discrimination on the basis of sex, race, color, handicap, religion, sexual orientation, or national and ethnic origin. Harassment of students on the basis of any of these characteristics contributes to a hostile environment that makes access to education for those subjected to it less than equal. Such discriminatory harassment is therefore considered to be a violation of the Fundamental Standard.
>
> 3. This interpretation of the Fundamental Standard is intended to clarify the point at which protected free expression ends and prohibited discriminatory harassment begins. Prohibited harassment includes discriminatory intimidation by threats of violence, and also includes personal vilification of students on the basis of their sex, race, color, handicap, religion, sexual orientation, or national and ethnic origin.
>
> 4. Speech or other expression constitutes harassment by personal vilification if it:
>
>   a) is intended to insult or stigmatize an individual or a small number of individuals on the basis of their sex, race, color, handicap, religion, sexual orientation, or national and ethnic origin; and
>
>   b) is addressed directly to the individual or individuals whom it insults or stigmatizes; and
>
>   c) makes use of insulting or "fighting" words or non-verbal symbols.
>
> In the context of discriminatory harassment by personal vilification, insulting or "fighting" words or non-verbal symbols are those "which by their very utterance inflict injury or tend to incite to an immediate breach of the peace," and which are commonly under-

stood to convey direct and visceral hatred or contempt for human beings on the basis of their sex, race, color, handicap, religion, sexual orientation, or national and ethnic origin.[48]

This regulation and others like it have been characterized in the press as the work of "thought police,"[49] but it does nothing more than prohibit intentional face-to-face insults, a form of speech that is unprotected by the First Amendment. When racist speech takes the form of face-to-face insults, catcalls, or other assaultive speech aimed at an individual or small group of persons, then it falls within the "fighting words" exception to First Amendment protection.[50] The Supreme Court has held that words that "by their very utterance inflict injury or tend to incite an immediate breach of the peace[51] are not constitutionally protected.

Face-to-face racial insults, like fighting words, are undeserving of First Amendment protection for two reasons. The first reason is the immediacy of the injurious impact of racial insults. The experience of being called "nigger," "spic," "Jap," or "kike" is like receiving a slap in the face. The injury is instantaneous. There is neither an opportunity for intermediary reflection on the idea conveyed,[52] nor an opportunity for responsive speech. The harm to be avoided is both clear and present. The second reason that racial insults should not fall under protected speech relates to the purpose underlying the First Amendment. If the purpose of the First Amendment is to foster the greatest amount of speech, then racial insults disserve that purpose. Assaultive racist speech functions as a preemptive strike. The racial invective is experienced as a blow, not a proffered idea, and once the blow is struck, it is unlikely that dialogue will follow. Racial insults are undeserving of First Amendment protection because the perpetrator's intention is not to discover truth or initiate dialogue but to injure the victim.[53]

The fighting words doctrine anticipates that the verbal "slap in the face" of insulting words will provoke a violent response with a resulting breach of the peace. When racial insults are hurled at minorities, the response may be silence or flight rather than a fight, but the preemptive effect on further speech is just as complete as with fighting words.[54] Women and minorities often report that they find themselves speechless in the face of discriminatory verbal attacks. This inability to respond is not the result of oversensitivity among these groups, as some individuals who oppose protective regulation have argued. Rather, it is the product of several factors, all of which reveal the non-speech character of the initial preemptive verbal assault. The first factor is that the visceral emotional response to personal attack precludes speech. Attack produces an instinctive, defensive psychological reaction. Fear, rage, shock, and flight all interfere with any reasoned response. Words like "nigger," "kike," and "faggot" produce physical symptoms that temporarily disable the victim, and the perpetrators often use these words with the intention of producing this effect. Many victims do not find words of response until well after the assault when the cowardly assaulter has departed.

A second factor that distinguishes racial insults from protected speech is the preemptive nature of such insults–the words by which to respond to such verbal attacks may never be forthcoming because speech is usually an inadequate response. When one is personally attacked with words that denote one's subhuman status and untouchability, there is little (if anything) that can be said to redress either the emotional or reputational injury. This is particularly true when the message and meaning of the epithet resonates with beliefs widely held in society.[55] This preservation of widespread beliefs is what makes the face-to-face racial attack more likely to preempt speech than are other fighting words. The racist name caller is accompanied by a cultural chorus of equally demeaning speech and symbols.[56]

The subordinated victim of fighting words also is silenced by her relatively powerless position in society. Because of the significance of power and position, the categorization of racial epithets as "fighting words" provides an inadequate paradigm; instead one must speak of their "functional equivalent."[57] The fighting words doctrine presupposes an encounter between two persons of relatively equal power who have been acculturated to respond to face-to-face insults with violence. The fighting words doctrine is a paradigm based on a white male point of view.[58] In most situations, minorities correctly perceive that a violent response to fighting words will result in a risk to their own life and limb. Since minorities are likely to lose the fight, they are forced to remain silent and submissive.[59] This response is most obvious when women submit to sexual speech or when the racist name caller is in a more powerful position–the boss on the job or the mob. Certainly, we do not expect the black women crossing the Wisconsin campus to turn on their tormentors and pummel them. Less obvious, but just as significant, is the effect of pervasive racial and sexual violence and coercion on individual members of subordinated groups who must learn the survival techniques of suppressing and disguising rage and anger at an early age.[60]

One of my students, a white, gay male, related an experience that is quite instructive in understanding the inadequacy and potential of the "fighting words" doctrine. In response to my request that students describe how they experienced the injury of racist speech, Michael told a story of being called "faggot" by a man on a subway. His description of the speech-inhibiting elements I have noted previously. He found himself in a state of semishock, nauseous, dizzy, unable to muster the witty, sarcastic, articulate rejoinder he was accustomed to making. He suddenly was aware of the recent spate of gay-bashing in San Francisco, and how many of these had escalated from verbal encounters.[61] Even hours later when the shock resided and his facility with words returned, he realized that any response was inadequate to counter hundreds of years of societal defamation that one word–"faggot"–carried with it. Like the word "nigger" and unlike the word "liar," it is not sufficient to deny the truth of the word's application, to say, "I am not a faggot." One must deny the truth of the word's meaning, a meaning shouted from the rooftops by the rest of the world a million times a day.[62] Although there are many of us who constantly and in myriad ways seek to counter the lie spoken in the meaning of hateful words like "nigger" and "faggot," it is a nearly impossible burden to bear when one encounters hateful speech face to face.

But there was another part of my discussion with Michael that is equally instructive. I asked if he could remember a situation when he had been verbally attacked with reference to his membership in a superordinate group. Had he ever been called a "honkie," a "chauvinist pig," or "mick"? (Michael is from a working-class Irish family in Boston.) He said that he had been called some version of all three and that although he found the last one more offensive than the first two, he had not experienced–even in that subordinated role–the same disorienting powerlessness he had experienced when attacked for his membership in the gay community. The question of power, of the context of the power relationships within which speech takes place, must be considered as we decide how best to foster the freest and fullest dialogue within our communities. It is apparent that regulation of face-to-face verbal assault in the manner contemplated by the Stanford provision[63] will make room for more speech than it chills. The provision is clearly within the spirit, if not the letter, of existing First Amendment doctrine.

The proposed Stanford regulation, and indeed regulations with considerably broader reach, can be justified as necessary to protect a captive audience from offensive or injurious speech. Courts have held that offensive speech may not be regulated in public forums such as streets and parks where a listener may avoid the speech by moving on or averting his eyes,[64] but the regulation of otherwise protected speech has been permitted when the speech invades the privacy of the unwilling listener's home or when the unwilling listener cannot avoid the speech.[65] Racist posters, flyers, and graffiti in dorms, classrooms, bathrooms, and other common living spaces would fall within the reasoning of these cases.[66] Minority students should not be required to remain in their rooms to avoid racial assault. Minimally, they should find a safe haven in their dorms and other common rooms that are a part of their daily routine. I would argue that the university's responsibility for ensuring these students received an equal educational opportunity provides a compelling justification for regulations that ensure them safe passage in all common areas. A black, latino, Asian, or Native American student should not have to risk being the target of racially assaulting speech every time she chooses to walk across campus.[67] The regulation of vilifying speech that cannot be anticipated or avoided would not preclude announced speeches and rallies where minorities and their allies would have an opportunity to organize counterdemonstrations or avoid the speech altogether.[68]

Psychic injury is no less an injury than being struck in the face, and it often is far more severe.[69] *Brown* speaks directly to the psychic injury inflicted by racist speech in noting that the symbolic message of segregation affected "the hearts and minds" of Negro children "in a way unlikely ever to be undone."[70] Racial epithets and harassment often cause deep emotional scarring, and feelings of anxiety and fear that pervade every aspect of a victim's life. Many victims of hate propaganda have experienced physiological and emotional symptoms ranging from rapid pulse rate and difficulty in breathing, to nightmares, post-traumatic stress disorder, psychosis, and suicide.[71]

A second injury identified in *Brown*, and present in my example, is reputational injury. "[L]ibelous speech was long regarded as a form of personal assault . . . that government could vindicate . . . without running afoul of the Constitution."[72] Although *New York Times* v *Sullivan* and its progeny have subjected much defamatory speech to constitutional scrutiny—on the reasoning that "debate on public issues should be uninhibited, robust and wide-open"[73] and should not be "chilled" by the possibility of libel suits—these cases also demonstrate a concern for balancing the public's interest in being fully informed with the competing interest of defamed persons in vindicating their reputation.[74]

Brown is a case about group defamation. The message of segregation was stigmatizing to black children. To be labeled unfit to attend school with white children injured the reputation of black children, thereby foreclosing employment opportunities and the right to be regarded as respected members of the body politic. An extensive discussion on the constitutionality or efficacy of group libel laws is beyond the scope of this essay.[75] However, it will suffice to note that whereas *Beauharnais* v *Illinois*,[76] which upheld an Illinois group libel statute, has fallen into ill repute;[77] and is generally considered to have been overruled implicitly by *Sullivan*, *Brown* remains an instructive case. By identifying the inseparability of discriminatory speech and action in the case of segregation, where the injury is inflicted by the meaning of the message, *Brown* limits the scope of *Sullivan*.[78] *Brown* reflects that racism is a form of subordination that achieves its purposes through group defamation.[79]

The third injury identified in *Brown* is the denial of equal educational opportunity. *Brown* recognized that black children did not have an equal opportunity to learn and participate in the school community if they bore the additional burden of being subjected to the humiliation and psychic assault that accompanies the message of segregation.[80] University students bear an analogous burden when they are forced to live and work in an environment where, at any moment, they may be subjected to denigrating verbal harassment and assault. The testimony of nonwhite students about the detrimental effect of racial harassment on their academic performance and social integration in the college commjnity is overwhelming.[81] A similar injury is recognized and addressed in Title VII's requirement that employers maintain a nondiscriminatory (nonhostile) work environment[82] and in federal and state regulations prohibiting sexual harassment on campuses as well as in the workplace.[83]

All three of these very tangible, continuing, and often irreparable forms of injury—psychic, reputational, and the denial of equal educational opportunity—must be recognized, accounted for, and balanced against the claim that a regulation aimed at the prevention of these injuries may lead to restrictions on important First Amendment liberties.

Blacks and other people of color are equally skeptical about the absolutist argument that even the most injurious speech must remain unregulated because in an unregulated marketplace of ideas the best ideas will rise to the top and gain acceptance.[84] Our experience tells us the opposite. We have seen too many demagogues elected by appealing to America's racism. We have seen too many good, liberal politicians shy away from the issues that might brand them as too closely allied with us. The American marketplace of ideas was founded with the idea of the racial inferiority of nonwhites as one of its chief commodities, and ever since the market opened, racism has remained its most active item in trade.[85]

But it is not just the prevalence and strength of the idea of racism that makes the unregulated marketplace of ideas an untenable paradigm for those individuals who seek full and equal personhood for all. The real problem is that the idea of the racial inferiority of nonwhites infects, skews, and disables the operation of the market (like a computer virus, sick cattle, or diseased wheat). Racism is irrational and often unconscious.[86] Our belief in the inferiority of nonwhites trumps good ideas that contend with it in the market, often without our even knowing it.[87] In addition, racism makes the words and ideas of blacks and other despised minorities less saleable, regardless of their intrinsic value, in the marketplace of ideas.[88] It also decreases the total amount of speech that enters the market by coercively silencing members of those groups who are its targets.[89]

Racism is an epidemic infecting the marketplace of ideas and rendering it dysfunctional. Racism is ubiquitous. We are all racists.[90] Racism is also irrational. Individuals do not embrace or reject racist beliefs as the result of reasoned deliberation.[91] For the most part, we do not recognize the myriad ways in which the racism pervading our history and culture influences our beliefs. In other words, most of our racism is unconscious.[92]

The disruptive and disabling effect on the market of an idea that is ubiquitous and irrational, but seldom seen or acknowledged, should be apparent. If the community is considering competing ideas about providing food for children, shelter for the homeless, or abortions for pregnant women, and the choices made among the proposed solutions are influenced by the idea that some children, families, or women are less deserving of our sympathy because they are not white, then the market is not functioning as either John Stuart Mill or Oliver Wendell Holmes envisioned it. In John Ely's terms there is a "process defect."[93]

Professor Ely coined the term "process defect" in the context of developing a theory to identify instances in which legislative action should be subjected to heightened judicial scrutiny under the equal protection clause. Ely argues that the courts should interfere with the normal majoritarian political process when the defect of prejudice bars groups subject to widespread vilification from participation in the political process and causes governmental decision makers to misapprehend the costs and benefits of their actions.[94] This same process defect that excludes vilified groups and misdirects the government operates in the marketplace of ideas. Mill's vision of truth emerging through competition in the marketplace of ideas relies on the ability of members of the body politic to recognize "truth" as serving their interest and to act on that recognition.[95] As such, this vision depends upon the same process that James Madison referred to when he described his vision of a democracy in which the numerous minorities within our society would form coalitions to create majorities with overlapping interests through pluralist wheeling and dealing.[96] Just as the defect of prejudice blinds the white voter to interests that overlap with those of vilified minorities, it also blinds him to the "truth" of an idea or the efficacy of solutions associated with that vilified group.[97] And just as prejudice causes the governmental decision makers to misapprehend the costs and benefits of their actions, it also causes all of us to misapprehend the value of ideas in the market.

Prejudice that is unconscious or unacknowledged causes even more distortions in the market. When racism operates at a conscious level, opposing ideas may prevail in open competition for the rational or moral sensibilities of the market participant. But when an individual is unaware of his prejudice, neither reason nor moral persuasion will likely succeed.[98]

Racist speech also distorts the marketplace of ideas by muting or devaluing the speech of blacks and other nonwhites. An idea that would be embraced by large numbers of individuals if it were offiered by a white individual will be rejected or given less credence because its author belongs to a group demeaned and stigmatized by racist beliefs.

An obvious example of this type of devaluation would be the black political candidate whose ideas go unheard or are rejected by white voters, although voters would embrace the same ideas if they were championed by a white candidate.[99] Racial minorities have the same experiences on a daily basis when they endure the microaggression of having their words doubted, or misinterpreted, or assumed to be without evidentiary support,[100] or when their insights are ignored and then appropriated by whites who are assumed to have been the original authority.[101]

Finally, racist speech decreases the total amount of speech that reaches the market. I noted earlier in this article the ways in which racist speech is inextricably linked with racist conduct. The primary purpose and effect of the speech/conduct that constitutes white supremacy is the exclusion of nonwhites from full participation in the body politic. Sometimes the speech/conduct of racism is direct and obvious. When the Klan burns a cross on the lawn of a black person who joined the NAACP or exercised his right to move to a formerly all-white neighborhood, the effect of this speech does not result from the persuasive power of an idea operating freely in the market. It is a threat, a threat made in the context of a history of lynchings, beatings, and economic reprisals that made good on earlier threats, a threat that silences a potential speaker.[102] The black student who is subjected to racial epithets is likewise threatened and silenced. Certainly she, like the victim of a cross burning, may be uncommonly brave or foolhardy and ignore the system of violence in which this abusive speech is only a bit player. But it is more likely that we, as a community, will be denied the benefit of many of her thoughts and ideas.[103]

Again MacKinnon's analysis of how First Amendment law misconstrues pornography is instructive. She notes that in concerning themselves only with government censorship, First Amendment absolutists fail to recognize that whole segments of the population are systematically silenced by powerful private actors. "As a result, [they] cannot grasp that the speech of some silences the speech of others in a way that is not simply a matter of competition for airtime."[104]

I wish to acknowledge the American Civil Liberties Union Biennial Conference, Stanford Law School, and the Duke University School of Law where tentative versions of this article along with Professor Strossen's article were presented. I am indebted to Stephen Arons, Thomas Grey, and Sylvia Law for their helpful comments on earlier drafts, to David Drummond, Marti Paschal, and Mark Niles for their research assistance, to Richard Delgado and Mari Matsuda for their trailblazing work on the subject of racist speech, and to countless others who have challenged and supported me in my efforts to understand this issue. The title of this article is inspired by the work by Chester Himes, If He Hollers Let Him Go *(1945).*

An earlier version of this article, along with an earlier version of Professor Strossen's article, "Regulating Racist Speech on Campus: A Modest Proposal?" 1990 Duke L. J. *484, were presented as papers for a plenary session of the 1999 Biennial Conference of the American Civil Liberties Union. Papers presented at this session served as a basis of discussion by delegates in small working groups who then proposed policy resolutions for adoption by the con-*

vention. Following a spirited debate, a resolution supporting narrowly framed restrictions of racist speech on campuses was defeated by the convention.

NOTES

    1. Karst, "Citizenship, Race, and Marginality," 30 *Wm. & Mary L. Rev.* 1, 1 (1988).

    2. The prevention of stigma was at the core of the Supreme Court's unanimous decision in *Brown* v *Board of Education*, 347 U.S. 483 (1954), that segregated public schools are inherently unequal. Observing that the segregation of black pupils "generates a feeling of interiority as to their status in the community," ibid. at 494, Chief Justice Warren recognized what a majority of the Court had ignored almost sixty years earlier in *Plessy* v *Ferguson*, 163 U.S. 537 (1996): The social meaning of racial segregation in the United States is the designation of a superior and an inferior caste, and segregation proceeds "on the ground that colored citizens are . . . inferior and degraded," ibid. at 560 (Harlan, J., dissenting); see also Black, "The Lawfulness of the Segregation Decisions," 69 *Yale L. J.* 421, 427 (1960); Brest, "The Supreme Court, 1975 Term–Forward: In Defense of the Antidiscrimination Principle," 90 *Harv. L. Rev.* 1, 8–12 (1976); Cahn, "Jurisprudence," 30 *N.Y.U. L. Rev.* 150, 158–59 (1955); Note that while formal, legally sanctioned segregation was the chief form of stigmatization prior to *Brown* and the Civil Rights Act of 1964, 28 U.S.C. §§ 1443, 1447 (1988). 42 U.S.C. §§ 1971, 1975a–1975d, 2000a to 2000h-6 (1988), the system has yet to be dismantled, and other stigmatizing mechanisms–including the exclusion of blacks from private clubs, privately enforced housing discrimination, and deprecating portrayals of blacks in the media–have reinforced its effects. See Lawrence, "Negroes in Contemporary Society," in *Man, Culture, and Society* 52, 59 (C. Lawrence ed. 1962).

    3. *Brown* is not a case about the right of black children to associate with white children. See Black, n. 2, 421, 427–29, responding to the argument put forward in Weschler, "Toward Neutral Principles of Constitutional Law," 73 *Harv. L. Rev.* 1, 31–34 (1959), that *Brown* was wrongly decided because it did not consider the nonassociational rights of white students.

    4. Although separate but equal was never a reality in the segregated school systems of America, the Court assumed an equality of resources in *Brown* and its companion cases in order to consider plaintiff's argument directly challenging the constitutionality of the separate but equal doctrine of *Plessy*. See *Brown*, 347 U.S. at 492.

    5. For discussion of the "cultural meaning" of segregation, see Black, n. 2; Lawrence, "Segregation 'Misunderstood': The Milliken Decision Revisited?" 12 *U.S. F. L. Rev.* 15 (1977); Wasserstrom, "Racism, Sexism, and Preferential Treatment: An Approach to the Topics," 24 *UCLA L. Rev.*, 581 (1977).

    6. It is important to note that *Brown* is a case about the state engaging in racist speech and that the First Amendment protects individuals, not the state. Stated another way, *Brown* invokes the Fourteenth Amendment, which prohibits *states*, and not *individuals*, from denying equal protection of the laws. Although this is true, I

believe that reliance on the state action doctrine in this context avoids the real issue. It also should be noted that antidiscrimination laws prohibiting segregation by private parties such as Title II of the Civil Rights Act of 1964, 42 U.S.C. §§ 2000a to 2000a-6 (1988) (public accommodations); Title VI, 42 U.S.C. §§ 2000d-I to 2000d-7 (1988) (federally assisted programs); Title VII, 42 U.S.C. §§ 2000e to 2000e-17 (1998) (equal employment opportunities), have not been held unconstitutional regulations of private individuals' speech or association.

7. Remarks by Nadine Strossen, ACLU General Counsel, responding to Professor Charles Lawrence at the 1989 ACLU Biennial Conference plenary session "Racism on the Rise," June 15, 1989. The "extreme" example cited by Professor Strossen is of a kind in which the Court has been reluctant to concede that the First Amendment has any relevance whatsoever. The law is not directed at anything resembling speech or at the views expressed. In such a case the regulation of speech is truly incidental to the regulation of conduct. Professor Strossen asserts that I "chide anyone who insists that *all* racist conduct that includes an expression component should be treated alike—namely, as protected speech." Ibid. This reading of my position clearly misses my point. I do not contend that all conduct with an expresive component should be treated as unprotected speech. To the contrary, my suggestion that racist conduct amounts to speech is premised upon a unique characteristic of racism—namely, its reliance upon the defamatory message of white supremacy to achieve its injurious purpose.

8. All communicative behavior is "100 percent action and 100 percent expression." Ely, "Flag Desecration: A Case Study in the Roles of Categorization and Balancing in First Amendment Analysis," 98 *Harv. L. Rev.*, 1482, 1495–96 (1975). Thus, the distinction between speech and conduct has little determinate content: "[A]ny particular course of conduct may be hung almost randomly on the 'speech' peg or the 'conduct' peg as one sees fit." L. Tribe, *American Constitutional Law*, § 12–7, at 927 (2d ed. 1988). Tribe has suggested that "[m]eaning might be poured into the speechconduct dichotomy by reference to a system of free expression that permits the identification of acts that should be protected by the First Amendment." Ibid.; see also *United States* v *O'Brien*, 391 U.S. 367 (1969). In *O'Brien* the Court stated that,

> [W]hen "speech" and "non-speech" elements are combined in the same course of conduct, a sufficiently important governmental interest in regulating the non-speech element can justify incidental limitations on First Amendment freedoms. . . . [We] think it clear that a government regulation is sufficiently justified it it is within the constitutional power of the Government; if it furthers an important or substantial governmental interest; the government interest is unrelated to the suppression of free expression; and if the incidental restriction on alleged first amendment freedoms is no greater than is essential to the furtherance of that interest.

Ibid. at 376–77.

9. The Court is clearest in its articulation of this understanding of the central purpose and meaning of segregation in *Loving* v *Virginia*, 388 U.S. 1 (1966). In striking down the Virginia statute prohibiting interracial marriage, Chief Justice

Warren noted that the state's purposes " 'to preserve the racial integrity of its citizens,' and to prevent 'the corruption of blood,' 'a mongrel breed of citizens,' and 'the obliteration of racial pride' [were] obviously an endorsement of the doctrine of White Supremacy." Ibid. at 7 (quoting *Naim* v *Naim*, 197 Va. 80, 90, 87 S.E.2d 749, 756 [1955]).

10. In *Plessy* v *Ferguson*, 163 U.S. 537 (1896), the Court upheld Louisiana's racial segregation of railroad passengers by rejecting the argument that segregation necessarily conveyed a message that blacks were inferior. "If this be so, it is not by reason of anything found in the act, but solely because the colored race chooses to put that construction upon it." Ibid. at 551. But *Brown* expressly rejected this rationale. In embracing the notion that "[s]eparate educational facilities are inherently unequal," the *Brown* Court, 347 U.S, 483, 495 (1954), implicitly adopted the reasoning advanced in Justice Harlan's dissent in *Plessy*, 163 U.S. at 560. Justice Harlan argued that provisions requiring separate facilities "in fact proceed on the ground that colored citizens are so inferior and degraded that they cannot be allowed to sit in the public coaches occupied by white citizens. . . ." Ibid.

11. See Black, n. 2; Lawrence, n. 5.

12. This analysis, which acknowledges antidiscrimination law as primarily the regulation of speech, is to be contrasted with the defense of pornography regulation that seeks to characterize the regulation of pornographic speech as the regulation of conduct. See MacKinnon, "Not a Moral Issue," 2 *Yale L. & Pol'y Rev.* 321, 340 (1984).

13. 42 U.S.C. §§ 2000a to 2000a-6 (1988).

14. See *Heart of Atlanta Motel, Inc.* v *United States*, 379 U.S. 241 (1964) (upheld Congress's authority under the commerce clause to compel owners of private property to grant access to individuals whom they wish to exclude); *Katzenbach* v *McClung*, 379 U.S. 294 (1964) (same).

15. See D. Bell, *Race, Racism, and American Law* (2nd ed. 1980). Bell suggests that any "decorative changes designed to maintain prior discriminatory policies" may be enjoined as a violation of Title II as a result of *United States* v *Boyd*, 327 F. Supp. 998 (S.D. Ga. 1971). D. Bell, at 100–101. See also *Green* v *County School Brd. of New Kent County*, 391 U.S. 430 (1968). The Court in *Green* held that "in desegregating a dual system a plan utilizing 'freedom of choice' is not an end in itself." Ibid. at 440.

In the summer of 1966 Robert Cover and I were working as summer interns with C. B. King in Albany, Georgia. One day we stopped for lunch at a take-out chicken joint. The establishment was housed in a long diner-like structure with an awning extending from each of two doors in the side of the building. A sign was painted at the end of each awning. One said, "white," the other, "colored." Bob and I entered the "white" side. When the proprietor took my order, I asked if he knew that the signs on his awnings were illegal under Title II of the Civil Rights Act of 1964. He responded, "People can come in this place through any door they want to." What this story makes apparent is that the signs themselves constitute an injury that violates the antidiscrimination principle even when the conduct of denial of access is not present.

16. See *Strauder* v *West Virginia*, 100 U.S. 303 (1880). According to Justice Strong, "The words of the amendment . . . contain a necessary implication of positive immunity, or right . . . to the colored race—the right to exemption from

unfriendly legislation against them distinctly as colored—exemption from . . . discriminations which are steps toward reducing them to the condition of a subject race." Ibid. at 307–38. Or course the equal protection clause only forbids governmental conduct that purposefully establishes or maintains while supremacy. But see nn. 22–46 and accompanying text (describing how the state action doctrine distorts our understanding of this problem).

17. Professor Kendall Thomas describes the way in which racism is simultaneously speech (a socialy constructed meaning or idea) and conduct by asking us to consider the concept of "race" not as a noun but as a verb. He notes that race is a social construction. The meaning of "black" or "white" is derived through a history of acted-upon ideology. Moreover, the cultural meaning of race continues to be promulgated through millions of ongoing contemporaneous speech/acts. Thus, he says, "we are raced." The social construction of race is an ongoing process. Comments of Kendall Thomas at panel on Critical Race Theory, conference on Frontiers of Legal Thought, Duke Law School, January 26, 1990.

18. C. MacKinnon, *Towards a Feminist Theory of the State*, 204 (1989).

19. Ibid.

20. Ibid.

21. The Civil Rights Cases, 109 U.S. 3, 20 (1883) (striking down the Civil Rights Act of 1875 on the ground that the Fourteenth Amendment did not empower Congress to prohibit racial discrimination by innkeepers, railroads, and places of public amusement); *Jones* v *Alfred H. Mayer Co.*, 392 U.S. 409, 439 (1968) (upholding Congress's use of the "badge of servitude" idea to justify federal legislation prohibiting racially discriminatory practices by private persons).

22. See n. 15 (story of "white" and "colored" signs).

23. John Ely has made the same observation about all speech. See n. 8. But I want to do more than merely convey the dilemma one faces in separating out the speech and conduct elements of communicative acts: I want to stress the complete overlap of the idea and practice of racism.

24. For a discussion of how conduct that violates the equal protection clause might be identified by reference to its cultural meaning within the society, see Lawrence, "The Id, the Ego, and Equal Protection: Reckoning with Unconscious Racism," 29 *Stan. L. Rev.* (1987), at 355–62,

25. Roughly stated,

[T]he [state action] doctrine holds that although someone may have suffered harmful treatment of a kind that one might ordinarily describe as a deprivation of liberty or a denial of equal protection of the laws, that occurrence excites no constitutional concern unless the proximate active perpetrators of the harm include persons exercising the special authority or power of the government of a state.

Michelman, "Conceptions of Democracy in American Constitutional Argument: The Case of Pornography Regulation," 56 *Tenn. L. Rev.* 291, 306 (1999). The doctrine embodies the notion in American life and law that racial discrimination can be accurately and properly divided into two spheres, "public" and "private." See D Bell, n.

15 at 104–10. Karl Klare notes that the separalion of state and civil society became a centerpiece of all liberal political theory and was important in the development of American constitutionalism. Klare's analysis shows how the state action limitation of the Fourteenth Amendment permitted a system of social and economic domination by prohibiting only those evils that could be directly connected to the in territorial exercise of state power. Entities such as corporations, universities, and labor unions are treated as private although their actions are public in scope and character. Klare, "The Quest for Industrial Democracy and the Struggle Against Racism: Perspectives from Labor Law and Civil Rights, Law," 61 *Or. L. Rev.* 157 (1982) (discussion of the structural similarities between the limitations contained in labor low and civil rights law). Klare argues that:

> [T]he practices constituting the "private sphere" of social and economic life are inextricably linked to and partially constituted by the rule of law. By the same token law is imbued with, when not captured by, the power relationships of social life. The law simply does not stand apart from the hierarchy of social life. Law and politics are implicated in the class and racial domination that characterize American society. There is no "core" or "infrastructure" of social or economic life that can be meaningfully described without reference to the role of law.

Ibid. at 193 (footnotes omitted).

26. Thus it is argued that a white family's decision to send its children to private school or to move to a racially exclusive suburb should be accorded respect in spite of the Fourteenth Amendment's requirement of nondiscrimination because their decisions are part of the right to individual familial autonomy. In this way, the state action rule's rather arbitrary limit on the scope of the antidiscrimination principle is transformed into a right of privacy–which is presented as the constitutional embodiment of an affirmative, neutral, and universally shared value. A new and positive image emerges–an image that has been abstracted from its original context.

27. I do not mean to suggest that privacy or autonomy has no normative value; there is some point at which the balance ought to be struck in its favor *after full consideration of the inequities that might accompany that choice.* What is objectionable about the privacy language that I am discussing here is that it ignores inequities and assumes we all share equally in the value being promoted.

28. The Court's treatment of the abortion controversy provides the most striking example of the fact that the right of autonomous choice is not shared by rich and poor alike. In *Roe* v *Wade*, 410 U.S. 113 (1973), the Court declared, in no uncertain terms, that the right of privacy "is broad enough to encompass a woman's decision whether or not to terminate her pregnancy." Ibid. at 153. Yet, in *Harris* v *McRae*, 448 U.S. 297 (1990), the Court with equal certainty asserted that "it simply does not follow that a woman's freedom of choice carries with it a constitutional entitlement to the financial resources to avail herself of the full range of protected choices." Ibid. at 316.

29. See Michelman, n. 25 at 306–307 (reflecting on the ambiguities in American constitutional legal thought concerning the governmental regulation of pornography).

30. Ibid.

31. Ibid. at 307. Michelman further argues that once the constitutional problem is properly posed it is far from obvious that the state commits the forbidden deprivation or denial by choosing the regulatory alternative.

> [S]o long as the state can fairly support a judgment that the infringements or liberty and equal protection consequent upon its choice for regulation or pornography are, in some appropriate sense, lesser than the infringements or liberty and equal protection consequent upon the opposite choice to leave pornography unregulated, that proregulation choice by the state would seem to come as close as humanly possible to good-faith compliance with the constitutional mandate. For the state simply to disregard the subversions of liberty and equal protection consequent upon a choice not to regulate—to set them aside as of no account—when it knows about those subversions and knows, too, how to avoid them by regulating, is for the state to choose to incur those subversions and thereby to cause them by even the strictest notions of legal causation. The issue of the state's liability for the resulting harm thus leaves behind the question of causation, to confront instead the question of justification by countervailing responsibilities, interests, or values (in this case consisting of the pornographer's claims to liberty and equal protection). On this analysis, the state's constitutional obligation would be to compare the constitutional values respectively at risk in the options that it confronts. The corresponding duty of a reviewing court would be to ascertain, within the limits of judicial institutional competence, whether the state has done so responsibly and in good faith.

Ibid. at 307–309 (footnotes omitted).

MacKinnon takes the argument a step farther, arguing that:

> The most basic assumption underlying First Amendment adjudication is that, socially, speech is free. . . . Free speech exists. The problem for government is to avoid constraining that which, if unconstrained by government, *is* free. This tends to presuppose that whole segments of the population are not systematically silenced socially prior to government action.

MacKinnon, n. 12 at 340.

32. Alan Freeman has described how much of civil rights law disguises value conflicts between victim and perpetrator groups by illustrating what is at stake in decontextualized neutral terms like "color blind" and "privacy." Freeman, "School Desegregation Law: Promise, Contradiction, Rationalization," in *Shades of* Brown: *New Perspectives On School Desegregation,* 70 (D. Bell ed. 1980).

33. Mari Matsuda gives us a small but powerful sampling of the millions of stories of racist verbal assault that could be told by victims of those assaults. Matsuda, n. 25. at 2326–31.

34. U.S. Const., Art. 1, § 2, cl. 3; § 9, cl. 1; Art 4, § 2., cl. 3.

35. *Dred Scott* v *Sanford,* 60 U.S. (19 How.) 393 (1857).

36. If one insists cm maintaining the state action distinction, then it might well be argued that under *Shelly* v *Kramer*, 334 U S. 1 (1948), there is state action when the First Amendment is invoked to protect racist fighting words that would not otherwise be protected

37. 339 U.S. 637 (1950).

38. "A Step Toward Civility," *Time*, May 1, 1989, p. 43.

39. Ibid.

40. See *Griffin* v *Prince Edward County School Bd.*, 377 U.S. 218 (1964) (ordering a county school system reopened; five years earlier it had been closed to avoid desegregation); *Norwood* v *Harrison*, 413 U.S. 455 (1973) (preventing a state from lending textbooks to students attending private white academies); see also *Runyon* v *McCrary*, 427 U.S. 160 (1976) (interpreting 42 U.S.C. § 1981 [1989] to outlaw race discrimination by private schools).

41. 42 U.S.C. §§ 2000a, 2000a-1 to 2000a-6 (1988).

42. *Heart of Atlanta Motel, Inc.* v *United States*, 379 U.S. 241, 258 (1964); see also *Roberts* v *United States Jaycees*, 469 U.S. 609, 624 (1994) (Court upheld the public accommodations provision of the Minnesota Human Rights Act). The *Roberts* Court explicitly rejected the freedom of association argument stating that "[t]he right to associate for expressive purposes is not, however, absolute. Infringements on that right may be justified by regulations adopted to serve compelling state interests, unrelated to the suppression of ideas, that cannot be achieved through means significantly less restrictive of associationai freedoms." Ibid. at 623.

43. 461 U.S. 574, 595 (1983).

44. Ibid. at 604.

45. Ibid.; see also *Runyon* v *McCrary*, 427 U.S. 160, 173–75 (1976) (interpreting 42 U. C § 1981 [1988] to outlaw race discrimination by private schools).

46. *Pittsburgh Press Co.* v *Pittsburgh Comm'n on Human Relations*, 413 U. S. 376 (1973) (upholding the regulation of sex-designated "Help Wanted" advertising)

47. I supported a proposal which would have been broader in scope by prohibiting speech of this nature in all common areas, excepting organized and announced rallies and speeches. It would have been narrower in its protection in that it would not have protected persons who were vilified on the hasis of their membership in dominant majority groups.

48. Fundamental Standard Interpretation: Free Expression and Discriminatory Harassment, adopted by Stanford University June 1990.

It is important to recognize that this regulation is not content neutral. It prohibits "discriminatory harassment" rather than just plain harassment and it regulates only discriminatory harassment based on "sex, race, color, handicap, religion, sexual orientation, and national or ethnic origin." It is arguably viewpoint neutral with respect to these categories, although its reference to "words which by their very utterance inflict injury . . . and which are commonly understood to convey direct and visceral hatred or contempt" probably means that there will be many more epithets that refer to subordinated groups than there will be words that refer to superordinate groups covered by the regulation.

49. Numerous news commentators have labeled as censorship any attempt to regulate verbal harassment: "Stanford's program of speech patrol is hardly the

worst. . . ." Len, "Legal Cornercutting Slices Away Civil Liberties," *Rocky Mountain News*, June 21, 1989, p. 11, col. 6; "[Lawrence's argument] exemplifies the ongoing attempt to give intellectual respectability to the spreading movement of censorship by liberals on campuses." Will, "Liberal Censorship," *Washington Post*, November 5, 1989, p. C7: "This is not the first time in recent years that some on the left have sought to silence those who disagree with them." Dembart, "At Stanford, Leftists become Censors," *New York Times*, May 5, 1989, p. A35.

50. The fighting words doctrine requires that the words be "directed to the person of the hearer." *Cohen* v *California*, 403 U.S. 15, 20 (1971). This requirement strikes a balance between our concern for protecting the individual from unavoidable personalized attack (one is not given an opportunity to avoid the speech by averting the eyes or leaving the room) and our concern for allowing space for even the most offensive speech in a public forum ("one man's vulgarity is another's lyric," ibid. at 25). I would argue that the face-to-face requirement be expanded in the case of racist verbal assaults to include those words that are intentionally spoken in the presence of members or the denigrated group. See nn. 52–68 and accompanying text.

51. *Chaplinsky* v *New Hampshire*, 315 U.S. 568, 572 (1942).

52. A defining attribute of speech is that it appeals first to the mind of the hearer who can evaluate its truth or persuasiveness The use of racial epithets lacks this quality; it is a form of "violence by speech." See J. Denver and J. Powell, *Caliban's Complaint: Racist Speech and the First Amendment*, (unpublished manuscript; available from author).

53. See Arkes, "Civility and the Restriction of Speech: Rediscovering the Defamation of Groups," 1974 *Sup. Ct. Rev.* 281, at 331; Delgado, "Words that Wound: A Tort Action for Racial Insults, Epithets, and Name-Calling," 17 *Harv. C.R. C.L. L. Rev.* 133 (1982), at 175.

54. It should not he necessary to urge victims of these insulting attacks to carry arms so that the "fighting words" rationale of these assaults can be more easily perceived by whites.

55. I have discussed this phenomenon in some detail in two articles that explore the nature of the injury of segregation and other racially stigmatizing actions. Segregation and other forms of racist speech injure victims because of their dehumanizing and excluding message. But each individual message gains its power because of the cumulative and reinforcing effect of countless similar messages that are conveyed in a society where racism is ubiquitous. See Lawrence, nn. 5, 24; see also Karst, "The Costs of Motive-Centered Inquiry," 15 *San Diego L. Rev.* 1163, 1163–66 (1978) (constitutional equal protection doctrine should focus on the pervastive social problem or racial inequality).

56. Mari Matsuda has noted that in framing a legal response to racist speech one must consider its role within the structural reality of racism in America.

> The implements of racism include: 1. Violence and Genocide; 2. Racial hate messages, disparagement, and threats; 3. Overt disparate treatment; and 4. Covert disparate treatment. . . .
>
> From the victim's perspective, all of these implements inflict wounds, wounds that are neither random nor isolated. Gutter racism, parlor racism,

corporate racism, and government racism work in coordination, reinforcing existing conditions of domination.

Matsuda, "Public Response to Racist Speech: Considering the Victim's Story," 87 *Mich. L. Rev.* (1989), at 2332–35.

57. Some civil libertarians will respond to my use of the "fighting words" doctrine by arguing that the doctrine itself is not good law. They will note that the reasoning in *Chaplinsky* v *New Hampshire*, 315 U.S. 568 (1942), has been implicitly abandoned. See Strossen, introductory remarks in notes above. Civil libertarians have always been critical of a doctrine which allows those who object to unpopular speech to exercise a veto on that speech by the threat of resort to violence. In response to the first point, I would note that at least as recently as *Cohen* v *California*, 403 U.S. 15 (1971), the Court indicated the continuing vitality of *Chaplinsky* in the context of face-to-face insults. In *Cohen*, the Court held that "the states are free to ban the simple use, without a demonstration of additional justifying circumstances, of so-called fighting words, those personally abusive epithets which, when addressed to the ordinary citizen, are, as a matter of common knowledge, inherently likely to provoke violent reaction." Ibid. at 20. More importantly, I am in substantial agreement with the civil libertarians who would not cease to protect speech that increases the propensity to violence of those who oppose the speech. Paradoxically, it is this clear and present danger of violence rationale that Professor Strossen cites as the part of the fighting words doctrine that remains good law. See introductory remarks in notes above. It also is worth noting that virtually every case in which the Court reversed the conviction charged with using offensive language directed at an individual, the reversal was based on the overbreadth of the statute and the potentially offended party was in a position of relative power when compared with the speaker. See, e.g., *Rosenfeld* v *New Jersey*, 409 U.S. 901 (1972); *Lewis* v *New Orleans*, 409 U.S. 913 (1972); *Brown* v *Oklahoma*, 408 U.S. 914 (1972) A majority of the Supreme Court was willing to vacate and remand those convictions for use of offensive language. But there is an alternative rationale for the "fighting words" doctrine that is more sound. Speech that preempts further speech rather than inviting response does not serve the purposes of the First Amendment and is therefore less deserving of protection. Furthermore, I believe that racists' fighting words and other face-to-face verbal assaults against persons from subordinated groups more closely fit this rationale than do garden variety fighting words.

58. The fighting words doctrine captures the "macho" quality of male discourse. It is accepted, justifiable, and even praiseworthy when "real men" respond to personal insult with violence. (Presidential candidate George Bush did well to emulate the most macho, and not coincidentally violent, of movie stars, Clint Eastwood, when he repeatedly used the phrase, "Read my lips!" Any teenage boy will tell you the subtext of this message: "I've got nothing else to say about this and if you don't like what I'm saying we can step outside.") The fighting words doctrine's responsiveness to this "male" stance in the world and its blindness to the cultural experience of women is another example of how "neutral" principles of law often reflect the values of those who are dominant. Black males also are well aware of the double standard that our culture applies to black and white men in responding to insult. Part of the culture of racial domination through violence–a culture of dominance that manifested itself in thousands of lynchings in the South and more recently

in the racial violence at Howard Beach and Bensonhurst–is the paradoxical expectation on the part of whites that black males will accept insult from whites without protest, yet they will become violent without provocation. These expectations combine two assumptions: First, that blacks as a group–and especially black males–are more violent and, second, that, as inferior persons, blacks have no right to feel insulted. One can only imagine the response of universities if black males started to respond to racist fighting words by beating up white students.

59. It is both uncommon and unlikely that whites will insult minorities with racial epithets in contexts where they are outnumbered or overmatched. Racial name calling is usually a sport engaged in by cowards who are certain of their ability to win the fight before they inflict the first blow.

60. For a discussion of submissiveness as a psychological defense, see Guthrie, "White Racism and Its Impact on Black and Non-white Behavior," *Journal of Non-White Concerns in Personnel and Guidance* 144 (1973). See also C. MacKinnon, *Sexual Harassment of Working Women: A Case of Sex Discrimination* (1979); S. Brownmiller, *Against Our Will: Men, Women, and Rape* (1975).

61. The National Gay and Lesbian Task Force includes verbal harassment among its categories of antigay violence. Hatfield, "Attacks on Gays Rising." *San Francisco Examiner,* June 7, 1989, p. A10, col. 2. Matsuda notes that racial violence is typically preceded by racist propaganda. Matsuda, n. 56 at 2335–41.

62. See *Bowers* v *Hardwick*, 478 U.S. 186 (1996). Chief Justice Burger, in his now-infamous concurrence, quoting Blackstone's characterization of sodomy "as an offense of 'deeper malignity' than rape, a heinous act 'the very mention of which is a disgrace to human nature,'" urged the Court to defer to the "millennia of moral teaching." Ibid. at 197. Mary Dunlap has called this one of the "gifts" of the Hardwick case–the recorded and published *admission* by the Supreme Court that we live in a profoundly homophobic nation. Remarks by Mary Dunlap, Stanford Law School symposium on *Bowen* v *Hardwick* (May 8, 1989).

63. See n. 48 and accompanying text.

64. See *Cohen* v *California*, 403 U.S. 15, 21 (1971) (holding that the state could not prohibit speech merely because it is offensive); *Erznoznik* v *City of Jacksonville*, 422 U.S. 205, 209 (1975) (overturning a city ordinance that deterred drive-in theaters from showing movies containing nudity).

65. See *Kovacks* v *Cooper*, 336 U.S. 77, 86 (1949) (right to free speech not abridged by city ordinance outlawing use of soundtracks on city streets); *FCC* v *Pacifica Found.*, 438 U.S. 726, 748 (1978) (limited First Amendment protection of broadcasting that extends into privacy of home); *Rowan* v *United States Post Office Dep't*, 397 U.S. 728, 736 (1970) (unwilling recipient of sexually arousing material had right to instruct Postmaster General to cease mailings to protect recipient from unwanted communication of "ideas").

66. At Stanford two white students posted a Sambo-like defacement of a Beethoven poster an a bulletin board outside of a black student's room in the black theme dorm. The university's office of general counsel held that the offending students could not be prosecuted under the university's fundamental standard because their actions constituted protected speech. Nowhere in their opinion did they mention the captive audience cases or the fact that the black students in this dorm might

have a justifiable expectation that they would not be subjected to this sort of vilification in what was now their home. Schwartz and Brest, "First Amendment Principles and Prosecution for Offensive Expression under Stanford's Student Disciplinary System," *Stanford Daily*, February 8, 1989, p. 9, col. 1.

67. According to Howard J. Ehrlich of the National Institute Against Prejudice and Violence, "[b]etween 20 percent and 25 percent of all minority students on campus have been victimized at least once during an academic year." Riechmann, "Colleges Tackle Increase in Racism on Campuses," *Los Angeles Times*, April 30, 1999, part 1, p. 36, col. 1. See also H. Ehrlich, *Campus Ethnoviolence and the Policy Options* (National Institute Against Prejudice and Violence, Institute Report No. 4, 1990), pp. 41–72.

68. Racist speakers planning organized events such as the Nazis march in Skokie or a spokesperson for the Klan would not be precluded from obtaining a permit to match or speak at designated times and places.

69. See *Fisher* v *Carousel Motor Motel, Inc.*, 424 S.W.2d 627, 630 (Tex. 1967) (award of $900 for racial slur on assault and battery grounds upheld; battery protects dignity as well as physical security); *Alcorn* v *Anbro Eng'g, Inc.*, 2 Col. 3d 493, 498, 468 p.2d 216, 218, 86 Cal. Rptr. 88, 90 (1970) (use of "niggers" sufficient to state a cause of action for "extreme and outrageous" intentional infliction of emotional stress); *Agarnal* v *Johnson*, 25 Cal. 3d 932, 944–46, 603 P.2d 59, 66, 160 Cal. Rptr. 141, 148–49 (1979) (same).

70. *Brown* v *Board of Educ.*, 347 U.S. 483, 494 (1954)

71. See Matsuda, n. 56, at 2335–41.(Physical and psychological harm of racist hate peech is significant). The effects of racial prejudice include displaced aggression, avoidance, retreat and withdrawal, alcoholism, and suicide. H. Kitano, *Race Relations*, 69–85 (2d ed. 1974). See also Delgado, n. 53, at 137–39 (noting, inter alia, high blood pressure, loss of self-worth, and special harm to children); G. Allport, *The Nature of Prejudice*, 142–60 (1954). Cf. Hafner, "Psychological Disturbances Following Prolonged Persecution," 3 *Soc. Psychiatry* 79 (1969) (discussing psychological symptoms including headaches, dizziness, social withdrawal, chronic depression, and anxiety neurosis in survivors of extreme persecution); Denis, "Race Harassment Discrimination: A Problem That Won't Go Away?" 10 *Employment Rel. L.J.* 415, 432–35 (1984) (discussing damages for psychic injury in race harassment cases).

72. L. Tribe, n. 8 §12-12, at 861. See *Chaplinsky* v *New Hampshire*, 315 U. S. 568 (1942) (classifying libel as wholly outside the scope of First Amendment protection); *Beauharnais* v *Illinois*, 343 U.S. 250 (1952) (including group defamation among unprotected libelous statements).

73. 376 U.S. 254, 270.

74. Implicit in the *Sullivan* rule is the proposition that the First Amendment establishes a right to speak defamatory truth. The *Sullivan* case,

> prohibits is public official from recovering damages for a defamatory falsehood relating to his or her official conduct unless he or she prove that the statement was made with "actual malice"—that is, with knowledge that it was false or reckless disregard of whether it was false or not.

Ibid. at 279–80. This privilege for good-faith critics of government officials was created in order to protect against the self-censorship of the speaker who fears that he has guessed wrong in his effort to speak the truth. Lawrence Tribe notes that "a rule that the First Amendment protects the right to utter the truth clearly does not suffice, because 'erroneous statement is inevitable in free debate,' and the only guarantee of legal safety under such a rule is silence." See L. Tribe, n. 8, § 12-12, at 864 (quoting *Sullivan*, 376 U.S., at 271–72).

But the self-censoirship rationale of *Sullivan* is inapplicable in cases involving speech which, rather than critiquing those in power, asserts the inferiority or in entire racially subordinated group. *Sullivan* is primarily a case about the unconstitutionality of labeling speech as seditious libel. It is concerned with censorship of criticism of government. The defamation of blacks or other racial minorities, as groups, does not involve criticism of government. Even when a racial epithet is used to attack a public official, the alleged inferiority of the racial group to which he belongs should not be held to be related to his fitness to hold the position. The individual who defames a racial group with racial epithets and stereotyped caricatures is not concerned that he may have "guessed wrong" in attempting to ascertain the truth. The racial epithet is the expression of a widely held belief. It is invoked as a statement or political belief—not as a statement of fact which may be proven true or erroneous. Moreover, if the *Sullivan* rule protects erroneous speech because of an ultimate concern for the discovery of truth, then the rule's application to racial epithets must be based an an acceptance of the possible "truth" of racism, a position which, happily, most First Amendment absolutists are reluctant to embrace. Professor Matsuda argues that "we [should] accept certain principles as the shared historical legacy of the world community. Racial supremacy is one of the ideas we have collectively and internationally considered and rejected." See Matsuda, n. 56, at 2360.

But *Sullivan* also held that "the central meaning of the First Amendment is profound national commitment to the principle that debate on public issues should be uninhibited, robust, and wide open." 376 U.S., at 270. Some civil libertarians argue that the status and attributes of various racial groups are public issues about which vigorous debate should be encouraged. This proposition is combined with the proposition that there is no such thing as a false idea to argue that *Sullivan* has necessarily overruled *Beauhamais* v *Illinois*, 343 U.S. 250 (1952). But are racial insults ideas? Do they encourage wide-open debate?

The solution might lie in establishing the equivalent of an actual malice requirement. Discussions that attempt to explore an issue of public concern would be protected, but group defamations that intentionally vilify a group or individual for purposes of harassment or intimidation would receive no protection.

75. There are compelling arguments to be made for the continuing viability and correctness of *Beauharnais*. See Arkes, "Civility and the Restriction of Speech: Rediscovering the Defamation of Groups," 1974 *Sup. Ct. Rev.* 281, 292 (One who rejects the notion of group libel must also reject that "certain minority groups in this country have in fact suffered injuries in the past as a result of racist stereotypes that have been perpetuated in the public mind."); see also Downs, "Skokie Revisited: Hate Group Speech and the First Amendment," 60 *Notre Dame L. Rev.* 629, 661–66 (1985) (statutes similar to the one in *Beauharnais* are unconstitutional unless the speech in question is racial vilification targeted at an individual or discrete group)

328 PART III: FREE SPEECH ON CAMPUS

76. 343 U.S. 250 (1952).

77. See L. Tribe, n. 8 § 12–17, at 926–27. See also *Collin* v *Smith,* 578 F.2d 1197, 1205 (7th Cir. 1978) (questioning whether *Beauharnais* remains a good law in the wake of the constitutionall libel cases), *cert. denied,* 439 U.S. 916 (1978).

78. See nn. 69–74 and accompanying text. The Court has recognized the inseparability of discriminatory speech and conduct in sustaining the regulation of sexist (and presumably racist) speech in *Pittsburgh Press Co.* v *Human Relations Commission,* 413 U.S. 376 (1973), where the Court held that sex-designated "help wanted" advertising columns could be prohibited since such ads "aided" unlawful sex discrimination in hiring. Ibid. at 389, 394. Similarly, regulation of racist advertising for home sales and rentals has been upheld against free speech claims.

79. For a discussion of the antidiscrimination principle of the equal protection clause and the centrality to that principle of the injury due to group defamation, see Lawrence, n. 24, at 350–51. He observes that:

The prevention of stigma was at the core of the Supreme Court's unanimous declaration in *Brown* v *Board of Education* that segregated public schools are inherently unequal. The social meaning of racial segregation in the United States is the designation of a superior and an inferior caste, and segregation proceeds "on the ground that colored citizens are . . . inferior and degraded."

Stigmatizing actions harm the individual in two ways: They inflict psychological injury by assaulting a person's self-respect and human dignity, and they brand the individual with a sign that signals her inferior status to others and designates her as an outcast.

Ibid. (footnotes omitted). See also Fiss, "Groups and the Equal Protection Clause" 5 *Phil. & Pub. Aff.* 107, 108, 129–70 (1976) (Common antidiscrimination doctrine is unduly limited to individualistic concerns, and to an assessment of the means as opposed to the ends of discrimination. A group disadvantaging principle would capture the equality ideal more completely).

80. In explaining why segregated educational facilities were inherently unequal, the *Brown* Court said, "To separate [Negro children] from others of similar age and qualifications solely because of their race generates a feeling of inferiority as to their status in the community that may affect their hearts and minds in a way unlikely ever to be undone." 347 U.S. 483, 494. The Court went an to quote the federal district court in Kansas which had found that "[a] sense of inferiority [engendered by segregated schools] . . . has a tendency to [retard] the educational and mental development of Negro children." Ibid.

81. Report of President's Ad Hoc Committee an Racial Harassment, University of Texas at Austin, November 27, 1999 (university president urged to initiate an investigation into the problem of racial harassment on the campus). The committee instituted hearings receiving both written and verbal testimony.

[M]any speakrs felt that they had experienced racism, resulting in deep feelings of personal anger, distress, and isolation in the academic community. Such experiences produce alienation from, rather than a supportive relationship with, the university. They also were concerned that there was no specific place to seek redress at the university for complaints of racial harassment.

Ibid. at 2; *Massachusetts Commission Against Discrimination. Report of University of Massachusetts Investigation,* 2 (1986) (investigation of 1986 racial incident on campus cited need to "review . . . the context of recent UMASS [racial] history," to better understand the factors that led to what most witnessing the incident characterized as a "race riot").

Note that many of these incidents go unrecorded because universities have not taken a stand against racist speech, defining it as a reportable offense or provided mechanisms or forums for reporting these incidents and their effect. A similar situation exists with regard to sexual harassment. See Sexual Harassment Survey, Student Affairs Research & Evaluation Office, University of Masuchusetts at Amherst (S89-C, February 1989). The University of Massachusetts study was designed to assess the feelings of students about sexual harassment and the mechanisms at the university to address their concerns. Although a majority of the students surveyed expressed first- or secondhand experience with sexual harassment, 34.2 percent of the women were unaware that there was a university policy prohibiting the harassment, and 60 percent were unaware of the university's specific grievance procedure. See also Kent, "The Silence of Survivors: Reporting Rape–Hazy Definition and Lack of Protocol Impede Reporting," *Stanford Daily,* February 29, 1990, p. 1, col. 2 ("[M]any people decide not to report acquaintance rape, and those who work with the issue say a main reason is that the university has no formal protocol for reporting highly sensitive cases like rape.").

82. For example, in *Meritor Savings Bank* v *Vinson,* 477 U.S. 57 (1986), the Supreme Court held that sexual harassment that creates a hostile or abusive work environment constitutes a violation of Title VII's prohibition against sex discrimination in employment. The Court referred to an EEOC guideline that defined sexual harassment as "[u]nwelcome sexual advances, requests for sexual favors, and other verbal and physical conduct of a sexual nature." Ibid. at 65. The Court also made clear that racial harassment would violate Title VII. Although the Court has noted that "mere utterance of an ethnic or racial epithet which engenders offensive fmlings in an employee" as not by itself actionable conduct under the statute, this is not because the racial epithet is protected by the First Amendment, but because the legislature has not determined that, standing in isolation, it is an act of employment discrimination. Ibid. at 67 (citing *Rogers* v *EEOC,* 454 F.2d 234 (5th Cir. 1971), *cert. denied,* 406 U.S. 957 [1972]).

83. See *Alexander* v *Yale University,* 631 F.2d 178, 184 (1980) ("In a Title IX suit, it is the deprivation of 'educational' benefits which, once proven, allows the court to afford relief. The statute recognizes that loss of educational benefits is a significant injury, redressable by law." However, the court ruled that the damages were too speculative to receive judicial remedy.).

84. The "marketplace of ideas" model sees speech as instrumental to democratic self-government. It argues that truth (or the best perspectives or solutions) can

be discovered through robust debate, free from government interference. In this model, the value of free speech lies not in the liberty interests of individual speakers, but in the societal benefits derived from unimpeded discussion. This theory has its origins in John Stuart Mill's *On Liberty*, ch. 2 (1859) (S. Collini ed. 1989). Justice Holmes established its place in First Amendment jurisprudence in his dissent in *Abrams* v *United States*, 250 U.S. 616 (1919):

> But when men have realized that time has upset many fighting faiths, they may come to believe . . . that the best test of truth is the power of the thought to get itself accepted in the competition of the market, and that truth is the only ground upon which their wishes can safely be carried out.

Ibid. at 630.

85. See Lawrence, n. 24, at 330 ("[Racism] is a part of our common historical experience and, therefore, a part of our culture. . . . We attach significance to race even when we are not aware that we are doing so. . . . Racism's universality renders it normal.").

86. Ibid. at 339–44; see nn. 91–92 and accompanying text.

87. See Lawrence, n. 24 at 341n. 101 (relating the story of a Mexican American law student who was complimented by a middle-aged white male interviewer: "You speak very good English." The student responded that her family has lived in Santa Barbara for four generations. The interviewer was unconscious of the racial stereotype underlying his intended compliment.).

88. Catharine MacKinnon argues, similarly, that pornography causes women to be taken less seriously as they enter the public arena. MacKinnon, n. 12, at 325–26, 335 (1984). See also Sunstein, "Pornography and the First Amendment," 1996 *Duke L. J.*, 589, 618–19 (analogizing the case for antipornography legislation to footnote 4 in *United States* v *Carotene Products*, 304 U.S. 144, 152 (1938), and recognizing "maldistribution of private power").

89. See nn. 53–57 and accompanying text.

90. See Lawrence, n. 24, where he describes America's racist heritage:

> Americans share a common historical and cultural heritage in which racism has played and still plays a dominant role. Because of this shared experience, we also inevitably share many ideas, attitudes, and beliefs that attach significance to an individual's race and induce negative feelings and opinions about nonwhites. To the extent that this cultural belief system has influenced all of us, we are all racists.

Ibid. at 322.

91. For a more detailed discussion of the irrationality of racism, see Lawrence, n. 20, at 331–36 (discussing the persistence of racist thinking despite personal experience that contradicts the racist belief; racist beliefs based on instinctive and unexplained distaste for members of the target group). Marie Jahoda notes that "racial prejudice, in its narrowest sense, is an attitude towards out-groups which refrains from reality-testing not just because the mental effort is too much but because the attitude itself fulfills a specific irrational function for its bearer." M. Jahoda, *Race Rela-*

tions and Mental Health, 11 (1960) (UNESCO publication). See also G. Allport, n. 71, at 85–87, 317–19.

92. I have explored the phenomenon of unconscious racism and its relationship to the jurisprudence of equal protection at some length elsewhere. See Lawrence, n. 24. In that article I noted two explanations for the predominance of unconscious racist beliefs and ideas:

> First, Freudian theory states that the human mind defends itself against the discomfort of guilt by denying or refusing to recognize those ideas, wishes, and beliefs that conflict with what the individual has learned is good or right. While our historical experience has made racism an integral part of our culture, our society has more recently embraced an ideal that rejects racism as immoral. When an individual experiences conflict between racist ideas and the societal ethic that condemns those ideas, the mind excludes his racism from consciousness.
>
> Second, the theory of cognitive psychology states that the culture— including, for example, the media and an individual's parents, peers, and authority figures–transmits certain beliefs and preferences. Because these beliefs are so much a part of the culture, they are not experienced as explicit lessons. Instead, they seem part of the individual's rational ordering of her perceptions of the world. The individual is unaware, for example, that the ubiquitous presence of a cultural stereotype has influenced her perception that blacks are lazy or unintelligent. Because racism is so deeply ingrained in our culture, it is likely to be transmitted by tacit understandings: Even if a child is not told that blacks are inferior, he learns that lesson by observing the behavior of others. These tacit understandings, because they have never been articulated, are less likely to be experienced at a conscious level.

Id. at 322–23 (footnotes omitted).

93. See J. Ely, *Democracy and Distrust: A Theory of Judicial Review*, 103–104, 135–79 (1980).

94. Ibid., at 152–58.

95. J. S. Mill, n. 84, at ch. 2.

96. *The Federalist*, no. 51, at 323–24, (J. Madison) (C. Rossiter ed. 1961).

97. J. Ely, n. 93, at 153.

98. See Lawrence, n. 24, at 347–49 (arguing that Ely's process defect theory is incomplete to the extent that it does not take into account the process distortions caused by unconscious racism).

99. Exit polls taken during the recent mayoral election in New York City and the gubernatorial election in Virginia overstated the support among white voters for the black candidates. The discrepancy has been attributed to a reluctance among white voters to admit, even anonymously, to not voting for a black candidate. Roarrithal, "Broad Disparities in Votes and Polls Raising Questions," *New York Times*, November 9, 1999, p. A1, col. 2.

Once again, the experience of one of my gay students provides the paradigmatic example of how ideas are less acceptable when their authors are members of a group that has been victimized by hatred and villification. Bob had not "come out" when he first come to law school. During his first year, when issues relating to heterosexism came up in class or in discussions with other students, he spoke to these issues as a sympathetic "straight" white male student. His arguments were listened to and taken seriously. In his second year, when he had "come out" and his classmates knew that he was gay, he found that he was not nearly as persuasive an advocate for his position as when he was identified as "straight." He was the same person saying the same things, but his identity gave him less authority.

100. See Davis, "Law as Microaggression," 98 *Yale L. J.* 1559, 1568 (1999) (describing a courthouse scene in which a white city attorney seizes upon the most pejorative interpretation of a black woman's question: "The inferiority of the black is more than an implicit assertion; it is a background assumption that supports the seizure of a prerogative.").

101. See G. Lopez, *The Well-Defined Academic Identity* (January 7, 1990) (unpublished manuscript, available from author) (AALS Law and Humanities panel speech on white revisionism of scholars of color); Delgado, "The Imperial Scholar: Reflections on a Review of Civil Rights Literature," 132 *U. Pa. L. Rev.* 561, 564–65 (1984); Weiss and Melling, "The Legal Education of Twenty Women." 40 *Stan. L. Rev.* 1299, 1336 (1988): "There were times when women made points, and they were ignored or trivialized. Five minutes later, a man would make the same point . . . and it was discussed"; Fox, "Women and Higher Education: Sex Differentials in the Status of Students and Scholars," in *Women: A Feminist Perspective* 239, 244–46 (J. Freeman 3d ed. 1989) (a "subtle and silent language differentiates males and females"; faculty encourages males while "reinforceing the invisibility of female students"); G. Steinem, "Men and Women Talking," in *Outrageous Acts and Everyday Rebellions,* 176 (1983) (gender differences in communication often due to sexism, not biology–to transform politics of talking" requires a feminist assault.

102. When speech directly threatens violence, as in the phrase "your money or your life" or in the phone call that takes responsibility for the terrorist bomb attack and threatens another, we recognize its inextricability from the accompanying conduct. It is more difficult to recognize the threat when the violence is systemic and need not be directly referenced in the speech, but the threat is just as effective, arguably even more so.

103. Catharine MacKinnon has noted that it is difficult to demonstrate empirically that pornography chills women's speech because "silence is not eloquent." C. MacKinnon, n. 18, at 206.

104. Id.

19

FROM "REGULATING RACIST SPEECH ON CAMPUS: A MODEST PROPOSAL?"

Nadine Strossen

Professor Lawrence has made a provocative contribution to the perennial debate concerning the extent to which courts and civil libertarians[1] should continue to construe the Constitution as protecting some forms of racist expression.[2] This recurring issue resurfaced most recently in connection with the increase of racial incidents at colleges and universities around the country.[3] In response, many of these institutions have adopted, or are considering,[4] regulations that curb "hate speech"–i.e., speech that expresses hatred or bias toward members of racial, religious, or other groups.

Civil libertarians are committed to the eradication of racial discrimination and the promotion of free speech throughout society.[5] Civil libertarians have worked especially hard to combat both discrimination and free speech restrictions in educational institutions.[6] Educational institutions should be bastions of equal opportunity and unrestricted exchange. Therefore, we find the upsurge of both campus racism and regulation of campus speech particularly disturbing, and we have undertaken efforts to counter both.[7]

Because civil libertarians have learned that free speech is an indispensable instrument for the promotion of other rights and freedoms–including racial equality–we fear that the movement to regulate campus expression will undermine equality, as well as free speech. Combating racial discrimination and protecting free speech should be viewed as mutually reinforcing, rather than antagonistic, goals.[8] A diminution in society's commitment to racial equality is neither a necessary nor an appropriate price for protecting free speech. Those who frame the debate in terms of this false dichotomy simply drive artificial wedges between would-be allies in what should be a common effort to promote civil rights and civil liberties.[9]

Professor Lawrence urges civil libertarians to "abandon . . . overstated rhetorical and legal attacks on individuals who conscientiously seek to frame a public response to racism while preserving our First Amendment liberties."[10] I join in this invitation, and I extend a corresponding one: Those individuals who espouse "new perspectives" on the First Amendment in an effort to justify hate speech regulations should avoid overstated attacks on those who conscientiously seek to preserve our First Amendment liberties while responding to racism.

In important respects, Professor Lawrence inaccurately describes, and unfairly criticizes, both traditional civil libertarians in general and the American Civil Liberties Union (ACLU) in particular. His argument depends on a "straw civil libertarian" who can be easily knocked down, but who does not correspond to the flesh-and-blood reality.[11] For example, contrary to Professor Lawrence's assumption, traditional civil libertarians do not categorically reject every effort to regulate racist speech. The ACLU never has argued that harassing, intimidating, or assaultive conduct should be immunized simply because it is in part based on words. Accordingly, traditional civil libertarians should agree with Professor Lawrence that some examples of racially harassing speech should be subject to regulation consistent with First Amendment principles—for example, the group of white male students pursuing a black female student across campus shouting, "I've never tried a nigger."[12]

Of course, traditional civil libertarians have urged that any restrictions on expressive activity must be drawn narrowly, and carefully applied, to avoid chilling protected speech. But, to a substantial extent, Professor Lawrence appears to endorse a similarly cautious approach. He stresses that he supports only limited regulations and invokes the recently adopted Stanford University code as a model.[13]

Insofar as Professor Lawrence advocates relatively narrow rules that apply traditionally accepted limitations on expressive conduct to the campus setting, his position should not be alarming (although it is debatable). In portions of his article, Professor Lawrence seems to agree with traditional civil libertarians that only a small subset of the racist rhetoric that abounds in our society should be regulated.[14] Although we may disagree about the contours of such concepts as "captive audience," "fighting words," or "intentional infliction of emotional distress" in the context of racist speech on carnpus,[15] these differences should not obscure strong common goals. Surely our twin aims of civil rights and civil liberties would be advanced more effectively by fighting together against the common enemy of racism than by fighting against each other over which narrow subset of one symptom of racism—namely, verbal and symbolic expressions—should be regulated.

What is disquieting about Professor Lawrence's article is not the relatively limited Stanford code he defends, but rather his simultaneous defense of additional, substantially more sweeping, speech prohibitions.[16] The rationales that Professor Lawrence advances for the regulations he endorses are so open-ended that, if accepted, they would appear to warrant the prohibition of *all* racist speech, and thereby would cut to the core of our system of free expression.

Although Professor Lawrence's specific proposed code appears relatively modest, his supporting rationales depend on nothing less immodest than the abrogation of the traditional distinctions between speech and conduct and between state action and private action. He equates private racist speech with governmental racist conduct.[17] This approach offers no principled way to confine racist-speech regulations to the particular contours of the Stanford code, or indeed to any particular contours at all. Professor Lawrence apparently acknowledges that, if accepted, his theories could warrant the prohibition of all private racist speech.[18] Moreover, although he stresses the particular evils of racism,[19] he also says that "much of my analysis applies to violent pornography and homophobic hate speech."[20] Thus, Professor Lawrence himself demonstrates that traditional civil libertarians are hardly paranoiac when we fear that any specific, seemingly modest proposal to regulate speech may in fact represent the proverbial "thin edge of the wedge" for initiating broader regulations.

As just explained, the relatively narrow Stanford code that Professor Lawrence endorses is incongruous with his broad theoretical rationale. The Stanford code also is at odds with Professor Lawrence's pragmatic rationale. The harms of racist speech that he seeks to redress largely remain untouched by the rule. For example, Professor Lawrence movingly recounts the pain suffered by his sister's family as a result of racist expression,[21] as well as the anxiety he endured as a boy even from the *possibility* of racist expression.[22] Yet the Stanford code clearly would not apply to any of the unspoken racist expressions that may lurk beneath the surface of much parlance in American life. Moreover, the regulation also would not apply unless the speech was directly targeted at a specific victim.[23] Therefore, it would not have relieved Professor Lawrence or his family of the traumas they experienced. Furthermore, the Stanford code would not address the racist incident at Stanford that led to its adoption.[24] Likewise, many additional campus racist incidents catalogued by Professor Lawrence and others would be beyond the scope of the Stanford code.

Two problems arise from the disharmony between the breadth of the racist-speech regulations endorsed by Professor Lawrence and the harm that inspires them. First, this disparity underscores the rules' ineffectiveness. The regulations do not even address much of racist speech, let alone the innumerable other manifestations of racism which—as Professor Lawrence himself stresses[25]—pervade our society. Second, this disharmony encourages the proponents of hate speech regulations to seek to narrow the gap between the underlying problem and their favored solution by recommending broader regulations. For example, Professor Mari Matsuda recently proposed a substantially more restrictive hate speech regulation on the theory that such a regulation is needed to redress the harm suffered by hate speech victims.[26] Professor Lawrence has indicated his approval of Professor Matsuda's approach. And the wedge widens.[27]

This article attempts to bridge some of the gaps that Professor Lawrence believes separate advocates of equality from advocates of free speech. It shows that—insofar as proponents of hate speech regulations endorse relatively narrow rules that encompass only a limited category of racist expression-these gaps are not that significant in practical effect. It also demonstrates that the First and Fourteenth Amendments are allies rather than antagonists. Most importantly, this article maintains that equality will be served most effectively by continuing to apply traditional, speech-protective precepts to racist speech, because a robust freedom of speech ultimately is necessary to combat racial discrimination. Professor Lawrence points out that free speech values as well as equality values may be promoted by regulating certain verbal harassment, and retarded by not regulating it.[28] But it also must be recognized that equality values may be promoted most effectively by not regulating certain hate speech and retarded by regulating it.[29]

Fighting Words

The fighting words doctrine is the principal model for the Stanford code, which Professor Lawrence supports.[30] However, this doctrine provides a constitutionally shaky foundation for several reasons: It has been substantially limited in scope and may no longer be good law; even if the Supreme Court were to apply a narrowed version of the doctrine, such an application would threaten free speech principles; and, as actually implemented, the fighting words doctrine suppresses protectible speech and entails the inherent danger of discriminatory application to speech by members of minority groups and dissidents.

Although the Court originally defined constitutionally regulable fighting words in fairly broad terms in *Chaplinsky* v *New Hampshire*,[31] subsequent decisions have narrowed the definition to such a point that the doctrine probably would not apply to any of the instances of campus racist speech that Professor Lawrence and others seek to regulate. As originally formulated in *Chaplinsky*, the fighting words doctrine excluded from First Amendment protection "insulting or 'fighting' words, those which by their very utterance inflict injury or tend to incite an immediate breach of the peace."[32]

In light of subsequent developments, it is significant to note that the first prong of *Chaplinsky*'s fighting words definition, words "which by their very utterance inflict injury," was dictum. The Court's actual holding was that the state statute at issue was justified by the state's interest in preserving the public peace by prohibiting "words likely to cause an average addressee to fight."[33] The Court stressed that "no words were forbidden except such as have a direct tendency to cause acts of violence by the person to whom, individually, [they are] addressed."[34] The Court also held that the statute had been applied appropriately to Mr. Chaplinsky, who had called a city marshal "a God damned racketeer" and "a damned Fascist."[35] It explained that these "epithets [are] likely to provoke the average person to retaliation, and thereby cause a breach of the peace."[36]

In *Gooding* v *Wilson*, the Court substantially narrowed *Chaplinsky*'s definition of fighting words by bringing that definition into line with *Chaplinsky*'s actual holding.[37] In Gooding, as well as in every subsequent fighting words case, the Court disregarded the dictum in which the first prong of *Chaplinsky*'s definition was set forth and treated only those words that "tend to incite an immediate breach of the peace" as fighting words. Consistent with this narrowed definition, the Court has invalidated regulations that hold certain words to be per se proscribable and insisted that each challenged utterance be evaluated contextually."[38] Thus, under the Court's current view, even facially valid laws that restrict fighting words may be applied constitutionally only in circumstances where their utterance almost certainly will lead to immediate violence.[39] Professor Tribe described this doctrinal development as, in effect, incorporating the clear and present danger test into the fighting words doctrine.[40]

In accordance with its narrow construction of constitutionally permissible prohibitions upon "fighting words," the Court has overturned every single fighting words conviction that it has reviewed since *Chaplinsky*.[41] Moreover, in a subsequent decision, the Court overturned an injunction that had been based on the very word underlying the *Chaplinsky* conviction.[42]

For the foregoing reasons, Supreme Court Justices[43] and constitutional scholars persuasively maintain that *Chaplinsky*'s fighting words doctrine is no longer good law.[44] More importantly, constitutional scholars have argued that this doctrine should no longer be good law, for reasons that are particularly weighty in the context of racist slurs.[45] First, as Professor Gard concluded in a comprehensive review of both Supreme Court and lower court decisions that apply the fighting words doctrine, the asserted governmental interest in preventing a breach of the peace is not logically furthered by this doctrine. He explained that:

> [I]t is fallacious to believe that personally abusive epithets, even if addressed face-to-face to the object of the speaker's criticism, are likely to arouse the ordinary law-abiding person beyond mere anger to uncontrollable reflexive violence. Further, even if one unrealistically assumes that reflexive violence will result, it is unlikely that the fighting words doctrine can successfully deter such lawless conduct.[46]

Second, just as the alleged peace-preserving purpose does not rationally justify the fighting words doctrine in general, that rationale also fails to justify the fighting words doctrine when applied to racial slurs in particular. As Professor Kalven noted, "outbursts of violence are not the necessary consequence of such speech and, more important, such violence when it does occur is not the serious evil of the speech."[47] Rather, as Professor Lawrence stresses, the serious evil of racial slurs consists of the ugliness of the ideas they express and the psychic injury they cause to their addressees.[48] Therefore, the fighting words doctrine does not address and will not prevent the injuries caused by campus racist speech. Even if there were a real danger that racist or other fighting words would cause reflexive violence, and even if that danger would be reduced by the threat of legal sanction, the fighting words doctrine still would be problematic in terms of free speech principles. As Professor Chafee observed, this doctrine "makes a man a criminal simply because his neighbors have no self-control and cannot refrain from violence."[49] In other contexts, the Court appropriately has refused to allow the addressees of speech to exercise such a "heckler's veto."[50]

The fighting words doctrine is constitutionally flawed for the additional reasons that it suppresses much protectible speech and that the protectible speech of minority group members is particularly vulnerable. Notwithstanding the Supreme Court's limitation of the doctrine's scope, Professor Gard's survey reveals that the lower courts apply it much more broadly. Since the Supreme Court only reviews a fraction of such cases, the doctrine's actual impact on free speech must be assessed in terms of these speech-restrictive lower court rulings. Professor Gard concluded that, in the lower courts, the fighting words doctrine "is almost uniformly invoked in a selective and discriminatory manner by law enforcement officials to punish trivial violations of a constitutionally impermissible interest in preventing criticism of official conduct."[51] Indeed, Professor Gard reported, "it is virtually impossible to find fighting words cases that do not involve either the expression of opinion on issues of public policy or words directed toward a government official, usually a police officer."[52] Even more disturbing is that the reported cases indicate that blacks" are often prosecuted and convicted for the use of fighting words.[53] Thus, the record of the actual implementation of the fighting words doctrine demonstrates that–as is the case with all speech restrictions–it endangers principles of equality as well as free speech. That record substantiates the risk that such a speech restriction will be applied discriminatorily and disproportionately against the very minority group members whom it is intended to protect.[54]

Professor Lawrence himself notes that many Supreme Court decisions that overruled fighting words convictions involved a "potentially offended party [who] was in a position of relative power when compared with the speaker."[55] As Professor Gard demonstrated, for each such conviction that was reviewed and overturned by the Supreme Court, many others were not.[56] Thus, Professor Lawrence and other proponents of Stanford's fighting words code must believe that the officials who enforce that code will do so in a manner that differs from the general enforcement pattern of similar regulations. They must have faith that Stanford officials, as opposed to other officials, are unusually sensitive to free speech rights in general, and to the free speech rights of minority group members and dissidents in particular.

Based on his analysis of the actual application of the fighting words doctrine, Professor Gard adheres to no such faith in the discretion of officials. In response to another legal academic's suggestion that the fighting words doctrine could be invoked to protect the aged and infirm from "the vilest personal verbal abuse,"[57] Professor Gard said that this was "a romantic vision that exists only in the imagination of a law professor."[58] Even assuming that Stanford officials might be unusually attentive to free speech values when implementing the fighting words doctrine, Stanford's use of that doctrine could fuel an increased use by other officials, who might well fail to implement it in a speech-sensitive fashion.[59]

Because of the problems with the fighting words doctrine, the committee that proposed a hate speech policy for the University of Texas expressly declined to use it as a model.[60] Likewise, recognizing the weakness of the public peace rationale, the proponents of the Stanford code have attempted to reinvigorate the other rationale that the Supreme Court enunciated in its *Chaplinsky* dictum, but has since abandoned–the notion that such words inflict psychic or emotional injury by their very utterance.[61] But this attempted "solution" to the problems flowing from the breach of the peace rationale causes another set of problems. First, the Supreme Court has never relied upon *Chaplinsky*'s psychic harm dictum to sustain a fighting words conviction.[62] Second, after it pronounced that dictum, the Court issued a line of decisions protecting speech that was allegedly offensive and that assertedly could have caused emotional or psychic injury.[63] Consequently, as Professor Gard stated, to revive *Chaplinsky*'s long-since-discredited second rationale "would turn the constitutional clock back at least [fifty] years.[64]

THE PROPOSED REGULATIONS WOULD NOT PASS CONSTITUTIONAL MUSTER[65]

The Regulations Exceed the Bounds of the Fighting Words Doctrine

As discussed above,[66] the fighting words doctrine is fraught with constitutional problems. As a result, it either has been abrogated *sub silentio* or probably should be. In any event, even assuming that the doctrine is still good law, it has been severely circumscribed by Supreme Court rulings. Because those limits are necessitated by free speech principles, they must be strictly enforced. Professor Gard's thorough study of the law in this area summarizes the Court's limitations on the fighting words doctrine:

> The offending language (1) must constitute a personally abusive epithet, (2) must be addressed in a face-to-face manner, (3) must be directed to a specific individual and be descriptive of that individual, and (4) must be uttered under such circumstances that the words have a direct tendency to cause an immediate violent response by the average recipient. If any of these four elements is absent, the doctrine may not justifiably be invoked as a rationale for the suppression of the expression.[67]

The operative language of the Stanford code provides:

> Speech or other expression constitutes harassment by personal vilification if it:
> (a)   is intended to insult or stigmatize an individual or a small number of individuals on the basis of their sex, race, color, handicap, religion, sexual orientation, or national and ethnic origin; and
> (b)   is addressed directly to the individual or individuals whom it insults or stigmatizes; and
> (c)   makes use of insulting or "fighting" words or non-verbal symbols. In the context of discriminatory harassment by personal vilification, insulting or "fighting" words or non-verbal symbols are those "which by their very utterance inflict injury or tend to incite to an immediate breach of the peace," and which are commonly understood to convey direct and visceral hatred or contempt for

human beings on the basis of their sex, race, color, handicap, religion, sexual orientation, or national and ethnic origin.[68]

A comparison of the Stanford code to the Supreme Court's four criteria for constitutional fighting words restrictions reveals that the code clearly does not satisfy one of the Court's criteria, and it may not satisfy the other three. Most importantly, as outlined above, since *Gooding* v *Wilson* the Court consistently has invalidated fighting words definitions that refer only to the content of words. Instead, it has insisted that these words must be evaluated contextually, to assess whether they are likely to cause an imminent breach of the peace under the circumstances in which they are uttered. Yet, the Stanford code punishes words which are "commonly understood to convey" group-based hatred. By proscribing certain words, without considering their context, the Stanford code violates Gard's fourth criterion, and for that reason alone falls afoul of the First Amendment.

The Stanford code also may fail to satisfy the Court's strict parameters for the fighting words doctrine in other respects. First, it does not expressly require that the prohibited speech "must constitute a personally abusive epithet," the first criterion in Professor Gard's list. Based on his analysis of cases that address the fighting words doctrine, Professor Gard concluded that "the utterance must constitute an extremely provocative personal insult"[69] in order to comport with free speech principles.[70]

Although the Stanford code may comply with the Court's second and third requirements, by prescribing that the prohibited speech be "addressed directly to the individual or individuals whom it insults or stigmatizes," both of these elements have been construed so strictly that they may not be satisfied by this provision. Some judicial rulings indicate that the second requirement, the face-to-face element, "is not satisfied by mere technical physical presence, but contemplates an extremely close physical proximity."[71] The third requirement has been interpreted to mean that "the offensive words must be descriptive of a particular person and addressed to that person."[72] The Stanford code does not require that the prohibited words describe the individual to whom they are addressed. Instead, under the Stanford code, the words may convey hatred for broad groups of people.

The Regulations Will Chill Protected Speech

Beyond its facial problems of violating neutrality principles and fighting words limitations, the Stanford code also will dampen academic discourse. . . .

In *Doe* v *University of Michigan*,[73] the United States District Court for the Eastern District of Michigan held that the University of Michigan's anti–hate speech policy violated the First Amendment because, as applied, it was overbroad[74] and impermissibly vague.[75] The court concluded that during the year when the policy was in effect, the university "consistently applied" it "to reach protected speech."[76] Moreover, because of the policy's vagueness, the court concluded that it did not give adequate notice of which particular expressions would be prohibited and which protected.[77] Consequently, the policy deterred members of the university community from engaging in protected expression for fear it might be sanctioned. This "chilling effect" of any hate speech regulation is particularly problematic in the academic environment, given the special importance of a free and robust exchange of ideas.

Moreover, the judge who ultimately found the Michigan rule unconstitutional did not share Professor Lawrence's opinion that it was poorly drafted and obviously overbroad. To the contrary, his opinion expressly noted that he would not have found the rule unconstitutionally overbroad merely based on its language. Rather, he found it unconstitutional in light of the enforcement record. These findings prove the relevance of the Michigan case not only to the Stanford situation, but also to all other campus hate speech regulations. Regardless of how carefully these rules are drafted, they inevitably are vague and unavoidably invest officials with substantial discretion in the enforcement process; thus, such regulations exert a chilling effect on speech beyond their literal bounds.

In the recent wave of college crackdowns on racist and other forms of hate speech, examples abound of attempts to censor speech conveying ideas that clearly play a legitimate role in academic discourse, although some of us might find them wrongheaded or even odious. For example, the University of Michigan's anti–hate speech policy could justify attacks on author Salman Rushdie because his book, *The Satanic Verses*,[78] was offensive to Muslims.[79]

Such incidents are not aberrational. Any anti–hate speech rule inescapably entails some vagueness, due to the inherent imprecision of key words and concepts common to all such proposed rules. For example, most regulations employ one or more of the following terms: "demeaning," "disparaging," "harassing," "hostile," "insulting," "intimidating," and "stigmatizing."[80] Therefore, there is real danger that even a narrowly crafted rule will deter some expression that should be protected[81]–especially in the university environment.[82] In particular, such a rule probably will "add to the silence" on "gut issues" about racism, sexism, and other forms of bias that already impede interracial and other intergroup dialogues.[83]

Additionally, it must be recognized that silencing certain expressions may be tantamount to silencing certain ideas.[84] As the plaintiff in *Doe* v *Michigan* argued:

> [T]he policy . . . is an official statement that at the University of Michigan, some arguments will no longer be tolerated. Rather than encourage her

maturing students to question each other's beliefs on such diverse and controversial issues as the proper role of women in society, the merits of particular religions, or the moral propriety of homosexuality, the University has decided that it must protect its students from what it considers to be "unenlightened" ideas. In so doing, the University has established a secular orthodoxy by implying, among other things, that homosexuality is morally acceptable, [and] that . . . feminism [is] superior to the traditional view of women. . . .[85]

The Michigan plaintiff was victimized directly by the "pall of orthodoxy"[86] that the university's anti–hate speech policy cast over the campus. As a graduate student specializing in behavioral psychology, he felt that the rule deterred him from classroom discussion of theories that some psychological differences among racial groups and between the sexes are related to biological differences, for fear of being charged with racial or sexual harassment.[87]

In addition to their chilling effect on the ideas and expressions of university community members, policies that bar hate speech could engender broader forms of censorship. As noted by Professor William Cohen of Stanford Law School, an anti–hate speech rule such as the one adopted by his university "purports to create a personal right to be free from involuntary exposure to any form of expression that gives certain kinds of offense." Therefore, he explains, such a rule "could become a sword to challenge assigned readings in courses, the showing of films on campus, or the message of certain speakers."[88]

THE PROPOSED REGULATIONS WOULD ENDANGER FUNDAMENTAL FREE SPEECH PRINCIPLES

The various proposed campus hate speech regulations, including the Stanford code that Professor Lawrence endorses, are inconsistent with current Supreme Court doctrine prescribing permissible limits on speech. More importantly, they jeopardize basic free speech principles. Whereas certain conduct may be regulable, speech that advocates such conduct is not, and speech may not be regulated on the basis of its content, even if many of us strongly disagree with—or are repelled by—that content.

Protection of Speech Advocating Regulable Conduct

Civil libertarians, scholars, and judges consistently have distinguished between speech advocating unlawful conduct and the unlawful conduct itself.[89] Although this distinction has been drawn in numerous different factual settings, the fundamental underlying issues always are the same. For example, within recent years, some pro-choice activists have urged civil libertarians and courts to make an exception to free speech principles in order to restrain the expressive conduct of antiabortion activists. Instead, civil libertarians have persuaded courts to prohibit assaults, blockages of clinic entrances, trespasses, and other illegal conduct by antichoice activists.[90] Similarly, civil libertarians and courts[91] have rejected pleas by some feminists to censor pornography that reflects sexist attitudes.[92] Instead, civil libertarians have renewed their efforts to persuade courts and legislatures to invalidate sexist actions.[93] A decade ago, civil libertarians and several courts–including the Supreme Court–rejected the plea of Holocaust survivors in Skokie, Illinois, to prohibit neo-Nazis from demonstrating.[94] Instead, civil libertarians successfully have lobbied for the enactment and enforcement of laws against anti-Semitic vandalism and other hate-inspired conduct.[95]

A pervasive weakness in Professor Lawrence's analysis is his elision of the distinction between racist speech, on the one hand, and racist conduct, on the other.[96] It is certainly true that racist speech, like other speech, may have some causal connection to conduct. As Justice Holmes observed, "[e]very idea is an incitement" to action.[97] However, as Justice Holmes also noted, to protect speech that advocates conduct you oppose does not "indicate that you think the speech impotent, . . . or that you do not care wholeheartedly for the result."[98] Rather, this protection is based on the critical distinction between speech that has a direct and immediate link to unlawful conduct and all other speech, which has less direct and immediate links. In Holmes's immortal words:

> [W]e should be eternally vigilant against attempts to check the expression of opinions that we loathe and believe to be fraught with death, unless they so imminently threaten immediate interference with the lawful and pressing purposes of the law that an immediate check is required to save the country. . . . Only the emergency that makes it immediately dangerous to leave the correction of evil counsels to time warrants making any exception to the sweeping command, "Congress shall make no law . . . abridging the freedom of speech."[99]

Justice Holmes's stirring phrases were penned in dissenting opinions. However, the Court enshrined his view as the law of the land in 1969, in *Brandenburg* v *Ohio*.[100] In a unanimous opinion overturning the conviction of a Ku Klux Klansman for an antiblack and anti-Semitic speech, the Court said that the First Amendment does "not permit a state to forbid . . . advocacy of the use of force or of law violation except where such advocacy is directed to inciting or producing imminent lawless action and is likely to incite or produce such action."[101]

It is impossible to draw a bright line between speech and conduct. It also may be difficult to determine whether certain speech has a sufficiently tight nexus to conduct to justify regulating that speech. Professor Lawrence, however, abandons the attempt to make any such distinctions at all. He treats even the most extreme, blatant discriminatory conduct as speech, including slavery itself.[102] Although undoubtedly harmful, the utterance of disparaging remarks cannot be equated fairly with the systematic denial of all rights to a group of human beings.[103] Professor Lawrence recognizes this and appropriately chides anyone who insists that *all* racist conduct that includes an expressive component should be treated alike—namely, as protected speech.[104] However, Professor Lawrence himself engages in precisely the same kind of oversimplification when he suggests that all conduct with an expressive component—which, in his view, includes *all* racist conduct and *all* racist speech[105]—should be treated alike, namely, as *unprotected* speech. Those of us who reject either extreme as unreasonably rigid should join forces in undertaking the essential, albeit difficult, task of line drawing.[106]

Proscription on Content-Based Speech Regulations

The indivisibility of free speech. It is important to place the current debate about campus racist speech in the context of earlier efforts to censor other forms of hate speech, including sexist and anti-Semitic speech.[107] Such a broadened perspective suggests that consistent principles should be applied each time the issue resurfaces in any guise. Every person may find one particular type of speech especially odious and one message that most sorely tests his or her dedication to free speech values. But for each person who would exclude racist speech from the general proscription against content-based speech regulations, recent experience shows that there is another who would make such an exception only for antichoice speech, another who would make it only for sexist speech, another who would make it only for anti-Semitic speech, another who would make it only for flag desecration, and so on.

The recognition that there is no principled basis for curbing speech expressing some particular ideas is reflected in the time-honored prohibition on any content-based[108] or viewpoint-based regulations. As stated by Professor Tribe, "If the Constitution forces government to allow people to march, speak and write in favor of peace, brotherhood, and justice, then it must also require government to allow them to advocate hatred, racism, and even genocide."[109]

The position stated by Professor Tribe is not just the traditional civil libertarian view, but it also is the law of the land. The courts consistently have agreed with civil libertarian claims that the First Amendment protects the right to engage in racist and other forms of hate speech.[110] Why is this so, and should it be so? Professor Lawrence rightly urges us to take a fresh look at this issue, no matter how well-settled it is as a matter of law. I have taken that invitation seriously and reflected long and hard upon his thought-provoking article and the questions it presents. Having done so, however, I conclude that the courts and traditional civil libertarians are correct in steadfastly rejecting laws that create additional new exceptions to free speech protections for racist expression.

One longstanding rationale for the view that speech must be protected, regardless of its content, is the belief that we need a free marketplace of ideas, open even to the most odious and offensive ideas and expressions,[111] because truth ultimately will triumph in an unrestricted marketplace.[112] The marketplace metaphor is subject to some criticism, as Professor Lawrence notes. Nevertheless, the marketplace of ideas does sometimes work to improve society: This has been particularly true with regard to promotion of racial equality. Moreover, there are other, independently sufficient, rationales for the content-neutral protection even of hate speech. Another important, more recently articulated, rationale is that freedom of expression promotes individual autonomy and dignity.[113] Professor Lawrence himself endorses an additional theory for the protection of racist speech, a view which recently was advanced by Dean Lee Bollinger: Free speech reinforces our society's commitment to tolerance and to combating racist ideas.

Although the foregoing theories may be acceptable in general, one might ask why they do not permit exceptions for racist speech. Racism in America is unique in important respects. For most of our country's history, racism was enshrined legally through slavery or de jure discrimination. The post–Civil War constitutional amendments guaranteed racial equality. More recently, all branches and levels of the government have sought to implement these constitutional guarantees by outlawing any vestiges of state-sponsored, as well as many forms of private, racial discrimination. Given our nation's special obligation to eradicate the "badges and incidents" of the formerly government-sanctioned institutions of racism, is it not appropriate to make broader exceptions than usual to free speech doctrines for racist speech? As Professor Rodney Smolla has noted, "Racist speech is arguably different in kind from other offensive speech, because the elimination of racism is *itself* enshrined in our Constitution as a public value of the highest order."[114]

The American commitment to eradicate racial discrimination is reinforced by a parallel international commitment, as expressed in such documents as the United Nations Charter,[115] the Universal Declaration of Human Rights,[116] and the International Convention on the Elimination of All Forms of Racial Discrimination.[117] Moreover, the United States is apparently alone in the world community in sheltering racist speech. Both under international agreements[118] and under the domestic law of many other countries[119] racist speech is outlawed.

In light of the universal condemnation of racial discrimination and the worldwide regulation of racist speech, it certainly is tempting to consider excepting racist speech from First Amendment protection. Episodes of racist speech, such as those cited by Professor Lawrence and others, make a full commitment to free speech at times seem painful and difficult. Civil libertarians find such speech abhorrent, given our dedication to eradicating racial discrimination and other forms of bigotry. But experience has confirmed the truth of the indivisibility principle articulated above: History demonstrates that if the freedom of speech is weakened for one person, group, or message, then it is no longer there for others.[120] The free speech victories that civil libertarians have won in the context of defending the right to express racist and other anti–civil libertarian messages have been used to protect speech proclaiming antiracist and pro–civil libertarian messages. For example, in 1949, the ACLU defended the right of Father Terminiello, a suspended Catholic priest, to give a racist speech in Chicago. The Supreme Court agreed with that position in a decision that became a landmark in free speech history.[121] Time and again during the 1960s and 1970s, the ACLU and other civil rights groups were able to defend free speech rights for civil rights demonstrators by relying on the Terminiello decision.

The slippery slope dangers of banning racist speech. To attempt to craft free speech exceptions only for racist speech would create a significant risk of a slide down the proverbial "slippery slope." To be sure, lawyers and judges are capable of–indeed, especially trained in–drawing distinctions between similar situations. Therefore, I agree with Professor Lawrence and other critics of the absolutist position[123] that slippery slope dangers should not be exaggerated. It is probably hyperbole to contend that if we ever stepped off the mountaintop where all speech is protected regardless of its content, then inevitably we would end up in the abyss where the government controls all our words.[124] On the other hand, critics of absolutism should not minimize the real danger: We would have a difficult time limiting our descent to a single downward step by attempting to prohibit only racist expression on campus. Applicable rules and supporting rationales would need to be crafted carefully to distinguish this type of speech from others.

First, we must think hard about the groups that should be protected. Should we regulate speech aimed only racial and ethnic groups, as the University of Texas is considering?[125] Or should we also bar insults of religious groups, women, gays and lesbians, individuals with disabilities, Vietnam War veterans, and so on, as do the rules adopted by Stanford and the University of Michigan? As the committee that formulated the University of

Texas's proposed rule pointed out, each category requires a separate evaluation, since each "raise[s] difrrent policy and legal concerns."[126] Therefore, we should not play fast and loose with the First Amendment by casually expanding the categories of proscribed hate speech.

Second, we must carefully define proscribable harassing speech to avoid encompassing the important expression that inevitably is endangered by any hate speech restriction. Censorial consequences could result from many proposed or adopted university policies, including the Stanford code, which sanctions speech intended to "insult or stigmatize" on the basis of race or other prohibited grounds. For example, certain feminists suggest that all heterosexual sex is rape because heterosexual men are aggressors who operate in a cultural climate of pervasive sexism and violence against women.[127] Aren't these feminists insulting or stigmatizing heterosexual men on the basis of their sex and sexual orientation? And how about a Holocaust survivor who blames all ("Aryan") Germans for their collaboration during World War II? Doesn't this insinuation insult or stigmatize on the basis of national and ethnic origin? And surely we can think of numerous other examples that would have to give us pause.

The difficulty of formulating limited, clear definitions of prohibited hate speech, that do not encompass valuable contributions to societal discourse, is underscored by the seemingly intractable ambiguities in various campus rules.[128] Even proponents of campus hate speech regulations recognize their inevitable ambiguities and contextualized applications,[129] with the result that the individuals who enforce them must have substantial discretion to draw distinctions based upon the particular facts and circumstances involved in any given case. Professor Richard Delgado, an early advocate of rules proscribing hate speech, acknowledged that the offensiveness of even such a traditionally insulting epithet as "nigger" would depend on the context in which it was uttered, since it could be a term of affection when exchanged between friends.[130] The imprecise nature of racist speech regulations is underscored further by the fact that even their proponents are unsure or disagree as to their applicability in particular situations.[131]

Once we acknowledge the substantial discretion that anti–hate speech rules will vest in those who enforce them, then we are ceding to the government the power to pick and choose whose words to protect and whose to punish. Such discretionary governmental power is fundamentally antithetical to the free speech guarantee. Once the government is allowed to punish any speech based upon its content, free expression exists only for those with power.

PROFESSOR LAWRENCE'S RATIONALES FOR REGULATING RACIST SPEECH WOULD JUSTIFY SWEEPING PROHIBITIONS, CONTRARY TO FREE SPEECH PRINCIPLES

Although Professor Lawrence actually advocates regulating only a relatively narrow category of racist speech, his rationales could be asserted to justify broader rules. Indeed, he himself appears to recognize that, if accepted, his approach could lead to outlawing all racist speech, as well as other forms of hate speech.[132] Since many universities and individuals now advocate broader-ranging regulations—and since Professor Lawrence also endorses restrictions that have a "considerably broader reach" than the Stanford code[133]—it is important to consider the problems with Professor Lawrence's more expansive rationales. His general theories about racist speech entail substantial departures from traditional civil libertarian and constitutional law positions.

Brown *and Other Cases Invalidating Governmental Racist Conduct Do Not Justify Regulating Nongovernmental Racist Speech*

Professor Lawrence intriguingly posits that *Brown v Board of Education,*[134] *Bob Jones University v United States,*[135] and other civil rights cases justify regulation of private racist speech.[136] The problem with drawing an analogy between all of these cases and subject at hand is that the cases involved either *government* speech, as opposed to speech by private individuals, or *conduct,* as opposed to speech.[137] Indeed, *Brown* itself is distinguishable on both grounds.

The Speech/Conduct Distinction

First, the governmental defendant in *Brown*—the Topeka, Kansas, Board of Education—was not simply saying that blacks are inferior. Rather, it was treating them as inferior through pervasive patterns of conduct, by maintaining systems and structures of segregated public schools. To be sure, a by-product of the challenged conduct was a message, but that message was only incidental. Saying that black children are unfit to attend school with whites is materially distinguishable from legally prohibiting them from doing so, despite the fact that the legal prohibition may convey the former message.

Professor Lawrence's point proves too much. If incidental messages could transform conduct into speech, then the distinction between speech and conduct would disappear completely, because *all* conduct conveys a

350 PART III: FREE SPEECH ON CAMPUS

message. To take an extreme example, a racially motivated lynching expresses the murderer's hatred or contempt for his victim. But the clearly unlawful act is not protected from punishment by virtue of the incidental message it conveys. And the converse also is true. Just because the government may suppress particular hate messages that are the by-product of unlawful conduct, it does not follow that it may suppress all hate messages. Those messages not tightly linked to conduct must still be protected.

Professor Lawrence's argument is not advanced by his unexceptionable observation that all human activity may be described both as "speech" and as "conduct." All speech entails some activity (e.g., the act of talking) and all conduct expresses some message.[138] First, this fact does not justify treating *any* speech-conduct as unprotected; second, it does not justify eliminating protection from the particular class of speech-conduct that Professor Lawrence deems regulable.

The fact that there is no clear distinction between speech and conduct does not necessarily warrant *limiting* the scope of protected speech-conduct;[139] instead, the lack of a clear distinction could as logically warrant *expanding* the scope of protection. Although one could argue–as does Professor Lawrence–that some speech is tantamount to conduct and should therefore be regulated, one could also argue that some conduct is tantamount to speech and therefore should not be regulated. This latter approach has characterized a line of Supreme Court decisions that protect various forms of conduct, ranging from labor picketing[140] to burning the American flag,[141] as "symbolic speech."

The absence of a clear distinction between speech and conduct also does not support Professor Lawrence's particular concept of regulable racist speech. Even assuming that his wholesale abandonment of the traditional distinction is warranted with respect to racist words and deeds, Professor Lawrence himself apparently concedes that this still would not justify the regulation of all racist words. To the contrary, he advocates regulating only a limited class of such words. But if Professor Lawrence does not draw the line between regulable and nonregulable racist speech on the basis of the speech/conduct dichotomy, on what basis does he draw that line? He does not offer a clear limiting principle for distinguishing the racist speech that should be regulated from the entire corpus of racist speech, which he views as conduct, and hence presumptively regulable under the speech/conduct approach.[142]

The Private Action/State Action Distinction

Even if *Brown* involved only a governmental message of racism, without any attendant conduct, that case still would be distinguishable in a crucial way from a private individual's conveyance of the same message. Under the post–Civil War constitutional amendments, the government is committed to eradicating all badges and incidents of slavery, including racial discrimination. Consistent with the paramount importance of this obligation, the Supreme Court has held that the equal protection clause bars the government from loaning textbooks to racially discriminatory private schools,[143] even though the Court had held previously that the establishment clause does not bar the government from loaning textbooks to private religious schools.[144] On this respect, the government's constitutional duty to dissociate itself from racism is even greater than its constitutional duty to dissociate itself from religion.[145] The government's supreme obligation to counter racism clearly is incompatible with racist speech promulgated by the government itself. Private individuals have no comparable duty.

Professor Mari Matsuda has argued that the government's failure to punish private hate speech could be viewed as state action insofar as this failure conveys a message that the state tolerates such speech.[146] Because the Court construes the establishment clause as prohibiting government action that conveys a message of state support for religion,[147] establishment clause cases constitute instructive precedents for evaluating Professor Matsuda's argument.[148] In the analogous establishment clause context, the Court repeatedly has held that the government's neutral tolerance and protection of private religious expression, along with all other expression, does not convey a message that the government endorses religion.[149] In its 1990 decision in *Board of Education of Westside Community Schools* v *Mergens*,[150] the Court expressly reaffirmed the crucial distinction between government and private speech, in the establishment clause context, in terms fully applicable to the racist speech controversy. The Court declared, "[T]here is a crucial difference between *government* speech endorsing religion, which the Establishment Clause forbids, and *private* speech endorsing religion, which the Free Speech and Free Exercise Clauses protect."[151] Paraphrasing this language and applying it to the campus hate speech context, one could say, "There is a crucial difference between *government* speech endorsing racism, which the Equal Protection Clause forbids, and *private* speech endorsing racism, which the Free Speech Clause protects."

In light of the government's special duty to dissociate itself from racism, one might try to distinguish private religious speech from private racist speech—much as the Court distinguished textbook loans to racially discriminatory private schools from the same kind of loans to private religious schools.[152] However, the direct, tangible, explicit government support of racially discriminatory schools through textbook lending programs is critically different from the indirect, intangible, implicit government support allegedly lent to racist conduct by the government's failure to outlaw private racist speech.[153]

Professor Lawrence makes a telling point when he says that our government never has repudiated the group libels it perpetrated for years against blacks and that it is insufficient for the government simply to cease uttering those libels.[154] One approach for promoting racial equality, which is consistent with free speech, is to urge the government to proclaim anti-racist messages.

Professor Lawrence also makes the persuasive point that there is no absolute distinction between state and private action in the racist sphere, insofar as private acts of discrimination (as well as government acts) also are unlawful.[155] This point, however, raises the other distinction discussed above—the distinction between words and conduct. Civil libertarians vigorously support the civil rights laws that make private discriminatory *acts* illegal,[156] but that is a far cry from making private *speech* illegal. The *Bob Jones* case, upon which Professor Lawrence seeks to rely,[157] illustrates these distinctions. What was objectionable there was the government conduct that supported and endorsed the private racist conduct—namely, the government's making of financial contributions, through the tax system, to racially discriminatory private educational institutions. Moreover, even if a private university could be prohibited from *taking* discriminatory actions—in the case of Bob Jones University, barring interracial marriage and dating—it still could not be prohibited from *advocating* such actions. The ACLU amicus brief in the *Bob Jones* case[158] made precisely these points in countering the university's claim that withdrawing its tax benefits would violate its First Amendment rights. The ACLU argued,[159] and the Court agreed,[160] that the university was still free to urge its students not to engage in interracial marriage or dating, and this was as far as its First Amendment rights extended. Prohibited racist acts are no different from other prohibited acts. The government may punish the acts, but it may not punish words that advocate or endorse them.

The other cases upon which Professor Lawrence premises his argument also do not authorize the regulation of private racist speech. For example, he attempts to analogize private racist speech to a local government's financing of allegedly "private" segregated (all-white) schools, after the government had closed down public schools in defiance of desegregation orders.[161] Lawrence misreads these cases as standing for the proposition "that defamatory message of segregation would not be insulated from constitutional proscription simply because the speaker was a non-government entity."[162] Another example is provided by *Griffin* v *Prince Edward County School Board*, in which the Supreme Court held that the governmental financing of segregated schools constituted prohibited state action.[163] In contrast, had individual school district residents urged their government to undertake such action, or expressed this opinion to black residents, that would have constituted protected private speech.[164]

The Nonintellectual Content of Some Racist Speech Does Not Justify Its Prohibition

In addition to his principal argument that private racist speech can be regulated because it is indistinguishable from governmental racist conduct, Professor Lawrence offers a second justification. He contends that "[a] defining attribute of speech is that it appeals first to the mind of the hearer who can evaluate its truth or persuasiveness,"[165] and that because certain racist speech lacks this quality, it should not be viewed as speech. This position is inconsistent with fundamental free speech values.

Lawrence's argument overlooks the teachings of such landmark Supreme Court decisions as *Terminiello* v *Chicago*[166] and *Cohen* v *California*,[167] which hold that protectible speech often appeals to the emotions as well as the mind. As early as 1948, the Court recognized that First Amendment protection is not restricted to the "exposition of ideas."[168] As Justice Douglas declared in a celebrated passage in *Terminiello*:

> [A] function of free speech under our system of government is to invite dispute. It may indeed best serve its high purpose when it induces a condition of unrest, creates dissatisfaction with conditions as they are, or even stirs people to anger. Speech is often provocative and challenging. It may strike at prejudices and preconceptions and have profound unsettling effects as it presses for acceptance of an idea. That is why freedom of speech, though not absolute, is nevertheless protected against censorship or punishment, unless shown likely to produce a clear and present danger of a serious substantive evil that rises far above public inconvenience, annoyance, or unrest. There is no room under our Constitution for a more restrictive view. For the alternative would lead to standardization of ideas either by legislatures, courts, or dominant political or community groups.[169]

Justice Harlan[170] echoed this theme in *Cohen* when he explained that protectible expression

> conveys not only ideas capable of relatively precise, detached explication, but otherwise inexpressible emotions as well. In fact, words are often chosen as much for their emotive as their cognitive force. *We cannot sanction the view that the Constitution, while solicitous of the cognitive content of individual speech, has little or no regard for that emotive function which practically speaking, may often be the more important element of the overall message sought to be communicated.*[171]

Together, *Terminiello* and *Cohen* recognize that speech often expresses the speaker's emotions and appeals to the audience's emotions. This generalization applies not only to the ugly words of racist vituperation, but also to the beautiful words of poetry. Indeed, much indisputably valuable language, as well as expressive conduct, has the intention and effect of appealing not directly or not only to the mind. Such language also seeks to and does engage the audience's emotions. If emotion-provoking discourse were denied protected status, then much political speech—which is usually viewed as being at the core of First Amendment protection—would fall outside the protected realm. The Court in *Terminiello* and *Cohen* rejected the restricted First Amendment paradigm of "a sedate assembly of speakers who calmly discussed the issues of the day and became ultimately persuaded by the logic of one of the competing positions."[172] Professor Lawrence reveals his narrower view when he asks, "[A]re racial insults ideas? Do they encourage wide-open debate?"[173] In light of the *Terminiello-Cohen* line of cases, Professor Lawrence wrongly implies that a negative response to these questions should remove racial insults from the domain of protected speech. Professor Lawrence also incorrectly implies that the response to these questions should be negative. Racial insults convey ideas of racial supremacy and inferiority. Objectionable and discredited as these ideas may be, they are ideas nonetheless.[174]

NOTES

1. There is no single "civil libertarian" or ACLU position on many of the issues discussed in this article. For example, Professors Lawrence and Strossen are both avowed civil libertarians and ACLU supporters, although they disagree on certain civil liberties issues.

On October 13, 1990, the ACLU's National Board of Directors adopted a policy opposing campus disciplinary codes against hate speech.

In addition to the national organization, the ACLU includes fifty-one statewide or regional "affiliates" which may all adopt their own policies. Although an affiliate's policies must be "in accordance" with those of the national organization, this requirement is designed "to obtain general unity, rather than absolute uniformity." See *Policy Guide of the American Civil Liberties Union*, at Policy No. 501 (rev ed. 1990) [hereinafter *ACLU Policy Guide*] Accordingly, some ACLU affiliates may adopt policies concerning the regulation of campus hate speech that are to some extent divergent from each other, and from the national ACLU policy. The ACLU California affiliates have adopted a policy that does not oppose the regulation of a limited class of campus hate speech, see Policy of ACLU California Affiliates Concerning Racist and Other Group-Based Harassment on College Campuses (adopted by ACLU of Northern California, March 8, 1990; ACLU of Southern California, March 21, 1990; and ACLU of San Diego and Imperial Counties, May 24, 1990; available from author). In contrast, for example, the Civil Liberties Union of Massachusetts has adopted a policy that opposes any content-based restrictions on campus speech.

To reflect the fact that civil libertarians may differ about the specific issues discussed in this article, the term "traditional civil libertarian" is used only to describe

the general view that much hate speech is entitled to First Amendment protection. All other, more specific views expressed in this article reflect the author's opinions. She does not purport to speak either for the national ACLU or for civil libertarians generally.

2. Consistent with Professor Lawrence's approach, this article focuses on racist speech, although the analysis generally applies to other forms of hate speech as well, such as sexist and homophobic speech, and speech vilifying religious or ethnic groups.

3. See Leslie, "Lessons from Bigotry 101," *Newsweek*, September 25, 1989, p. 48 (documents incidents at 250 colleges and universities since fall 1986). See also *Civil Rights Division of Antidefamation League of B'nai B'rith Policy Background Report— Campus Anti-Bias Codes, a New Form of Censorship?* 1 (1999) (in 1988 there were more reported incidents or anti-Semitic harassment on United States campuses than in any prior year). For a listing of some recent incidents of campus racism, see Matsuda, "Public Response to Racist Speech: Considering specific the Victim's Story," 87 *Mich. L. Rev.* 2320, 2333 n. 71 (1989).

For some possible explanations for this wave of campus racism, see Steele, "The Recoloring of Campus Life," *Harper's*, February 1989, p. 47

4. See *Carnegie Foundation for the Advancement of Teaching, A Special Report: Campus Life, in Search of Community* 20 (1990), at 19 (60 percent of the chief student affairs officers surveyed in 1989 reported that their campuses had written policies on bigotry, racial harassment, or intimidation, and another 11 percent said they are working on such policies).

5. See generally *ACLU Policy Guide*, n. 1, at Policy Nos. 301–31 (ACLU policies advocaitng equality for racial and other historically disempowered groups). For a summary of the ACLU's efforts to implement these policies, see n. 6.

6. It has long been an ACLU priority to combat racial discrimination in education. For example, during the 1920s and 1930s, the ACLU assisted with the NAACP's formulation of a nationwide legal campaign against segregated education. See S. Walker, *In Defense of American Liberties: A History of the ACLU* 88–90 (1990). The Southern California ACLU successfully challenged school segregation as early as 1946. See ibid. at 239. The ACLU's recent efforts in this category include its representation of the plaintiffs in *Brown* v *Board of Educ.*, 892 F.2d 851 (10th Cir. 1989) (*Brown III*), which challenged the de facto segregation of Topeka, Kansas, public schools. See also Memorandum from john a. powell to Ira Glasser and the Executive Committee, March 10, 1990, at 3–4 (hereinafter powell, Memorandum) (listing cases in which ACLU National Legal Department currently is challenging racial discrimination in education; available from author).

7. For example, the ACLU represented the plaintiff in *Doe* v *University of Mich.*, 721 F. Supp. 852 (E.D. Mich. 1989). which successfully challenged the University of Michigan's anti–hate speech policy as violating the First Amendment. The ACLU also has initiated a lawsuit challenging the University of Wisconsin's hate speech regulation. See Grabble, "Student Coalition Sues UW over Racial Harassment Rule," *Milwaukee Journal*, March 30, 1990, p. 8B, col. 1. Prior to the adoption of both rules, the ACLU sought to persuade the universities to formulate narrower restrictions.

8. At times, Lawrence recognizes that these goals are in fact mutually rein-forcing, see Lawrence at 310, n. 57, but at other times, he seems to view them as incompatible. See ibid. at 305–306, 315. This is a major unresolved tension in his article.

9. See Gale & Strossen, "The Real ACLU," 2 *Yale J. L. & Feminism* 161, 171–84 (1990). Some themes in the present article were previously explored in the Gale & Strossen essay. Professor Strossen thanks Professor Gale for her permission to draw upon this earlier piece in the present one.

10. See Lawrence at 481 of original text.

11. In Professor Lawrence's composite view, "traditional" civil libertarians dis-play the following "typical" propensities. First, they argue that all speech should be absolutely protected, at least if it "stops short of violence." See Lawrence at 307. Second, they recognize that no insults or fighting words are protected free speech, unless they are racial in nature. See Lawrence at 436, 437, 476 of original text. Third, they do not acknowledge that racist speech inflicts real harm. See Lawrence at 306. Fourth, they are more committed to the values reflected in the Constitution's free speech clause than to those reflected in its equal protection clause. See Lawrence at 306. Fifth, they do not support, and indeed "often" oppose, "group expressions of condemnation" of racist speech. See Lawrence at 477 of original text. Sixth, they "typically ... elect to stand by" while universities draft constitutionally vulnerable hate speech regulations. They "wait [to] attack [such] poorly drafted and obviously overbroad regulations." Ibid.

The foregoing stereotypes are presented through unsupported assertions and are belied by the facts recited throughout this article. Professor Lawrence also makes incorrect and misleading statements specifically about the ACLU and its members. See Lawrence at 473, 476, and nn. 163–64 of original text.

Professor Lawrence qualifies his depiction of the "traditional" civil libertarian or ACLU member in one important respect: He repeatedly suggests that civil libertar-ians and ACLU members who are members of minonty groups (or perhaps women) differ from others in their positions on free speech and equal protection issues. See Lawrence at 466 of original text.

Such racial stereotyping is both factually inaccurate and antithetical to equality principles. The inaccuracy is illustrated by the fact that two ACLU officials, both black, recently engaged in a public debate against each other in which one opposed all campus hate speech regulations. See M. Meyers, "Banning Racist and Other Kinds of 'Hate' speech on the College Campus" (outline for a debate with john a. powell at Hofstra University, Hempstead, Long Island, January 25, 1990; available for the author). Both of thew officials agree that the effort to shape appropriately narrow hate speech restrictions entails an undesirable diversion of resources firom the essential task of shaping underlying attitudes Interviews with Michael Meyers and john a. powell, in New York City (August 18, 1990).

12. Lawrence at 306 (quoting "A Step Toward Civility," *Time*, May 1, 1989, p. 43).

13. See Lawrence at 308, n. 47. Stanford University recently adopted a rule defining some expression as prohibited "harassment by vilification." Stanford Uni-versity, Fundamental Standard interpretation: Free Expression and Discriminatory

Harassment (June 1990) (hereinafter Stanford Code and Comments). The rule, which was principally drafted by Professor Thomas Grey, is quoted in the text accompanying n. 68.

At various points in his article, Professor Lawrence endorses regulations of broader scope, see n. 16. However, he stresses his proposed variation of the Stanford code, which would apply to "all common areas" and would "not . . . protect persons . . . vilified on the basis of their membership in dominant majority groups." Lawrence at 308, n. 47. Therefore, throughout the remainder of this article, references to the regulation endorsed by Professor Lawrence refer to this formulation, unless expressly indicated otherwise.

14. See Lawrence at 308, n. 47

15. Civil libertarians have a range of opinions as to when, if ever, these concepts may legitimately be employed to restrict speech. See text accompanying nn. 30–64. The only doctrinal concept advanced by Professor Lawrence as a justification for regulating campus hate speech that the ACLU expressly and categorically rejects is group defamation. See *ACLU Policy Guide*, n. 1, at Policy No. 6(c).

16. See, e.g., Lawrence at 308, n. 47 (supports variation on Stanford code which was broader than the one adopted in that it would apply to all common areas); ibid. at 456–57 of original text (urges regulation of racial epithets that do not involve face-to-face encounters, where victim is captive audience); at 309, n. 50 (argues that fighting words include not only those addressed face-to-facc, as undercurrent doctrine, but should "be expanded in the cale or racist verbal assaults to include those words, that are intentionally spoken in the presence of members of the denigrated group"); at 312, n. 74, 75 (endorses regulation of group defamation).

17. See Lawrence at 301–307.

18. See ibid. at 307. ("This precedent [*Brown* v *Board of Educ.*, 347 U.S. 493 (1954), and its progeny] may not mean that we should advocate the government regulation of all racist speech. . . .")

19. For example, Lawrence argues that racist speech and conduct are unique because of the direct link between speech or act and harm:

> I do not contend that *all* conduct with an expressive component should he treated as unprotected speech. To the contrary, my suggestion that racist conduct amounts to speech is premised upon a unique characteristic of racism–namely its reliance upon the defamatory message of white supremacy to achieve its injurious purpose.

Ibid. at 302, n. 7.

It is difficult to understand how racism is unique in terms of the asserted link between its message and its harm. Surely the same connection would exist between any form of group hatred and its resulting harm. For example, sexism relies on the message of male supremacy; homophobia relies on the message of heterosexual supremacy.

20. See n. 16.

21. See Lawrence at 459–61 of original text.

22. Ibid. at 482–83 of original text.

23. See text accompanying n. 68 (quoting Stanford code).

24. See Gottlieb, "Banning Bigoted speech: Stanford Weighs Rules," *San Jose (Calif.) Mercury News*, January 7, 1990, p. 3 (Professor Thomas Grey, who drafted the Stanford code, said "his rule probably wouldn't apply to one of the most publicized racial incidents at Stanford, when a white student left on a black student's door a poster of Beethoven drawn as a black caricature"). The broader variation of the Stanford code, which Professor Lawrence endorsed, see Lawrence at 308, n. 47, apparently would have applied to this Stanford incident, see ibid. at 311, n. 66, but not to the incident endured by his sister or to his boyhood ordeal.

25. See Lawrence, at 313–15 See, e.g., ibid. at 313: "Racism is ubiquitous. We are all racists."

26. See Matsuda, n. 3

27. See Lawrence at 481, n. 169 of original text.

28. See Lawrence, n. 57.

29. See text at 365–96.

30. See Lawrence at 308–309. See also text accompanying n. 68.

31. 315 U.S. 568 (1942).

32. Ibid. at 572 (emphasis added).

33. Ibid. at 573.

34. Ibid.

35. Ibid. at 569.

36. Ibid. at 574.

37. 405 U.S. 518, 523 (1972) (where appellant had said to police officers, "White son of a bitch, I'll kill you," "You son of a bitch, I'll choke you to death," and "You son of a bitch, if you ever put your hands on me again, I'll cut you all to pieces." Court reversed conviction under law that it found overbroad in light of *Chaplinsky*).

38. See, e.g., *Karlan* v *City of Cincinnati*, 416 U.S. 924, (1974); *Rosen* v *California*, 416 U.S. 924 (1974); *Kelly* v *Ohio*, 416 U.S. 923 (1974); *Lucas* v *Arkansas*, 416 U.S. 919 (1974); *Brown* v *Oklahoma*, 408 U.S. 914 (1972); *Lewis* v *New Orleans*, 408 U.S. 913 (1972); *Rosenfeld* v *New Jersey*, 408 U.S. 901 (1972). Professor Lawrence twice states that *Cohen* v *California*, 403 U.S. 15 (1971), quoted approvingly *Chaplinsky*'s language that certain words could be classified as unprotected fighting words per se, without regard to the circumstances in which they were uttered. See Lawrence at 310, n. 57. But this citation does not support the continuing validity of that language, in light of the Court's subsequent rulings in *Gooding* and other fighting words cases.

39. See, e.g., *Eaton* v *City of Tulsa*, 415 U.S. 697, 699 (1974) (per curiam) (reversing contempt of court conviction for witness' use of word "chickenshit," since there was no showing that it posed imminent threat to administration of justice); *Hess* v *Indiana*, 414 U.S. 105, 109 (1973) (per curiam) (reversing disorderly conduct conviction where statement during antiwar demonstration–"We'll take the fucking street later [or again]"–was not directed at any particular person or group and there was no showing that violence was imminent).

40. L. Tribe, n. 58, § 12-18, at 929 and n. 9. A strictly limited fighting words concept is consistent with the views of Zechariah Chafee, whose writings provided the definition of "fighting words" that the Court adopted in *Chaplinsky* v *New Hamp-*

shire, 315 U.S. 568, 572. See Z. Chafee, *Free Speech in the United States* 151–52 (1941). In the same book, shortly after the passage proposing this definition, Chafee quali- fied his account of fighting words:

> This breach of peace theory is peculiarly liable to abuse when applied against unpopular expressions and practices. It makes a man a criminal simply because his neighbors have no self-control. . . . Thus . . . these crimes of injurious words must be kept within very narrow limits if they are not to give excessive opportunities for outlawing heterodox ideas.

Ibid.

41. See nn. 38–39.

42. Compare *Cafeteria Employees Local 302* v *Angelos*, 320 U.S. 293, 295 (1943) (use of word "fascist" is "part of the conventional give-and-take in our economic and political controversies" and hence protected under federal labor law) with *Chap- linsky*, 315 U.S. at 573–74 (conviction affirmed on ground that words "God damned racketeer" and "damned Fascist," when addressed to police officer, were likely to provoke violent response). See also Note, "First Amendment Limits on Tort Liability for Words Intended to Inflict Severe Emotional Distress," 85 *Colum. L. Rev.* 1749 (1995). The author stated that:

> The principle that the advocacy of ideas is subject in regulation when such advocacy is intended to and likely to incite immediate violence remains good law. The continued validity of the application of this principle to the facts in *Chaplinsky*, however, is questionable because the addressee in *Chaplinsky* was a police officer. It is possible that the Court would now hold that because of his special training, the likelihood of a police officer responding violently is too remote for words addressed to a police officer to constitute "fighting" words.

Ibid. at 1768 n. 98 (citations omitted). Accord *Lewis* v *City of New Orleans*, 408 U.S. 913, 913 (1972) (Powell, J., concurring) (suggested that Court should apply separate standard when addressee of alleged fighting words is police officer).

43. *Gooding* v *Wilson*, 405 U.S. 518, 537 (1972) (Blackmun, J., dissenting, joined by Burger, C.T.) ("[T]he Court, despite its protestations to the contrary, is merely paying lip service to *Chaplinsky*.").

44. See, e.g., Gard, "Fighting Words as Free Speech," 58 *Wash. U. L. Q.* 531, 536 (1980) (post-*Chaplinsky* Supreme Court decisions have rendered fighting words doctrine "nothing more than a quaint remnant of an earlier morality that has no place in a democratic society dedicated to the principle of free expression"); Shea, "'Don't Bother to Smile When You Call Me That'–Fighting Words and the First Amend- ment," 63 *Ky. L. J.* 1, 1–2 (1975) ("majority of the U.S. Supreme Court has gradually concluded that fighting words, no matter how narrowly defined, are a protected form of speech"). See also letter from Professor Gerald Gunther to Professor George Parker, Chair of the Student Conduct Legislative Council at Stanford University (May 1, 1989), reprinted in *Stanford Univ. Campus Rep.*, May 3, 1989, p. 18 [hereinafter Gun- ther letter [May 1, 1989]]. In his letter, Professor Gunther stated that:

[T]here has been only *one* case in the history of the Supreme Court in which a majority of the Justices has ever found a statement to be a punishable resort to "fighting words." (That case was *Chaplinsky* v *New Hampshire*, a nearly fifty-year-old case involving words which would very likely not be found punishable today.) More important, in the nearly half century since *Chaplinsky*, there have been repeated appeals to the Court to recognize the applicability of the "fighting words" exception.... [I]n every one of the subsequent attempted rehances on that exception, the Supreme Court has refused to affirm the challenged conviction. In short, one must wonder about the strength of an exception which, while theoretically reconsidered, has ever since 1942 not been found apt in practice.

45. See, e.g., n. 42, at 1757 n.44 (*Chaplinsky* may well reflect concerns peculiar to the decade when it was decided, rather than enduring First Amendment principles).

46. See Gard, n. 44, at 580.

47. H. Kalven, *The Negro and the First Amendment* 14–15 (1965).

48. See Lawrence, at 312–15.

49. Z. Chafee, n. 40, at 151.

50. See, e.g., *Gregory* v *City of Chicago*, 394 U.S. 111 (1969) (holding that there was constitutionally insufficient evidence to support disorderly conduct convictions for civil rights demonstrators who failed to disperse upon police order; Court refused to consider evidence noted by Justice Black in dissent that hostile crowd of one thousand spectators was growing unmanageable in spite of efforts of one hundred uniformed police officers); *Cox* v *Louisiana*, 379 U.S. 536, 550 (1965) (reversed civil rights demonstrators' breach of peace convictions, finding insufficient evidence to support local officials' claims that spectator violence was imminent, where there were one hundred to three hundred "muttering" spectators); *Terminiello* v *Chicago*, 337 U.S. 1 (1949) (where race-baiting speaker attracted "angry and turbulent" crowd, Court reversed breach of peace conviction).

51. Gard, n. 44, at 590.

52. Ibid. at 548 Accord ibid. at 568.

53. See, e.g., *Lewis* v *City of New Orleans*, 415 U.S. 130 (1974) (state court upheld conviction on basis of fighting words doctrine in situation in which police officer said to young suspect's mother, "[g]et your black ass in the goddamned car," and she responded, "you god damn mother fucking police—I am going to [the Superintendent of Police] about this."); *Street* v *New York*, 394 U.S 576 (1969) (black man who protested against shooting of civil rights leader James Meredith by burning American flag and saying, "If they let that happen to Meredith we don't need an American flag," was convicted under statute that criminalized words casting contempt on United States flag; Supreme Court rejected contention that conviction could be justified on fighting words rationale; ibid. at 592); *Edwards* v *South Carolina*, 372 U.S. 229, 236 (1963) (state court upheld convictions of civil rights demonstrators for holding placards stating "I am proud to be a Negro" and "Down with Segregation"; Supreme Court rejected contention that convictions could be justified on fighting words doctrine); *Weller* v *City of St. Petersburg*, 245 So. 2d 685 (Fla. Dist. Ct. App.

1971). *rev'd, City of St. Petersburg* v *Walker*, 261 So. 2d 151 (Fla. 1972) (black man was convicted for shouting "pig" at passing police car, and state supreme court upheld conviction based on fighting words doctrine).

54. See Gard, n. 44, at 566 ("Many commentators have recognized that [the] problem of discriminatory enforcement is particularly acute in the fighting words context. [One very real] danger is . . . that the penal law will be selectively invoked against members of racial or other minority groups and speakers who espouse ideological views unpopular with enforcement officials.") (footnote omitted) See also ibid. at 571 (doctrine creates danger that the common meaning ascribed to words by certain subcultures will be punished based on "myopic ethnocentricity" of officials who enforce rules); Karst, "Equality as a Central Principle in the First Amendment," 43 *U. Chi. L. Rev.* 20, 38 (1975) ("[S]tatutes proscribing abusive words are applied to members of racial and political minorities more frequently than can be wholly explained by any special proclivity of those people to speak abusively.").

55. Lawrence at 310, n. 57.

56. See Gard, n. 44, at 564.

57. Shea, n. 44, at 22.

58. Gard, n. 44 at 564.

59. Professor Lawrence recognizes the potential danger that any speech-restricting precedent "would pose for the speech of all dissenters," and that such a dangerous precedent "might . . . include general societal tolerance for the suppression of speech." Lawrence, at 458 and n. 106 of original text.

60. See Report of the President's Ad Hoc Committee on Racial Harassment, University of Texas at Austin 17 (November 27, 1989).

61. See Stanford Code and Comments, n. 13, at 3. The pertinent part of the Stanford Code and Comments states that:

> The Supreme Court's phrase [in *Chaplinsky*] "insulting or 'fighting' words" is often shortened to simply "fighting words," an expression which . . . may . . . have certain misleading connotations. First, the expression may imply that violence is considered an acceptable response to discriminatory vilification. . . . Second, exclusive focus on the actual likelihood of violence might suggest that opponents of controversial speech can transform it into forbidden "fighting words" by plausibly threatening violent response to it. . . . Finally, the "fighting words" terminology might be thought to imply that extreme forms of personal abuse become protected speech simply because the victims are, for example. such disciplined practitioners of non-violence . . . that they do not . . . pose an actual and imminent threat of violent retaliation. Such a limitation might be appropriate under a breach of peace statute, whose sole purpose is to prevent violence, but does not make sense in an antidiscrimination provision such as this one.

62. See Gard, n. 44, at 577.

63. See, e.g., *United States* v *Eichman*, 110 S. Ct. 2404, 2409 (1990) (prosecution for burning American flag in violation of Flag Protection Act of 1989, Pub. L. No. 101-131. 103 Stat. 777, held inconsistent with First Amendment protection of expres-

sive conduct); *Hustler Magazine* v *Falwell*, 485 U.S. 46 (1988) (First and Fourteenth Amendments prohibit public figures from recovering damages for intentional infliction of emotional distress due to caricature publication without showing false statements of fact made with "actual malice"); *Spence* v *Washington*, 418 U.S. 405 (1974) (conviction for hanging flag upside down with peace symbol taped on held invalid; statute held to be impermissible infringement on protected expression); *Cohen* v *California*, 403 U.S. 15 (1971) (First and Fourteenth Amendments require state to show compelling reason to make public display of four-letter expletive a criminal offense); *Street* v *New York*, 394 U.S. 576 (1969); *Terminiello* v *City of Chicago*, 337 U.S. 1 (1949) (Court reversed breach of peace conviction where race-baiting speaker attracted "angry and turbulent" crowd).

64. Gard, n. 44, at 577.

65. As a private institution, Stanford University is not directly bound by First Amendment standards. However, many private academic institutions make policy choices to adhere to standards that are consistent with their notions of academic freedom.

66. See text accompanying nn. 30–64.

67. Gard, n. 44.

68. Stanford Code and Comments, n. 13.

69. Gard, n. 44, at 536.

70. See also ibid. at 541: "The importance of the content-focused personally abusive epithet element cannot be overestimated. . . . In essence it guarantees that the expression of ideas, no matter how offensive or distasteful, will be afforded constitutional protection."

71. Ibid. at 559 (citing In re S.L.J., 263 N.W.2d 412, 420 [Minn. 1978]) (when alleged fighting words were spoken "from more than fifteen feet away rather than eye-to-eye, there wss no reasonable likelihood that they would tend to incite an immediate breach of the peace"); *Garvey* v *State*, 537 S.W.2d 709, 710 (Tenn. Crim. App. 1975) (face-to-face requirement was not met when defendant, while driving past police station, shouted "sooey" at police officer).

72. Gard, n. 44, at 561 (emphasis added).

73. 721 F. Supp. 852 (E.D. Mich. 1989).

74. See *City of Houston* v *Hill*, 482 U.S. 451, 458 (1987) (regulation of speech will be unconstitutionally overbroad if it "reaches a substantial amount of constitutionally protected conduct") (citing *Hoffman Estates* v *The Flipside, Hoffman Estates, Inc.*, 455 U.S. 499, 494 [1982]).

75. In particular, the term "stigmatize," also used in the Stanford code, specifically was held to be unconstitutionally vague. *Doe*, 721 F. Supp. at 867.

The void-for-vagueness doctrine is enforced especially strictly in the First Amendment context. See *Kolender* v *Lawson*, 461 U.S. 352, 358 (1983); *Hoffman Estates*, 455 U.S. at 499; *Smith* v *Goguen*, 415 U.S. 566, 573 (1974); *Grayned* v *City of Rockford*, 408 U.S. 104, 109 (1972).

76. See *Doe*, 721 F. Supp at 865. The court cited the following examples of protected speech which had been subjected to the policy: a statement by a graduate student in the School of Social Work, in a research class, expressing his belief that homosexuality was a disease and that he intended to develop a counseling plan for

changing gay clients to straight; the reading of an allegedly homophobic limerick, which ridiculed a well-known athlete for his presumed sexual orientation by a student in the School of Business Administration during a class public-speaking exercise, ibid.; and a statement by a student during an orientation session of a preclinical dentistry class, widely regarded as especially difficult, that he had heard that minorities had a hard time in the course and that they were not treated fairly, ibid. at 865–66.

77. See ibid. at 867.

78. S. Rushdie, *The Satanic Verses* (1988).

79. See Statement of the Washtenaw County Branch, American Civil Liberties Union, on the University of Michigan Policy "Discrimination and Discriminatory Harassment by Students in the University Environment" 6 (May 25, 1989).

Other examples of academic discourse that have been labeled censurable as hate speech include the following: a group of students complained that a faculty member had created a hostile atmosphere by quoting racist comments originally made at the turn of the century, even though the professor said that was not his intention, see ibid. at 4; another group of students contended that the former students' complaint about the professor had itself created a hostile atmosphere, see ibid. at 5; a law student suggested that judicial decisions reflecting adverse stereotypes about blacks should not be studied in law school courses, see Shaw, "Caveat Emptor," *N.Y. L. Sch. Rep.*, April 1999, p. 3; a Jewish professor was penalized for suggesting to his black students that they should celebrate the anniversary of their ancestors' liberation from slavery under the Thirteenth Amendment, just as Jews celebrate their ancestors' liberation from slavery during Passover, see Hentoff, "Campus Court-Martial," *Washington Post*, December 15, 1988, p. A25, col. 2; students complained about a professor's statement that black students are not sufficiently critical of human rights violations by black African governments, see McKinley, "Minority Students Walk Out Over a Teacher's Remarks," *New York Times*, October 4, 1989, p. B3, col. 5.

80. See *Doe* v *University of Mich.*, 721 F. Supp. 852, 867 (E.D. Mich. 1989) (holding unduly vague the terms "stigmatize," "victimize," " 'threat' . . . to an individual's academic efforts," and "interfering with an individual's academic efforts").

81. Regarding the chilling effect of a University of Connecticut anti–hate speech rule utilizing some of these terms, see Brief of Amicus Curiae in Support of Plaintiff's Motion for Preliminary Injunction at 9–10 and n. 10, *Wu* v *University of Conn.*, No. Civ. H-89-649 PCD (D. Conn. January 25, 1990) (submitted by ACLU). In its brief, the ACLU stated that:

Given [the rule's] ambiguities, a . . . student could plausibly fear prosecution for voicing an opinion that members of the Unification Church . . . are "cultists"; that Zionists are "imperialists" or that Palestinians are "terrorists"; that evangelical ministers are "hustlers" and their followers are "dupes"; or that homosexuals are "sick." Most ironically of all, a homosexual rights activist could perhaps be prosecuted for declaring that Catholics are "bigots" if they follow their Church's teaching that homosexuality is a sin. . . . Similarly, a black activist student leader might reasonably hesitate to characterize other black students, who are deemed insufficiently supportive of black causes, as "Uncle Toms." . . .

82. See letter from Professor William Cohen to Professor George Parker, Chair of the Student Conduct Legislative Council at Stanford University (May 1, 1989); reprinted in *Stanford Univ. Campus Rep.*, May 3, 1989, p. 18.

83. Ibid. See also Letter from Pierre Bierre, research computer scientist in the Neuropsychology Laboratory of the Departments of Psychiatry and Psychology, to George Parker, Chair of the Student Conduct Legislative Council, Stanford University (March 16, 1989), reprinted in *Stanford Univ. Campus Rep.*, Mar. 22, 1989, p. 20: "As any conflict counselor knows, the first step to resolve conflicts is to get people to open up and share unedited gut feelings, however irrational they may seem, and the second step is to remove the listening 'blocks' that prevent the other side from hearing those feelings."

84. As Justice Harlan observed in *Cohen v California*, 403 U.S. 15, 26 (1971), "[w]e cannot indulge in the facile assumption that one can forbid a particular word without also running the substantial risk of suppressing ideas in the process."

85. Affidavit of John Doe in Support of Plaintiff's Motion for Preliminary Injunction at para. 14, *Doe v University of Mich.*, 721 F. Supp. 852 (E.D. Mich. 1989) (No. 89-71683) [hereinafter Doe Affidavi].

86. *Keyishian v Board of Regents*, 385 U.S. 589, 603 (1967). See also *West Virginia State Bd. of Educ. v Barnette*, 319 U.S. 624, 642 (1943), which declared that:

> If there is any fixed star in our constitutional constellation, it is that no official, high or petty, can prescribe what shall be orthodox in politics, nationalism, religion or other matters of opinion or force citizens to confess by word or act their faith therein. If there are any circumstances which permit an exception, they do not now occur to us.

87. See Doe Affidavit, n. 85 at paras. 7–11.

88. Cohen letter (March 10, 1989), n. 82. Professor Cohen cited the following examples of potential censorship under this construction: a challenge by evangelical Christians to the film *The Last Temptation of Christ* (Barbara De Fina, released by Universal and Cineplex Odeon Films 1998); a challenge by blacks to D. W. Griffith's film *The Birth of a Nation* (Epoch Producing Corporation 1915); or a speech by Professor Shockley on racial differences.

89. See *Brandenburg v Ohio*, 395 U.S. 444, 456–57 (1969) (Douglas, J., concurring): "The line between what is permissible and not subject to control and what may be subject to regulation is the line between ideas and overt acts."

90. Compare S. Walker, n. 6, at 349 (discussing ACLU representation of antiabortion demonstrators) with *National Abortion Fed'n v Operation Rescue*, No. CV 89-1181 AWT (C.D. Cal. August 29, 1989) (holding antiabortion demonstrators in contempt for violating order previously obtained by Southern California ACLU to protect abortion clinics and patients from assaults and other illegal conduct).

91. In *American Booksellers Ass'n v Hudnut*, 771 F.2d 323, 334 (7th Cit.), *aff'd*, 475 U.S. 1001 (1985). the Supreme Court summarily affirmed the Seventh Circuit ruling

invalidating an ordinance based upon model legislation drafted by feminist procensorship leaders Andrea Dworkin and Catharine MacKinnon.

92. See generally A. Dworkin, *Pornography: Men Possessing Women* (1981) (pornography is not mere expression but method of domination of women); MacKinnon, "Pornography, Civil Rights, and Speech," 20 *Harv. C.R.-C.L. L. Rev.* 1 (1995) (same). Some feminists reject the notion that censoring pornography advances women's equality; they believe, to the contrary, that censoring pornography perpetuates archaic stereotypes about women. See Strossen, "The Convergence of Feminist and Civil Liberties Principles in the Pornography Debate" (Book Review). 62 *N.Y.U. L. Rev.* 201 (1987) (reviewing *Women Against Censorship* [V. Burstyn ed. 1985]) (book demonstrates falseness of dichotomy between feminist and civil libertarian principles, since goal of both is society in which individuals are treated justly).

93. For a description of ACLU efforts to combat sex discrimination, see Gait and Strown, n. 9, at 168–84.

94. *Collin* v *Smith,* 447 F. Supp. 676 (N.D. Ill.), aff'd, 578 F.2d 1197 (7th Cir.), *cert. denied,* 439 U.S. 916 (1978); *Village of Skokie* v *National Socialist Party,* 69 Ill. 2d 605, 373 N.E.2d 21 (1978).

95. See letter from Morton Halperin to author, at 2 (February 5, 1990) (ACLU strongly supported federal legislation directing FBI to gather statistics on hate crimes) (available from author).

96. See Lawrence at 302–304. See, e.g., ibid. at 302, n. 7 ("racist conduct amounts to speech"); ibid. at 441 (*"Brown's* declaration that segregation is unconstitutional amounts to a regulation of the message of white supremacy"); ibid. at 303, n. 23 ("I want to stress the complete overlap of the idea and practice of racism "); ibid. at 444 of original text ("[T]he Court recognized the inseparability of idea and practice in the institution of slavery"); ibid. at 304 (*"Brown* mandates the abolition of racist speech."); ibid. at 305 (*"Brown* is a case about group defamation.").

97. *Gitlow* v *New York,* 268 U.S. 652, 673 (1925) (Holmes, J., dissenting).

98. *Abrams* v *United States,* 250 U.S. 616, 630 (1919) (Holmes, J., dissenting).

99. Ibid. at 630–31.

100. 395 U.S. 444 (1969) (per curiam)

101. Ibid. at 447.

102. See n. 96.

103. Slavery, as well as de jure segregation and other phenomena that Professor Lawrence assimilates to hate speech by students or faculty members, also are distinguishable on the additional ground that the former emanated from the government, and the latter from private individuals. Regarding the significance of this distinction, see text accompanying notes 143–64.

104. See Lawrence at 307.

105. See ibid. at 301–307.

106. Indeed, Professor Lawrence himself emphasizes that he advocates regulating only a narrow class of racist speech. See ibid. at 308, n. 47. Therefore, he apparently recognizes that his equation between racist speech and racist conduct–whatever theoretical appeal it might have–is not relevant to the task of deciding *which* subset of racist speech should be restricted. However, while rejecting the

speech/conduct line between protected and unprotected expressive activity, he offers no other. For a further discussion of this issue in the particular context of Professor Lawrence's argument that *Brown* v *Board of Education* sanctions regulating racist speech, see text accompanying nn. 134–42.

107. See nn. 89–95 and accompanying text.

108. See, e.g., *Police Dept. of Chicago* v *Mosley*, 408 U.S. 92, 95 (1972) ("[A]bove all else, the First Amendment means that government has no power to restrict expression because of its message, its ideas, its subject matter, or its content."). Courts will sustain a content-based speech regulation only where the government can prove that it "is necessary to serve a compelling state interest and that it is narrowly drawn to achieve that end." *Widmar* v *Vincent*, 454 U.S. 263, 270 (1981). This stringent showing can rarely be made. See, e.g., *Carey* v *Brown*, 447 U.S. 455, 465 (1980) (statute prohibiting peaceful picketing in residential neighborhoods not narrowly tailored enough to promote state's asserted interests in (1) promoting privacy of home, and (2) providing special treatment for labor).

109. L. Tribe, *American Constitutional Law* (2d. ed. 1988), § 12–8, at 838 n. 17.

110. Justice Holmes enunciated this position in *United States* v *Schwimmer*, 279 U.S. 644, 654 (1929) (Holmes, J., dissenting): "If there is any principle of the Constitution that more imperatively calls for attachment than any other it is the principle of free thought–not free thought for those who agree with us, but freedom for the thought that we hate."

111. See, e.g., *Watts* v *United States*, 394 U.S. 705, 709 (1969) (per curiam) (refers to a " 'profound national commitment to the principle that debate on public issues should be uninhibited, robust, and wide-open, and that it may well include vehement, caustic, and sometimes unpleasantly sharp attacks.' The language of the political arena . . . is often vituperative, abusive, and inexact" [quoting *New York Times Co.* v *Sullivan*, 376 U.S. 254, 270 (1964)]). The Supreme Court recently reaffirmed that the First Amendment does not allow authorities to "prohibit the expression of an idea simply because society finds the idea offensive or disagreeable." *Texas* v *Johnson*, 109 S. Ct. 2533, 2544 (1989) (invalidating conviction for burning United States flag to express idea).

112. In a widely quoted dissent, Justice Holmes championed this rationale for free speech as "the theory of our Constitution":

> [W]hen men have realized that time has upset many fighting faiths. they may come to believe even more than they believe the very foundations or their own conduct that the ultimate good desired is better reached by free trade in ideas–that the best test of truth is the power of the thought to get itself accepted in the competition of the market, and that truth is the only ground upon which their wishes safely can be carried out.

Abrams v *United States*, 250 U.S. 616, 630 (1919) (Holmes, J., dissenting). See also *Cohen* v *California*, 403 U.S. 15, 24 (1971) (free expression "will ultimately produce a more capable citizenry and more perfect polity"); *New York Times*, 376 U.S. at 270.

113. See *Cohen*, 403 U.S. at 24: "[N]o other approach [than protecting free speech] would comport with the premise of individual dignity and choice upon which our political system rests"; Richards, "Free Speech and Obscenity Law:

Toward a Moral Theory of the First Amendment," 123 *U.P. L. Rev.* 45, 62 (1974) (freedom of expression permits and encourages individual's exercise of autonomy).

114. R. Smolla, *Free Speech in Open Culture* (tentative title, forthcoming).

115. U.N. Charter art. 1, par. 3.

116. Universal Declaration of Human Rights, arts. 2, 7, 16, G.A. Res. 217 (III), 9 U.N. GAOR (3d Sess. pt. 1) at 71, U.N, Doc. A/810 (1948).

117. Opened for signature March 7, 1966, 660 U.N.T.S. 195.

118. For example, the International Convention on the Elimination of All Forms of Racial Discrimination, ibid. art. 4(a), requires states to "declare as an offence punishable by law all dissemination of ideas based on racial superiority or hatred, [and] incitement to racial discrimination."

119. See Kretzmer, "Free Speech and Racism," 8 *Cardozo L. Rev.* 445, 499–506 (1987) (reviewing European anti–hate speech laws).

120. As Thomas Paine wrote during our country's formative period: "He that would make his own liberty secure, must guard even his enemy from oppression, for if he violates this duty, he establishes a precedent that will reach himself." (quoted in American Civil Liberties Union, *Why the American Civil Liberties Union Defends Free Speech for Racists and Totalitarians* 2 [n.d.] [hereinafter ACLU pamphlet]).

121. *Terminiello* v *Chicago*, 337 U.S. 1 (1949) (ACLU appeared amicus curiae); see also *Brandenburg* v *Ohio*, 395 U.S 444 (1969) (per curiam) (upholding free speech rights of Ku Klux Klan leader represented by ACLU).

122. See, e.g., *Brown* v *Louisiana*, 383 U.S. 131, 135 (1966); *Cox* v *Louisiana*, 379 U.S. 536, 552 (1965).

123. See Minow, "On Neutrality, Equality, & Tolerance: New Norms for a Decade of Distinction," *Change*, January/February 1990, at 17.

124. As Professor Lawrence notes, see C. Lawrence, Presentation at ACLU Biennial Conference, introductory note, the Court has long upheld certain content-based speech regulations, such as those governing obscenity, without eviscerating all free speech rights.

125. See Report of President's Ad Hoc Committee on Racial Harassment, University of Texas at Austin 17 (November 27, 1989) (authored by Committee chaired by Mark G. Yudof, Dean, and James A. Elkins, Centennial Chair in Law, University of Texas School of Law).

126. Ibid.

127. See Duggan, Hunter, and Vance, "False Promises: Feminist Antipornography Legislation in the U.S.," in *Women Against Censorship* 130, 134, 138–39, 146–47 (V. Burstyn ed. 1985); Snitow, "Retrenchment Versus Transformation: The Politics of the Antipornography Movement," in ibid. at 118.

128. See text accompanying nn. 73–83.

129. See Matsuda, n. 3, at 2373.

130. Delgado, "Words that Wound: A Tort Action for Racial Insults, Epithets, and Name-Calling," *Harv. C.R.-C.L. L. Rev.* 133, 179–80 (1982). According to Professor Delgado,

[A]n epithet such as "You damn nigger" would almost always be found actionable, as it is highly insulting and highly racial. . . . "Boy," directed at a young black male, might be actionable, depending on the speaker's intent, the hearer's understanding, and whether a reasonable person would consider it a racial insult in the particular context. "Hey, nigger," spoken affectionately between black persons and used as a greeting, would not be actionable. An insult such as "You dumb honkey," directed at a white person, could be actionable but only in the unusual situations where the plaintiff would suffer harm from such an insult.

Ibid.

131. For example, during a discussion about the University of Wisconsin rule regulating hate speech, even advocates of the role disagreed as to whether it would (or should) apply to the following hypothetical situation: A white student sits down next to a black student and says, "I want you to know that I'm a racist and hate the idea of blacks being here at the university," but does not use any racist epithet. Telephone interview with Eunice Edgar, Executive Director of ACLU of Wisconsin (November 14, 1989). See also Gottlieb, n. 4 (Professor Thomas Grey, who drafted Stanford code, "said his rule probably wouldn't apply to one of the most publicized racial incidents at Stanford, when a white student left on a black student's door a poster of Beethoven drawn as a black caricature." [emphasis added]).

132. See text accompanying nn. 17–20.

133. Lawrence at 311. See also n. 16.

134. 347 U.S. 483 (1954).

135. 461 U.S. 574 (1983).

136. See Lawrence at 301–307.

137. Regarding the significance of this distinction, see text accompanying nn. 96–103.

138. See Lawrence at 302, n. 8.

139. For example, as Professor Lawrence observes, ibid., John Hart Ely has described all communicative behavior as "100 percent action and 100 percent expression." Ely, "Flag Desecration: A Case Study in the Roles of Categorization and Balancing in First Amendment Analysis," 88 *Harv. L. Rev.* 1482, 1495–96 (1975). This does not lead Professor Ely, however, to conclude that all speech should be regulated, nor does it lead him to conclude that the speech/conduct distinction is irrelevant to First Amendment analysis. Rather, he suggests that, in evaluating the constitutionality of a government regulation of certain conduct, the analytical focus should not be on whether that conduct should be classified "speech" or "action." Instead, he urges, the relevant inquiry should be whether the regulation is aimed at the expressive aspect of such conduct. If so, it is presumptively unconstitutional. If not, it is presumptively constitutional. Ibid. at 1496–97. This is the analysis that the Court enunciated in *United States* v *O'Brien*, 391 U.S. 367, 391–92 (1968) (upholding statute that criminalized the destruction of draft cards where governmental interest was limited to the noncommunicative aspect of defendant's conduct).

Under the Ely-*O'Brien* analysis, *Brown* does not involve the regulation of the expressive aspect of speech-conduct. Under the *O'Brien* test, as Professor Ely paraphrased it, "[t]he critical question . . . [is] whether the harm that the state is seeking to avert is one that grows out of the fact that the defendant is communicating . . . or rather would arise even if the defendant's conduct had no communicative significance whatsoever." Ely, at 1497. Analysis reveals that school segregation would be invalidated apart from its communicative significance.

One can imagine situations in which the act of requiring schools to be racially segregated did not convey the message of white supremacy which Professor Lawrence views as the central meaning of school segregation. See Lawrence at 303, 312–13. Yet *Brown* surely would hold that such segregated schools violate the equal protection clause. For example, a black student who had been raised in a different culture marked by black supremacy, and then moved to the United States and attended a racially segregated school, might well interpret school segregation as conveying the message of white inferiority. Would *Brown* not demand that this student should nonetheless attend a desegregated school? As another example, a community might come to view racial diversity much the way it regards religious diversity, so that the choice to attend a religiously segregated school would be viewed as conveying no more stigmatizing a message than the choice to attend a religiously segregated school. Would *Brown* not insist, nevertheless, that no public schools could be racially segregated, even if the option of attending them was completely voluntary? See *Green* v *County School Bd.*, 391 U.S. 430 (1968) (rejected "freedom-of-choice" plan for desegregation).

140. See, e.g., *Thornhill* v *Alabama*, 3 10 U.S. 98 (1940) (peaceful picketing to publicize labor dispute is constitutionally protected free speech).

141. See *United States* v *Eichman*, 110 S. Ct. 2404, 2409–18 (1990); *Texas* v *Johnson*, 109 S. Ct. 2533, 2539 (1989) (Flag burning is "conduct sufficiently imbued with elements of communication to implicate the First Amendment.").

142. The fact that Professor Lawrence also rejects the state action doctrine as a limiting principle on government's regulatory power further expands the range of speech that he would allow to be restricted. See Lawrence at 304–307.

Scholars constantly grapple with the complex problems of how to separate regulable from nonregulable speech. For recent efforts, see C. Baker, *Human Liberty and Freedom of Speech* (1989); K. Greenawalt, *Speech, Crime, and the Uses of Language* (1989); H. Kalven Jr., *A Worthy Tradition: Freedom of Speech in America* (1998); F. Schauer, *Free Speech: A Philosophical Enquiry* (1992). Yet I am unaware of any that provide a more coherent basic approach than the Court's current general framework: A government regulation aimed at speech or expressive conduct is presumptively unconstitutional unless "it furthers an important . . . governmental interest . . . [that] is unrelated to the suppression of free expression . . . [and] the incidental restriction on . . . First Amendment freedoms is no greater than is essential to the furtherance of that interest." *United States* v *O'Brien*, 391 U.S. 367, 377 (1968). If speech is integrally interrelated with, or incites, violent or otherwise unlawful conduct, government regulation would be permitted under the *O'Brien* formulation.

143. *Norwood* v *Harrison*, 413 U.S. 455, 471 (1973).

144. *Board of Educ.* v *Allen*, 392 U.S. 236, 249 (1968).

145. See *Norwood*, 413 U.S. at 470: "However narrow may be the channel of permissible state aid to sectarian schools, . . . it permits a greater degree of state assistance than may be given to private schools which engage in discriminatory practices."

146. See Matsuda, n. 3, at 2378–79.

147. See, e.g., *County of Allegheny* v *ACLU*, 109 S. Ct. 3086, 3101 (1989) (establishment clause inquiry is whether government is "conveying or attempting to convey a message that religion or a particular religious belief is *favored* or *preferred"*).

148. Professor Lawrence also suggests the analogy between establishment clause doctrine and the law governing race discrimination. See Lawrence at 447 of original text ("for over three hundred years, racist speech has been the liturgy of America's leading established religion, the religion of racism").

149. *Board of Educ.* v *Mergens*, 110 S. Ct. 2356 (1990) (interpreting Equal Access Act, 20 U S.C. §§ 4071–4074 (1988), which prohibits public secondary schools from denying meeting space to religious and other clubs on the basis of speech content, expresses neutrality towards religion). *Widmar* v *Vincent*, 454 U.S. 263, 271–72 (1981) (when university has created a forum generally open to student groups, its content-based exclusion of religious speech violates principle that regulation should be content neutral).

150. 110 S. Ct. 2356 (1990).

151. Ibid. at 2372 (emphasis added).

152. See text accompanying nn. 143–44.

153. See *Norwood* v *Harrison*, 413 U.S. 455, 466 (1973) (state may not grant "tangible financial aid . . . if it has a significant tendency to facilitate, reinforce, and support private discrimination"); ibid. at 467 (state must not give "significant aid" to racially discriminatory private institutions); ibid. at 469 (discriminatory private schools may not receive "material aid" from state).

154. Lawrence at 305–306.

155. See Lawrence at 307.

156. The ACLU joined an amicus brief filed by a coalition of civil rights organizations in *Patterson* v *McLean Credit Union*, 109 S. Ct. 2363 (1989), endorsing the Court's earlier interpretation of 42 U.S.C. § 1981 (1988) as outlawing private race discrimination, see *Runyon* v *McCrary*, 427 U.S. 160, 173 (1976) (section 1981 reaches private acts of discrimination).

157. See Lawrence at 311.

158. Brief of the American Civil Liberties Union and the American Jewish Committee, Amici Curiae in support of Affirmance at 37–38, *Bob Jones Univ.* v *United States*, 461 U.S. 574 (1983) (Nos, 81-3, 81-1).

159. Professor Strossen was counsel of record for the ACLU and the American Jewish Committee, amici curiae, advocating government denial of tax benefits to racially discriminatory educational institutions.

160. See *Bob Jones*, 461 U.S. at 603–604: "Denial of tax benefits will inevitably have a substantial impact on the operation of private religious schools, but will not prevent those schools from observing their religious tenets." Accord *Runyon*, 427 U.S. at 177 (42 U.S.C. § 1981 [1988] forbids private, commercially operated, non-sectarian schools from denying admission based on race, but such schools remain free "to inculcate whatever values and standards they deem desirable.").

161. See Lawrence at 306, n. 40.

162. Ibid. at 306.

163. 377 U.S. 218, 233 (1964).

164. Equally unpersuasive is Professor Lawrence's attempted reliance on cases upholding prohibitions upon race-designated advertisements for employees, home sales, and rentals, see Lawrence at 307 and n. 46, 312 n. 78. As the Supreme Court ruled, in *Pittsburgh Press Co.* v *Human Relations Comm'n*, 413 U.S. 376, 391 (1973), these advertisements constituted integral elements of the prohibited discriminatory conduct—i.e., refusing to hire women. Ibid. at 388–89. Therefore, these advertisements fit within the general category of speech that may be regulated on the ground that it constitutes an essential element of an unlawful act.

165. Lawrence at 309, n. 52.

166. 337 U.S. 1 (1949).

167. 403 U.S. 15 (1971).

168. *Winters* v *New York*, 333 U.S. 507, 510 (1948) (reversing conviction for selling crime magazines under statute prohibiting publication of "stories of . . . bloodshed, lust, or crime" as obscene, ibid. at 508). The Court concluded that expression devoid of "ideas," but with entertainment value, was protected, because the line between the informing and the entertaining is too elusive for the protection of that basic [First Amendment] right. . . . What is one man's amusement, teaches another's doctrine." Ibid. at 510,

169. *Terminiello*, 337 U.S. at 4–5 (citations omitted). For a very different view, compare Lawrence at 302: "Regulations that require civility of discourse in certain designated forums are not incursions on intellectual and political debate."

170. It is noteworthy that these two ringing endorsements of constitutional protection for offering provocative speech were written by Justices at opposite ends of the Court's ideological spectrum. The agreement on this issue between Justice Douglas, a noted liberal, and Justice Harlan, a respected conservative, indicates that their views represent a solidly entrenched consensus about free speech tenets.

171. *Cohen*, 403 U.S. at 26 (emphasis added). Professor Tribe eloquently described how Cohen supports a more generous vision of protectible speech than just the intellectually oriented speech that Professor Lawrence would protect: "Justice Harlan's opinion for the majority [in *Cohen*] implicitly rejected the hoary dichotomy between reason and desire that so often constricts the reach of the First Amendment." L. Tribe, n. 109 § 12-1 at 787–89.

172. Rutzick, "Offensive Language and the Evolution of First Amendment Protection," 9 *Harv. C.R.-C.L. L. Rev.* 1, 18 (1974). Compare Lawrence at 309: "The racial invective is experienced as a blow, not a proffered idea, and . . . it is unlikely that dialogue will follow."

173. Lawrence at 312, n. 74.

174. Professor Matsuda, n. 3 at 2360, acknowledged that racist speech conveys an idea when she stated that "racial supremacy is one of the *ideas* we have collectively and internationally considered and rejected" (emphasis added). Professor Lawrence recognized the same point when he quoted this sentence from Matsuda. Lawrence at 312, n. 74.